MOUNTAIN DHARMA

MOUNTAIN DHARMA

Meditative Retreat and the
Tibetan Ascetic Self

David M. DiValerio

Columbia University Press

New York

Columbia University Press
Publishers Since 1893
New York   Chichester, West Sussex

Copyright © 2025 Columbia University Press
All rights reserved

Library of Congress Cataloging-in-Publication Data
Names: DiValerio, David M., author.
Title: Mountain Dharma : meditative retreat and the
Tibetan ascetic self / David M. DiValerio.
Description: New York : Columbia University Press, [2025] |
Includes bibliographical references and index.
Identifiers: LCCN 2025006752 (print) | LCCN 2025006753 (ebook) |
ISBN 9780231220217 (hardback) | ISBN 9780231220224 (trade paperback) |
ISBN 9780231563123 (ebook)
Subjects: LCSH: Asceticism—Buddhism—History. | Meditation—Buddhism—
History. | Buddhism—Tibet Region—History.
Classification: LCC BQ6200 .D583 2025 (print) | LCC BQ6200 (ebook) |
DDC 294.3/444709—dc23/eng/20250312

COVER DESIGN: Milenda Nan Ok Lee
COVER ART: Nicholas Roerich (1874–1947), *Guru Guri Dhar* (1931). Public domain.
Image courtesy of the Nicholas Roerich Museum, New York, NY.

GPSR Authorized Representative: Easy Access System Europe, Mustamäe tee 50, 10621
Tallinn, Estonia, gpsr.requests@easproject.com

For my mother

CONTENTS

Acknowledgments ix

Introduction 1

1. The Prescriptive Literature for Individual Retreat 24

2. Locating the Ascetic Self 44

3. Isolating the Ascetic Self 69

4. Nourishing the Ascetic Self 93

5. Preserving the Ascetic Self 116

6. Forming the Ascetic Self 136

7. The Tibetan Ascetic Self in Time 160

Conclusion 183

....

Appendix. Prescriptive Texts for Individual Retreat 189

Notes 193

Works Cited 237

Index 247

ACKNOWLEDGMENTS

Research for this project began in earnest during a sabbatical in the 2017–2018 academic year, which I spent at the University of Virginia. Thanks to Kurtis, for giving support of all kinds; to David, for taking an interest; and to John, for encouragement. Paul Dafydd Jones and Charles Mathewes graciously allowed me to join their Luce Seminar, "Religion, Theology, Theory, and Modernity," which has provided some of the intellectual underpinnings of this work.

In 2020–2021, I was a fellow at the University of Wisconsin–Milwaukee's Center for 21st Century Studies. My thinking about this project advanced considerably during this year of sustained conversation with my colleagues Ivan Ascher, Douglas Haynes, Jenny Kehl, Gladys Mitchell-Walthour, and Sara VanderHaagen, along with Richard Grusin and Maureen Ryan. I received feedback on an early draft of the manuscript from Xin Huang, Aragorn Quinn, Hilary Snow, and Mike Wert, as participants in the Critical Asian Humanities Reading Group, a collaboratory supported by C21; from Kati Fitzgerald, Michael Sheehy, and Tawni Tidwell, as members of a Tibetan contemplative and medical traditions reading group that ran for two years; and from Chris Cantwell and Sarah Schaefer, members of a religion-themed reading group whose name is not fit for print. All four of these communities provided crucial intellectual and social lifelines during the pandemic. Michael has been an especially important interlocutor since the earliest days of this project.

Flavio Geisshuessler, Christian Wedemeyer, and my colleague, Ben Campbell, each gave a pointed suggestion early in my research that would prove critical to the final form of this book. Timely conversations with Alex Gardner, Eric

Haynie, Jennifer Jordan, Rachel Pang, Andy Quintman, Brenton Sullivan, and Steve Weinberger allowed me to keep moving forward.

Thanks to William Edmundson, Cameron Fontaine, Terri Piszczor, Jamee Pritchard, and Rebecca Schnabel for their willingness to accompany me on the journey during our 2020 graduate seminar, "Technologies of the Self."

The writing of this book was greatly facilitated by a year-long research fellowship furnished by the Robert H. N. Ho Family Foundation and administered by the American Council of Learned Societies, which was taken in 2021–2022.

This book simply would not exist without the work done by the Buddhist Digital Resource Center. This organization's indispensability to the preservation of Tibetan literary culture continues to far exceed the recognition it receives. This research also uses a number of texts conserved by the Nepal–German Manuscript Preservation Project, working in partnership with the Nepal Research Center and the National Archives of Nepal. I was able to access these texts thanks to a travel grant from UWM's Graduate School. A big thank you to Kathleen Koch for her reliable work in the Office of Research.

Wendy Lochner deserves special acknowledgment for her heroic efforts over the year and a half that it took to get this manuscript through the peer review process. I thank the two anonymous reviewers for their thoughts and suggestions. Talking through the manuscript with Tommy Symmes, my developmental editor and valued friend, was a real joy. Leslie Kriesel's thoughtful and judicious copyediting greatly improved the final product. Thanks to Karl Ryavec for lending his skill in creating a custom map.

I will forever owe a debt of gratitude to my psychoanalyst, E.N., who has shown me the very meanings of patience, generosity, and compassion. He deserves a great deal of credit for bringing this book into the world.

Warm appreciation to the many friends who so enrich my life in Milwaukee, over dinners, holidays, games, visits to beer gardens, while taking in the arts, watching our teams, enjoying the shores of Lake Michigan, and much more, in both sun and snow. In particular I would like to recognize Max Rondolino, Pascale Engelmeijer and Ziggy, Dan Paskowitz and Sarah, Dan Kern, Diego Diaz Martinez and Carolyn Lee, Kate Negri and Jon Schutkin, Rick and Shannon Popp, Nick Fleisher and Christine Evans, Itzi Lazkano, and André Allaire.

Thanks to Sonam for always thinking to call, because I never do. Congratulations on the completion of your PhD. Alyson Prude and Jann Ronis remain steadfast frineds.

This book was written while we were all living in a kind of extended retreat. When Kay Wells and I closed on our house in early March 2020, we hadn't the faintest idea of how the world or our lives were about to change. She has lovingly and forbearingly supported me through every step of the deeply affecting process that has culminated in this book. The nearly three years between when I submitted the manuscript and when it was finally published included some particularly trying times, when it seemed this work might never see the light of day. Thank you for everything that you are and everything that you have done to help me through it all.

INTRODUCTION

In the *Elementary Forms of the Religious Life*, Émile Durkheim describes religious asceticism as the intensive practice of "negative" observances that separate an individual from the profane, ordinary world, thereby positioning them nearer to the sacred. "The pure ascetic," he wrote in 1912, "is a man who raises himself above men and who acquires a special sanctity through fasts, vigils, retreat, and silence—in a word, more by privations than by acts of positive piety (offerings, sacrifices, prayers, etc.)." Asceticism being an "essential element" of religious life, every religion possesses "at least the seed" of the phenomenon. Durkheim observes that although it tends to serve as preparation for positive forms of religiosity, in certain instances asceticism "escapes that subordination and becomes central, the system of prohibitions swelling and aggrandizing itself to the point of invading the whole of life." This results in what he designates "systematic asceticism." Durkheim names the Buddhist saint as the leading exemplar of this phenomenon.[1]

The vocabulary used to refer to Tibetan Buddhism's paramount ascetic undertaking—the act of going into individual long-term meditative retreat—suggests that Durkheim is not misguided in describing asceticism as "negative" in the specific way he uses that term. Tibetans speak and write about going into retreat using words like *gcod*, *spong*, and *blos gtong*, which are expressive of severing, abandoning, renouncing. *Mtshams*, the word that translates as "retreat," in the sense of a purposeful withdrawal from ordinary activities, literally means a demarcation or boundary. This accentuates how in the Tibetan context, retreat is in an essential way about the boundary between the practitioner and the profane world from which they are separated.

While religious asceticism may look to outside observers like a cutting off or an end, for the practitioner that seeming end in actuality marks the beginning of a new way of being. This book is about what goes on in the space that is created upon renouncing ordinary life. More so than a question of how any individual may have navigated these concerns, our interest is to explore the system of norms—the culture of asceticism—that informs how the undertaking has been understood and pursued, as a Tibetan religiocultural practice extending across doctrinal, sectarian, and temporal divisions. Using the example of individual long-term meditative retreat in Tibetan Buddhism, this study details how, rather than being an island unto themselves or a disembodied consciousness, the religious ascetic exists in a world of positive relations—to places and things, to other people, and to their own being. The central question is how Tibetan meditator-intellectuals have understood these relationships, and how they have therefore understood the personhood of the ascetic. This study takes the view that religious asceticism, even when it espouses a rhetoric of extreme self- and world abnegation, is in fact a site of perpetual self-formation, through both the creative production of discourse and subsequent practice shaped by that discourse. In a departure from Durkheim, the term "positive" is not used to refer to ordinary religious activity, but rather to the activities and relationships through which the personhood of the ascetic is formed. The "negative" and "positive" aspects of ascetic practice as I use those terms are not opposed to each other; rather, the positive refers to what an individual enacts and embodies in their attempt to achieve the negatively defined ideal.

To approach this from a different angle, we can say that in devoting the entirety of one's being to achieving an ultimate realization of the Buddhist view of no self, new selves are produced along the way. This book contributes to our understanding of the history of religions in Asia and elsewhere by focusing on the processes through which such selfhoods have been produced, specifically in an ascetic context.

The religious culture of the Tibetan-speaking world offers the historian of religion a singular opportunity to study an ascetic tradition in a historical frame. A robust emphasis on practicing meditation in the context of a long-term retreat—whether in solitude or alongside a dozen or so peers; in a cloister, a cabin, or a cave; for a period of a year or three or ten—has been a defining characteristic of Tibetan Buddhism throughout its entire history. Over the past millennium an uncountable number of women and men have chosen to take on such a commitment in pursuit of spiritual advancement, often enduring great physical trials in the process. Some became so known for their reclusiveness that it provided the basis for a praiseful title, like *mtshams pa*, "retreatant," *ri khrod pa*, "one who stays in mountain hermitages," and *brag phug pa*, "cave dweller." A small subset of these yogins and yoginis would be acclaimed by later generations for the depths of their sacrifices and the heights of their realization. Some of the Himalayan world's greatest cultural heroes and heroines have obtained their charisma in this way. The Tibetan practice of meditative retreat cuts across all sectarian and even religious boundaries, being taken up by Nyingmapas, Kadampas, Kagyupas, Jonangpas, Sakyapas, Gelukpas, Rimépas, and practitioners of Bön. From a traditional Tibetan perspective, to meditate earnestly is to enter long-term retreat. While for some Tibetans intensive meditation in retreat has been a lifelong pursuit, for others it is a circumscribed endeavor complementary to other avenues of religious self-development, such as the rigors of monastic scholasticism. Unlike scholasticism, retreat has long been open to nonmonks, to women, and to individuals lacking an extensive religious education, including the nonliterate.

Although there are comparable ascetic traditions across the Asian religious landscape—the wandering *sādhu*s of Hinduism, Theravada Buddhist monks and nuns withdrawing to the forest for meditation, Daoist masters seeking immortality in the mountains, the *yamabushi* or "mountain prostrators" of Japan's Shugendo—long-term retreat on and around the Tibetan plateau is unique for how widely it has been practiced, for how long that has been the case, and for how well documented it is. This is a tradition unbroken at any point for the last thousand years, persisting even through the horrors of the Cultural Revolution. One could argue that in discussions of how the Buddhism of Tibet differs from the Buddhism(s) of other parts of Asia, this emphasis on long-term meditative retreat should be mentioned alongside Tibetan Buddhism's coevolution with autochthonous Tibetan religious practices and beliefs, outsized monastic tradition, and unique system of reincarnate lamas, all of which have been subject to sustained scholarly investigation. Yet the importance of long-term retreat in Tibet has escaped the attention of the broader academic study of religion almost entirely: in the second edition of the *Encyclopedia of Religion,* published in 2005, the word "Tibet" does not appear in the entry for "retreat" or for "eremitism" (the practice of being a hermit).[2] As Tibet's is perhaps the most robust and longest-standing tradition of religious reclusion that the world has ever seen, this is a striking omission—symptomatic, perhaps, of a dearth of exposition on Himalayan asceticism by the field of Buddhist studies.

The subject matter of this book is properly referred to as "individual long-term meditative retreat." To address the three adjectives in turn, this study focuses specifically on *individual* retreat, and therefore does not attempt to account for the Tibetan tradition of communal meditative retreat, in which a group of men or women do a long retreat together. Such communal retreats have typically played a seminary-like function for trainees in different traditions within the Himalayan religious world. An extremely consequential development for Tibetan Buddhism as it is practiced around the world today is Jamgön Kongtrül's (1813–1899) instituting a particular version of a communal retreat lasting specifically for three years and three fortnights, during which a class of meditators proceeds through a set curriculum of instruction and practice under their lama. Although the basic model predates him, the fact that it is now practiced on at least four continents stems from this famous polysectarian polymath's activity. Kongtrül's impact on the retreat tradition will be discussed in chapter 7, but communal retreat deserves further study in its own right, since many aspects of ascetic practice addressed in this book assume very different contours for meditators residing in defined communities, which are often long-standing institutions possessing communal wealth. The kind of meditative retreat that is the subject of this book is referred to as "individual" rather than "solitary" because, despite maintaining an ideal of utter solitude, the tradition has allowed for a significant degree of elasticity when it comes to a retreatant's interpersonal relationships. Much of Tibetan retreat practice historically was performed by men and women doing individual retreats in close proximity to one another, never fully cut off from the world outside.

What is meant by *long-term* can be best conveyed by examples of individuals' or groups' sequestering themselves for the sake of intensive religious practice for periods of time that emerge as short- or medium-term in comparison, for which the wide world of Tibetan Buddhism and Bön provides myriad occasions. The best studied is the Tibetan Buddhist practice of *nyungné* (*smyung gnas*), sometimes called the "fasting ritual," which brings lay men and women to a monastery for three days of intensive ritual practice in a group setting, paired with abstention from food, drink, and conversation—all in the service of ridding themselves of negative karma and propitiating the bodhisattva of compassion, Avalokiteśvara.[3] Widespread in Tibetan Buddhism is the expectation that a trainee will complete a hundred thousand repetitions of each of four or five "preliminary practices" (*sngon 'gro*) as necessary preparation for tantric practice; some individuals withdraw from ordinary activities for a period of months to complete this ordeal in an environment free of distractions. Later, a fully initiated man or woman might conduct a retreat lasting weeks or months in order to recite a deity's mantra hundreds of thousands of times as part of an "approach–accomplishment" or "service–practice" (*bsnyen sgrub, sevāsādhana*) ritual. Some practitioners of the Great Perfection (in its Bön or Nyingma forms) and the Kālacakra undertake a "dark retreat" (*mun mtshams*), in which the meditator is confined to a chamber utterly devoid of light, typically for forty-nine days, in order to catalyze visionary experiences.[4] Treasure revealers (*gter ston*) may sequester themselves for some time before attempting to extract a long-dormant text or holy object from the physical landscape. There are stories of great masters secluding themselves for weeks or months as they approach the moment of death.[5] There are also short- and medium-term retreat practices specific to the monastic tradition: one is the summer retreat, dating all the way back to the time of the Buddha, when monks and nuns are expected to remain in one place for the duration of the monsoon season. Monks working their way through the scholastic curriculum would sometimes remove themselves to caves or hermitages to limit distractions while they memorized texts.[6] Also widespread is the convention of simply withdrawing from normal activities for a period of time to avoid distraction and focus on religious practice. Today, the Fourteenth Dalai Lama regularly goes into such a retreat in his quarters in Dharamsala.

Within Tibetan religious culture, men and women might isolate themselves for periods of days, weeks, or months for a wide range of religious ends. Distinguishable from all of these is the practice of disengaging for a more extended period of resolute ritual and meditative practice. It cannot be stated definitively what qualifies as a "long-term" retreat because few of the principal texts used in this study specify how long a retreat should last. As will be shown in chapter 1 and elaborated upon in chapter 7, the tradition has often spoken of an ideal of three years, or three years and three fortnights or months. Individuals also undertake retreats of far longer duration, including making a vow to remain in retreat for the remainder of their life. For the purposes of this book, a retreat is "long-term" by virtue of its being of sufficient length to entail certain practical considerations—where to do it, how to feed oneself, how to endure threats to one's bodily well-being—that do not arise with respect to shorter periods of disengagement from the world. The focus is the tradition's navigation of the practical concerns inherent to the endeavor of individual long-term retreat.

As for what *meditative* practice consists of, the contemplative and ritual practices that are the central purpose of an individual long-term retreat are not categorically different from those performed by Tibetan Buddhists and Bönpos in other contexts. The recitation of liturgies, the propitiation of protector deities, mind training (*blo sbyong*), guru yoga, deity yoga, Cutting (*gcod*), the Path and Fruit, manipulating the psychophysical winds and drops of the yogic body (*rlung, prāṇa; thig le, bindu*), the Six Yogas of Naropa, the Kālacakra, posttantric practices like the Great Perfection and the Mahāmudrā—this is only a sampling of what composes the Tibetan world of contemplative practice, in and outside of retreat. Popular teachings, scholarly studies, or translations of Tibetan or Sanskrit texts may provide more information on any of these. But they by no means constitute the totality of what an individual living in long-term retreat would be occupied with, for outside of each day's formal practice sessions they will be taken up with a whole range of activities relating to sustaining and caring for their bodies, preserving the integrity of the retreat, and much else. This book explores the norms, values, and beliefs that shape these aspects of the meditator's comportment, and thereby structure retreat as a lived activity. Focusing on the ideas and practices that in effect give a meditative retreat its form, as opposed to the meditations performed inside the retreat, can provide new understanding of retreat itself as a transhistorical cultural and religious practice. I propose that these practices pertaining to more quotidian concerns, which are from a certain perspective incidental to the contemplative practices that are the central purpose, are in fact what define retreat. Moreover, the components that give shape to individual long-term retreat derive from and perpetuate specific conceptions of personhood for the meditator, making the history of retreat in Tibet the history of what can be thought of as the Tibetan ascetic self.

The principal source material for this study is literature produced by the Tibetan Buddhist tradition that provides instruction on how to live in an individual long-term retreat. This corpus comprises texts composed between the twelfth century and the early part of the twentieth, including works by authors of various schools and lineages, with an emphasis on the products of the Kagyu sect, who have prioritized meditative retreat more than any other school of Tibetan Buddhism. Although this study crosses sectarian lines, it is concerned almost exclusively with retreat in Buddhism, not incorporating any texts of retreat instruction deriving from Bön. The twenty-nine texts used here include detailed primers for how to live and practice in retreat, assemblages of encouragement for retreatants, and more informal works, such as a handful of spiritual songs exhorting meditators to take pleasure in a life of purposeful solitude, all ranging from a few pages in length to many hundreds. The appendix lists these sources in full, in the approximate chronological order of their composition. Chapter 1 provides an introduction to this little-studied body of literature. Throughout this book, my discussion of the contents of this prescriptive literature is contextualized by references to other Tibetan literary sources, including hagiography, historical chronicles, and instructions for other kinds of religious practice. I address how the prescriptive literature for individual long-term retreat complements or offers a different perspective on findings presented in prior scholarship on various facets of trans-Himalayan religions.

To characterize the methodology employed in this study, I will describe some potentially fruitful approaches to studying individual long-term retreat that lie outside its purview. One possible approach, in the vein of much of the work in Tibetan Buddhist studies published over the past two decades, would be to look systematically at hagiographies and historical accounts to glean what we can about the history of retreat practice and its place in the Tibetan religious imaginary. A broader cultural history of individual long-term retreat would also be illuminating, the historical record being replete with examples of how Tibetans have selected retreat from a repertoire of behaviors in order to achieve various not strictly otherworldly ends. Most famously, after the Fifth Dalai Lama's death in 1682, his prime minister successfully conspired to keep his death a secret for the next fifteen years by deploying the ruse that he was in meditative retreat in the Potala palace. During this time the exact same artifice was being used to conceal the death of Bhutan's ruler, Zhabdrung Ngawang Namgyel (1594–1651), which was not made public for more than fifty years. As Michael Aris has summed it up, "we are faced with the odd situation that during these years the Tibetan and Bhutanese states were both ruled by corpses, in a manner of speaking."[7] Retreat has been used as a means to politely decline invitations, to avoid potentially embarrassing situations, and to move out of the way of danger. Entering into retreat has long constituted a means of healing or preserving life force, for oneself or someone else. There is a tradition of going into a multiyear retreat after the death of one's mother or father.[8] Having completed some length of time in retreat has been a qualification, formally or less so, for holding certain religious offices in the Himalaya.[9] None of the prescriptive texts used in this study suggest entering retreat for any of these reasons, instead focusing on more rarefied personal religious aims. Nevertheless, the existence of these examples in the historical record speaks to individual long-term retreat's place among the repertoire of behaviors whose legibility defines Tibetan culture. Visitors to central Tibet today will chance upon locations regarded as having been sites of retreat for Tibet's earliest Buddhist kings, dating back to the seventh century, and for the Indian tantric saint known as Padmasambhava or Guru Rinpoché (ca. eighth–ninth cent.), and his consort Yeshé Tsogyel. This signals the role meditative retreat plays in Tibet's founding mythos.[10]

Another worthwhile approach would be to look at attitudes toward long-term retreat, as embodied in the figure of the yogin, that are conveyed in popular entertainments like Tibetan opera and smaller-scale performances by traveling dramatic troupes.[11] One could look systematically at long-term retreat through the eyes of its critics: in a poetic composition skewering every sector of the Tibetan religious world, the enigmatic firebrand Drukpa Künlé (b. 1455) facetiously describes how he visited a community of long-term retreatants who were consumed with impatience, constantly asking, "How many more days?"[12] A systematic examination of Euro-American perceptions of the Tibetan ascetic tradition could include, for example, Herman Melville's *Moby-Dick*: on account of his being conspicuously absent from the *Pequod*'s deck during the early part of that fateful journey, Captain Ahab is described as having "hidden himself away with such Grand-Lama-like exclusiveness."[13] More recently, seeking out an ascetic at the entrance to his presumably Himalayan cave in order to benefit from his wisdom has been a remarkably persistent trope throughout decades of single-panel comics: the intrepid seeker makes their way to a craggy mountaintop to ask the sage a question of ultimate existential importance, only to be surprised by the banality of the response. Once aware that the Jedi are essentially *siddha-bodhisattva*s and that Ewoks speak an intelligible form of Tibetan, one begins to see the extraordinary extent to which the mighty recluse-sage Yoda is based on the preeminent anchorite and master of tantric yoga Milarepa (1028/40/52–1111/23), a founding saint of the Kagyu school.[14]

Our understanding of meditative retreat in Tibet would be improved vitally by further research on specific institutions or locales that have been hubs of retreat practice, individual or communal, often for many centuries. For example, part of a chapter of José Cabezón and Penpa Dorjee's history of Sera monastery in Lhasa is devoted to the numerous hermitages associated with this famed bastion of Geluk scholasticism. While some date to as far back as the Tibetan imperial period, most were founded in the eighteenth century. The authors show that after the death of its founder, a hermitage would become the property of his subsequent incarnations. Because those reincarnations typically did not espouse the same contemplative interests as their predecessor, or due to the demands placed on reincarnate lamas (*tulku*, spelled *sprul sku*) in general, after just one or two generations the hermitages most often became "prototypical ritual monasteries," where communal ritual rather than individual meditation was the focus. As Cabezón and Dorjee conclude, "The historical lesson here is a simple one: it is difficult for hermitages to remain meditation-oriented institutions so long as succession is through the trulku system."[15] Such a clearly documented case of the routinization of meditative charisma is but one example of the important insight into the history of religions that can be gained by focusing on specific Himalayan institutions devoted (for a time, at least) to the practice of retreat.

These kinds of inquiry entail looking at the phenomenon of meditative retreat from the outside, as it were. By contrast, the present study attempts to understand the tradition of individual retreat from the inside, using materials written by and for long-term retreatants. In this way this project may be thought of as an intellectual history of eremitic and ascetic practice in Tibet. These texts are meant to instruct, each expressing an author's understanding of what is most essential for a potential retreatant to know. As prescriptive texts, they are expressions of ideals to be strived toward and interpretive frameworks to be invoked, rather than accounts of ascetics' firsthand experiences or descriptions of what a retreatant's daily life actually looked like. This study sets out to analyze the prescriptions these texts offer regarding certain pragmatic aspects of life in retreat, with an eye toward how problems are framed and what solutions are offered. These being persistent problems that can rarely be resolved completely, a meditator-author's instruction is usually an exercise in reconciling competing values and aims. In reconstructing conversations that have taken place around the practice of individual retreat, we will be dealing with beliefs about what is or is not possible, what one should or should not strive toward, and what does and does not matter in navigating those possibilities. The individual chapters to follow are organized around trends and ruptures observed in the tradition's discourse about these pragmatic concerns, including the ongoing reimagining of the retreat endeavor and of the ascetic's very personhood.

There are critical facets of individual long-term retreat and the literature offering instruction for its practice that simply are not addressed here, including material, political, gender, geographic, social, biographical, physiological, psychological, literary, and other aesthetic considerations. The example from Cabezón and Dorjee offers a glimpse of what taking a different approach to studying Tibet's retreat tradition might reveal. It also highlights the fact that investigation of the plateau's thousand-year history of monasticism remains an ongoing project, even in the wake of a succession of widely renowned and methodologically varied monographs on the topic over the past few decades. By contrast, the study of Tibet's anchoritic tradition is in its infancy. I invite other scholars to pick up where this book leaves off.

Insofar as it aims to reconstruct to the extent possible the specific ways of seeing, thinking, and behaving that have provided the contours of eremitism in Tibet historically, this project is a study of the habitus of Tibet's subculture of asceticism and tantric practice, to invoke the explanatory framework popularized by Pierre Bourdieu. The notion of habitus allows us to see how an individual occupying a specific position in the world of human affairs is acculturated to and shaped by certain norms that they may then affect and reproduce, thereby shaping other individuals. The result of this process is a set of mores that is passed on over time, yet always subject to change. Bourdieu writes that "habitus could be considered as a subjective but not individual system of internalized structures, schemes of perception, conception, and action common to all members of the same group or class and constituting the precondition for all objectification and apperception." This "system of structured, structuring dispositions" is "constituted in practice and is always oriented toward practical functions."[16]

Greatly influencing how this study goes about reconstructing the Himalayan eremitic habitus historically through an examination of the "positive" aspects of religious asceticism—positive insofar as they are ways of seeing and acting that define the personhood of the individual meditator—are the second and third volumes of Michel Foucault's *History of Sexuality*, as anomalous as that may sound. The final third of Foucault's intellectual career was devoted to reexamining the development of modern Western notions of sexuality, tracing continuities and discontinuities relating to the rise of Christianity. But having famously come to the conclusion that "sex is boring," in his final years Foucault adjusted his focus to what he had come to think of as a more fundamental issue: the history of the human person.[17] Foucault came to see that before we can properly grasp what was novel about Christianity's treatment of sexuality, we must first understand what was novel about Christianity's conceptions of issues like desire, truth, and the makeup of human personhood. This requires first establishing how these matters were thought of in ancient Greece and Rome. With this aim Foucault conducted the research that would be presented in the second and third volumes of the series, published in French in 1984, whose titles are rendered in English as the *Use of Pleasure* and the *Care of the Self*. This research grew out of Foucault's reading of texts showing the specific ways that *aphrodisia* or amorous enjoyments were thought of in the ancient Western world, with special attention to related aims, associations, and potential dangers. Together these texts bespeak these societies' evolving discourses about sexual activity and related concerns, in which the public (that is, the male, free public) participated collectively; how any single individual understood or experienced these concerns is a separate matter. The materials that Foucault found most revealing treat in a prescriptive manner issues related to how to live a good life—how to live in a way that is enjoyable, well ordered, and healthy. In addition to sexual activity, these texts address ideas and practices related to beauty, marital relations, home economics, friendship, citizenship, medicine, and daily physical comportment, including ways of relating to food.

By mining materials offering prescriptions for how to live well, Foucault is able to uncover underlying ideas about how the human person was constituted in a specific cultural and historical context. This led him to describe a hermeneutical category that he referred to as "technologies of [the] self." These are "techniques which permit individuals to effect, by their own means [Foucault adds in one version of this lecture: or with the help of other people], a certain number of operations on their own bodies, on their own souls, on their own thoughts, on their own conduct, and this in a manner so as to transform themselves, modify themselves, or to attain a certain state of perfection, of happiness, of purity, of supernatural power, and so on."[18] In their pursuit of some desired manner of being in the world—health, happiness, holiness—people are in a constant process of self-maintenance and becoming; the diverse means by which they do this are technologies of self. Foucault observes that "as there are different forms of care, there are different forms of self."[19] Using this hermeneutic, we can examine discrete techniques of caring for and cultivating oneself to reveal the conceptions of human personhood that they perpetuate or are based upon. Those conceptions of subjectivity can then be historicized.

Foucault's widely dispersed late-career lectures and writings as well as subsequent decades of work by scholars across a range of academic fields show that the highly elastic category of "technologies" or "techniques of self" has been understood and applied in three distinct ways, each tied to a different sense of what can be expressed by the Greek term *askēsis* or asceticism. The primary way that Foucault deployed "technologies of self" is to refer to formal practices that a person might self-consciously engage in for personal betterment, including procedures for observation, self-examination, directed contemplation, confession, journaling, and letter writing. In this respect, Foucault follows Pierre Hadot's inquiry into the shaping of individuals through "spiritual exercises" in the ancient world, a category Hadot had modeled after the Catholic contemplative practices codified by Ignatius of Loyola (1491–1556). Hadot and Foucault were especially interested in how these practices connect an individual to truth and shape them as a moral subject. A person performing such exercises with the intention of self-transformation can be seen as practicing *askēsis*, a kind of training, or "the effort that the individual was urged to bring to bear on himself," in Foucault's words.[20] We can call this sense 1 of "technologies of self," which is the most restrictive understanding of the term. But as historian of religion Steven Collins has pointed out, all cultures must teach their children literally everything—how to walk, eat, deal with waste, speak, dress, interact with other people and the physical world. The innumerable and mostly informal means by which cultures do this give us sense 2 of "technologies of self." As applied practices that shape an individual as a member of society, and deriving from that society, these are directly related to Bourdieu's category of habitus. Internalizing and living by these guardrails constitutes *askēsis* in a second, quite different meaning of the term. Midway between the specificity of sense 1 and the universality of sense 2 lies sense 3 of what can be meant by "technologies of self": techniques of self-formation tied to particular disciplines or vocations—athletics, military training, performing magic, certain arts, occupying a particular social niche—that require, as Collins puts it, "a training or education which produces a certain kind of individual who possesses skills, physical and mental, which others do not."[21] Historians have examined, for example, how in premodern times the process of becoming a member of the royal court, in India and Europe alike, involved fashioning oneself as a specific kind of person through the assumption of particular manners of dress, physical comportment, and speech.[22] This is the reproduction of the habitus for occupying a specific position in society—or for trying to escape from it. Over the last few decades a number of scholars have used the hermeneutic of "technologies of self" to guide their examination of the vocation of religious asceticism, the kind of *askēsis* epitomized by the lifestyle of the Desert Fathers of fourth-century Christianity. As an attempt to reconstruct the discipline of meditative reclusion in Tibet, this study is primarily about "techniques of selfhood" in sense 3, and its associated sense of what is expressed with the word "asceticism." However, as the Tibetan tantric eremitic vocation is simultaneously constituted by both contemplative practices for self-transformation and sundry informal means of shaping a person's behavior, this study is also concerned with technologies of self in senses 1 and 2, and their related forms of *askēsis*. In general, religious asceticism lends itself very readily to exploration through the hermeneutic of the technologies of self in all three senses at once, because it is about making a dramatic and highly visible break with one's former life and subjecting oneself to a new set of self-transformative operations, both more and less formal, toward the goal of becoming a more perfect being.[23]

As Collins has noted, both Foucault and Hadot expressed an interest in the applicability of these hermeneutics to the study of Buddhism, in particular its contemplative practices and its monastic tradition.[24] With the present work, I hope to demonstrate the value of pursuing this line of inquiry, as well as the richness of the Tibetan literary archive in support of such a project.

Of particular importance to how Foucault conducts his inquiry into the history of the (Western) self is the hermeneutic of problematization, which is to ask how something becomes "an object of concern, an element for reflection, and a material for stylization" of a person's behavior.[25] This entails examining a text to isolate how its author understands some particular concern as registering for the imagined reader, this often being implicit in the prescriptions given for dealing with that concern. With the hermeneutic of problematization, we are interested in the question of *on what specific grounds* the matter at hand is or isn't viewed as constituting a problem for the individual, and *how intensely* the matter is regarded as a problem, which is typically indexed by the degree of elaboration to which it is subjected. To Foucault's formulation I would add that in some cases we must go the further step of evaluating how a given text treats multiple possible ways of problematizing a concern vis-à-vis *one another*—whether one problematization is denied in favor of another, whether different problematizations are hierarchized or combined. This is essential to tracking diachronic arcs within the discourse.

To use one example from the *Use of Pleasure* to demonstrate this approach, based on his reading of prescriptive texts from around the fourth century BCE, including influential treatises attributed to Hippocrates (ca. 460–ca. 370), Foucault describes how in ancient Greece, sexual activity was problematized in such a way that the relative propriety of an individual's sexual conduct was viewed as an outcome of "an interplay of qualities—dryness, heat, moisture, cold—between the body and its milieu." In this setting, sexual acts were thought of and treated in terms of their warming, cooling, drying, and moistening effects on an individual's corporeal being, and needed to be moderated accordingly. This rendered sex an issue that intersected with such concerns as a person's clothing, diet, hygiene, and exercise habits, but also with the weather and the time of year. Completely absent is any concern for what specific acts are committed or with whom: those differences simply did not register, were not legible in this particular discourse about sex. Having been drawn into relief, this society's specific way of problematizing sexual activity—and more important, the notions of the human person on which it is based—can now be viewed in comparison with those of other societies and historicized.[26]

This methodology holds the person at its center, attempting to systematically establish the considerations in relation to which their activity is oriented and their subjectivity is produced. Within literatures of self-cultivation, any specific method of problematizing some concern will be defined in large part by what it does or does not raise above the threshold of consideration for the individual who is to put those prescriptions into practice. To some extent, we are using the textual evidence to gain a sense of what was thinkable or unthinkable at a certain time and place, and what that meant for the production of selfhood. A distinct advantage of the hermeneutic of problematization is that it can bring to light constituent elements of an author's thinking that the author is not directly interested in or concerned with, revealing unexamined tendencies of thought.

For example, although caves have long been the paradigmatic setting for individual long-term retreat in Tibet, prescriptive retreat texts also mention the use of thatched huts, tents, and small cabins made of wood or stone.[27] Few authors directly address the implications of doing a retreat while residing in these different kinds of structure, but two that do provide a telling contrast. The commentarial appendix to Yangönpa Gyeltsen Pel's (1213–1258) *Blazing Jewel: The Mountain Dharma That Is the Source of All Good Qualities*, an influential and comprehensive retreat manual that will be described in detail in chapter 1, includes the statement that doing a retreat in a recently constructed hut may be preferable to doing a retreat in a cave. This is because an old structure can carry a negative influence or "taint" (*grib*) left over from a previous inhabitant, which may prove harmful. Four centuries later, in a shorter retreat manual titled *Garland of Critical Points for the Precious Mountain Dharma*, Lhatsün Namkha Jikmé (1597–1650)—also known as Künzang Namgyel, or the Madman of Kongpo—espouses a very different view, asserting that meditators "of the superior type" will be able to abide in caves and other "unfabricated, naturally existing" dwellings, just as the great masters of the past had done. Meditators who are of only middling capacities may need to resort to manmade structures. This is not ideal, because constructing and dwelling in such a shelter can lead to feelings of possessiveness, which may result in the squandering of one's religious progress.[28] The two authors have framed the question of what kind of structure the meditator should reside within in different ways, raising different concerns above the threshold of consideration for the retreatant: for Yangönpa, the foremost concern is that a supernatural residue may be left in the dwelling, which may adversely affect a later inhabitant. For Namkha Jikmé, the concern is the inhabitant's potential feelings toward the structure, as framed by the overarching Buddhist goal of detachment. Underlying these differing instructions with respect to the retreat dwelling are differing ideas about what forces the meditator is most affected by and the concerns in relation to which they should orient their behavior. For an individual seeking instructions for how to do a retreat, a different notion of what constitutes their experience in the world will be conveyed depending on whether they follow Yangönpa's or Namkha Jikmé's directives about the retreat dwelling. Focusing on how an author has problematized a particular concern allows us to connect specific prescriptions with the systems of thought, both formal and informal, to which they are related.

The central chapters of this book explore how dozens of authors have respectively problematized six orienting concerns in a meditator's comportment during an individual long-term retreat: place, other people, food, various kinds of danger, the spiritual lineage, and time. The aim is to highlight shared interpretations, underlying tensions, and observable changes in the discourse over time. Certain concerns, values, and even basic ways of seeing and thinking gain and ebb in their salience to the retreatant's conduct—at least according to idealizing textual presentations of that conduct. In many instances, this is a matter of contrasting how authors differently posit a conceptual boundary—around the meditator, around the retreat, between right and wrong behaviors—and how the ascetic is to maintain that boundary through limits on their behavior. Throughout, it will be useful to pay special attention to the language and metaphors through which the tradition has expressed itself.

Together these chapters trace a genealogy of the Tibetan "ascetic self." I use this term to refer to the form of selfhood cultivated by the individual during their time in retreat based on the sum total of prescriptions they subscribe to, as well as the different versions of that self that have existed over the many centuries of the Himalayan retreat tradition. The Tibetan ascetic self is established through how the meditator has historically been encouraged to understand and comport themselves in relationship to a number of different dimensions: the spatial, the interpersonal, the material, the bodily, the temporal. Ultimately the Tibetan ascetic self emerges as a shifting, historically contingent entity that is constituted in relation to diverse interpretations of practical concerns. This ascetic self sits at the center of—is produced by and reproduces—the Tibetan eremitic habitus.

I am not the first scholar to foreground the category of the "ascetic self." I direct the reader's attention to Gavin Flood's 2004 book, the *Ascetic Self: Subjectivity, Memory, and Tradition*, and Niki Kasumi Clements's *Sites of the Ascetic Self: John Cassian and Christian Ethical Formation*, from 2020. Flood's work is a comparative study of religious asceticism, based on Christian, Hindu, and early Theravada Buddhist scriptural traditions, taking up some of the same issues and themes as the present study but from a more macro-level and phenomenological perspective. *Mountain Dharma* has a great deal in common with Clements's study, given its focus on "the mechanisms involved in formation, arguing a view of asceticism as a means of self-cultivation as opposed to self-renunciation," relying on the hermeneutic of the technologies of self in order to do so.[29]

In his treatment of the retreat dwelling, Lhatsün Namkha Jikmé attaches heightened value to residing in a naturally existing structure like a cave, and he praises the forebears of his tradition for having done so. The fact that his august predecessor Yangönpa states a clear preference for a manmade structure suggests that Namkha Jikmé may have harbored a misperception about the ideals that gave shape to the eremitic pursuit in earlier centuries. This disparity highlights an issue that will figure prominently in this study: how the ascetic may be defined as existing in a certain relationship to the dimension of time through ideas and values that are attached to specific modes of ascetic abiding. A central argument concerns a phenomenon that I refer to as "lived deferential reverence." As we track what successive generations of authors of prescriptive retreat texts have portrayed as being possible or impossible to achieve ascetically at the time of their writing, a clear tendency emerges: in the latter centuries of the tradition, authors state with increasing frequency that there is a superior way of ascetic abiding that was once possible, as exemplified by the exploits of past masters of the Buddhist contemplative tradition, but is no longer feasible, as demonstrated by the imperfect asceticism to be observed during one's own time. These latter-day authors then prescribe what they present as a less ideal form of ascetic abiding. This dynamic has important implications for the Tibetan ascetic self. For one, it makes a statement upholding the greatness of the accomplishments of the enlightened forefathers of the meditative tradition, to whom the latter-day contemplative is related through lineal descent. But while reaffirming the goal of achieving that same greatness, it asserts the impossibility of doing so in the present. This has historically served to justify changes in how asceticism is practiced. Even more significant, I argue, is how making such a statement places the prescribed form of asceticism in a historical frame: the very process of living by that attenuated form now reinforces a sense of historical consciousness, as the gap between the imagined, ideal asceticism and the lesser version actually practiced serves as a continual reminder of the distances in time and ability that separate the past masters from the meditator in the present. In this way, the form of asceticism that one lives by becomes an expression of a deferential relationship to that which the tradition most reveres. This attitude of lived deferential reverence, expressed in developments in many different facets of the anchoritic pursuit, becomes more prominent in the latter centuries of the tradition, suggesting the growth of a historical consciousness over time. This book argues that lived deferential reverence, as a specific way of seeing the world and beings within it that gets instantiated through various modes of activity performed by individuals—thereby rendering commonplace and true the ideas that underlie it—becomes, over time, a critical organizing part of the Himalayan ascetic habitus. Lived deferential reverence can be seen as a way of problematizing some concern—or as may be more accurate, a constituent part of such a problematization. I propose lived deferential reverence as a pattern of thought and behavior likely to play an organizing role in other long-standing traditions of religious asceticism as well.[30] Tracking this pattern of lived deferential reverence with respect to diverse facets of the eremitic endeavor provides the basis for a transhistorical argument about the category of enlightenment that I develop over the course of this book, to be addressed most directly in its final two chapters.

Chapter 1 provides an introduction to the prescriptive literature that is the central source material for this study, while also providing some indications of what an individual meditative retreat traditionally consisted of. The chapter begins by describing and comparing three of these texts and their respective presentations of the retreat endeavor: Yangönpa Gyeltsen Pel's *Blazing Jewel*, the most influential prescriptive retreat text of the premodern Tibetan world, which I characterize as a retreat *manual*; Karma Chakmé's (1608/10/13–1678) *Mountain Dharma: Direct Advice on Retreat*, the second most influential, which I refer to as a retreat *handbook*; and Drakar Lozang Pelden's (1866–1928) *Garland of Pearls: The Mountain Dharma Requisite for All Dharma Practitioners Staying in Isolated Places*, which I describe as a retreat *guide*. Some observations about the broader corpus of prescriptive retreat literature are then made, as well as a few caveats delineating the limits of this study.

When embarking upon a long-term retreat, one of the first considerations that a meditator must contend with is where to do it. Chapter 2, "Locating the Ascetic Self," compares how retreat texts have treated the question of what locales are suitable or unsuitable for long-term retreat, and what those instructions reveal about these authors' understandings of the ascetic self. After reviewing the essentially universal expectation that an individual should meditate in a place of interpersonal isolation, the chapter focuses on three fundamentally different ways that authors have instructed the practitioner to go about evaluating the suitability of a potential retreat location, which are based on different understandings of how the individual relates to their physical surroundings. These three prescribed modes of geospatial awareness can be described, respectively, as experiential, geomantic, and reverential. The last of these maintains that what makes a potential retreat location suitable is its having been inhabited by a great meditator in the past. This view came to dominate in the latter centuries of the retreat tradition, reflecting an increase in thinking about the ascetic as existing in relation to the past masters of the tradition. The personhood of the meditator is established in part through their relationship to the dimension of time, deriving from the way the physical environment is made legible to them.

With a location decided on, the boundaries of one's retreat will be engendered by the observance of limitations in one's interpersonal relationships. Chapter 3, "Isolating the Ascetic Self," considers the prescriptions given for maintaining interpersonal boundaries during a retreat by examining how retreat texts have problematized relations with family, with the faithful laity, with the retreat attendant, and with other retreatants. Over time, authors assume the ascetic to inhabit different sociological realities—a heroic loner, for example, or a ritualist serving a host of lay clients. Another important shift is a growing acceptance of the fact that an individual will most likely do their retreat in a place occupied by other meditators, necessitating detailed prescriptions to regulate interactions between them. Some authors of the nineteenth and early twentieth centuries would even go so far as to say that the presence of other ascetics is essential to an individual meditative retreat, showing the expansion of retreat discourse to accommodate the dictates of celibate monasticism, made necessary by the benighted circumstances in which we are understood to now live. Together, these intersecting trends entail a dramatic reconceptualization of the fundamental nature of individual retreat over time.

A critical concern throughout the duration of an individual long-term retreat is the food by which the meditator will be sustained. Chapter 4, "Nourishing the Ascetic Self," examines the different ways that food has been problematized by authors of prescriptive retreat texts. The tradition has shown relatively little interest in what the food is or how it is consumed, focusing far more on how it is acquired. The specifics become critically important in rendering the retreatant's ascetic conduct ethical or unethical, with food emerging, I argue, as the preeminent moral concern. While hailing the alchemical technique of "essence extraction" (*bcud len*) as a means to transcend the need for ordinary human foodstuffs, authors of retreat texts are quick to discount the practice as a realistic possibility in their present moment. To then break the retreat to go begging for sustenance, with all the dangers brought on by doing so, becomes an expression of the ascetic's diminished standing relative to the earlier generations of the lineage.

Also of concern throughout an individual retreat are a variety of threats to the meditator's physical well-being. Chapter 5, "Preserving the Ascetic Self," looks at how exegetes of the tradition have problematized threats to the meditator, including sickness, cold temperatures, and physical harm caused by nefarious individuals. The chapter explores the techniques prescribed for counteracting these threats as producing a distinct subculture of healing and self-preservation, formulated amid the specific circumstances of long-term reclusion. The collective discourse is remarkably consistent in the kinds of techniques offered for averting such a diverse array of dangers, suggesting that the retreat tradition has fostered and is fundamentally based upon a model of selfhood defined by the mutability of its corporeality, which I refer to as an imaginal self. This manner of relating to the self is produced in part through how technologies for dealing with potential bodily harms are hierarchized relative to one another, which ensures that higher Buddhist and ascetic values are recognized even when they cannot be adhered to in actual fact.

Framing the entire endeavor of retreat, from start to finish and beyond, is the meditator's relationship to the spiritual lineage. Chapter 6, "Forming the Ascetic Self," considers eremitic ways of relating to the eminent yogins of earlier generations, to the lama, and to one's disciples. This chapter identifies a constitutive element of Tibet's ascetic subculture by highlighting how the tradition offers certain relational circularities based on visualization and emulation that serve to close the loop between meditator, guru, and more enlightened masters of generations past, thereby overcoming imperfections in the transmission lineage, made necessary due to the specific circumstances of meditating in isolation. Prescriptive retreat texts instantiate lived deferential reverence through the authorial stances assumed by their creators, with author and reader alike being established as existing in a particular moment in time through their positioning relative to the prospect of enlightenment.

To form a bridge to the present, chapter 7, "The Tibetan Ascetic Self in Time," looks back at the history of long-term retreat from the perspective of our present moment, in which the ideal of meditating for a period of three years and three fortnights or months constitutes a powerful normalizing force in globalized Tibetan Buddhism. This chapter traces a history of the ideal of practicing for three years and three fortnights: its articulation in tantric scriptures around the turn of the first millennium, its ambiguous place in individual retreat practice over centuries, and its rise to ubiquity in both communal and individual retreat. This has occurred thanks in large part to the retreat program instituted by Jamgön Kongtrül in 1860, which provides resolution to many of the challenges that had been central to individual retreat discourse and practice for centuries. I argue that the remarkable success of Kongtrül's model of retreat is evidence of the attitude of lived deferential reverence, such that the very endeavor of retreat, undertaken in these specific parameters, has come to express feelings of distance from and reverence for the meditation masters of generations long past.

The conclusion briefly reflects upon some key findings of this study, then turns to address a question on the margins of and yet integral to the entire project.

In parallel to how this study elaborates upon the positive aspects of attempting to achieve the negative renunciatory ideal, it brings attention to the rich intellectual history of what is in one narrow sense an anti-intellectual tradition. Tibet's eremitic subculture has throughout its history defined itself in contradistinction to the high intellectual tradition of monastic scholasticism. Hagiographic representations of great yogins commonly argue through narrative accounts or spontaneous songs that learning Buddhist truths through meditative experience is superior to learning them from familiarity with philosophical discourse; the vast learning of the *geshé* (*dge bshes*) is lampooned in a manner that argues in favor of a meditative pedagogy that supersedes reliance on books.[31] In this very specific way, the retreat tradition may be anti-intellectual. But this by no means precludes anchoritism from being intellectual in a different sense, as the challenges inherent to the eremitic pursuit have provoked creative and thoughtful exegesis over centuries. In the course of this book I hope to bring out the intellectual richness of this tradition, in spite of its self-conscious distancing from the centers of monastic learning, to demonstrate that the historian of religion's inquiry need not be governed by what the tradition may outwardly portray as possessing or lacking intellectual depth.

This study also advances an argument through the fundamental way it problematizes meditation as a phenomenon to be studied. The research for this book has been undertaken as interest in meditation has been on the rise in the Euro-American world and beyond. At present, meditation and/or mindfulness is commonly prescribed for the mentally and physically well, but also for the depressed, the sick, the old, and the dying. Meditation and/or mindfulness is even for American elementary schoolers—a development that, in the broad sweep of Buddhist history, is especially worthy of note. The methods of delivery for instruction are more varied than at any previous moment in the history of Buddhist contemplation. The institutions that provide access to meditation include public schools, universities, hospitals, corporate human resource departments, churches, yoga studios, and Buddhist centers. The instructors include doctors, psychologists, yoga instructors, experienced lay meditators, and monks and nuns, whether Buddhist by birth or by choice. Internet-based how-tos and apps provide sources of expertise while allowing us to be our own gurus. Playing a complementary role are academic centers dedicated to the scientific study of contemplative traditions, which support and funnel into certain trajectories medical, public health-related, psychological, sociological, and Buddhological research. Underlying the enthusiasm for this kind of academic work (on the institutional level, and for a great many, on a personal level as well) are an interest in how the Western medical understanding of the self may be advanced through this encounter and how the power of meditation may be harnessed to solve both personal and social ills.

I believe that the two trends, the popular and the academic, coalesce in their relating to Buddhist meditation in a way that can be characterized as instrumentalist. These discourses define meditation by what medically or socially quantifiable effects it can be proven to have. David McMahan sees meditation as having become subject to "the modern cult of calculability in which something is only real when it is measurable and measured."[32] The creation and expansion of the academic field of contemplative studies, sustained by its diverse participants, serves to institutionalize this fundamental way of problematizing meditation as an object of study. The operative truth at the center of these discourses—holding them together and getting proved through their activities—is the medical, psychological, and sociological efficacy of meditation. Complicating this picture, many Tibetan lamas are very keen to draw from these findings, with the goal of making their teaching more effective, creating a feedback loop between the two spheres.

As undeniable as meditation's salubrious effects may be, other approaches to understanding meditation can be of significant value for historians, scholars of religion, institution builders, practitioners, and contemplative studies investigators. In their instrumentalist approach, the popular and academic discourses tend to treat meditation as an ahistorical phenomenon, paying little attention to how it has been affected by the cultural, social, or historical contexts in which it has traditionally existed. Harold Roth provides some insight into why this is the case, presenting contemplative studies today as a corrective to an overly historical approach to the study of religion that has dominated the field for decades—that historical approach having been a corrective to an overly Protestant, theological, and ahistorical bent of an earlier era.[33]

Related to all of this, Buddhist studies has addressed through study and translation the diversity of meditative practices and understandings of the path of self-transformation articulated by 2,500 years of Buddhist tradition, providing a thorough understanding of the *contents* of meditation practices from most corners of Buddhist Asia—although new troves continue to be discovered.[34] Yet there has been almost no attempt to systematically consider the specific *contexts* in which meditation has been practiced in Asian societies. Who is meditating, at what point in their lives, with whom, and to what end? Integral to the question of context is how the personhood of the meditator has been formed. Absent a discussion of these kinds of details in traditional Buddhist societies, modern observers may naturally assume that meditation was practiced far more widely than it actually was, and that its purpose has remained a constant. This study aims to demonstrate how viewing a form of meditation as a meaningfully different thing if performed in a temple or a cave, alone or in a group, with aspirations of transcendence or merely for some emotional relief, as a rite of passage or a lifelong endeavor, can open new ways of seeing Buddhist and Asian religious history. What would happen if we included as subjects schoolchildren in Kentucky, hospice residents, NBA players preparing for a game, or a CEO using Headspace on her morning subway ride? With this book I hope to encourage further systematic examination of the contexts in which Buddhist meditation has been practiced, both to fill certain gaps in our understanding of the history of the tradition and to lend insight into how new selves are being fashioned out of their relationship to meditation in the present. This project aligns fundamentally with the direction eloquently laid out by McMahan in his 2017 article "How Meditation Works: Theorizing the Role of Cultural Context in Buddhist Contemplative Practices," and further expanded upon in his 2023 book, *Rethinking Meditation: Buddhist Meditative Practice in Ancient and Modern Worlds*. I believe the present study largely heeds that call, having many of the same motivating convictions and employing similar theoretical perspectives.

In a comparable fashion, tantra, as part of the broader ritual and contemplative traditions of Asia (Buddhist, Hindu, Jain), has long posed a pointed methodological problem for historians of religion. This book demonstrates how the elusive phenomenon of tantra can be gotten at, in part, through a systematic examination of the contexts in which it was practiced historically.

Finally, two notes about the form of the present text. First, some of the passages translated in the chapters to follow, which I have conveyed as prose, are lines of nonrhyming verse in the original Tibetan. This modification is to prevent excessive line breaks distracting from what is being expressed. All translations are my own unless otherwise noted.

Second, throughout most of the book I talk about the Tibetan retreat tradition in the past tense; since none of my principal source material derives from our current period, I am to some extent talking about a bygone form of the practice. But individual and communal long-term retreat are both alive and well, and much about how they were practiced in the past still holds true today. I hope to explore these matters further, through a more comprehensive study of the role of communal long-term retreat in globalized Tibetan Buddhism. The genesis of this book was an encounter with the living tradition in the fall of 2001, when I conducted a rudimentary investigation of how Jamgön Kongtrül's communal three-year, three-fortnight retreat program was being implemented at Bokar Ngedön Chökhor Ling monastery in Mirik, West Bengal, under the direction of the late Bokar Rinpoché—the principal disciple of Kalu Rinpoché and a direct inheritor of Kongtrül's lineage. Though brief, my encounter with Bokar Rinpoché and a few of the wonderful people in his monastic community was utterly formative. In retrospect, I see that the last twenty-four years of my life have been spent in search of answers to questions about the Tibetan eremitic tradition that arose for me at that time.

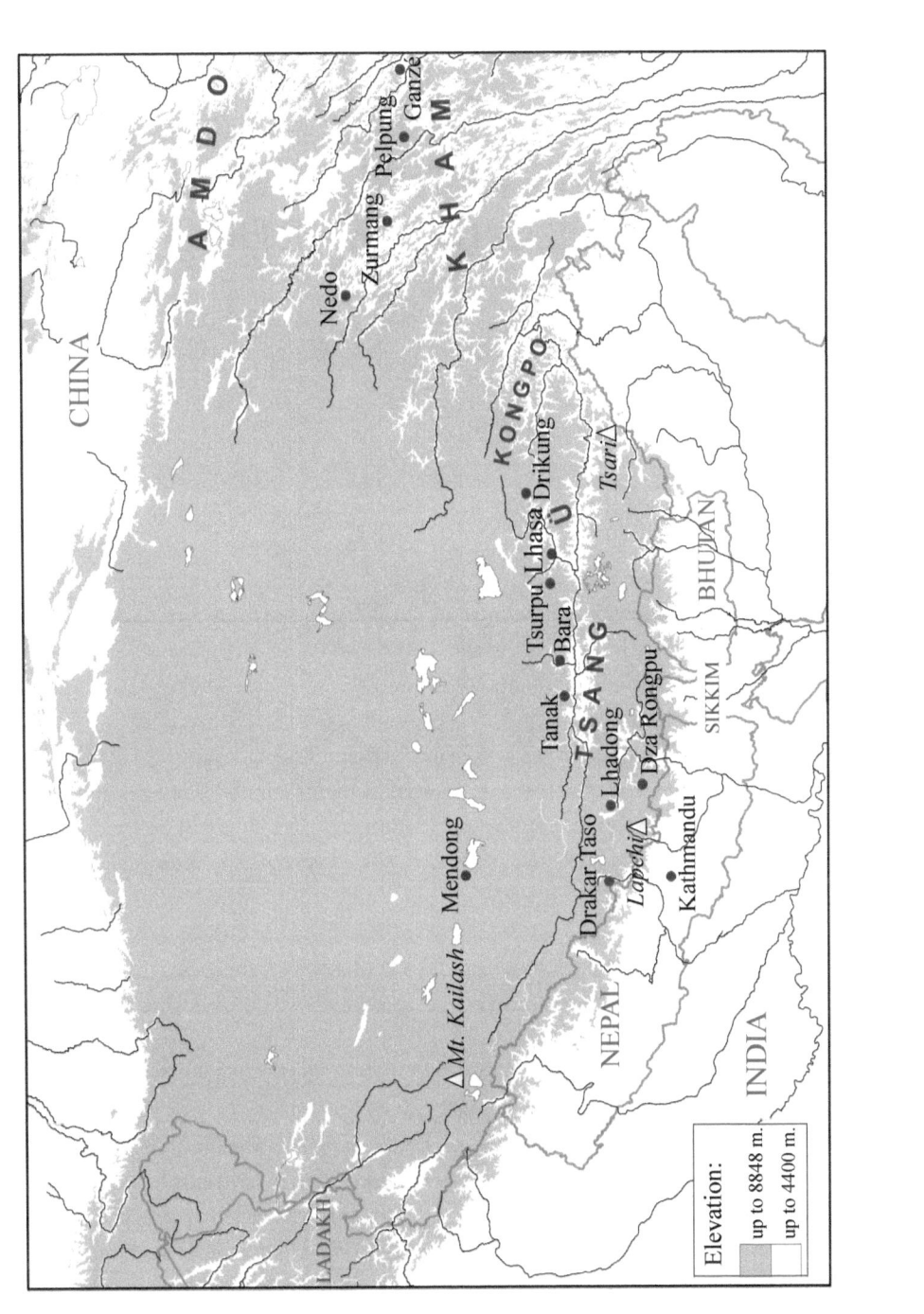

CHAPTER 1

THE PRESCRIPTIVE LITERATURE FOR INDIVIDUAL RETREAT

The principal source material for this study, listed in the appendix, includes twenty-nine texts by twenty-two authors representing Nyingma, Kadampa, Geluk, and various Kagyu orientations, hailing from all geographic corners of the Tibetan-speaking world, composed between the twelfth century and the early decades of the twentieth.[1] Although many of these authors were among the most renowned thinkers and prolific writers of their times, others are little known. To provide an introduction to this body of literature, this chapter will begin by describing in detail two of the most influential texts, and then a third, less well-known example. These are three of the longest texts offering prescriptions for retreat, and each will be cited many times in the chapters to follow. All bear the title of *ri chos*, "mountain Dharma." Dating from the thirteenth, seventeenth, and early twentieth centuries, they represent three different sectarian orientations, and take three very different approaches to providing instruction. While discussing these texts, I will also highlight the basic parameters of retreat as presented by each author, including the central practices to be performed and the schedule for doing so. This rough sketch of what an individual retreat consists of will be fleshed out over the chapters to follow.

The discussion will then extend to address some important points concerning the prescriptive retreat literature as a whole. A few more individual texts will be briefly described, the remaining ones to be introduced as they come up in later chapters. The last part of the chapter will stake out some caveats marking the limits of this study.

The most influential prescriptive text for individual long-term retreat in the premodern period is Yangönpa Gyeltsen Pel's thirteenth-century *Blazing Jewel:*

The Mountain Dharma That Is the Source of All Good Qualities, which is accompanied by a commentarial resource called the *Great Appendix*. Yangönpa (so named after completing one of his early retreats at a hermitage in southwestern Tibet known as Yangön) is one of the most revered Kagyu masters of his era. Born in the Latö area of Tsang, he remained in southwestern Tibet his entire life. He began his education at the age of five or six and entered Lhadong monastery at nine. Between the ages of around eleven and twenty-two he trained under the famed ascetic Kodrakpa Sönam Gyeltsen (1182–1261), after which he took full monastic ordination. He would go on to train under Götsangpa Gönpo Dorjé (1189–1258) of the Drukpa Kagyu, Sakya Paṇḍita (1182–1251), and Chenga Drakpa Jungné (1175–1255), the fourth abbot of Drikung. Having completed numerous long-term retreats during those years, later in life Yangönpa settled into a pattern of spending four months each summer in strict retreat at Namkha Ding hermitage, and four months each winter in retreat at Lhadong. In between, he was compelled to tend to divers worldly affairs, such as dispensing instruction, providing materially for his community, and mediating disputes in the region. He lived during the time of the Mongol incursion into central Tibet, beginning in 1240, which would dramatically shift the Tibetan political landscape for the next century and beyond.[2]

Yangönpa's *Collected Works*, which are devoted mainly to providing instructions for yogic practice, comprise some 1,700 pages, much of which was set to paper by his close disciple, Chenga Rinchen Den (b. 1202). In 125 folio sides, the *Blazing Jewel* can be described as a *manual* for individual meditative retreat, insofar as it provides a systematic how-to, proceeding step by step while also describing the thoughts and attitudes that should be cultivated continually. In order, its seven chapters address what qualities the potential retreat candidate should exemplify; where to do a retreat; the practices to be undertaken, the central ones being the Six Yogas of Naropa and the Mahāmudrā (this chapter makes up two-thirds of the entire text); the removal of obstructions to spiritual progress; further improvement practices (*bogs dbyung, bogs 'don*); the five "Paths" (*lam, mārga*) or stages of spiritual progress; and liberation, including an exposition on the three "bodies" (*sku, kāya*) of buddhahood. Whereas many other retreat texts only refer to the ritual and meditative practices to be performed, assuming that instruction will be received through some other means, Yangönpa includes actual directions for some of these practices, particularly detailed for exercises manipulating the psychophysical winds of the yogic body, and the Mahāmudrā, which is presented as the supreme contemplative practice, meant to culminate in an understanding of the emptiness of all phenomena. The organization of the text is both sequential and hierarchical, creating up to nine levels of nested subject headings, all clearly marked. The chapter on spiritual obstructions provides a good example of Yangönpa's highly ordered manner of exposition. He begins by addressing the long-term, universal cause of any obstacle to spiritual progress that an individual might experience, which is mistakenly grasping at a (non)existent self. He then proceeds to the more proximate causes of obstacles, of which there are five categories: bad motivations, broken vows, interpersonal relationships, disorder in the psychophysical winds, and demonic influences. Yangönpa discusses each of these separately, to help the meditator understand the nature of the problem. After this, the chapter discusses how to prevent obstacles from arising in the first place. The final section details how to diagnose and counteract an obstacle should one nevertheless arise; such obstacles are broken down into six groups, depending on the phase of spiritual progress in which the meditator is likely to encounter them. The reader is left with the impression that every possible outcome has been covered. Equipped with the theoretical and practical understanding this manual provides, the meditator may feel fully prepared for their time in retreat.

In its form and approach, Yangönpa's *Blazing Jewel* bears a meaningful resemblance to texts of the Stages of the Path (*lam rim*) genre, about which more will be said below. The 175 folio sides of the *Great Appendix,* cited in the introduction, are of a quite different nature. This appendix or supplement (*lhan thabs*) comprises 36 commentarial asides, which are indicated as corresponding to specific places in the main text. This makes the *Great Appendix* in effect a series of endnotes providing further elaboration on topics mentioned in the central exposition. Many of these commentarial asides end with a statement like "so he [Yangönpa] has said." They were written down by Chenga Rinchen Den, who in another text describes the *Great Appendix*'s origins: he petitioned his guru for further clarification on certain key points in the *Blazing Jewel*, which Yangönpa would give only on condition that they be written down and preserved. Yangönpa would check Chenga's transcription and correct any mistakes.³ In its colophon, the *Great Appendix* is characterized as a key that unlocks the *Blazing Jewel*, providing access to the treasures contained within.⁴

Yangönpa's retreat manual and its appendix are commonly treated as a single work.⁵ They have traditionally been grouped with two other texts—the *Secret Explanation of the Vajra Body* and a text on the *bardo* or intermediate state between lives—the three being collectively known as the "Mountain Dharma Trilogy" (*ri chos skor gsum*). Throughout this study, references to Yangönpa's *Mountain Dharma* denote the retreat manual and its appendix.

In the *Blazing Jewel*, Yangönpa favors quoting luminaries of the early Kagyu tradition who were his direct forbears, namely Milarepa, Lama Zhang (1122–1193),

Götsangpa, and above all his guru, Kodrakpa. Preserved throughout the text are a plethora of brief interlinear notes of unspecified provenance, many of which are concerned with identifying the source of a specific teaching.[6] Striking a humble stance, Yangönpa describes the *Blazing Jewel* as something he wrote to hopefully be of benefit to a few disciples. He reaffirms that this is directed toward his students by punctuating sections of instruction with statements like, "Take this to heart, my sons!" (or "my children"; in Tibetan, *bu*).[7]

As for the details of retreat practice, Yangönpa stipulates that the prerequisites that make one fit to "meditate alone in the remoteness of a mountain hermitage" are being an able-bodied person who has given up attachment to the world, has received the four ritual empowerments (*dbang, abhiṣeka*) of Unexcelled Yoga tantra, has trained under a qualified lama, has had some meditative experience, is prepared to be alone, possesses the physical strength and the mental fortitude to endure the hardships of retreat, maintains their vow-based ethics unhypocritically, and remains committed to working for the benefit of sentient beings.[8] Although nowhere stated explicitly, it seems that Yangönpa's assumed reader is a male monastic, not necessarily maintaining the vow of celibacy, and squarely within the Kagyu tradition.

After securing permission from their lama, the practitioner goes to the location for the retreat and performs rituals meant to protect them and to ensure the fruitfulness of their practice. After spending the first month or so on the four preliminary practices, the individual will devote the bulk of formal practice time to the Perfection phase meditations with signs (the Six Yogas of Naropa, here consisting of *tummo*, luminosity, illusory body, dreaming, transference of consciousness, and guru yoga) and without signs (the Mahāmudrā of the ground, of the path, and of the fruit). Save for stipulating that the first month should be devoted to the preliminary practices and that those newly training in *tummo* (*gtum mo*) or inner heat should devote one month to it, Yangönpa provides no specific time frames: neither the *Blazing Jewel* nor the *Great Appendix* states how long a retreat should last.[9] However, in both his last testament and another short text, Yangönpa asserts that the superior undertaking is to complete a retreat lasting nine years, the middling is to do one for six, and the ordinary is to do three.[10] The root text mentions that one should begin a retreat at the beginning of the lunar month, which in the Tibetan cultural world is an auspicious time.[11]

Regarding daily life during retreat, Yangönpa is particularly detailed concerning the contemplations the meditator must perform upon waking up in the morning, before ingesting anything, when the mind and the psychophysical channels are clear.[12] They are to visualize themselves in the form of the tutelary deity or *yidam* (*yi dam*) and consume a blessed pill. They then go for refuge and contemplate their good fortune to be able to practice the Dharma. They also contemplate the impermanence of life, which makes Dharma practice necessary. The retreatant then does practices aimed at preserving their own life, including a visualization of the buddha Amitāyus. They are to dress while generating divine pride, then wash up while visualizing a host of deities and reciting a ritual formula, by which they are purified and the tantric empowerments are refreshed. The retreatant's schedule for the remainder of the day will include either four or six formal sessions of meditative practice; a standard of four sessions predominates throughout the history of the tradition.[13] Yangönpa also describes the essential procedures for doing prostrations and making offerings on a daily basis, as well as the monthly cycle of offering ritual cakes or *tormas* (*gtor ma*), by which the Dharma protectors and the local deities are appeased.

The day's end means the beginning of a crucial period of activity for the retreatant. In preparation for sleep, the meditator does the *Kusulu* (or *Kusali*) Accumulation (*ku su lu'i tshogs*; from the Sanskrit *kuśala*, meaning "right, proper, suitable, good"), which is a form of Cutting; confesses if they have broken any vows during the day; and then assumes what is referred to as the "lion's lying posture" (*seng ge'i nyal thabs*).[14] While falling asleep the meditator is to maintain a visualization and reaffirm their intention of recognizing what is to follow as being a dream. If done properly, the time until waking can then be spent practicing luminosity or dream yoga—to travel the universe, prepare for death, and learn the truth of the illusoriness of existence.

Yangönpa's *Mountain Dharma* holds a special importance in the history of individual long-term retreat in Tibetan Buddhism, having been transmitted, studied, and used by meditators for centuries.[15] The chapters that follow return many times to this earliest of the major prescriptive retreat texts, providing a more complete sense of Yangönpa's take on retreat and his particular understanding of the ascetic self.

Four hundred years later, in eastern Tibet, the great exegete Karma Chakmé (1608/10/13–1678, who often styled himself Rāga Asya, the Sanskrit rendering of Chakmé, "without attachment") would compose the second most important instruction for individual retreat in the premodern period: *Mountain Dharma: Direct Advice on Retreat*. As a youth in Kham, Karma Chakmé received an education grounded in the Nyingma. He did his first short-term retreat, focusing on Avalokiteśvara, at the age of thirteen. In time, he would complete such a cycle of practice for a hundred different deities.[16] As a teenager Karma Chakmé traveled to central Tibet to take ordination and train in the Kagyu. His illustrious teachers included the Sixth Red Hat, Chökyi Wangchuk (1584–1630), and the Tenth Karmapa, Chöying Dorjé (1604–1674). As a teacher, Karma Chakmé's most important activities derived from his relationship with Mingyur Dorjé (1645–1667): after mentoring and transmitting Nyingma teachings to the boy, Karma Chakmé played a crucial role in compiling a cycle of treasure teachings (*gter ma*) that Mingyur Dorjé revealed, known as the Sky Dharma (*gnam chos*). Karma Chakmé helped establish both the Pelyul lineage of the Nyingma and the Nedo sub-branch of the Kagyu, named after the location of a monastery he founded.[17]

Karma Chakmé's *Collected Works* comprise a Himalayan-proportioned sixty volumes. His *Direct Advice on Retreat* is the thirty-second volume, and at 840 folio sides is the Mount Everest of individual retreat instructions. As will be detailed at the beginning of chapter 3, the work is the product of a collaborative process in which Karma Chakmé dictated to his student Tsöndrü Gyatso over a period of five months the sundry instructions that would make up the text.[18] The fifty-three chapters are entirely in verse, reflecting the liturgical nature of much of the content. While the root text of Yangönpa's *Blazing Jewel* is intricately structured, Karma Chakmé's text is far less so: the individual chapters each stand on their own as discrete teachings or practices, with the overall structure created by the ex post facto ordering of those chapters by Tsöndrü Gyatso. Many chapters are presented as teachings delivered in response to a question by Tsöndrü Gyatso about some particular aspect of Dharma practice.[19] As the record of separate teachings on specific points given orally, written down and arranged by a disciple, Karma Chakmé's *Direct Advice on Retreat* is similar in form to Yangönpa's *Great Appendix*.

As structured by Tsöndrü Gyatso, Karma Chakmé's *Direct Advice on Retreat* progresses through preparatory topics like reflecting upon the rarity of a human life, maintaining vows, and completing the preliminary practices (chapters 2–12); where and how to do a retreat (13–16); practices like the Kusali Accumulation, generating longevity, and the "lower" forms of tantric practice, including Kriya, Cārya, and Yoga tantra (17–20); funerary practices and rites for protection from nefarious beings (21–25); Unexcelled Yoga tantra (26); more advanced and esoteric forms of identifying with a deity via *sādhana* (*sgrub thabs*, "means of accomplishment") and other types of yogic practice (27–33); aspects of yogic experience and conduct, including signs of progress, avoiding well-known "places of deviation" (*gol sa*) from the true path, removing obstacles, further improvement practices, and various facets of comportment, both in and outside of a retreat setting (34–40); death and death-related practices (41–44); instructions for practices related to the Dharma protectors (45–52); and finally, the proper manner of dedicating merit (53). *Direct Advice on Retreat* includes instructions for those taking the very first steps in the Dharma, as well for those who, after many years of practice, find themselves the object of devotional activity.[20] A significant proportion of the text deals with death and dying, including how to lead a faithful client through the dying process, how to intervene on behalf of the deceased, and how to determine the proper location for the disposal of a corpse. The text gives a great deal of instruction for rituals performed for other people, whether living or dead. This highlights that Karma Chakmé expects the retreatant to continue to interact with the world outside, fulfilling obligations in an economy of ritual responsibility.

If Yangönpa's *Mountain Dharma* can be described as a retreat *manual* (with its systematic, step-by-step approach, prescribing a retreat consisting of specific practices), Karma Chakmé's can be regarded as a retreat *handbook*, insofar as it is a useful reference containing practical instructions on many things relating to retreat but does not present itself as a start-to-finish program to be adhered to, having been composed piecemeal and accommodating various forms of retreat, to be described presently. Although explicitly titled *Direct Advice on Retreat*, the text is better thought of as a compendium of instructions for the full range of ritual practices that an accomplished and respected anchorite may have reason to perform, both during and after retreat.[21]

While Yangönpa's *Blazing Jewel* takes a one-size-fits-all approach, assuming a specific kind of practitioner, Karma Chakmé's *Direct Advice* offers instruction to different kinds of individuals doing retreats of varying sorts. The text is formulated as a resource for practitioners of both the Nyingma and the Kagyu, reflecting its author's participation in both sectarian traditions. Karma Chakmé refers primarily to aspects of the Kagyu but also includes discussions of their Nyingma correlates (often, for example, discussing the Mahāmudrā and then the Great Perfection manner of approaching some question).[22] This shows the author's expectation that the audience will include practitioners located in either tradition, both of which he treats as fully legitimate. In the colophon, Karma Chakmé explains that he composed this text driven by a vision of a future time when people will wander in mountain hermitages practicing the exoteric and esoteric traditions, the Nyingma and the New schools (*gsar ma*), "all rolled together as one."[23]

In addition, Karma Chakmé's text describes the basic contours of a retreat as practiced by six different tiers of people, completely separate from the question of their sectarian affiliation. These instructions are conveyed in the sixteenth chapter, which bears the title "Direct Advice on Retreat" (*mtshams kyi zhal gdams*), repeating the title of the handbook as a whole. The initial stages of a retreat will be the same for all six kinds of practitioner: the individual will spend between three and seven days meditating assiduously on each of the four mind turnings: the rarity of a human rebirth, the uncertainty of the time and manner of death, the workings of karma, and the faults of samsara. They will then spend about a week on each of the four preliminary practices, here consisting of taking refuge, Vajrasattva purification, mandala offerings, and guru yoga. This will be followed by some days of ritual practices intended to prevent obstacles during the retreat to follow.

From here, Karma Chakmé describes six divergent paths, as different kinds of people will employ different kinds of practices. There are two general categories of practitioner, the *kusali* and the *paṇḍita*. The *kusali* is an ordinary practitioner, animated primarily by faith. As Karma Chakmé explains elsewhere in the text, *kusali* is a Sanskrit term used to denote a yogic practitioner whose lifestyle has become so simple that outside of meditation they are concerned with only three kinds of behavior: eating (*ku*), sleeping (*sa*), and defecating (*li*).[24] (The Tibetan tradition uses the Indic term *bhusuku* in precisely the same way.) Within this general category of ordinary, faith-directed practitioner, an individual will belong to one of three tiers, based on their mental capacities: the limited, the middling, and the superior. The second general category is the *paṇḍita*, a rare being of great learning and ability, animated by a deep understanding of the Dharma rather than mere faith in it. There are three tiers of *paṇḍita* as well.[25]

For the least sophisticated of the six types, the *kusali* of limited faculties, whom Karma Chakmé assumes to be nonliterate, the day begins with waking early and loudly supplicating the lama. The first formal practice session, which ends at dawn, includes the recitation of some short prayers, repeating Avalokiteśvara's six-syllable mantra while visualizing oneself as the deity in the pure realm of Sukhāvatī, the practices of calm abiding and insight meditation (*śamatha* and *vipassanā*), and examining the nature of the mind. Afterward the retreatant will do a few hundred prostrations and eat a meal. There will be three additional sessions in the course of the day, consisting of different practices, depending on what kind of training the individual has received. The final session, which begins after sunset, may include the recitation of the mantra for Padmasambhava or Vajrapāṇi and may close with the Kusali Accumulation. Whether sitting upright (*tsog bu*) or lying in the lion's posture, the *kusali* should fall asleep while visualizing at their heart the guru in the form of the tutelary deity and quietly reciting the six-syllable mantra. This is conducive to seizing control of the experience of sleep, in order to continue practicing throughout the night. For the humblest of the six kinds of practitioner, each day of the retreat is to be regarded as the same as the one before: "No matter how many years or months you stay there, you break it down as if you were meditating for a single day."[26]

For *kusali*s of middling and then superior capacities, Karma Chakmé describes daily routines with increasing levels of elaboration, making use of their broader knowledge of the Dharma and greater mental acuity. Taking the form of retreat just described as a starting point, individuals of middling capacities would add longevity practices, ritual cake practices, protector deity practices, and the recitation of more extensive liturgies. These practitioners may have any of a variety of tutelary deities as the focus of their retreat. Each formal session will primarily consist of reciting the mantra of that deity while doing a visualization. Karma Chakmé adds that the middling *kusali* might read a few pages of text during the break between the first and second meditation sessions. *Kusalis* of superior capacities engage with more advanced yogic practices like *tummo*. For this kind of practitioner, Karma Chakmé has increased expectations for attunement to their actions and bodily processes, which are subject to a higher degree of ritualization. Certain ritual procedures should be added in order to multiply manyfold the positive effects of ritual actions undertaken throughout the day. The practitioner should do the "yoga of eating" (*zas kyi rnal 'byor*) when consuming food, and should not drink water they have not ritually consecrated. Even getting up to relieve oneself is turned into an opportunity for making merit: through an ordered process of visualization, dedication, and the recitation of a mantra, the retreatant's waste is transmuted into an offering that satisfies the thirst and hunger of the *pretas* or hungry ghosts (*yi dwags*). *Kusalis* of lesser capacities are not expected to attend to and ritualize their behavior in so granular a fashion.[27]

For rare individuals of great intelligence and broad learning, who have obtained transmissions and empowerments for many tantric systems and whose powerful minds can fully penetrate the Dharma—rather than merely having faith in it based on how it appears—the retreat endeavor takes on a very different character. These *paṇḍitas* will perform ambitious ritual cycles that represent the highest of the "approach–accomplishment" category of deity-oriented practices. The most capable of the three types of *paṇḍita* will have no trouble acquiring the extensive material resources and ritual assistants—suggesting retreat for these rare individuals may not be solitary—needed to complete the full version of such a practice, known as "Great Accomplishment" or "communal practice" (*sgrub chen, mahāsādhana*) for Nyingmapas and "Accomplishment Offering" or "practice worship" (*sgrub mchod, sādhanapūja*) for the Kagyu and the other New schools. As presented by Karma Chakmé, this practice involves constructing a sand mandala and performing millions of recitations of a deity's mantra, all while visualizing the deity, over a period of about a month.[28] There will be four or three or two main sessions of practice daily, depending on the ability of the practitioner, each consisting of the recitation of a liturgy followed by numerous repetitions of the mantra. In ordinary circumstances Great Accomplishment or Accomplishment Offering entails the unbroken, twenty-four-hours-per-day recitation of the mantra throughout the duration of the rite, achieved through the combined efforts of a team of ritualists, but this expectation does not hold in the context of retreat. The end of the weeks-long cycle is marked by the ritual closing of the mandala and then a *homa* or fire pūjā ritual. All of this constitutes religious practice "with elaborations." Karma Chakmé then instructs that the *paṇḍita* should devote one week to yogic practices focusing on the channels and winds, which is practice "without elaborations," then spend one week examining the nature of the mind, which is "thoroughly without elaborations." This final phase constitutes "taking a break" (*ngal bso*) from the more demanding practices already undertaken.[29] After completing one such cycle, which is a deep engagement with both the Generation and Perfection phases (*bskyed rim, rdzogs rim*) of tantric practice, the superior *paṇḍita* may move on to do the same basic cycle of practice for a different enlightened deity.

Karma Chakmé details that *paṇḍita*s who are of only middling capacities will have less understanding of the practices and less material resources at their disposal, and will therefore do a less elaborate form of such a ritual, known as the "Lesser Accomplishment" (*sgrub chung*), which does not require a full sand mandala. The least capable among the *paṇḍita*s are those who, for any of a variety of reasons, choose to practice continually focusing on a single deity, rather than moving from one to the next.

Karma Chakmé writes of the value of doing intensive practice on a single deity for the space of about a month; only the most capable practitioners can persist for a longer period without their mental state growing stale. Individuals who alternate between the forms of practice with and without elaborations will be able to continue making progress, doing a number of such ritual cycles in succession. In this critical sixteenth chapter Karma Chakmé does not state how long a retreat should last. However, elsewhere in the text he refers to retreats of three years and three fortnights in duration.[30] Karma Chakmé was himself residing in a permanent retreat at the time of composing the text. As for the daily schedule, Karma Chakmé explains that practitioners who have trouble maintaining the visualizations during four daily sessions should resort to doing six shorter sessions. Meanwhile other practitioners will find that as they become ever more habituated to practice, their schedule can be consolidated into just two sessions, one taking up the daylight hours and the other the night.[31]

Karma Chakmé is heavily influenced by the Pure Land strain of Buddhism, which posits that, in addition to striving toward enlightenment through the various standard means, a person can generate the intention to take their next rebirth in a perfected realm where escape from the samsaric process can be achieved more easily via direct contact with a buddha. An entire chapter of *Direct Advice on Retreat* is devoted to a discussion of these enlightened realms. Here Karma Chakmé argues that Sukhāvatī is the supreme among the Pure Lands, because of how easy it is to be reborn there, absolute faith not even being required. Karma Chakmé's enthusiasm for Pure Land imbues his handbook with ideological and ritual content not found in many other prescriptive retreat texts used in this study.[32]

In terms of influence, no prescriptive retreat text of the premodern period comes close to Yangönpa's and Karma Chakmé's respective *Mountain Dharmas*. But a contrasting style of offering retreat instruction comes in the final text, the *Garland of Pearls: The Mountain Dharma Requisite for All Dharma Practitioners Staying in Isolated Places*, by Lozang Pelden Tenzin Nyendrak (1866–1928), the third incarnation of the lineage associated with Drakar Jangchub Ling monastery, in Ganzé, Kham. After being recognized as a reincarnation at the age of four, Lozang Pelden began his education, in time taking ordination as a monk in the Geluk tradition. From ages seventeen to twenty-two he would train at Drepung Loseling in Lhasa. There he engaged the great Nyingma exegete Ju Mipam (1846–1912) in debate, which would contribute greatly to his legacy. He also received teachings in the Nyingma and Sakya traditions. Drakar Lozang Pelden spent the remainder of his life in eastern Tibet, establishing a half-dozen religious institutions and reaching a great number of followers, including the laity and both female and male clerics. In the early twentieth century he was appointed to a leadership position in the administration of Geluk monasteries throughout Kham under Zhao Erfeng (1845–1911), and later under the Chinese Frontier Authorities. In this capacity he tried to institute a series of reforms, raising the expectations for monastic behavior. Lozang Pelden also had contacts with a number of Europeans in the area. His popularity seems to have led to some uneasy relationships, his life being peppered with conflicts, culminating in the period from 1919 to 1922 when he lived in exile in Amdo. He had significant contact with the Bönpo meditator and writer Shardza Tashi Gyeltsen (1859–1933/35).[33]

The religious institutions established by Drakar Lozang Pelden tended to be semiformal "encampments" (*sgar*), common in the region. Monks, nuns, and laypeople would arrive, attracted by his teachings, and later return to their home monasteries or worldly obligations. Some of these communities were considered hermitages, and many training under Lozang Pelden practiced in retreat. While staying at the religious encampment of Getar Lung, which he established in Drango in 1903, Lozang Pelden composed the *Garland of Pearls*, in 278 folio sides, contained within the third of his twenty-volume *Collected Works*. The *Garland of Pearls* does not lay out a specific meditative or ritual program, let alone provide actual instruction for those practices, but does mention that the retreatant is expected to adhere to the daily schedule of four meditation sessions and should refrain from venturing out of their cell to cook, get water, or meet visitors, except during the breaks between sessions.[34] The handful of instances where Lozang Pelden mentions a specific religious practice all refer to those that fit within the Geluk tradition, but the text expresses no specific sectarian alignment. Signaling a universalist intent, the title indicates that it is to be regarded as "requisite for all Dharma practitioners staying in isolated places." As sources of authority, Lozang Pelden tends to draw quotations from the writings of Kadam and Geluk masters like Atīśa (982–1054), Potowa Rinchen Sel (1027/31–1105), and Tsongkhapa Lozang Drakpa (1357–1419), and from canonical sources and commentaries. Compared to Yangönpa's start-to-finish retreat manual and Karma Chakmé's wide-ranging handbook, the *Garland of Pearls* offers far less in terms of direct instruction, instead providing a thorough body of advice on how and how not to live in retreat. Throughout this study I refer to this and other texts written in a similar style as retreat *guides*.

The *Garland of Pearls* eschews organization in terms of chapters or marked sections, instead offering guidance on a succession of concerns pertinent to the retreat endeavor, flowing from one topic into the next, often circling back to reinforce points already made. Persistent concerns include the need to separate oneself from home and family; repelling visitors; avoiding improper, hypocritical relationships with patrons; relating to the lama and Dharma siblings; and maintaining an attitude of *bodhicitta*. While most other prescriptive retreat texts achieve their form by unfolding concrete prescriptions, Lozang Pelden's tries to equip the meditator with an understanding of the most ideal form of religious life, which they can then try to embody. Lozang Pelden conveys his vision by making contrasts between what are in his opinion proper and improper ways of conducting oneself. For example, in a number of places he makes a point of contrasting how ordinary people behave with respect to some aspect of life—productive labor; relating to servants and retinues; facing illness, old age, and death—and how a proper Dharma practitioner will behave.[35] Rather than taking the purity of one's asceticism for granted, Lozang Pelden extemporizes on the full range of forms that one's comportment might take, rightly or wrongly. Because of this, his exposition ends up talking a great deal about lay life and lower forms of religiosity. By contrast, Yangönpa's *Blazing Jewel* says nothing about the world outside the retreat.

Much of what Drakar Lozang Pelden writes about in the *Garland of Pearls* is how to be a proper Buddhist cleric in a fairly general fashion, not specific to the retreat endeavor. The instructions regarding retreat are again conveyed through contrasts. Over eight pages Lozang Pelden thoroughly distinguishes between genuine and lesser retreatants: an individual of the latter category may be motivated by thoughts of attaining praise and material resources, set up their retreat at an insufficient physical remove from their home village or monastery, or break their retreat to visit family or patrons. They will continue to find enjoyment in food, clothing, and material things. Ultimately, such a person's behavior is driven by conceptual thoughts. This is a path that ends with broken spiritual commitments or *samayas* (*dam tshig*) and perhaps even a rebirth in hell. By contrast, the genuine retreatant will cut off the succession of conceptual thoughts. Having abandoned all intentions for activities of this life, they will stay in a mountain hermitage, just like the accomplished masters of the past. They will cut off interpersonal relationships and take real joy in practice. As a result, they will generate signs of success and make progress toward buddhahood.[36]

Drakar Lozang Pelden makes two other kinds of distinction at length in order to characterize what he regards as the correct form of retreat practice. First is possessing the proper kind of Dharmic learning prior to beginning. He criticizes those who downplay the necessity of such an education, who maintain that being able to endure ascetic trials is the essence of practice. On account of their not knowing the way out of the darkness of ignorance, Lozang Pelden compares these people to marmots hibernating on a wintry mountainside. As he argues over the course of twelve pages, meditators possessing the proper learning will be able to avoid mistaken understandings and will progress quickly. Along the way he also makes a point of critiquing those who spend their entire religious careers studying but never bother to meditate, which he likens to accumulating a lot of food without ever tasting it.[37] The second distinction is between correct and incorrect retreat practice, on the grounds of maintaining the proper focus on the emptiness of all phenomena. He quotes Potowa's saying that "if you don't remember emptiness, it's like building a house on ice."[38] Interrelated with this is the issue of unduly prioritizing tantric practice and neglecting the rigors of the exoteric. Lozang Pelden treats these issues exhaustively over more than twenty pages.[39]

Drakar Lozang Pelden's *Garland of Pearls* gives the sense of a meditator who is somehow constantly embattled, navigating a difficult path that narrowly avoids the pitfalls by which all their efforts could go to waste. He seems to regard the very endeavor of retreat as under threat: some fifteen pages near the end of the text are devoted to quotations from sutras and Tibetan masters about the necessity of practicing in retreat, giving the sense that the undertaking must in general be defended.[40]

The respective *Mountain Dharmas* of Yangönpa, Karma Chakmé, and Drakar Lozang Pelden exemplify three different approaches to providing instruction for how to conduct a long-term meditative retreat, which I have labeled a retreat manual, a retreat handbook, and a guide to retreat. As such, they display three different levels of specificity in prescribing the content of the retreat program. These writings also represent three different sectarian identities: one strictly Kagyu, one drawing from Kagyu and Nyingma traditions and addressing practitioners of both simultaneously, and one by a classically trained Gelukpa working in the Geluk monastic administration, who conceived of himself as expressing a more universal Buddhist message. Some of the differences between these texts and their respective understandings of retreat highlighted here reflect broader trends in the history of the Tibetan ascetic self. For one, in the progression from Yangönpa's one-size-fits-all retreat to the dual sectarianism of Karma Chakmé to the nonspecific, universalist-leaning retreat of Lozang Pelden, we see a suggestion of how the discourse has opened up and expanded over time.

To extend our consideration to the broader corpus of prescriptive literature for individual retreat that is the principal source material for this study, the titles of two-thirds of these texts contain the phrase "mountain Dharma" (*ri chos*). Rather than a formal marker of genre, this is better understood as a term of art indicating the eremitic endeavor.[41] Chapter 2 will describe the associations conveyed by the word "mountain" in this usage.

The description of the three works above establishes the normal range of expository approaches taken in this genre of literature. A outlier is the *Necklace for Those Wanting Liberation, Called "Mountain Dharma: The Garland of Beryl,"* by Künga Namgyel (1567–1629), the fourth of the Trungpa incarnation lineage of Zurmang, who was an important teacher of Karma Chakmé and a disciple of Zurmang Lekshé Drayang, who will be introduced in chapter 2. This short guide to retreat consists of 108 separate directives for the meditator to live by, organized as ten sets of ten followed by one set of eight, including categories like "the ten aspects of whipping the mind," "the ten ways of practicing mendicancy," and "the ten aspects of combining the practice of meditation into one thing." Each directive is described in a single line of nine-syllable verse. Together, these prescriptions depict a retreat program only in the broadest strokes. Offering little in terms of exposition, the text as a whole seems intended to function mnemonically.[42]

In connection to this point, texts offering prescriptions for individual long-term retreat tend to provide no clear indication of their intended use—whether they are to be studied in detail prior to the start of a retreat, to be read and referred to during a retreat, or to be a normalizing resource for gurus guiding their disciples in retreat. There is a consensus within the tradition that meditative retreat is not a time for reading. In his sixty-folio-side manual cited in the introduction, the *Garland of Critical Points for the Precious Mountain Dharma*, Lhatsün Namkha Jikmé writes that to have "many different texts" in one's retreat will create an undue complexity or distraction that must be abandoned in order to focus single-pointedly on meditation.[43] Karma Chakmé mentions the guru's providing the retreatant with instructions for their meditation practices during the first week of a retreat, if staying nearby, ephemerally written on a dust-covered slate. If the student is staying farther away, some notes (*zin bris*) on the practices may be necessary.[44] But he cautions against reading too much, arguing that retreat is not a time for textual study. If literate, the retreatant may make a habit of reading daily from the writings of the *siddha*s of the past or other beneficial texts, although Karma Chakmé stipulates that this should be "not a lot, but three or four pages" per day.[45] Karma Chakmé's spiritual heir, Karma Ngedön Tenkyé (b. late nineteenth century), who hailed from western Tibet—popularly known as Mendong Tsampa Rinpoché (*sman sdong mtshams pa rin po che*), referring to his status as a dedicated retreatant from Mendong—mentions in his thirty-three-folio-side, *Instruction Pointing Out the Mountain Dharma, the Path to Liberation,* that the retreatant may "write letters, look at texts, and study a little bit, if needed," during the afternoon break, alongside tending to the fire and eating and drinking.[46]

Given this general sentiment that retreat is not a time for serious reading and the fact that none of the twenty-nine principal texts used in this study expresses a clear expectation that it will be brought into the retreat for consultation, one gets the impression that this literature tended to be engaged with outside of and prior to the retreat proper. A number of these texts include a refrain along the lines of, "Listen, my [spiritual] sons!," or are identified as having been composed at the request of a disciple; this suggests they were intended primarily to be read by potential retreat candidates, rather than by the lamas guiding them.

Across these texts, reference is sometimes made to the existence of earlier "mountain Dharma" works. Earlier texts offering prescriptions for long-term retreat are quoted or briefly discussed, but not with great frequency. Amid a broader Tibetan literary culture in which the refutation of already-articulated views and borrowing (often unattributed) are commonplace, works offering prescriptions for retreat show a limited tendency to draw from, quote, or respond to their precursors.[47] I know of no full written commentary on an earlier text offering prescriptions for individual retreat. The intellectual history of ascetic practice in Tibet that is pieced together in this study, then, is not primarily of individual authors responding directly and consciously to one another, but rather of a succession of thinkers returning again and again to offer new solutions to the same perennial challenges in the anchoritic undertaking.

One area of agreement among the three long *Mountain Dharmas* described above is the presumption of a male readership, which is pervasive throughout the broader corpus of prescriptive retreat literature. Drakar Lozang Pelden has been recognized as a pioneer in expanding the nunhood in eastern Tibet, as he had many female disciples, and some of the religious institutions he established were specifically for nuns. In the third volume of his *Collected Works*, directly after the *Garland of Pearls* and a shorter retreat guide called the *Garland of Flowers*, which will also be used in this study, there is a text in fifteen folio sides titled the *Steps to Liberation: Discipline for Female Monastics*, which provides guidelines for female clerics. Included therein are a handful of points specific to women practicing in retreat.[48] That a female audience is addressed separately suggests that the *Garland of Pearls* and the *Garland of Flowers* are both primarily intended for male readers, although not necessarily excluding women. In parallel fashion, in the record of Yangönpa's final testament, after exhorting his followers to pursue a life of asceticism and retreat, he gives a few words of encouragement specifically for "female meditators" (*sgom ma*).[49] Prescriptive retreat texts often talk about the necessity of avoiding women and what the meditator should do if he comes into contact with one; these texts do not provide instructions to female retreatants should they encounter men.[50] The only text used in this study specifically for female practitioners is a charter establishing behavioral guidelines for the community of female meditators at Drakar Taso—and therefore not strictly about individual retreat—written in 1816 by the community's male abbot.[51] In the course of my research I have not found any text offering instructions for individual long-term retreat written by a woman, nor any full text offering instructions specifically for female retreatants.[52] Although women have practiced retreat continuously throughout the history of the tradition, this is not represented in the existing prescriptive literature. This kind of androcentrism has predominated throughout the history of Indian and Tibetan Buddhism.

This charter document for the community of retreatant-nuns at Drakar Taso helps delineate the types of materials used in this study. Berthe Jansen and Brenton Sullivan have recently used the systematic reading of prescriptive monastic charter documents, sometimes called "monastic constitutions" or "monastic guidelines" (*bca' yig,* short for *khrims su bca' ba'i yi ge*), to shed new light on the history of Tibetan Buddhist monasticism. We have at our disposal a number of such charters written to provide structure for specific institutions devoted to the practice of meditation, where retreats of varying lengths would be practiced. These texts typically lay out behavioral guidelines for the community, including punishments for infractions; the duties of individuals fulfilling roles within that community, like the appointed disciplinarian and chant leader; and the daily, monthly, and annual schedules to be adhered to. Because they provide direction for communal rather than individual retreats and because their respective ambits are limited to specific meditative communities, I draw only selectively from this body of literature, citing just a few examples. These documents will prove essential in research focusing on the institutional, political, material, gender, geographic, and social facets of retreat practice historically, which fall outside the scope of the present project. The titles of some of the texts that make up my principal source material contain some permutation of *bca' yig* or *khrims su bca' ba'i yi ge*, but are included in this study because they are addressed to practitioners of individual long-term retreat in general, rather than the inhabitants of a specific meditative community. In my translations of text titles, I render *bca' yig* and *khrims su bca' ba'i yi ge* as "guidelines."

The second caveat is that this study does not attempt to take into account instructions for retreat practice that are offered in texts with a different primary purpose. For example, Tibetan Buddhist texts on the Stages of the Path, modeled on Atiśa Dīpaṃkara's *Lamp for the Path to Enlightenment*, strive to lay out a comprehensive program of self-transformation, describing the steps from the earliest turning of the mind to the fruits of buddhahood. Popular in every sect of the Tibetan Buddhist tradition, landmark examples include Gampopa's (1079–1153) *Jewel Ornament of Liberation*, Sakya Paṇḍita's *Clarifying the Sage's Intention*, Tsongkhapa's various compositions in the genre, and more recently Patrul Rinpoché's (1808–1887) *Words of My Perfect Teacher*. Such texts have variously been treated as material to be intensively studied and practiced early in one's spiritual career while performing the preliminary practices, or as pertaining throughout religious life. As such, these works have provided fodder for short- and medium-term retreats while also being widely studied and practiced outside of retreat contexts. Some Stages of the Path texts provide instructions on aspects of how to conduct a retreat. Other kinds of practice text also provide partial instructions for retreat. One famous example is Nupchen Sangyé Yeshé's (ninth–tenth century) *Lamp for the Eye of Contemplation*, an exposition on meditation theory from an early Nyingma perspective. It offers guidance on proper locations for intensive meditation and states that during such practice the yogin should have the "four compatible reliances" (*mthun pa bsten pa bzhi*): his master, a sexual consort, Buddhist texts, and a servant. The text provides other significant details regarding how the meditator should care for their physical well-being.[53]

Although a consideration of these and other prescriptive materials would undoubtedly add to our understanding of the history of Himalayan eremitism, this book's principal source material is limited to texts that have as their primary intent providing instruction on how to conduct retreat, with all the practical concerns thereby entailed. For example, while Atīśa's and Tsongkhapa's writings in the Stages of the Path genre provide content for the retreat program imagined by Drakar Lozang Pelden, his *Garland of Pearls* and *Garland of Flowers*, devoted specifically to questions of how to do such a retreat, are more centrally relevant.

The third caveat is that this study makes only limited use of shorter, informal texts that address how to do retreat, such as spiritual songs, poetry, letters, and accounts of dialogues between gurus and disciples. A rich example of this kind of material is the *Collected Songs* of Dordzin Namkha Dorjé (1486–1553), a yogin of the Barawa Kagyu, based in the Shang valley in Tsang. The Barawa Kagyu descended from Yangönpa's activities: its founder, Barawa Gyeltsen Pelzang (1310–1391), was considered a reincarnation of Yangönpa. Namkha Dorjé both received and transmitted the *Mountain Dharma* trilogy, as well as other works by Yangönpa.[54] In one song, delivered in response to a disciple's prosaic request for "a five-stanza composition about how to practice, after having abandoned this life," Namkha Dorjé gives a directive to "practice ... in mountain hermitages, without grasping at self, just as in the life stories [or examples, *rnam thar*] of the past masters of the Kagyu." Another song, given in response to a request for instruction on generic facets of Dharma practice, includes the following advice:

> If you manage to establish a mountain hermitage that conforms to
>   Dharma practice,
> even if it be away from your homeland, relations, and so on,
> someone will revere and respectfully serve you.
> So wander among mountain hermitages without bias.[55]

For Namkha Dorjé, to practice Buddhism is to meditate in retreat. But merely withdrawing to a mountain hermitage may not be sufficient, for such a place can easily become a locus of human activity and lose its ascetic bearing, necessitating the further austerities of itinerancy. Although this kind of material may be gleaned for indications of how eremitic asceticism has been thought of historically, this study does not engage thoroughly with this vast literature, instead prioritizing longer texts that elaborate upon the challenges of retreat more expansively, conveying their authors' understandings of the ascetic endeavor in greater detail.[56]

The final caveat is to recognize the enormous importance of oral discourse in Tibet's subculture of individual long-term retreat. This body of exposition would have consisted of lore and instructions passed down from generation to generation, as well as contextually dependent directives, encouragement, or insight given in the moment from master to student, reflecting their individual predilections and needs. This oral discourse would have mediated between texts like those relied on in this study and what a meditator would have actually practiced, filling critical gaps in the prescriptions provided in those texts. The extent to which the textual sources at our disposal may reflect this oral discourse remains an open question. Yangönpa's *Blazing Jewel*, for example, includes scores of points of instruction, sometimes in the form of a quotation, that are noted as deriving from Yangönpa's various teachers. This renders the manual partially reflective of the more intimate oral discourse about retreat at the time. On certain important points, Yangönpa instructs the reader to request further information from their lama.[57] Karma Chakmé's *Direct Advice on Retreat* is entirely the record of teachings given orally. Other prescriptive retreat texts used in this study are also likely directly influenced by oral teachings received or given by their respective authors. The oral discourse of retreat instruction would have at times included discussions of the contents of these very texts: the more prominent, like Yangönpa's and Karma Chakmé's *Mountain Dharmas*, typically would not have been used by meditators who had not received the ritual reading transmission (*lung*) for them. The moment of giving or receiving such a transmission would have provided an occasion to discuss the text.

For these reasons we should not think of the oral discourse of retreat and that preserved in prescriptive texts as unrelated or not mutually influential. Nevertheless, many important and intimate conversations about the practice of individual long-term retreat surely have been lost. Although we lack knowledge of certain details about retreat as it was understood, talked about, and practiced in the distant past, we do have access to an expansive record of the thought world in which retreat was undertaken. This includes the vocabularies and conceptual categories employed, the perceived relationships between things, and the values and ideas orienting those relations. The next six chapters are an attempt to systematically reconstruct what we can of that world of thought, and of the ascetic self that sits at its nexus.

CHAPTER 2

LOCATING THE ASCETIC SELF

A meditator cannot begin a retreat without first making a decision about where to do it. This entails two separate issues: the physical structure to be inhabited, and where that structure is located. The first of these concerns has been addressed only sparsely by exegetes of the tradition. The second, by contrast, is taken up in almost every text providing instruction for the practice of individual retreat. This chapter examines the prescriptions that authors of retreat texts have offered regarding where to do a retreat and why, in order to understand how the Tibetan ascetic self has been conceived of as existing in relation to the dimension of space. Although the negative aspect of the issue of place—the need to withdraw physically from the world of ordinary human affairs—has remained a constant throughout the history of the Tibetan ascetic tradition, on the more positive side—namely, how the ascetic should decide upon a particular place of isolation—there have been some significant changes over time. This evolution in thinking about how the meditator relates to physical space, happening over centuries, has entailed a major reimagining of the Tibetan ascetic self as a being in both spatial and temporal dimensions.

When demonstrating the hermeneutic of problematization, the introduction considered two instances from among what little the prescriptive literature says regarding the potential benefits or drawbacks of residing in a cave, tent, hut, or cabin during a retreat. The tradition has also been fairly reticent regarding the interior space of the retreat dwelling. It is expected that the chamber will feature an altar that serves as the focal point of ritual practice. The cell may also have places to store resources like food, water, and firewood.[1] One feature that the tradition has shown a particular concern for is the place where the meditator will sit and/or lie down to meditate and sleep. Retreat texts commonly mention preparing the spot by drawing a *svastika*, a traditional symbol of steadfastness, on the ground beneath where the individual will sit or lie, and inscribing the place above with powerful diagrams (*yantra*) or spells (*mantra*) for the protection of life.[2] In his *Direct Advice on Retreat*, Karma Chakmé mentions that a person who grows sleepy during meditation sessions should affix a text or a devotional statue to a pillar inside the retreat chamber, which they can circumambulate twenty or so times in order to regain lucidity. One should be careful to circumambulate in wide enough circles to avoid getting dizzy and passing out.[3] Karma Chakmé also mentions that a retreatant who find themselves struggling to remain diligent in their practice can write reminders in large letters on the interior walls of their dwelling, including messages like DEATH and DO NOT BE DISTRACTED, a custom that he says he observed among meditators in central Tibet.[4]

While the arrangement of the retreat chamber in the earthly dimension is typically treated sparingly, if at all, authors of prescriptive texts for individual retreat regularly mention the ritual procedures required to render that space habitable. Such a process may include visualizing a "circle of protection" (*[b]srung 'khor, [b]srung ba'i 'khor lo*) or offering ritual cakes to the lama, the Dharma protectors, or local deities, who are propitiated for protection, the prevention of obstacles, or the furnishing of material resources for the duration of the retreat.[5] Karma Chakmé instructs that when offering a ritual cake to the local deities, the meditator should supplicate them to preserve the integrity of the space as follows: "Until such time as I exit from this retreat, do not allow outside obstacles to enter, and do not allow that which is accomplished in here to escape outward. Protect the *samaya*s of the one who stays here."[6] As part of the process of setting up the retreat, many texts mention making a cairn of white stones or putting up a sign outside the dwelling, which plays an important role in maintaining interpersonal boundaries, as will be discussed in chapter 3.

The retreat dwelling has generally gone unproblematized by authors of prescriptive retreat texts, the few remaining exceptions to be pointed out below. This suggests that the dwelling tended to be regarded as a matter of expediency. The Drukpa Kagyupa Mipam Püntsok Sherap (1654–1715) active in Mustang—known as the Reincarnation of Taktsé or the Mendicant of Taktsé—epitomizes this attitude when he writes in his sixty-folio-side manual, *Refined Honey That Extracts the Essence of Accomplishment in the Profound Mountain Dharma*, that the reader should do a retreat "in whatever meditation house you possess that is agreeable to your mind."[7] The lack of attention to the retreat dwelling suggests a major difference between the ascetic culture of Tibet and that of Buddhist India, for, as Kazi Ashraf has convincingly shown, in the South Asian context,

"The ascetic hut, the sine qua non of asceticism, condenses the rich imaginary and complex practices of the ascetic tradition.... In the ideation, imagination, and representation of the ascetic hut, we are drawn to the heart of the ascetic project, to its fundamental deliberations and practices."[8]

While in Tibet the dwelling itself is not regarded as being of sufficient consequence to merit great elaboration, the question of where it might be located is addressed often and in considerable detail, representing a rich body of deliberation regarding the nature of the ascetic self. We will first consider some notions of space that have been held as self-evident throughout the long history of Tibetan eremitism, then turn to some more distinctive and historically significant ways of understanding the relationship between the meditator and the physical world they inhabit.

The tradition's most axiomatic thinking about space can be discerned through the vocabulary used to refer to the anchoritic endeavor in general. One term used throughout the entire history of the tradition to characterize the proper physical setting for an individual retreat is *dben pa* (pronounced "wen-pa" in the dialect of central Tibet), which most essentially means empty, in the sense of being devoid of something.[9] By extension, it also means "isolated," "secluded," or a place that is characterized as being isolated or secluded. This term appears in a handful of formulations commonly used to refer to the locale for a retreat, such as *gnas dben pa, dben gnas,* and *dben sa*. While in the vast majority of instances the term is used without specifying what such a place should be devoid of or isolated from, the exceptions show precisely what connotations the term carries. As the Third Karmapa, Rangjung Dorjé (1284–1339), wrote in his twenty-three-folio-side manual, *Mountain Dharma: The Quintessence of Nectar,* a location suitable for retreat is "devoid of the ways of men" (*skye bo'i rgyun lugs dben*) and "devoid of distractions" (*'du 'dzis dben pa*). Drakar Lozang Pelden characterizes such a location as being "devoid of human comings and goings" (*mi yi rgyu 'grul gyis dben*). One author affirms that the "places of isolation" (*dben gnas*) praised time and time again in the highest possible terms by the Buddha and his associates are "isolated places, empty valleys free of people or dogs" (*dben mi med khyi med lung stong*).[10] It is significant that dogs are mentioned, suggesting that in order to be suitably "empty" a place does not need to be free of undomesticated animals, only domesticated ones. These examples show that the word *dben* refers to the ideal of inhabiting a location that is at a physical remove from the civilized world.

Just as ubiquitous in the Tibetan discourse about anchoritism is the word *ri*, meaning "mountain." A term used almost synonymously with *dben gnas* and its various permutations is *ri khrod* (its two syllables meaning "mountain" and something like "locale"), which gets translated as "hermitage" or "retreat," or more literally, "mountain hermitage," "mountain retreat." The one who resides there, a *ri khrod pa*, is a hermit, an anchorite, a recluse, a retreatant. Within this discourse, the eremitic lifestyle is commonly referred to as "wandering" or "roaming" (*'grim, rgyu*) in the mountains or among mountain hermitages.

The Buddhist cosmology adopted from India posits that a mountain constitutes the axis of the physical world. For Tibetans, mountains have also traditionally been places of purity and power, the abodes of the gods, their snowy upper reaches untainted by human presence. On and around the Tibetan plateau, mountains have also been regarded and worshiped *as* gods.[11] Mountains have become symbols of Buddhistness, being likened to *stūpa*s, and of Tibetanness, as Tibetans have throughout their history differentiated themselves from the peoples living in environs surrounding and below the plateau. A triangular white mountain features prominently on the Tibetan flag, used since 1916. A reference to mountains in an eremitic context may invoke some mixture of these meanings. But even more integral to the sense conveyed is the fact that in such a usage *ri* functions semantically in a way very similar to *dben*. Tibetan culture has long featured a predilection for thinking, speaking, and behaving in terms of vertical hierarchies: a person touches a Dharma book or a photo of the lama to their head, to honor it and receive its blessing, while always being careful not to sit with their feet extending in the direction of the altar. The spiritual or worldly hierarchy among people is marked by the respective heights of the seats offered to them. From the perspective of linguistic anthropology, this aspect of Tibetan cultural practice can be seen to derive from their living in dramatically vertically differentiated landscapes. For example, directions are commonly offered in the form of heading "up" or "down" the valley. This carries over to affect how Tibetans speak of nonspatial things as well, such as the "upper," "middle," or "lower" part of a month or a day. A two-volume Tibetan dictionary is divided into "upper" and "lower" parts. The polite way to say that a cleric has given up their monastic status is to say that they "fell to a lay state" (*skya bab*).[12]

In this specific geographic, cultural, and linguistic context, "mountain" acquires its meaning in large part through the negation of what it is not: the ordinary space of human habitation down below. The valley floor provides the location for agriculture, the trials and tribulations of family and village life—all the ordinary human undertakings that perpetuate samsara. Mountains, meanwhile, offer the very opposite, being a natural refuge from those kinds of distractions, a place of striving to attain a higher mode of being. The discourse surrounding long-term retreat is run through with expressions reflecting this binary and hierarchical manner of thinking about topography. One author contrasts the village with the isolated mountain hermitage, likening them respectively to a fiery pit and a cool pavilion, a hellish realm and a divine one.[13] Meanwhile, an individual's commitment to anchoritism may be recognized with the title of "one who does not descend from the mountain."[14] Prescriptive retreat texts commonly use not "descending" (*'bab*) to the village as a way to refer to the anchoritic endeavor as a whole.[15] Chapter 3 gives further examples of how prescriptive retreat texts refer to the village as the *other*, the place that must be shunned in order to conduct a legitimate retreat. Also relevant here is the fact that throughout the Tibetan eremitic literature are references to striving to live in a wandering mode, unattached to any particular place, avoiding human contact, and thereby being "like a deer" or "like an injured deer" (*ri dwags bzhin, ri dwags rma bzhin*). The word translated as "deer" is a compound that has "mountain" as its first syllable.[16]

By virtue of all these associations, in both the discourse of retreat practice and that of the broader Tibetan culture in which it circulates, remaining "in the mountains" expresses synecdochally the whole of the eremitic ideal. In this way the "mountain" of the "mountain Dharma" functions in a way very similar to the "forest" or "wilderness" (*vana, araṇya*) of the ascetic tradition of the early centuries of Buddhism in India, and more recently in the Theravada societies of Southeast Asia, where the "forest monks" have established themselves as the true inheritors of the ascetic and meditative tradition.[17] A close parallel can be found in the "desert" of the early Christian anchorites, who came to be known as the Desert Fathers. This association lives on today through references to the "deserts" that surround Carthusian monasteries in both France and England. "Hermit" and "eremitism" derive from the Greek *erēmos*, which refers to wild and uninhabited spaces.[18] In the Tibetan context, it is the "mountain" that represents the *other* space where asceticism is to be performed. Like the ascetic's hut in South Asia, the Tibetan mountain is not just a mountain but a vehicle for thought.

There are countless passages in the prescriptive literature for individual retreat that address the virtues of practicing in mountainous locales where a meditator can be separated from society, congruent with Durkheim's understanding of asceticism as a "negative" religious observance. This most widely held attitude about place in Tibetan eremitism can be best observed in the long-standing tradition of writing poetic compositions intended to provide inspiration or encouragement through praise for residing in undomesticated spaces. This literature may be viewed as something of a subgenre within the prescriptive literature for long-term retreat. One of the earliest authors whose work is used in this study, Jikten Sumgön or Jikten Gönpo Rinchen Pel (1143–1217), founder of the Drikung branch of the Kagyu, composed a song titled *Wandering Alone in Mountain Hermitages for the Sake of Sentient Beings*, where he argues for the superiority of anchoritism over the laxer religiosity of monastery life, stating that "experiential realization increases in a remote mountain hermitage" (*ri khrod dgon pa*). In his fourteenth-century *Words of Joy in a Forest Grove*, Longchenpa Drimé Özer (1308–1364), a great luminary of the Nyingma, offers an extended praise of withdrawing to "the forest of nirvana" or "peacefulness" (*zhi ba'i nags*) while expounding on the limitations inherent to remaining in "the village of existence" (*srid pa'i grong*). He writes that "the forest has been universally praised by the Victors," and that "the attainment of awakening by all the Victors of the three times / only occurs while staying in forests— / never while staying in a town or other distracting place" (as translated by Timothy Hinkle).[19]

Later there would coalesce a tradition of composing songs about "taking joy in isolation" (*dben par dga' ba*). These songs may highlight features of life in a mountainous setting, in some cases arguing that such circumstances are especially conducive to religious advancement. Other songs of the genre are more general praises of the anchoritic undertaking. The song by the first Tewo Lungzang Nangwa, Ngawang Lozang Samten (1687–1748/49), titled *Song of Taking Joy in Isolation: Exhorting My Own Mind Toward Virtue*, is made up of verses like the following:

> In general, the lifetime of a transmigrating being is a flash of lightning.
> In particular, there is no certainty to life in this world.
> Now, for the sake of doing Dharmic things for what remains of your
>   life,
>   it is good to wander among mountain hermitages in isolated places.

The last line (*gnas dben pa'i ri khrod 'grim na bzang*) is repeated throughout.[20] An excellent example of the genre is the Third Changkya, Rölpé Dorjé's (1717–1786) *Long Dharmic Song About Taking Joy in Isolation*. After lamenting how easy it is for a person to squander their precious opportunity to practice the Dharma, he turns to praise staying in a place of isolation, surrounded by nature and purposefully separated from meaningless activities and from people concerned with this life. Rölpé Dorjé describes this as the distilled essence of what the Buddha taught.[21] Writings like these argue in favor of anchoritism by treating removal to a mountainous, socially isolated location as a spiritual panacea, the single solution to all the potential shortcomings in one's religious practice. By remaining there amid those circumstances, the retreatant will surely advance spiritually.

A final example showing the unchanging nature of this impulse toward reclusion in the Indo-Tibetan Buddhist tradition is *Beneficial Moon: A Dharma Address*, by the famed autobiographer and poet from Amdo, Shabkar Tsokdruk Rangdröl (1781–1851). Composed in 1812 for the benefit of individuals practicing in retreat at the renowned holy mountain Tsari, where Shabkar was residing at the time, the text is a guide to retreat comprising many hundreds of quotations drawn from Indian and Tibetan sources, selected and arranged to make arguments about a number of specific aspects of the eremitic enterprise. Shabkar's own words are confined to brief passages between quotations. Rather than laying out a specific retreat program or imparting practical instructions, the text is a bastion of encouragement about meditating in isolation. The question of place figures prominently throughout. The basic argument that Shabkar makes aligns with the sentiment expressed many times throughout the tradition: establishing oneself in an isolated place is a religious cure-all, since it creates a situation where one's good qualities will naturally increase, and there will be no occasion for any negative behavior. Shabkar's strategy for conveying this is to present a litany of 125 quotations praising a life of isolation drawn from the entire history of the Buddhist tradition. In the course of *Beneficial Moon* he quotes more than twenty different Tibetans on this topic, representing every major Tibetan Buddhist school, with Milarepa, Lama Zhang, and Shar Kelden Gyatso (1607–1677) featuring most prominently. Shabkar quotes at least eight Indian masters, both tantric and nontantric, featuring Śāntideva and Atīśa. Most notably, he marshals thirty quotations from fifteen different Buddhist sutras to reinforce his point. The sutra he quotes most frequently in this connection is the *King of Samādhi Sūtra*, including such passages as the following (as translated by Peter Alan Roberts):

> I rejoice in those who live in the forest,
> Always alone and solitary like a rhinoceros,
> Always with pure livelihood and few activities,
> Without acting hypocritically for the sake of reputation.[22]

References to remaining solitary "like a rhinoceros" or "like a rhinoceros horn" (this difference stemming from an ambiguity in the Pāli word) constitute a refrain in the sutra literature.[23] Through these quotations from sutras and the writings of Indian Buddhist luminaries, Shabkar explicitly assimilates the Tibetan ideal of seeking solitude in mountains with the subcontinent's rhetoric of finding it in forests. He thereby encourages his nineteenth-century reader to identify with and see themselves as directly connected to earlier generations of practitioners, stretching all the way back to the Buddha in the fifth century BCE, thanks to their shared ascetic pursuit. In this way Shabkar highlights a fundamental way of thinking about space that has remained a constant throughout the entire history of Indian and Tibetan Buddhist asceticism.

The basic orientation toward place described in the previous section is concerned with creating a physical separation between the individual and the world of ordinary human affairs, as a necessary precondition for meditative practice. But the Tibetan eremitic tradition has had much more to say about how to behave in relation to the dimension of space. By examining the prescriptions regarding where to do a retreat and why with a particular attunement to how individual authors have differently problematized the issue of place, we see that the tradition has espoused varying modes of geospatial awareness, which reflect and sustain distinct conceptions of the ascetic self. Here we will consider three strains in the tradition's thinking about this issue.

The first of these strains is exemplified in one of the earliest retreat texts considered in this study, by Chegom Sherap Dorjé (1124–1204), also known as Chegom Zhikpo, Chegom Dzongpa, and Khakyong Drakpa. Born in Tanak, he is associated with the Kadam, although his career to an extent predated the formation of strong Tibetan Buddhist sectarian identities.[24] The twelve-page *Lamp for Fortunate Mountain Hermits*, a manual in nine-syllable verse, places the location of the retreat as the most central concern in the anchoritic endeavor.[25] The text is structured around providing answers to questions a person might have about living in an isolated, mountainous place: What are the religious benefits of living there? What are the drawbacks of not doing so? Why shouldn't a person regard living in such a place as likely to be filled with hardships? Should one not be concerned about acquiring the material means to sustain oneself—and about falling ill, growing sad due to loneliness, or being bothered by pernicious spirit entities? One by one, Chegompa allays all such concerns. He argues that while the retreatant lives in isolation, all six of the "perfections" (*pāramitā*) to strive for under the Mahayana will naturally increase, along with improvements in every kind of meditation. Not withdrawing to such a place is to remain in a world of distractions (*'du 'dzi*), where one's bad qualities will tend to increase. While living in a cave or under a rocky overhang, a meditator has nothing to worry about, for a house that has not been built by human labor is indestructible, like a vajra. The natural world provides fruits and nutritional essences. Stream water is pure and free of insects. Responding to the question of why living in the isolation of retreat does not lead to feelings of loneliness, Chegompa paints a resplendent picture of a human life lived in communion with nature: a person who remains in a mountain hermitage is serenaded by birds and bees. In time, these creatures will understand that the retreatant is not a threat, and will begin to come close in a playful and relaxed manner. The meditator may be soothed by the pleasant sounds of deer, horses, yaks, and herdsmen calling out to one another as they gather on the bank of a lake below. Associates such as these, who lack any notion of attachment or hatred, provide a form of companionship superior to anything that can be found in the world of ordinary human affairs. In short, what may seem to be the challenges of mountain living are in fact its virtues.[26]

While a great deal of what Chegompa has expressed is fully congruent with songs of "taking joy in isolation" and the basic Indian and Tibetan Buddhist attitude toward ascetic spaces, there is a particular slant to his treatment of how the meditator relates to their surroundings that makes his presentation distinctive. This is reflected most clearly in Chegompa's explanation of how even while living in the solitude of retreat, a meditator can continue to have access to Dharma instruction:

> When one stays in a remote mountain hermitage, the vegetation and the forest change in color, on account of the changing of the four seasons. The flowers, new and old, replace one another by turns; the seasons, male and female, dry out the plant life; the winds scatter the fruits; and birds assemble at these heaps of sticks—and thus the phenomena of impermanence and change are taught to the solitary person. The way the streams emerge and dry up, increase and decrease; the way the oceans and lakes melt or freeze; how the waterfowl gather or disperse; how the birds and deer migrate without certainty; how all beings are born and die; how they harm one another; the way the sun and moon and stars appear and decline, are clear or obscured; the way the years and months continue onward without stopping for a single day, and so on—these all teach the suffering of the impermanence of compounded things. Phenomena are like dreams or illusions, lacking truth, and teach the Dharma of not being attached to things that are baseless and impermanent.

In a similar vein, Chegompa mentions that if the meditator should become afraid during the night, this can provide an occasion to remember the lama's instructions and thereby become more certain of Dharmic truths.[27]

These passages give a picture of an individual who does not merely inhabit the lush and frightening world of a mountain forest but instead relates intimately to those surroundings through the way they continually instruct the meditator in the higher truths of Buddhism, both day and night. The *Lamp* does not describe a specific meditation program to be followed or many other aspects of the retreat endeavor commonly addressed in the prescriptive literature. Filling many of those roles is the mountain itself, which provides sustenance and instruction to the retreatant, indeed structuring their very life. To frame the enterprise of meditative retreat via this emphasis on learning *from* the mountain renders the relationship between the individual and their geospatial environment pedagogical or educative, and essentially cognitive. The *Lamp*'s instructions for a retreat assume and foster what we can call an *experiential* mode of geospatial awareness.

Other Tibetan authors describe the retreatant as relating to their surroundings in a way akin to this, perhaps without granting the notion as central a place as Chegompa. For example, in his *Words of Joy in a Forest Grove*, Longchenpa mentions that while staying in a forest for meditation, an ascetic will observe changes in the foliage due to seasonal change, which will serve as a reminder of impermanence and other Buddhist truths. Observing the passing of months and seasons provides a reminder of one's own mortality. Reflections on the surface of a pond illustrate the illusory nature of phenomena.[28]

This basic way of relating to one's surroundings during contemplative practice has a particularly venerable Buddhist heritage. The second chapter of Buddhaghosa's Theravada classic, the *Visuddhimagga* or *Path of Purification*, written in Pāli in the early fifth century, offers prescriptions for thirteen different forms of ascetic practice (*dhutaṅga* in Pāli, *dhūtaguṇa* in Sanskrit) for monastics, which include wearing only cast-off rags, eating only alms, roving about with no fixed residence, and dwelling only in the forest. Most directly pertinent is the ascetic practice of dwelling at the foot of a tree (*rukkhamūlika*). Remaining there, Buddhaghosa writes, the meditator cannot help but observe changes in the tree's foliage caused by the progression of the seasons, which serves as a lesson in impermanence. Living in such a place will also prevent any feeling of attachment to a habitation. This list of *dhutaṅga* practices has a long and complex history in early South Asian Buddhism, being alternately prescribed and condemned as too extreme, having been proposed as necessary vows for monks to adhere to by the Buddha's (evil) interlocutor (cousin) Devadatta, which became the cause of controversy and schism. Showing that these ideas have lived on in the tradition, Drakar Lozang Pelden discusses this classical list of ascetic observances in his post-1903 *Garland of Pearls*, echoing the experiential understanding of how the meditator relates to their surroundings.[29]

Like the more general attitude about the value of remaining in mountainous spaces described earlier in this chapter, this first mode of geospatial awareness treats those spaces in a generic manner: although unpeopled mountainous environs are praised for their benefits to an individual's practice, there is no indication that any particular mountain locale might serve differently from any other. This is a non-site-specific way of considering the question of where to do a retreat. The two other ways by which the natural topography has become legible in the Tibetan eremitic tradition—both more prominent within the discourse than this first one, and less canonical—are site-specific, maintaining that the meditator is affected, positively or adversely, by certain facets of their physical surroundings. But the question on what grounds the individual is affected has been answered in two different ways, a distinction of great consequence in the history of the Tibetan ascetic self.

The second notable strain in the eremitic problematization of space is best exemplified by Yangönpa's treatment of how to decide upon a suitable location for a retreat, written just a few decades after Chegompa's *Lamp*. Yangönpa mentions that this topic had been addressed in many instructions for meditative practice, but his presentation is based on the teachings of his guru Kodrakpa, and in accordance with his own experience. This very dense, two-folio-side chapter is given near the beginning of the *Blazing Jewel*, then revisited in six folio sides of commentary in the *Great Appendix*. Yangönpa begins by stating that there are three qualities that make a potential retreat site suitable or unsuitable: whether or not it "accords with your mind," whether or not it is auspicious, and whether or not it is free of worldly distractions (*'du 'dzi*, the same word used by Chegompa in this connection). He then discusses potential retreat locations based on a mode of geospatial awareness that we can somewhat imperfectly refer to as *geomantic*, or more precisely, *topomantic*. The word used by Yangönpa to refer to this manner of looking at things is *sa dgra*, meaning "ground antagonism"; other authors use the related term *sa dpyad*, "ground analysis." Yangönpa begins by talking about how locations possessing particular characteristics (*mtshan nyid*) are conducive to the generation of certain faults or good qualities in the mental continuum of the meditator. First is the physical makeup of the terrain: a rocky mountain is dominated by a feeling of sadness and supports the practices of *tummo* and illusory body. Slate or snow mountains are dominated by a feeling of clarity, and aid in meditation on the dependently arisen nature of phenomena and the practice of luminosity, although they pose the danger of disordering one's psychophysical winds. Less experienced meditators tend to prefer a grassy mountain or a forest, which are conducive to staying put. Individuals who have not yet obtained realization or who have lapsed *samaya*s will not be able to stay in highly empowered places (*gnas chen*) like charnel grounds. For those with some degree of attainment, staying in an inhospitable place can be very beneficial for making further spiritual progress. A site can be inappropriate because of its posing a threat to the meditator's life or physical well-being, by virtue of its falling under the domain of a *gyelpo* or other kind of terrestrial spirit, being haunted, or being on a path trodden by tax collectors or ruffians (or perhaps *yeti*s).[30]

After this initial list of considerations, Yangönpa presents a second grouping based on a somewhat different logic. If the site is on a mountain that resembles a person sitting upright with legs crossed, this will be conducive to establishing oneself in meditative *samādhi*s. If it resembles a lotus in bloom, it will be conducive to realization. If ground and sky are seen to meet in the shape of an inverted triangle, it promotes achieving *siddhi*s (supernatural powers understood as signs of spiritual progress), but there is the danger that residing in such a spot will foster lustful feelings. If the ground resembles a flayed corpse, a charnel ground, or a mandala, it is a blessed place, conducive to gaining *siddhi*s, but may produce spiritual obstacles as well. It is auspicious if the mountain behind the site is a high one. The presence of a mountain in the cardinal directions from the site can respectively render it auspicious, desirable, optimal for accumulating resources, or harmful to the meditator's life force. Higher ground to the west means the meditator will accumulate fame, while an opening to the west will result in obstacles. A meditator should avoid a location in a deep ravine unreached by the sun, which will prove bad for their physical health and prevent them from being able to seize control of their dreams or make spiritual progress. Finally, Yangönpa devotes a few lines to local spirit entities: places under the control of a white *nāga* or *mentsun* spirit will be found suitable, while places inhabited by *senmo*, rock ogresses, or *tsen* will present difficulties. He states specifically that if the place is inhabited by a *gyelpo* spirit, it will be the cause of faults in one's understanding.[31]

The *Great Appendix*'s commentary on this chapter—something dictated by Yangönpa, or a summary thereof—further increases the range of considerations to be accounted for in evaluating a potential retreat site, extending in the macro and micro dimensions simultaneously. It begins with a discussion of the relative levels of material development of different nations, comparing Tibet to Mongolia, India, Kashmir, Persia, and Yunnan. The discussion then shifts to potential features of the specific locale: the shape of the valley, the presence of snow and water, the color of the mountainside, whether the region is peaceful or enveloped in war, the shape of the ground itself, and what lies in the cardinal directions. Included here are instructions for negating certain factors by drawing diagrams that serve as antidotes. Next are features of the retreat cell—in what direction the door lies, the orientation of its pillars and beams—and how they may affect the meditator's experiences. Getting closer to the person of the meditator, the passage addresses the "geomancy of clothing" (*gos kyi sa dgra*): the hat a meditator wears is significant because it constitutes a dependent connection (*rten 'brel*) with the lama. The hem of their clothing pertains to the question of resources. The seams are connected to whether or not there will be obstacles to the retreat. Ornaments relate to achieving benefit to other beings. And so on. The final category addressed, very briefly, is the geomancy of the retreatant's own body (*lus kyi sa dgra*). Mentioned here are the importance of the yogic channels and the physical yogic exercises (*'khrul 'khor*).[32]

On the topic of where to do a retreat and why, Yangönpa presents a dizzying array of considerations to be taken into account simultaneously. Given how carefully structured the rest of the *Blazing Jewel* is, this passage stands out as a kind of data dump: some subheadings might help make sense of this presentation, but Yangönpa provides none. If we reorganize what Yangönpa has provided across the *Blazing Jewel* and its *Appendix*, we can say that moving outward concentrically, the meditator should be attentive to the bearing of their own body, the clothing that enwraps it, the room they inhabit, the form of the mountainside they sit upon, their immediate environment, the contours of the terrain their retreat looks out on, and even perhaps what region of the earth they reside in. No clear directives are given that would allow a person to weigh vis-à-vis one another the many different factors. How should a meditator feel about their circumstances if, say, the hem of their garment is ragged but their hat is in good condition, in a snowy, wooded place that resembles a lotus flower, with an opening to the west, on a mountain of medium height, which might look like a seated meditator if viewed from a certain angle? These considerations are united into a coherent system by the fact of their existing in relationship to the physical person of the meditator in the present moment, whether proximately or at a distance. The dimensions of the meditator's experience on which these factors may have an effect are diverse as well, including access to material resources, relative happiness, clarity or torpor of mind, gaining supernatural powers, and lustful thoughts. All of these are subsumed under the more general consideration of whether they will positively or negatively affect spiritual progress. The *Great Appendix* explains the principle at the heart of this geomantic reality as follows: "The external and the internal, the container (*snod*) and its contents (*bcud*), appearances and thought: because of the fact that they are inseparable from one another, being of a single nature, whatever fault or good quality there may exist in the external world, the container, the support (*rten*)—such a fault or good quality will be produced in the mental continuum of a sentient being, which is the supported (*brten*)."³³ In this view, internal and external penetrate each other absolutely. Yangönpa's presentation suggests a particularly porous, unbuffered form of the self, living in a highly enchanted world, to use Charles Taylor's formulations.³⁴ The fine-grained attunement to the physical environment that Yangönpa instructs the meditator to cultivate necessitates a heightened sensitivity to the meditator's own experiences in the moment, as it is in the interaction between the external and internal domains that lived outcomes are produced.

Yangönpa's treatment of geomancy has been cited and referred to by later authors, making it perhaps the most enduring passage of his *Mountain Dharma*.³⁵ More important for our purposes, throughout much of the subsequent history of retreat discourse in Tibet, authors would continue to offer prescriptions for where to do a retreat based on making the landscape legible through geomantic considerations, drawing upon various precedents and sources of authority. The Third Karmapa's *Quintessence of Nectar*, written a few decades after Yangönpa's retreat manual, describes how to determine the suitability of a potential meditation site in similar terms.³⁶ Sönam Chödzin's (b. 1688) *Reminder for Those Who Wander in Isolated Mountain Hermitages: Direct Advice That Is the Ship for Great Liberation* conveys a geomantic mode of geospatial awareness that reflects its Sikkimese author's perspective from the southern periphery of the Tibetan world. In addition to describing geomantic factors like those reviewed above, Sönam Chödzin mentions that individuals who meditate on Padmasambhava tend to go to Sikkim, those who abandon their homelands go to Mount Kailash, those who focus on the yogas of the channels, winds, and drops go to Tsari, and those from the frontier of the Tibetan world (*mtha' mi*) go to Mongolia.³⁷ Yangönpa's *Great Appendix* and Sönam Chödzin's presentation show how this geomantic worldview fosters a kind of cosmopolitanism, as examining how one's environs may affect one's spiritual prospects gives way to consideration of how other locations, even quite far away, might affect them differently.

In the story of how Karma Chakmé's retreat handbook came to be composed, it is related that its compiler, Tsöndrü Gyatso, specifically stated that he lacked the knowledge to determine the geomantic suitability of the hermitage where he had been practicing meditation and wished to be educated on the matter.³⁸ Karma Chakmé obliges with the fifteenth chapter, which, in seventeen folio sides, is the most extensive discussion of geomancy in any text used for this study. Here I will provide an overview of Karma Chakmé's treatment, followed by some analysis. (My reading of this section relies greatly on the record of the commentary delivered orally by Khenpo Karthar Rinpoché between 1999 and 2003.³⁹) The first of the chapter's six sections provides an introduction to geomancy, including a theory for the mechanisms behind it; operative factors are the five material elements of the physical world, and the constitutive elements of a person's consciousness and life force. The second section presents a list of the divine, human, and textual sources for the various schools of geomantic thinking, which Karma Chakmé asserts can be subsumed under two larger traditions: the Chinese and the Indian. The third section details a litany of geomantic considerations that includes but goes beyond what Yangönpa offered, including the shape of the mountains surrounding a site; what lies in the cardinal directions; the configurations of running water, paths, and trees; the relative heights vis-à-vis one another of the mountains viewed from the location; building *tsa-tsa* houses, placing *mani* stones, and planting trees to counteract certain geomantic features—and a great deal more. The contents of this section are presented as an attempt to organize and simplify the overwhelming amount of discourse on the topic, as "an oral instruction that can be held in your hand."[40] The fourth section addresses the geomantic considerations to be taken into account when dealing with corpses. The fifth section is a presentation of geomancy that has a man-made dwelling as the central reference point, in two parts: the first regarding habitations for concerted religious practice in general (referred to here as *sgrub gnas*), including monasteries; and the second addressing habitations for meditative retreat specifically (*sgrub khang*). The former discusses how to determine the relative suitability of a location depending on whether the individual will be engaged in any of the four tantric activities of taming, expanding, empowering, or fierce activity, which are the basis for a specific strain of geomantic thinking within the retreat tradition.[41] It also addresses the interior space of the dwelling, such as in what directions lie the doorway, water vessels, and hearth; and the arrangement of pillars, beams, the resting place, and the altar. The latter part of the fifth section—on dwellings for meditative retreat specifically—offers an alternative set of factors, describing how the arrangement of the chamber can place the meditator in or out of favor with the protector deities, and in what direction their head should lie when sleeping, relative to the direction in which the guru resides. Also mentioned are the ideal dimensions of the interior of such a dwelling. The sixth and final section of the chapter presents a whole different set of geomantic considerations needed for practitioners of Cutting, who have reason to seek out haunted locations rather than avoid them.

There are five aspects of Karma Chakmé's treatment of geomancy meriting special mention. First, as with Yangönpa, only when discussing geomantic forces are prescriptions given concerning the interior of the retreat dwelling. Here Karma Chakmé even goes so far as to describe the ideal size of the internal space: it should measure twelve by seven in the unit known as the "Sugata's span." This repeats a normative description of a monk's cell going back to the Vinaya.[42] This suggests that it is primarily when invoking this particular manner of thinking about the meditator and their relationship to the dimension of space that the details of the retreat dwelling rise above the threshold of consideration. Second, Karma Chakmé recognizes multiple major traditions of geomantic thinking, each of which has its own subschools and sources of authority. The sources of the Chinese tradition include teachings related by different emanations of Mañjuśrī, various emperors and scholars, and even Confucius himself; the Indian tradition goes back to the sutras and tantras. Karma Chakmé also recognizes the existing discourse about geomancy within Tibet's prescriptive retreat literature, stating, "As for geomancy for those doing meditation, there are many 'mountain Dharma' geomancies."[43] He does not, however, state which of these authoritative traditions or texts he may have drawn from, or how he regards his treatment in relation to them. Overall, whereas Yangönpa merely mentions the existence of a body of discourse about geomancy, Karma Chakmé provides what he presents as his own definitive understanding that distills the wisdom of all these traditions—an attempt to systematize and provide a roadmap for the existing discourse. Third, in Karma Chakmé's presentation, there are different entire traditions of geomantic thinking for practitioners engaging in specific activities, such as meditating, doing Cutting, or participating in the disposal of corpses. No clear indication is given for how an individual is to negotiate the multiple nesting and interrelated domains of geomantic consideration—his instructions for the retreat dwelling somehow fitting into or alongside the requirements for religious dwellings in general, which fit within the more general geomantic considerations. Fourth, the individual has the ability to change the geomantic conditions of a place, such as by making certain decisions about the orientation of a structure when building it or doing things like making *tsa-tsa* houses or piles of *mani* stones, or planting trees. This adds further variability to the issue.

Finally, Karma Chakmé's presentation of geomancy includes temporal considerations. In the third section of the chapter, Karma Chakmé writes about the profile of the horizon when viewed from the perspective of the potential retreat site, which is to be seen as divided into twelve sectors, which correspond to the twelve animals of the duodecennial calendrical cycle. If the sky in any sector should appear to be pierced by a point, this will prove deadly to a person born in the corresponding year who might reside in that place. If in the direction associated with the animal of the year of a person's birth there happens to be a topographical feature that resembles that animal, it will be especially good for the individual.[44] This added consideration creates a further, rather dramatic means of connecting person and place.

Yangönpa's terse presentation of geomancy was complex; Karma Chakmé's, from four hundred years later, is considerably more so—this despite his intention to present a condensed and simplified teaching. Given the sheer number of factors to take into account, the many ways to interpret those factors, and the complexity of potential interactions among them, the geomantic mode of geospatial awareness gives way to an unwieldy multiplicity that is just as likely to produce uncertainty as to resolve it. There is evidence that members of Tibet's eremitic tradition have found the geomantic view too complicated to be fully satisfying or convincing. In his 108-page retreat manual, *Words on the Mountain Dharma: The Melody Producing Nothing but Good*, Zurmang Lekshé Drayang (b. sixteenth century) of Zurmang Dutsi Til monastery in the Nangchen region of Kham, seat of the Trungpa incarnations, devotes a chapter to the question of what to take into consideration when seeking a location for a retreat. Despite repeating some of Yangönpa's assertions about different features of the terrain and how they may affect a person, Lekshé Drayang expresses skepticism about this general way of problematizing the environment, writing that with regard to the circumstances of one's retreat, "it is discussed as if all of them come only from critical aspects of the terrain itself. However, because of the importance of the power of karma from previous lives, it is never entirely certain." Layering the dimension of an individual's personal karmic trajectory on top of the challenge of weighing the countless geomantic factors vis-à-vis one another perhaps produced a system too complicated to navigate with confidence. Other commentators would similarly describe geomancy as an unreliable or unwieldy way of thinking about place.[45]

In the latter centuries of eremitism in the Himalaya, a third strain in conceiving of the relationship between the individual and physical space came to occupy a more central position within Tibet's ascetic discourse, suggesting a significant shift in the Tibetan eremitic habitus and in thinking about the nature of the ascetic self. While Karma Chakmé's extensive treatment of geomantic considerations constitutes the fifteenth chapter of his handbook, the sixteenth chapter, "Direct Advice on Retreat," gives his most forthright instructions for the practice of retreat. Here Karma Chakmé offers a very different set of considerations to be taken into account when deciding on a location. He states that certain places were long ago blessed by the heroes (*dpa' bo*) and the *ḍākiṇī*s, were later visited by the Indian saint Padmasambhava, and then re-identified (*ngos bzung*) sometime after that by Tibetan *mahāsiddha*s. There are hundreds of such places that are regarded as major sites (*gnas chen*) and thousands regarded as lesser ones (*gnas phran*). Karma Chakmé asserts that meditating in one of these places for a single day is superior to meditating for an entire year in a place that is not so empowered. These constitute the very best locations for a retreat. If one cannot stay in such a place, there are other sites where past masters of the Kagyu have meditated or at least visited. Presenting this view as canonical and normative, Karma Chakmé states that the need to meditate in a place with such a connection to the past "has been taught by all." Reminiscent of Yangönpa's statement about the potential downside of meditating in a previously occupied cave, Karma Chakmé describes how although a site may have at one time been empowered in such a way, it can be corrupted if occupied by an individual with a broken *samaya*. The presence of such a person leaves a harmful, polluting taint, which can impede the spiritual progress of a later inhabitant. A highly realized and powerful meditator may be able to counteract this defilement and revitalize the place, but a lesser being will not have that ability and therefore should resort to meditating somewhere else.[46] Other retreat texts also mention the importance of avoiding a site that has been inhabited by an individual with a broken *samaya*, expanding the list of human activities by which a potential retreat space may become defiled to include black magic, the brewing of alcohol, and more.[47]

Despite his comprehensive treatment of geomancy in the chapter just prior, here Karma Chakmé makes no reference to it. Occupying pride of place in his main instructions for retreat is an entirely different way of thinking about space, one that prioritizes the question of who (divine or human) might have done what in a particular location at some time in the past. This perspective, which I refer to as the *reverential* mode of geospatial awareness, would become increasingly prominent in the latter centuries of the Tibetan eremitic tradition. Writing a few decades before Karma Chakmé, Lhatsün Namkha Jikmé's brief presentation of how to decide on a place for meditation in his *Garland of Critical Points for the Precious Mountain Dharma* states that a site "should have been blessed by the presence of *siddha*s in the past, and be a place indicated in prophecies."[48] Zurmang Lekshé Drayang, a contemporary, takes this a step further: in his list of the kinds of locations that are *unsuitable* for retreat, he mentions haunted places, places visited by predators, wolves, and bandits, and also "places where *siddha*s of the past did not set their feet." He adds that all of this is to be known from the teachings of the tradition.[49] The fact that Lekshé Drayang asserts that the *absence* of a characteristic can render a location unsuitable for retreat may suggest that it had become a taken-for-granted aspect of how place was seen and thought of in Tibetan eremitic discourse.

In his early eighteenth-century treatment of how to decide on a retreat location, Mipam Püntsok Sherap, distilling what was taught by the past masters, first mentions the twenty-four holy sites discussed in the tantras, about which, in his own words, "nothing more need be said." Outside of these, "there are the places where the previous Kagyupas meditated, including the locations prophesied to Milarepa by Marpa [1012–1097], and so on. There are also the places blessed by Padmasambhava." Should one not have access to such a location, a handful of other considerations then become operative: whether or not the material necessities can be accumulated, whether or not the place is currently occupied, and, very similar to the advice from Yangönpa and others, whether the makeup of the location—"forest, slate, and so on"—accords with one's disposition.[50] In the early twentieth century, Karma Ngedön Tenkyé would write in his *Instruction Pointing Out the Mountain Dharma* that when evaluating the relative suitability of a potential retreat site, "the absolute best kind is a mountain abode blessed by the *siddha*s of the past." For those who do not have access to such a place, Karma Ngedön Tenkyé gives an exposition on what kinds of location are and are not suitable, with attention to questions of distancing oneself from the homeland, whether or not the locals act favorably toward the Dharma, whether or not the necessary material conditions are easy to find, and the other religious practitioners residing in the area.[51]

These many examples show how in the latter centuries of the Tibetan eremitic tradition, a new value came to be most prominent in determining the suitability of a potential retreat site: whether or not a specific place had been occupied in the past by one or more highly accomplished individuals. This idea must be differentiated from statements in which wild spaces are praised generically as the venue for past masters' spiritual successes, examples of which were highlighted earlier in this chapter. By contrast, the authors cited here are referring to a *specific* place, and whether or not such a master may have spent time there. This is a way of conceiving of the retreatant's relationship to space that is site-specific (although not person-specific), but on a completely different basis from the geomantic mode. In this third strain of thinking, the primary basis for elaboration upon a location is not its physical details or how they may affect an individual, but rather the question of what may have occurred there in the past. In this view, potential meditation sites are regarded less as sites whose details are to be mapped and more as vessels conveying imprints that were created in the past. In this reverential mode of geospatial awareness, the topography becomes legible through the adoption of a historical perspective. This way of thinking about the retreatant's relationship to the physical world entails a flattening of space and of the individual in the present moment, in favor of an increased elaboration of space and of the individual in a historical frame.

The reverential mode of geospatial awareness is the only one among the three that defines the meditator in relationship to other people. It also serves to define the meditator as a historical being, existing in relationship to historical time in a way not entailed by modes of geospatial awareness that were more prevalent in the earlier centuries of the tradition. These two things are directly related. The rise of this manner of problematizing space and its accompanying form of historical consciousness exemplifies the phenomenon of lived deferential reverence, as presented in the introduction. The difference in time and status between the latter-day ascetic and the enlightened forbears of the tradition is made manifest through the very act of choosing a retreat location. Those past masters possessed sufficient greatness to open new sites for meditative practice, leaving a presence so powerful that it could affect a person's meditative outcomes hundreds of years later. The spiritual prospects of the latter-day meditator depend upon it. The need to rely on a place so empowered in the past reminds the meditator of their own comparative dearth of spiritual potency. Authors of retreat texts detail how latter-day individuals can ruin a retreat site, meaning that we have power and agency, but tending only in the wrong direction. From the very moment the practitioner chooses a location for their retreat based on this particular manner of thinking about space, the gaps in time and in ability that exist between them and their enlightened forebears are manifested and reaffirmed. This is the development of lived deferential reverence—a structured, structuring disposition—as part of the habitus of asceticism in Tibet. Other instances, as we will see in the chapters to follow, are expressed even more directly.

The growth in the perceived value, if not the necessity, of doing a retreat in a location that had been inhabited by some past master also shows the eremitic tradition's role in the millennium-plus-long endeavor of taming and organizing the Tibetan landscape. This project goes all the way back to the seventh century, with the construction of temples like the Jokhang in Lhasa that are regarded as pinning down the unruly demoness that is the ground of Tibet, and the eighth or ninth century, when Padmasambhava tamed the autochthonous spirits of the plateau, turning them into servants of the Dharma. This work would be continued by many generations of Tibetan cultural producers through a variety of interrelated yet distinct means, as scholars have become increasingly aware. In the 1990s, a number focused on the importance of guidebook literature (*gnas yig*), which provides latter-day pilgrims and meditators with an understanding of why a particular location is in fact a holy and empowered place they can interact with if they choose to visit. This was a process of inscribing the landscape with meaning and instructing people to visit and ritually interact with places imbued with special significance. More recently, Andrew Quintman and Rachel Pang have directed attention to the ways writing Tibetan hagiographic and autobiographical literature relating to ascetic meditators like Milarepa and Shabkar Tsokdruk Rangdröl has contributed to mapping the Tibetan landscape and creating a shared identity for Tibetan peoples. Quintman describes this as "a dialogical relationship between a life story recorded on paper and a life imprinted on the ground." He also alludes to the importance of "praxis-oriented traditions" that "form and reform the landscape."[52] In this chapter we have seen how the prescriptive literature for individual long-term retreat offers yet another perspective on this process of giving meaning to the Himalayan topography. The increasing prevalence of the reverential mode of geospatial awareness in the latter centuries of the individual retreat tradition shows that the activity of retreatant-authors and individual meditators contributed to and became imbricated with this large-scale and collective process of transforming how Himalayan peoples see, think about, talk about, and interact with the physical space around them.

There is no neat historical transition from one manner of problematizing place to the next, as authors sometimes offer prescriptions based on the experiential, geomantic, and reverential modes of geospatial awareness within a single text. The rise of a new approach to an ascetic concern does not mean that preexisting ones will lose their currency. We must therefore be sensitive to where the author places their emphasis—the intensity with which they problematize an issue in a particular way—and how they treat and hierarchize different manners of problematizing an issue vis-à-vis one another. Nor do these three modes of geospatial awareness represent the full range of ways authors have addressed the location for a retreat. The seven-folio-side *Mountain Dharma: The Vase of Nectar*, by Pakmodrupa Dorjé Gyelpo (1110–1170), one of the earliest texts used in this study, is largely devoted to the question of place. This founding father of the Kagyu prescribes a mode of geospatial awareness based mainly on the presence or absence of nonhuman spirit beings, *ḍākinī*s in particular, among other topographical and environmental considerations. In his instructions for how a practitioner of middling capacities should decide upon a retreat location, Pakmodrupa stipulates that it should be at the peak of three mountains, at the confluence of three rivers, in an auspicious place that generates a good feeling, or in a location where much spiritual accomplishment has been already achieved—the last of these considerations alongside, but not above, the other kinds of variables.

This is the only suggestion of the reverential mode of geospatial awareness in the text, and it is buried among prescriptions deriving from other ways of thinking about space. Meanwhile, in a record of teachings by his disciple Jikten Sumgön presented under a similar title, *Mountain Dharma: The Large Vase of Nectar*, considerations regarding where to do retreat are primarily filtered through the categories of the Eight Great Charnel Grounds, the Twenty-Four Sites, the Thirty-Two Places of Accomplishment, and so on, based on Indian tantric lore.[53]

One discussion of potential meditation locations meriting further attention is that offered by Longchenpa at the beginning of his fourteenth-century *Finding Rest in Meditation*, which seems to combine in a complex way the experiential, the geomantic, and other modes of geospatial awareness, including considerations of the roles played by spirit beings and the time of year. More detailed study will be required to disentangle these threads and better understand this text's place in the history of the Himalayan ascetic tradition's thinking about space.[54]

Tantric Tibetan eremitism also espouses practices and views that inculcate a sense of the ultimate fungibility of one's surroundings. Many prescriptive texts state that, subsequent to deciding on a location and entering into retreat, a meditator should cultivate what has been translated as "pure vision" or "sacred outlook" (*dag snang*) toward their environment. Yangönpa describes this as the "postattainment practice of purifying the realm," which is a key element of the Generation phase of *sādhana*, the most basic form of the deity self-identification practice, at the core of tantra. When practicing pure vision, toward the goal of achieving an all-encompassing self-association with the tutelary deity, the meditator is to imagine the physical world around them as perfect and divine, inhabited by perfect and divine beings—just as the tutelary deity resides amid such utopian circumstances. Yangönpa instructs, "You meditate on the physical world—the container—as a divine palace, and on sentient beings—the contents—as the tutelary deities." The meditator is to strive to remember at all times that all living beings are born of the enlightened consciousness that is buddhahood, and thus functionally equivalent to tutelary deities. Everything that appears is a reflection of awareness. And because all appearances are the meditator's own mind, all of the good seen around them is understood to reside inside their own mind. Coming to fully see their surroundings in this way contributes to the meditator's obtaining all the wonderful qualities of a buddha.[55] The practice of pure vision as outlined by Yangönpa shows a crucial implication of the absolute interpenetration of the internal and the external—what is in effect a correlate of the porousness of the self foregrounded by the geomantic mode of geospatial awareness: an assertion of the meditator's ability to re-create themselves, other beings, and the world around them through purposeful tantric visualization. By practicing pure vision, intended as a means to transcend distinctions and differential experiences that could stand in the way of achieving full self-identification with the deity, a distinctive, imaginal form of selfhood is cultivated, as will be addressed more directly in chapter 5. Appealing to a similar dynamic, in his *Large Vase of Nectar*, Jikten Sumgön describes a procedure for turning any location into a holy place like Tsari, Lapchi, or Mount Kailash through a process of willfully striving to see it as such.[56] While a way of relating to the environment, this is also a way of relating to one's own being.

In thirty-four pages, the *Heart of the Esoteric Instruction That Completely Untangles the Mountain Dharma*, by the Second Red Hat, Kachö Wangpo (1350–1405), makes a distinctive contribution to the tradition by critiquing the existing "mountain Dharma" discourse for its treatment of place. The text focuses on how to properly "identify the mountain" (*ri bo ngos gzung*), the mountain in this context having external, internal, and secret meanings, all interrelated. Kachö Wangpo writes about the mountain as being free of the enemies that are the afflictive emotions and the thief that is sloth, and being the ladder to a higher rebirth, the door to great esoteric wisdom, the source of all good qualities, the place where all the Victors gather—worded so ambiguously that he seems to be saying both that the mountain possesses these qualities and that the presence of these qualities is the mountain. With a similar ambiguity, he writes about the parts of the yogic physiognomy as being the mountain and the mountain as being the parts of the yogic physiognomy. Throughout the text Kachö Wangpo complicates ordinary understandings of the internal and the external, and the conventional and the ultimate. The view that mountains are the only appropriate setting for meditation, he argues, is wildly mistaken, it also being necessary to practice among human habitations: the meditator should try to experience mountains and lowlands, isolated places and peopled ones, as all being the same. He critiques those who have formulated "mountain Dharmas" based on the most exacting kind of conceptual thought, falling into partiality through quoting from a great many scriptural sources. In closing he writes that if a person meditates on a mountainside for an entire world age without the proper aim, then like bears, marmots, and rabbits, they will find no liberation. Those who flee to the mountain out of fear of the world yet lack the understanding that samsara is already liberated will never attain wisdom. Although they may adhere to a hundred different vows, if they haven't had instruction on the nature of the mind, they are no different from monkeys dwelling on a hillside. Those who stray from the correct approaches to tantra or meditation on emptiness will not progress toward liberation. But thanks to the *Heart of the Esoteric Instruction*, which expresses the definitive secret that is the essence of the "mountain Dharma," they may hope to obtain "a bliss that is immovable like a mountain."[57]

While nearly every prescriptive text for individual long-term retreat is in agreement about the necessity of withdrawing to a place of interpersonal isolation, there is great diversity in how authors have thought about the meditator's relationship to their surroundings. Among these, three prominent strains have emerged: an experience-based understanding of the relationship between the meditator and their environment, a topography-based geomancy, and the view, gaining in force over centuries, that an overriding factor in determining the suitability of a location as a retreat site is its having been used by a great meditator in the past. These views emphasize, respectively, the importance of being on *a* mountain; the traits of *one particular mountain*, intersecting with the *mental, emotional, and karmic state* of a *particular meditator*, at a *particular moment in time*; and finally, *what may have taken place* on a given mountain at an earlier moment in time, a consideration undertaken in a reverential mood. Unlike the first two, the third serves to define the ascetic as existing in relationship to historical time. The fact that the prescriptive literature gives voice to yet other ways of problematizing the dimension of space, including ones that serve to undermine assumptions about the physical world's specificity and immutability, establishes this as one of the questions provoking the greatest diversity of thought in retreat discourse. The dimension of space, it would seem, has constituted a blank canvas onto which foundational contours of the ascetic's selfhood have been projected.

This chapter demonstrates how a religiocultural formation defined by reclusiveness and interiority can be examined through the systematic reading and comparison of texts offering prescriptions for its practice. Insofar as the principal source material for this study is prescriptive, the findings are at the level of ideals, indicative of prevailing notions of how eremitism should be practiced, rather than at the level of description of how it was actually enacted and lived. But this kind of idealizing prescription must be seen as having affected actual ascetic practice and self-understanding, even if not directly or without the mediating effect of human interpretation. While it may be difficult to imagine a meditator adhering perfectly to all of Yangönpa's directions for geomantically evaluating a potential retreat site, an individual simply attempting to choose a location based on the instructions offered in the *Blazing Jewel* would be actively training themselves to view their surroundings, and themselves, through a geomantic lens.

Five hundred years later, a practitioner would likely be more concerned with the history of the site, geomancy having become a secondary or tertiary consideration. In this way, the prescriptive texts used in this study filtered down to affect actual ascetic practice and self-understanding, even if not providing direct representations thereof. These texts can be seen as reflecting and actively shaping the eremitic habitus, as their authors provide conceptual resources for meditators, affecting ways of seeing, acting, and being.

And as we have seen, while these conceptual resources may be ways of characterizing the world around them, on a more fundamental level they are about the meditator, as an always-incomplete being formed continually through interpretive processes and practical action. The act of choosing a retreat location based on any of the modes of geospatial awareness reviewed in this chapter, motivated by the aim of attaining a state of spiritual elevation, becomes a practical technique of acting upon one's own conduct and thoughts in a way that fosters an altered subjectivity—a technology of self. By comparing different techniques offered by the tradition across many generations, we have begun to see some of the contours of the multifaceted genealogy of the Tibetan ascetic self.

CHAPTER 3

ISOLATING THE ASCETIC SELF

The dozens of Tibetan texts offering prescriptions for individual long-term retreat allow us to observe, at a level of detail that may not be possible for any other premodern Asian ascetic tradition, how Himalayan meditator-intellectuals have over many centuries grappled with the tension between the ideal of reclusion and the inevitability of interaction with other humans. This chapter sets out to better comprehend what exactly the Tibetan eremitic tradition has understood reclusion to look like, as suggested by the prescriptions for maintaining it. Tracking changes in how interpersonal relationships have been problematized allows us to see an important arc in the history of individual retreat practice, which is interrelated with the genealogy of the Tibetan ascetic self.

The collaborative process that spawned Karma Chakmé's *Mountain Dharma: Direct Advice on Retreat* provides an object lesson in the fundamental tensions that will be systematically examined in this chapter—as well as the idiosyncratic ways they have been negotiated. The opening section of the handbook relates how, subsequent to Karma Chakmé's vow to remain permanently in meditative retreat (*tshe mtshams*), at the end of 1665 his disciple Tsöndrü Gyatso arrived at the portal to his chamber to request instructions for how he himself might do retreat.[1] Tsöndrü Gyatso's resolve to intensify his meditation was a consequence of his recently having endured an illness that brought him near the point of death, causing him to confront his lack of spiritual attainment. Karma Chakmé at first declined to provide retreat instructions, denying his authority to speak on the matter by pointing out the stark gap between, on the one hand, the true asceticism practiced by the past masters of the Kagyu, and on the other, the more moderate form he had enacted, still living close to his homeland and relations.

(This passage will be translated in full in chapter 6.) In the wake of further prodding from Tsöndrü Gyatso, and after making numerous disclaimers about the limitations of his qualifications, Karma Chakmé agreed to give teachings on how to do retreat. Over the next few months, Tsöndrü Gyatso would sit outside this portal during the gaps between the master's meditation sessions and diligently record the instructions given to him. Readers of *Direct Advice on Retreat* are continually reminded of the process of this mountainous text's production; most of its fifty-three chapters begin with the command, "Tsöndrü Gyatso, listen to this!" and end with a colophon detailing at what time on which day that teaching was given.

Tsöndrü Gyatso sitting on the ground outside his guru's cell on a winter night, scribbling by the light of a butter lamp the words being spoken to him through a hatch, is an image that neatly exemplifies one specific understanding of what interpersonal isolation should ideally consist of. This will provide a useful point of comparison with other understandings of isolation, articulated by exegetes both before and after Karma Chakmé, for establishing a genealogy of eremitic reclusion in the Tibetan world.

As noted in the introduction, the Tibetan word for retreat, *mtshams* (which translates the Sanskrit *sīma*), means a border or a boundary.[2] Prescriptive retreat texts offer little detailed treatment of such boundaries in the physical dimension. Although this body of literature makes occasional reference to the practice of physically sealing the meditator inside their chamber, typically with a wall of rocks and mud, none of the texts read for this study engages in any discussion of the merits or the practical challenges of living in such a manner.[3] A physical demarcation more commonly mentioned is the *mtshams [m]tho*. Often this refers to a "retreat cairn," a small pile of stones the meditator creates outside their retreat to mark the boundary with the profane world that lies beyond. Other authors prescribe erecting a *mtshams [m]tho* in the form of a sign bearing text conveying to potential visitors the eremitic conditions being adhered to within or the length of the retreat being undertaken, or listing the names of people who may be allowed inside. Some commentators of the tradition understand this as involving both kinds of boundary, in the form of a cairn with a sign attached to it.[4]

Physical boundary markers such as these tend to be mentioned only in passing in Tibetan eremitic discourse. Meditator-intellectuals of the tradition problematize and discuss in vastly greater detail the maintenance of boundaries in the interpersonal realm, in which physical barriers like the *mtshams [m]tho* may play a role. This chapter examines the different ways that exegetes of the tradition have problematized interpersonal relations, as evidenced by the specific mechanisms they present as salient to maintaining boundaries between the retreatant and four categories of other individuals with whom they might interact: family members, the broader laity, attendants, and other meditators. The tradition's prescriptions for how a retreatant should relate to their guru and disciples will be addressed in chapter 6. As authors have returned to this issue over many centuries, they have come to very different conclusions when weighing the potential benefits and drawbacks of different kinds of interpersonal interaction—as well as when considering the more fundamental question of the extent to which interpersonal isolation is even possible or truly desirable. Over time, more moderate stances have been adopted for cutting off interpersonal relations, which necessitates more detailed prescriptions for how to navigate the relationships thereby entailed. Over the time period considered in this study there has been a clear redefinition of the ascetic as a being in the social world, which has meant a significant reimagining of the endeavor of individual retreat itself.[5]

The prescriptive retreat text most resolute in portraying a meditator who lives without interpersonal relations of any kind is also one of the earliest. Yangönpa instructs in his thirteenth-century *Blazing Jewel: The Mountain Dharma That Is the Source of All Good Qualities* that at the beginning of a retreat, the yogin should cultivate the following thoughts: "Having severed all concern for the things of this life, I will be very diligent in my meditation. I will not come into contact with anyone, neither by voice nor by face. I will not go outside, and will only ever be alone. With the doorway walled up (*sgo brtsigs*), I will not wander about during the daylight hours. Let no obstacle enter into this strict retreat."[6] I find this passage, intended to establish the basic interpersonal architecture for the retreat to follow, to be ambiguous on some crucial points, including what precisely the walling up of the door is meant to entail, and how to interpret the parallel statements about not going outside and not going outside during the day. The line rendered as the second sentence above—*ngag dang gdong pa yang mi la mi 'phrad*—is clear enough in the Tibetan, but difficult to translate into concise and accurate English. The meaning conveyed is that you intend not to hear the voice or see the face of anyone else, or to allow your own to be heard or seen.

The association between human interaction and "obstacles" (*bar chad*) suggested in this passage is strengthened in the text that follows. Nearly all subsequent mentions of interacting with other people are contained within the *Blazing Jewel*'s fourth chapter, on obstructions to religious progress.[7] One potential cause of obstacles is interpersonal relations—literally, "those with whom you associate" (*grogs*). In Yangönpa's view, this is because interacting with others can lead to attachments or to the adoption of incorrect understandings. There is also the risk that the meditator will interact with someone who has broken a *samaya* or ethical vow, which can obstruct one's spiritual progress. In his discussion of obstacles, Yangönpa writes, "At the time when you are doing strict meditation, coming into contact with anyone at all will bring on a harmful taint. Even if the contact does not involve a face, this can happen from hearing a voice." He concludes, "It is important that you not meet faces with anyone. It has been said that you should use an eye cover, or go about keeping your eyes half-closed." This eye cover (*mig ra* or *mig dra*) is a blindfold-like covering made from yak hair, normally worn to prevent snow blindness.[8] Four centuries later, Karma Chakmé was still very committed to this ideal of neither seeing others nor being seen—even while he discoursed at length verbally. His handbook provides instructions for doing a recitation and washing your face with water that has been empowered by a spell in order to undo the "facial contamination" (*gdong grib*) that can result from being seen by another person, or worse, from seeing them. Karma Chakmé respectively refers to these two possibilities during an approach–accomplishment retreat as a "hole" and a "tear" (*bug pa, ral ba*), showing that by adhering to the dictates for maintaining the prescribed interpersonal boundaries, the ascetic was understood as creating a kind of protective envelope around themselves. Its integrity could be breached, necessitating repair.[9] Yangönpa and Karma Chakmé seem to have held rather different ideas about how speech factors into the maintenance of an eremitic bubble around the retreatant, as will be discussed below.

For Yangönpa, interpersonal interaction during the normal course of a retreat is viewed exclusively through the lens of obstacles. Save for during the liminal period of performing three highly advanced tantric practices (the Secret Practice, the Public Practice, and the Practice of the Observance), interpersonal interaction of any kind—even merely having your face seen by another person, or hearing their voice—should be avoided at all costs, because it is likely to be harmful to the retreatant.[10] Problematizing interpersonal interactions through a logic of obstacles and harmful taints is consistent with Yangönpa's general conception of the ascetic self, which, as in his instructions for understanding the physical environment through geomantic considerations, particularly emphasizes evaluating circumstances in various dimensions in terms of their relative conduciveness or deleteriousness to a meditator's spiritual progress. Yangönpa treats the ascetic as something of a conduit through which these different kinds of forces pass, fostering a heightened attunement to such external circumstances and how can they affect the practitioner's internal states. This requires one to maintain something akin to what Foucault refers to, coming from the ancient

Greek context, as "circumstantial vigilance."[11] Their porous, unbuffered condition makes the ascetic a highly vulnerable being who must shun human interaction for their own self-preservation, keeping an inviolable interpersonal boundary around them.

———

In stark contrast to Yangönpa, in the centuries to follow authors would provide increasingly detailed treatments of how and how not to interact with other people during a retreat, signaling a tacit acceptance of such kinds of contact and a shift in the norms and expectations that constitute the Tibetan eremitic habitus. This has opened the door to successive reconceptualizations of what individual long-term retreat should be. Yangönpa's expectation of a completely solitary meditator who shuns exchanging words with or seeing other people would become an outlier in the history of the tradition, conceptually relegated by later generations to being a more respectable form of asceticism achievable only in times long past.

The kind of interpersonal relationship most universally problematized in prescriptive retreat texts is with the members of one's family. This is so axiomatic a concern that cutting off ties to homeland and family comes to stand in synecdochally for the entire renunciatory ideal. In *Direct Advice on the Mountain Dharma: The Ocean of Wonders*, the famous Nyingma ascetic and treasure revealer Jikmé Lingpa (1729/30–1798) states it plainly: "My straightforward advice is this: if you succeed in utterly abandoning craving for your homeland and possessions, half of the Dharma will already be done." This declaration is reminiscent of a moment in the *Hundred Thousand Songs* of Milarepa when Rechungpa (1084–1161) asks the great yogin about his previous statement that "by abandoning your homeland, half of the Dharma will be accomplished." This phrase has echoed throughout Himalayan eremitism into modern times.[12]

As noted above, when making the case to Tsöndrü Gyatso for why he lacked the authority to instruct anyone in how to do retreat, Karma Chakmé specifically mentioned that he still lived in the area where he had been born, surrounded by relations and acquaintances. Within the *Direct Advice on Retreat*, however, Karma Chakmé argues that if an ascetic were to abandon their homeland only to develop an attachment to someplace else, then that new place must be abandoned. By the same token, if a meditator has no attachment to their homeland, then they can remain there without detriment to their practice. This idea, which represents a kind of doubling down on the true meaning of renunciation, has been expressed in other retreat instructions as well.[13] While most retreat texts refer without complication to the need to cut ties to home, Shabkar writes about this ad nauseum in *Beneficial Moon*, devoting more than one tenth of the text to this topic. He weaves together more than seventy quotations and examples from the lives of past masters to reemphasize the necessity of renouncing family, such as Tsangpa Gyaré's (1161–1211) instruction to "abandon the homeland, which is the root of all attachment and aversion. Abandon the family, which is the root of all suffering."[14] The many pages of the *Beneficial Moon* dedicated to this topic are a veritable compendium of the endless ways authors in the Indo-Tibetan Buddhist tradition have tried to articulate this fundamental orienting ideal.

Although the tradition speaks unanimously about the goal of cutting off relations with homeland and family, individual authors offer varying prescriptions for actually maintaining such a separation during a retreat. Statements on how retreatants are to negotiate relations with their families are frequently folded into directives about how to relate to the broader laity, so they will be treated together here. Practically speaking, the question of how to maintain this kind of separation during a retreat comes down to two issues: potentially choosing to depart from retreat in order to call upon family or the lay faithful, and the more pernicious problem of their coming to visit.

Drakar Lozang Pelden treats the issue of how to negotiate interpersonal relationships with the lay world in great detail across his two early twentieth-century guides to retreat. The shorter *Guidelines for Renunciant Meditators: The Beautiful Garland of Flowers, the Mountain Dharma of Esoteric Instruction That Is Easy to Grasp*, opens with a thorough discussion of why it is imperative that a contemplative renounce all ties to home. Lozang Pelden describes the meditator's homeland and familial relations as causes of continual annoyance: they threaten to drag one into other peoples' problems, which can agitate the mind and cause one to be reborn in hell. Therefore, the homeland should be regarded as like a prison or a pit of flames. Lozang Pelden also points out that on account of visiting their homeland too frequently, a mountain hermit (*ri khrod pa*) may come to resemble a villager (*grong gseb pa*). For these reasons, the meditator should formally vow not to break their retreat to visit home unless they have been given specific permission by their lama. In Lozang Pelden's version of retreat, the lama is expected to play an essential gatekeeping function, as the meditator should neither go out begging nor welcome a guest without express permission.[15] Putting in place a different kind of gatekeeping mechanism, in his twelfth-century *Lamp for Fortunate Mountain Hermits*, Chegom Sherap Dorjé discourages the meditator from accepting any invitation to break their retreat to visit faithful villagers unless the meditator has had an extrasensory perception (*mngon shes*) confirming that doing so would prove a critical intervention in the spiritual lives of those individuals at that precise moment. Otherwise, one should write off the invitation as a demonic deception and not take "a single step from your hermitage." Accepting such an invitation will lead to additional requests in the future, so that in time the retreatant will be "carried off by Māra," the Demon.[16]

As will be seen in chapter 4, a retreatant's need for food has been consistently viewed as drawing them into the orbit of other people, rendering food an object of elevated moral concern. The tradition recognizes that the meditator may face other reasons for departing from their retreat as well. Under normal circumstances it may be easy enough to ignore calls from the outside world and keep to one's retreat. But authors of retreat prescriptions often mention the challenge that arises when a meditator receives news that a relation or a patron is in poor health or near death, and thus in need of a ritual intervention. In *Beneficial Moon*, Shabkar makes the specific point that a meditator should not break their retreat in order to attend to an ill or dying family member, citing at length the most towering personages of Tibetan Buddhist history who all left home and never saw their parents again, including Atiśa, Marpa, Milarepa, and Tsongkhapa.[17] Karma Chakmé espouses the same ideal, writing that as a rule, "Even if a kinsman or someone you love is at the point of death, you can only make dedications and prayers. It is not acceptable to go there." In spite of this, Karma Chakmé also concedes that if it should happen that a person such as the meditator's mother, father, Dharma sibling, or patron is gravely ill or dies, and provided that the meditator is not at the time in the midst of an intensive ritual undertaking, they may have no choice but to leave their retreat and go there to recite prayers to benefit the ailing person, or to perform a transference of consciousness ceremony for the deceased. In such a case, the meditator should leave at night and return by morning, in order to minimize the number of people encountered out in the world. A series of recitations, visualizations, and other ritual actions are to be done in preparation for departing one's chamber and breaking the sanctity of the retreat; another procedure is prescribed for when the meditator returns, in order to restore it.[18]

Karma Chakmé's instructions for leaving the retreat stipulate that if the meditator is at the time engaged in remaining silent (*ngag mtshams*, literally "speech boundary"), then they should speak to no one but the sick or dying person. Nyingmapas commonly observe a vow not to speak while carrying out approach–accomplishment retreats, the span of which is defined by the amount of time it takes to complete a certain number of recitations of the deity's mantra. The logic behind requiring silence is that ordinary speech can pollute or disrupt the ritual spells that have been uttered. In line with this, Karma Chakmé maintains that if the retreatant does not refrain from ordinary speech during the period of performing such a ritual, then the number of recitations must be increased threefold.[19] Silence has been prescribed for other reasons as well. Karma Ngedön Tenkyé, who positioned himself as a spiritual and intellectual heir of Karma Chakmé and similarly adopted a Kagyu–Nyingma identity, writes in favor of refraining from speaking during retreat as follows:

> Conversation is another obstruction to the Dharma: too much meaningful talk is a cause of afflictive emotions. Too much *un*meaningful talk is a cause of taking rebirth as a chattering beast. For those who talk too much, critical faults (*nyes ltung*) fall like rain. For those who maintain silence (*smra bcad*, literally "sever speech"), many such faults will be naturally prevented. Therefore, keeping distinct such things as, on the one hand, joking around, idle conversation, [undue] inquisition, and on the other, the profound Dharma and the Six Syllable [mantra], it is worthwhile to maintain silence except for reciting the Six Syllable.

No stranger to such technologies of reclusion, Karma Ngedön Tenkyé, as is related in a biographical sketch, "passed a period of many years while maintaining silence, doing sealed retreats, and so on."[20] In his *Garland of Beryl*, under the mnemonic category of "the ten aspects of comportment for training continually," the Fourth Trungpa, Künga Namgyel, another Kagyupa with strong Nyingma connections, offers this directive: "In retreat on a mountain, you sever speech, isolate the mind, and create a perimeter" around you (*ri mtshams smra bcad sems dben khor yug bya*).[21] As we saw above, the Kagyupa Yangönpa included as one of the fundamental conditions of the retreat the intention of not hearing anyone's voice or allowing one's own to be heard. He also mentions "a strict severing of speech" (*smra bcad dam pa*) as one of the steps to temporarily implement should the retreatant experience impediments to their ability to do recitations quickly. This would seem to be an intensification of a commitment to not speaking that is already in place, perhaps temporarily ceasing to even pronounce prayers and mantras aloud.[22] The details of all this being somewhat unclear, for understanding how different authors define reclusion, it is sufficient to track whether or not their respective models of retreat include a prescription for silence, how that prescription is articulated, and whether silence is presented as a general condition to be adhered to or as limited to a specific ritual application. Generally speaking, across the many generations of texts written subsequent to Yangönpa's, the ideal of silence becomes less part of the universal conditions of retreat and more of a marked and circumscribed undertaking. As we will see in the course of this chapter, some versions of individual retreat, including Karma

Chakmé's, allow for a great deal of talking. Historically, the eremitic technology of silence seems to have had more currency among the Nyingma than in the other sects.

To return to the question of interacting with one's family and the broader laity, as Drakar Lozang Pelden eloquently puts it in his *Garland of Flowers*, "Having in that way abandoned the homeland and gone to stay in an isolated place, you may find that people from the homeland come running up to you."[23] His longer *Garland of Pearls* treats this issue in particular detail, addressing at length the actively defensive posture that the retreatant must assume to keep the outside world at bay. Lozang Pelden recognizes that the ascetic will likely be dependent upon family and the lay faithful for material support, a dynamic that sustains a perpetual threat to their isolation. This produces an inherently fraught situation requiring careful navigation. As for how a retreatant should act toward those who arrive bearing provisions or gifts, Lozang Pelden instructs that the meditator should speak to them enough to be polite, but not engage them in conversation. One method for dealing with local patrons is to pretend to be insane, after which people will arrive "less and less." Only a select few individuals, such as male familial relations who have traveled from far away, may be allowed inside the retreat, provided that the meditator has gotten permission from their lama. Anyone else—all female relations, relations who live nearby, other people arriving with donations of food and clothing, elderly locals who pass their time repeating mantras and visiting clerics—should be met only outside, at the boundary marked by the *mtshams m[tho]* or retreat cairn.[24] In Lozang Pelden's presentation, the cairn plays a crucial role in maintaining limits in interpersonal interactions. Writing around the same time, Karma Ngedön Tenkyé prescribes a similar approach: he stipulates that the retreatant should only allow visitors who come bearing water, wood, or offerings. The retreatant should not do anything to prepare for these relatives' or patrons' arrival. If the retreatant cannot avoid setting a pot to boil, they should give only bad hospitality. The rules are different, however, if the retreatant is sick or elderly.[25]

About relating to the public, Karma Chakmé provides very brief instructions for cultivating the "behavior of an injured deer," which is to shun all human contact, and the "behavior of a madman," pretending not to recognize visitors or understand what they may be asking, to discourage them from coming back.[26] But the capacious *Direct Advice on Retreat* concerns itself with other basic models of life in retreat as well, to be pursued or abandoned as the practitioner moves in and out of periods of intensive ritual practice. More than one fifth of the handbook is devoted to providing instruction for ritual interventions to be performed for other people. Yangönpa framed all interactions with other people as potential causes of "obstacles"; Karma Chakmé, writing four hundred years later, assumes a very different sociological reality. In all, he depicts the meditator as a spiritual agent most likely to have ritual obligations to family members and acquaintances, which may compel them to exit the retreat or to receive visitors in need. This renders the fundamental parameters of the retreat more fungible. Based on this, Eric Haynie has characterized Karma Chakmé's understanding of the sociology of retreat as "orbital," as his *Direct Advice on Retreat* "explicitly prescribes a renunciate ideal, and simultaneously includes chapters detailing practices by which a retreatant can attend to worldly, social affairs."[27] The broader scope of the present study allows us to observe that, relative to other exegetes of the tradition writing both before and after him, Karma Chakmé assumes a great deal more interaction with ritual clients. Relative to other authors within the tradition, Karma Chakmé compensates for this with an increased concern for procedures and checks on the meditator's behavior that serve to maintain and restore the boundaries of the retreat, as they would otherwise seem to be violated. For example, Karma Chakmé addresses the possibility of a retreatant contracting a harmful taint through physical contact, touching people who present themselves at the retreat hatch to receive the meditator's blessing. This taint can be counteracted through burning incense and reciting ritual formulas.[28] Many further examples show how Karma Chakmé suggests maintaining interpersonal boundaries, or restoring them after they have been violated. He also suggests how the interpersonal boundaries of the retreat will change as the meditator moves in and out of periods of more intensive ritual practice, as assumed by his model of retreat for practitioners of the *paṇḍita* type.

The ninth chapter of Karma Chakmé's *Direct Advice on Retreat* provides a rich example of his understanding of the retreatant's likely need to interact with the faithful laity. This chapter provides instructions for three different visualization rituals, drawn from different corners of Tibetan Buddhism, meant to "clear away an obstacle" that may be afflicting a person who has fallen ill or is in an otherwise compromised state. The first intervention involves visualizing a deity who produces a nectar that purifies the afflicted person and removes the obstacle. The second centers around visualizing a goddess who bathes the sick person in liquid, filling them up like a crystal vase. In the third, the meditator visualizes him- or herself in the form of the deity who emanates the purifying nectar. In each case, the divine power accessed through visualization is transmitted to the ailing person through imagined bodily contact with a fluid. Each rite includes soliciting the deity to aid the individual, who is called out by name. Although each is referred to as a rite to guarantee the well-being of a sick person (*nad pa*), Karma Chakmé lists a number of other kinds of challenging circumstances that these rites might protect against, such as drowning, falling from a cliff, enemies, bandits, and warfare. "Sickness" is a metaphor through which various kinds of dangers and challenges defining the human condition are expressed.

Particularly illuminating is the explanation Karma Chakmé gives for why the retreatant will probably need the rituals described in this ninth chapter, a state of affairs that he puts in an explicitly historical frame. Karma Chakmé observes that we live in a time characterized by the presence of the five kinds of degeneration in the world (*snyigs ma lnga*), which means that people commonly are subject to illness, external harms, and various kinds of obstacles in their lives. In search of relief, laypeople are moved to make offerings to religious practitioners, accompanied by requests for the performance of healing or protection rituals. Those described by Karma Chakmé in this chapter are generally applicable, low-output, risk-free spiritual interventions that the retreatant can perform on such occasions, and thereby fulfill their duty to individual patrons.[29] In sum, whereas Yangönpa asserts that other people can only constitute obstacles for the porous personhood of the retreatant (and is all but silent on the issue of needing to rely on the outside world for sustenance), Karma Chakmé understands the ascetic as inevitably living in a relationship of exchange with other people, for whom the meditator represents a vector for the removal of various ills. Here Karma Chakmé invokes the narrative of inevitable degradation that is at the heart of Buddhist eschatological cosmology, thereby asserting that this configuration of the relationship between the meditator and the laity, and the concomitant porousness of the retreat, is a product of the historical moment in which they live.

Other chapters of Karma Chakmé's handbook also reflect this basic client-oriented conception of the retreatant, providing models for interacting with people throughout diverse areas of concern. Similar in intent to the ninth chapter, the eighteenth chapter provides instructions for rites for preserving life (which includes granting protection from illness, enemies, armies—basically any external harm, from brigands to drowning to falling from heights) for "you, your guru, your patrons, or others."[30] The thirty-sixth chapter, on removing obstructions, lists remedies for a few dozen bodily ailments, which Karma Chakmé makes clear can be performed either for oneself or for someone else.[31] Karma Chakmé presents Cutting as a method for curing an illness in oneself or someone else, and also as a means to change the weather in a beneficial way, such as by stopping hail or relieving a community from drought, necessitated by rain having become infrequent in the "degenerate age" (*snyigs dus*, similar to the Indian notion of the Kali Yuga) when the text was written.[32] Chapter 40 provides instructions on various modes of activity to benefit other people, including teaching disciples and imparting blessings, and sharing one's spiritual gifts with as many people as possible. Karma Chakmé's retreatant will be fully prepared to tend to others' final needs as well—by helping one find a path to heavenly Sukhāvatī during the dying process, conducting funerary rites, and interring a corpse in a geomantically acceptable location.[33]

A different kind of interpersonal relation, raising a different set of concerns, is with the "retreat attendant" (*mtshams g.yog, sgrub pa'i g.yog*). This is a person, monastic or lay, who has taken on the responsibility of seeing to the retreatant's practical needs, thereby allowing them to focus more exclusively on their meditation. Drakar Lozang Pelden presents the question of the anchorite's relationship with the attendant as a key criterion in making their asceticism either legitimate or illegitimate. In the *Garland of Pearls* he writes that while worldly people with the means to do so will accumulate ever more servants, true Dharma practitioners will do the opposite and take care of themselves. A meditator who continues to rely on servants "like a worldly person" will experience obscurations that prevent them from seeing the true nature of reality; this kind of attachment could even send a person to a hell realm in the next life. Lozang Pelden takes a hard stance, pointing out that when a meditator serves as their own attendant, there are the advantages of not needing to conceal their face and not needing to worry about the attendant's state of mind or whether or not they will obey, or how their words might stir up the mental continuum. "It's easier, you don't accumulate faults, and it accords with the life stories of the superior ones" (*gong ma'i rnam thar dang mthun pa*), among other "inconceivable advantages."[34] In the shorter *Garland of Flowers*, he depicts a situation in which a retreatant may be in the process of teaching a young cleric how to read and write. The retreatant might then be tempted to have the student make a fire or fetch water as a kind of payment. Lozang Pelden discourages this, saying, "You should stay alone, content with serving as your own attendant."[35]

Other meditator-intellectuals of the tradition have been more accepting of reliance on an attendant to facilitate one's contemplative practice, but nevertheless insist on maintaining certain strictures to ensure the separation that defines the retreat endeavor. In Jikmé Lingpa's *Direct Advice on the Mountain Dharma: The Ocean of Wonders*, which is unique for how it interweaves prescriptions with descriptions of how Jikmé Lingpa lived during his own retreat undertaken in central Tibet starting in 1757, he avers that during those three years he did not speak a single word through the portal to his chamber, and his retreat attendants never crossed the threshold into his inner sanctum.³⁶ Karma Chakmé concurs with Lozang Pelden that it is ideal to forego having an attendant—"the supreme kind of practitioner are those who care for themselves, alone"—but if a retreatant is to have one, there are standards to be adhered to. For one, the *Cakrasaṃvara Tantra*'s statement about having a woman serve you while meditating applies only to *mahāsiddha*s who have gained perfect control over the psychophysical channels and winds. For Karma Chakmé's presumed monk reader, it is inappropriate to be alone with a woman, and to have one in your chamber for even a moment is a major infraction. Thus the yogin should issue an order to the Dharma protectors that if a human woman should cross the threshold into his retreat, they should expel her. (This does not apply if she be a *ḍākiṇī* goddess composed of light.) As for the retreat attendant, summarizing what is recorded in the tantras, Karma Chakmé lists the qualities that would make an individual unsuitable, including having broken *samaya*s, harboring negative views about the lamas of their Dharma tradition, being insane, sinful, or deceitful, or having an illness, such as leprosy. A good retreat attendant will be attentive, have faith in the Dharma, and strive to perform well. It is ideal if the meditator can remain unseen by the attendant. If the meditator is at that time maintaining a vow of silence, they should communicate with the attendant through notes written on a dust-covered slate. If the attendant is nonliterate, this presents a particular challenge: the meditator can attempt to silently mouth the words to them, which unfortunately requires their face being seen. If the retreatant fails to make themselves understood in that way, they can resort to something called "half-speech" (*phyed ngag*), which is to talk while keeping one's teeth clenched tight.³⁷

Karma Chakmé also explains that at the moment of officially setting the boundary of the retreat, the attendant must be inside with you. If you anticipate that anyone else may need to cross the boundary and enter the retreat at any later time, you should write that person's name on a piece of paper and wrap it around a rock, and imagine or visualize (*bsgom*) that they are in your presence. As such, when you perform the "circle of protection" visualization that establishes the retreat, they will be inside the protected space with you.³⁸

As reviewed thus far, in the centuries after Yangönpa's *Blazing Jewel*, the concern to provide the anchorite with guidance on how to relate to their family, to the lay faithful, and to the retreat servant compelled exegetes to continually reimagine and redraw the boundary that defines the retreat, the integrity of which is sustained through the maintenance of physical, behavioral, and most of all conceptual boundaries—leaving retreat only when the circumstances are deemed most dire, offering visitors hospitality that falls below the standard of propriety, or experimenting with protocols, from more to less favored, for interacting with the retreat attendant. Although the need for such a virtual peripersonal encasement remains constant throughout the history of the eremitic tradition, notions of where the operative *mtshams* is to be drawn and how it is to be maintained have varied significantly from one author to the next.

Another kind of interpersonal relationship whose negotiation was of particular consequence to the history of eremitism in Tibet is between retreatants themselves. There have been many different ways of treating the issue, ranging from a wary acceptance of the likelihood of needing to reside in proximity to other meditators to the bold claim that their presence is integral to one's own personal practice. This process of redefining isolation and redrawing the essential retreat boundary vis-à-vis other meditators is the focus of the remainder of this chapter.

Writing a century after Yangönpa, the Second Red Hat, Kachö Wangpo, presents solitary retreat and retreat within a loose community as equally satisfactory options: "It is acceptable to either stay with associates who have the same goals as you, or to stay with no associates whatsoever." Karma Chakmé would write that doing a retreat in total solitude is best, but if a meditator must reside in a space where other retreatants are present, "you should confine yourself alone, not meeting one another with your faces." As with a similar statement from Yangönpa mentioned above, the phrase *ngo mi gtugs pa* is difficult to render properly in English, here meaning neither seeing anyone else's face nor having yours seen by them. Expressing a similar view concerning fellow meditators, in the early twentieth century Karma Ngedön Tenkyé asserted that retreatants may reside—his wording is significant—"separately alongside other practitioners of a concordant type" (*rigs mthun rang rang so sor mnyam du sdod*).[39]

Statements such as these show the persistence of the ideal of pure solitude throughout the history of the Tibetan retreat tradition, even while authors of prescriptive texts have allowed for the likelihood of having to live in proximity to other meditators. The prospect of conducting an individual retreat in a location occupied by other ascetics raises issues requiring careful navigation. This is best shown by the Zurmang exegete Lekshé Drayang's detailed treatment of the matter in *Words on the Mountain Dharma: The Melody Producing Nothing but Good,* from around the sixteenth century, which devotes one of its eight chapters to the topic of "relating to fellow Dharma practitioners." Lekshé Drayang begins by stating that practitioners doing retreats in the same vicinity should ideally accord with one another in five basic ways: their views, their conduct, the kind of meditation they perform, their Dharma tradition, and how they acquire their sustenance. Being too different in any of these respects is likely to result in disagreements and negative feelings. He gives the example of how, if meditators practicing alongside one another have different doctrinal views, "when they talk about Dharma or compare their respective experiences, they may grow contemptuous of one another and end up breaking their *samayas*." Lekshé Drayang treats this expectation as constituting a high bar, concluding that "these days it's very rare to find those with whom you accord in these five ways," suggesting that this state of affairs is a product of historical circumstances.[40]

The ideal of perfect harmony in these five areas being so elusive, Lekshé Drayang provides detailed guidelines for avoiding improper relations with fellow practitioners. As a general statement, he asserts that a person with bad conduct will be a cause of distraction to others, and various bad karmas will accumulate within the community. For example, if a meditator behaves in such a way that the other retreatants develop an unfavorable view of them, this leads to an increase in afflictive emotions. But Lekshé Drayang also mentions the good influence that a retreatant can have on others: "By contrast, a yogin who skillfully maintains a perfect reputation can be a positive example for all of the members of the mountain hermitage or the meditation complex. The blessing of his realization will be transferred to others. At the very least, he can have positive relations with whomever he interacts with." Lekshé Drayang adds, "Even if you cannot gather [fellow practitioners] who accord with you in the five ways, it is important that you make an good example of yourself. [In that way,] even the worst fellow practitioners can be brought into contact with excellent practice."[41] In Lekshé Drayang's view, in our present world age a meditative retreat is not likely to take the form of anchorites merely conducting individual retreats in proximity and in parallel; they will affect one another in significant ways, thereby constituting a community of meditators. Together they form an ecosystem, to which they all contribute and by which they are individually affected.

In spite of the good influence that retreatants can potentially have on one another, Lekshé Drayang makes sure to expound upon the evils of unnecessary conversation. The only appropriate kind of conversation is that directed toward improving one's religious practice; all talk about meaningless and worldly things is to be avoided. Lekshé Drayang observes that there are many practitioners who talk too much, and even for a great meditator, the enjoyment of conversation can become a serious obstacle. He goes so far as to state, "Each hour of talk can create the residual poison of a mental latency that lasts for many years." Talking too much to fellow practitioners can also damage a retreatant's reputation, diminishing their status in the eyes of the lama, Dharma siblings, patrons, and local rulers. For two people to renounce all worldly activities, enter meditative retreat, and then to engage in constant conversation—that is "the work of Māra." For canonical backing, he quotes the Buddha as recorded in the *Sūtra to Inspire Noble Aspirations*.[42]

Lekshé Drayang also discusses the problem of feeling jealous of other practitioners—specifically, of what kind of praise or material support they may receive. He depicts the very negative thoughts that might go through a practitioner's mind, along with specific thoughts to cultivate in order to counteract them. For example: "If some individuals of worse religious practice than you, who secretly harbor faults, are looked up to and given offerings by certain other individuals, which you yourself do not receive, then without being unhappy, you should cultivate a feeling of joy toward the patrons." Cultivating pure vision toward other practitioners can help counteract this negativity. Other authors also discuss the importance of this.[43]

Lekshé Drayang's prescriptions for relating to other meditators reflect an ascetic culture in which it is accepted that anchorites will do individual retreats, parallel and near to one another, forming a coherent community. The hermit is thought of as a social being who will interact with, influence, have feelings about, and have a reputation among other retreatants. Nevertheless, Lekshé Drayang's chapter on "relating to fellow Dharma practitioners" is primarily about maintaining interpersonal boundaries in order to prevent those interactions from having too negative an effect on one's spiritual standing or the community. Lekshé Drayang seems to regard such a situation as particularly fraught, eliciting detailed prescriptions on his part and necessitating vigilant self-policing by the meditator.

As evidence of the normalization of thinking about the retreatant as a social being, in the early seventeenth century Lhatsün Namkha Jikmé (a Nyingmapa who specifically mentions cutting off all speech and bricking oneself inside one's retreat) writes in his *Garland of Critical Points for the Precious Mountain Dharma* that there are five relationships by which the retreatant's position is defined: their relationship with their lama, with their patrons, with their Dharma siblings, with the retreat attendant, and with themselves. Namkha Jikmé includes prescriptions for and hazards to avoid in each of these relationships. His discussion of how to maintain an appropriate connection with patrons, for example, notes that receiving their material kindness obligates the ascetic to meditate sincerely; when the patron is ill, the ascetic should attend to them at their bedside, and if necessary perform the postmortem rites. Maintaining a relationship with patrons poses a danger, however, because it can increase the meditator's desire for food and beer. A hermit must be careful not to welcome visitors to their retreat, lest it become little more than a glorified guesthouse. In relating to Dharma siblings, one should avoid unnecessary speech, be sure not to fall into distraction, and avoid writing things that might create enemies and lead to engaging in Dharmic refutations.⁴⁴ Namkha Jikmé's interest in systematizing these five relationships shows how far the tradition had progressed toward normalizing the concept of the retreatant existing in connection to other kinds of people, both inside and outside of the eremitic community, while nevertheless insisting on the maintenance of limits on interpersonal interactions integral to defining a retreat.

———

Tracing what prescriptive retreat texts have said about how retreatants should relate to one another brings to light a significant change in the latter centuries of the eremitic tradition, signaled in a retreat guide by a rough contemporary of both Lekshé Drayang and Namkha Jikmé, Lozang Chökyi Gyeltsen (1567/68/70– 1662), the Fourth Panchen Lama. The *Beryl Ladder for Ascending to the Palace of the Three Bodies: Guidelines for Earnest Mountain Hermits* is intended for those who, having come to see samsara as an iron cage blazing with fire, decide to "stay in an isolated mountain ravine, living like a sage of old" (*drang srong*, which translates the Sanskrit *ṛṣi*). These individuals will abandon their home area, monastery, relations, and Dharma siblings, and will vow to live in isolation. Lozang Chökyi Gyeltsen describes a kind of spontaneously forming retreat community not unlike that depicted by Lekshé Drayang, but which relies explicitly on the dictates of celibate monasticism to ensure the community's integrity:

> If you have arrived at a community (*sde*) of peers of chaste conduct [i.e., celibate monks] with whom you are the same in terms of outward markers, views, and practices, you should abandon feelings of like, dislike, and of competitiveness toward one another.
> In order to not harm your principal practice of the *prāti*[*mokṣa* vows, i.e., monasticism], because they are the root of the Teaching of the scriptures and in actual practice, without neglecting the tradition of the Three Bases [of the monastic community, *gzhi gsum*: fortnightly confession, the summer retreat, and the ending of the summer retreat], you must act in ways that accord with the Dharma that you hold in common, and follow a common set of rules.
> You should generate the thought that all sentient beings in general are your teachers. More specifically, there is the very great fault of those of chaste conduct getting angry at one another, which, according to [Śāntideva's] *Compendium of Training*, is taught in many sutras. Therefore you should think of them as your instructors and practice pure vision.

> If staying in that mountain hermitage with those peers improves your virtuous practice, then keep it as your base, because doing a lot of moving from place to place disrupts your practice of virtue. But if it does not improve your virtuous practice, then as Potowa said, "Roam everywhere, like the sun and the moon."[45]

The picture here is of independent and itinerant yogins who form a temporary, evolving community defined by their collective adherence to the monastic discipline. Lozang Chökyi Gyeltsen writes from the perspective of a mainstream Gelukpa, in which the dictates of the Vinaya, to which each individual monk is expected to have voluntarily submitted, play a critical role in defining a community of retreatants and ensuring proper behavior by its members.

This view of the role of monastic discipline in individual retreat practice was not exclusive to Gelukpas, or even to Buddhists. The Bönpo visionary Shardza Tashi Gyeltsen, mentioned in chapter 1 as an interlocutor of Drakar Lozang Pelden, addressed this issue directly, and using thinking and terminology similar to those of the Fourth Panchen. The passage in question is contained within the longer of two biographies of Tashi Gyeltsen by his disciple Kelzang Tenpé Gyeltsen (1897–1959), and is presented as a quotation from the master, directed toward the inhabitants of a hermitage he had founded. To paraphrase based on William Gorvine's translation, Shardza Tashi Gyeltsen is recorded as saying that a yogin who remains in total solitude in the mountains "like a lion" is not required to adhere to the monastic code of conduct, because his behavior, no matter what it may be, affects only himself. However, when there forms a community based in a particular place, adherence to those guidelines becomes necessary. Otherwise, there is the likelihood of discord in thought and action between individual members. Shardza critiques those living in his day who neglect the unifying dictates of the daily and occasional religious services of the monastic community: "Turning away from the rules of the monastery, it seems they imagine being a hermit or a practitioner amounts to just beating a drum by themselves at their own time. Because the view and conduct of such people is discordant, they become immoral friends for one another." The goal is to "maintain the continuity of a practice community with the pure discipline consistent with the intention" of the founders of the tradition, "avoiding conduct made up by ourselves."[46] While granting validity to the path of the solitary meditator, Shardza here expresses the view that individual practitioners coming together must adhere to these monastic vow–based behavioral expectations.

Drakar Lozang Pelden would go a step beyond the Fourth Panchen and Shardza Tashi Gyaltsen to state that a communal retreat is actually *superior* to one in perfect isolation—a topic about which he maintains there is a major misconception. The reasoning he presents is that living among others helps a practitioner conform to their monastic ethics, whereas residing in complete solitude leaves open the door to aberrant and inappropriate behavior. Lozang Pelden argues that when a practitioner lives under the guidance of their lama and Dharma siblings, their external behavior must naturally conform to the normalizing influence constituted by those other people, which will make it easier to maintain strictness in one's internal mental state. Such a meditator will avoid slackness and maintain their training out of timidity or a sense of anxiety (*bag tsha*). Naturally, the virtues of such a one will "increase like a lake in summer." By contrast, a hermit who goes it alone will have more difficulty remaining mindful of their mental state. In Lozang Pelden's view, such an individual, "due to falling under the influence of patrons, teachers, and other bad associates, will be stained by critical faults in the three sets of vows. Each day the inconceivable mass of sins increases, like Mount Meru." And so the rare freedoms and advantages of a human life will be wasted. He concludes, "That which is called 'practicing the Dharma' is not to be done separately (*logs su*). There is no form of the Dharma superior to that of those who accord themselves with their lama and their peers, this discipline of according oneself."[47]

In light of Drakar Lozang Pelden's prescriptions about various kinds of interpersonal relationships as reviewed in the course of this chapter, it would seem that his model of retreat is a strictly defined community of practitioners living together and mutually enforcing one another's ethical behavior—but while strictly limiting other kinds of interpersonal relations and keeping servants, well-wishers, and family members at bay. Lozang Pelden's instructions here reflect a fully and purposefully communal model of retreat, in which the *mtshams* is drawn not around the individual anchorite but around the community to which he or she belongs. Relations with other people are not to be strictly avoided, but may in fact play an indispensable role in the life of the individual retreatant—as long as all parties are committed to the dictates of monasticism. Their coming together is not merely a matter of convenience or a sign of the ever-worsening times, but an asset to their personal religious practice.

These three examples from the seventeenth to early twentieth centuries express the view that, when done properly, long-term retreat and monasticism are intimately related, with the strictures of monasticism playing an essential role in ensuring the maintenance of the critical interpersonal boundaries around the retreatant. This is a kind of cenobitic eremitism. The significance of these authors' taking this stance comes into relief when we consider attitudes toward monasticism that prevailed in earlier centuries of Tibetan anchoritism. Nearly all of the prescriptive retreat texts used in this study were composed by men living as monks, and while not stipulating that retreat is reserved for career clerics, many retreat texts assume such a status for their readers. But the understanding of monasticism's role in determining the form of the retreat was for a long time very different from that espoused by the Fourth Panchen, Shardza, and Lozang Pelden. For example, in his thirteenth-century treatment of personal ethical conduct, Yangönpa discusses the three sets of vows—monastic, bodhisattvic, and tantric—which respectively enable a person to achieve the state of a Hearer, a bodhisattva, and a buddha. He mentions briefly the different interpretations by Tibetan Buddhists of how those sets of vows relate to one another, aligning himself with the view that the "higher" sets of vows subsume the "lower" ones, in an evolutionary manner. But the relative importance of the different sets of vows vis-à-vis one another is context dependent: when staying in a place of isolation, the meditator can do tantric practice "exclusively" (*'ba' zhig byed*), holding tantric expectations as primary (*gtso cher bsrung*). When residing among other people, however, the meditator must hold the monastic and bodhisattvic vows as primary. If anything, Yangönpa seems to regard the monk's vows as posing something of a challenge to the supreme form of religious practice. There is no suggestion that the form of the retreat itself should be determined by the expectations and practices of monasticism.[48] A century after Yangönpa, Kachö Wangpo would take a similar stance regarding the three sets of vows.[49]

In the fifth chapter of *Direct Advice on Retreat*, Karma Chakmé takes a historically informed approach to this issue, discussing the different ways representatives of the various sects of Tibetan Buddhism have prescribed navigating the potential tensions caused by the opposing dictates of the different sets of vows. In line with his ecumenical approach, Karma Chakmé does not clearly espouse one particular view. Later in the text he quotes his teacher, the Sixth Red Hat, Chökyi Wangchuk, as describing the ideal form of practice as follows:

> Externally, fully ordained in the vows of individual liberation
>   [i.e., celibate monasticism];
> internally a bodhisattva;
> secretly a tantric yogin:
> a thrice-qualified bearer of the vajra.
> Thinking of it, I am oh so glad!

Karma Chakmé comments: "As for those kinds of activities, whether you're meditating in retreat, staying in a village, a monastery, or wherever, you enact them perfectly and unflaggingly. That in fact is not very hard." Karma Chakmé here espouses the view that maintaining one's monastic ethics is the same kind of undertaking regardless of context: one carries this personal ethics internally in all different modes of life, including while in retreat. Showing that in his view monastic practice must be made to conform to the parameters of retreat, in his instructions on the rule-recitation and confession ceremony (*gso sbyong, poṣadha*) that must be performed by all monks on a fortnightly basis, Karma Chakmé specifically addresses how an individual can properly do this while residing in retreat, and thus separated from the community of monks among which the ceremony is customarily done.[50]

Throughout much of the history of Himalayan eremitism, the relationship between monasticism and individual retreat was rather undefined, the two being as it were incidental to each other. Monkhood was seen as a building block for an individual's spiritual practice, to possibly be carried into retreat and maintained as one would in any other mode of life. Under this approach, certain monastic practices like the ordinarily communal fortnightly confession ceremony would have to be altered. This stands in contrast to the view expressed by some latter-day exegetes of the tradition who understood long-term retreat and monasticism as existing in a fundamentally different kind of relationship. In this view, the very form that a retreat takes is determined by what may best help a meditator preserve their status as a monastic, which is considered indispensable to their religious and existential standing. Whereas for most of the history of retreat in Tibet, an individual's monastic status was regarded as a personal affair, a concern internal to the practitioner, among these later authors there is movement toward externalizing the clerical role such that it determines the shape of the meditative community and the retreat itself. This latter-day trend (at least within some communities) is reflected in other changes in retreat discourse as well, most clearly in a certain way of problematizing the food consumed by a retreatant, to be shown in chapter 4.

Much of what this chapter has documented is a shift in Tibetan ascetic discourse and practice from a model based on the ideal of solitary retreat to an acceptance of parallel and then communal forms of retreat. In some circles, the dictates of monasticism would play an important role in defining such a communal mode. In spite of such a trend, communal and monastic forms of retreat have in no way supplanted the older individualistic model, as individual and not explicitly monastic forms of retreat have been valued and practiced continually into the present. Thus when authors of later retreat texts offer prescriptions based on new ideas about the nature of solitude, these constitute not repudiations of earlier models but rather evidence of the evolution of Tibetan religious culture through the expansion of the repertoire of acceptable forms of eremitic practice.

A significant factor in this expansion to include parallel, communal, and monastic forms of retreat is a deferential justification maintaining that ascetic practice is subject to temporal considerations. In varying degrees of explicitness, many latter-day authors suggest that the model of the completely solitary meditator constitutes an idealized version of retreat, attainable in times past but now realizable only by the rarest of ascetic heroes, if at all. This attitude is exemplified by the Fourth Panchen Lama's reference to living in interpersonal isolation like "a sage of old," and by Drakar Lozang Pelden's stating that not relying on a retreat attendant "accords with the life stories of the superior ones." This attitude is implicit in Karma Chakmé's criticism of his own inability to remove himself from his homeland, which places him in a lower category than the great past masters of the Kagyu. Also, when explaining the symbiotic relationship between the retreatant and the laity, Karma Chakmé associates it with living during the time of the five degenerations. Similarly, Lekshé Drayang suggests that an ascetic's expectations relating to interpersonal isolation should be modified in light of temporal circumstances.

A more explicit statement about how our position in time affects our ascetic horizons, including vis-à-vis the question of achieving interpersonal solitude, is given by Ngawang Tenzin Norbu (1867–1940/49?), of Dza Rongpu, a Nyingma monastery in southern Dingri, near Mount Everest. The second section of his seventy-three-folio-side *Charter: Direct Advice on the Mountain Dharma*, dated to 1914, addresses how to practice religion while living in isolation. It begins with the following statement: "As for renouncing all the wonderful things of this life and practicing the Dharma, it is difficult for us Dharma pretenders of the degenerate age to equal any part of the external or internal conduct of the superior ones who came before" (*sngon byon gong ma*). This statement refers to the idea, pervasive in Buddhist cultures, that beginning sometime after the passing away of Śākyamuni Buddha, his Dharma would gradually disappear from the world, in parallel to the worsening of the human condition. In light of this and given our position in time, Ngawang Tenzin Norbu states that all we can realistically aspire to do is live in such a way that we are not accumulating sins and downfalls, and will not have cause for regret at the moment of death. Over the next two folio sides, he makes a series of contrasts between the ideal version of religious practice that once was and the diminished version that we can strive toward in these benighted times. Although it is difficult to renounce all activities of this life, pass our time in religious activity, and live only by begging, as long as we possess a small amount of food and clothing, we can stay in a mountain hermitage. Although it is difficult to know and maintain all the vows of monasticism, we can at least strive not to harm others and to be assiduous in the fortnightly confession. Although it is difficult to know and maintain all the tantric *samayas*, we can strive to understand everything we see and hear as the play of the three bodies of buddhahood. Finally, he writes, "Although it may be difficult to spend our whole lives wandering only in the mountains like a rhinoceros, while we reside in remote places, mountain hermitages, and so forth, regarding our kinsmen or anyone else, whether their position be elevated or lowly, we should abandon feeling too close or antagonistic toward them, maintaining our independence." In short, as samsara progresses in its preordained process of degeneration and essential facets of the ideal form of asceticism exemplified by the great sages of previous generations become all but impossible to enact, we can maintain a spirit of reclusion as a sort of internalized discipline, even if not fully manifested outwardly in our lifestyle. Perhaps interconnected with this view, Ngawang Tenzin Norbu argues that the monastic discipline must play a central organizing role in the comportment of the ascetic, due to living "during this time when the Teachings have nearly subsided."[51]

In these examples we see that authors in recent centuries of the Tibetan eremitic tradition have increasingly demonstrated an attitude of lived deferential reverence by accepting and even prescribing for their readers a form of ascetic practice that they regarded as farther from ideal than what had been enacted long before, when the world and the people in it were closer to perfect. The specific form of the hermit's practice, undertaken in relation to a horizon of possibility that is always receding, serves to mark their place in both historical and eschatological time.

———

With the goal of understanding how interpersonal relations have been problematized within the retreat tradition, this chapter has examined the specific mechanisms that authors have prescribed for maintaining limits in a meditator's interactions with their family and the broader laity, with the retreat attendant, and with other meditators—means of preserving the sacred core of the retreat from incursions by the profane outside. While the ideal that the meditator should limit interpersonal interactions as much as possible has remained a constant, meditator-intellectuals have assumed very different models for how the retreatant may actually exist in the world: Yangönpa's heroic loner who shuns all interaction absolutely; Karma Chakmé's unseen ritualist for hire, who is sometimes silent and inaccessible; Zurmang Lekshé Drayang's meditator as a member of a community of retreatants; and Drakar Lozang Pelden's retreatant as member of a monastic community, solitude being the path to squandering the precious opportunity that is a human life. These are four starkly different ways of imagining and defining the ascetic self, sociologically and interpersonally, representing dramatically different ideas of what individual long-term retreat is or should be.

Across all the successive reconceptualizations of reclusion, the need to maintain boundaries in the interpersonal realm remains unchanged. Whether the boundary is drawn around an individual or around a group to which they belong, separation from ordinary existence is maintained through the observance of limitations in one's interactions with other people. The full and final abandonment of the world may remain as an objective, but the actual lived practice of eremitism entails a continual stream of small, procedural ways of keeping the world beyond one's doorstep at bay, each a practical mechanism that contributes to the positive definition of the ascetic self.

CHAPTER 4

NOURISHING THE ASCETIC SELF

This chapter examines both general attitudes and specific prescriptions relating to material concerns in the eremitic endeavor, which play a defining role in the history of the Tibetan ascetic self. Throughout the literature offering instruction for individual long-term retreat there is pervasive use of stock phrases, varying according to geographical and historical linguistic patterns across the Tibetan-speaking world, that mean "food and clothing" (such as *zas gos, lto gos, lto rgyab*). In his early eighteenth-century *Direct Advice That Is the Ship for Great Liberation,* Sönam Chödzin writes that the meditator "will survive on whatever food and clothing they receive."[1] The phrase *mthun rkyen*, literally "conducive circumstances," carrying the sense of "the things one needs," is commonly used to refer to food and clothing as well.[2] Throughout the history of the tradition, these twinned material concerns have been consistently mentioned in connection to how they constitute potential points of attachment to the world. The meditator's ability to overcome such attachments is a critical determinant in making their asceticism either authentic and worthwhile or false and potentially harmful. Exemplifying this attitude, in his early twentieth-century *Instruction Pointing Out the Mountain Dharma,* Karma Ngedön Tenkyé asserts that when beginning a retreat

> your mindset is the most important thing. Therefore, regarding any desires you may harbor relating to your reputation, to competitiveness or pride, or if you think about how in time everyone will come to have faith in you, as a result of which you will acquire nice food and clothing—if, thinking in such a way, you take to a mountain hermitage and meditate, then even though you may strive

diligently in your asceticism (*dka' thub*), because your thinking is improper, the endeavor will become non-Dharmic.

Statements of this kind, emphasizing a meditator's need to examine their true motivations and abandon attachments to material things, are commonplace in the prescriptive literature for individual retreat.[3] They call to mind how, according to the standard version of his *Life* written in 1488 by the Madman of Tsang (1452–1507), shortly before his death Milarepa is storied to have instructed his disciples to "renounce all thoughts of food, clothing, or conversation."[4] This text in fact charts Mila's journey to enlightenment through changes in his relationships to food and clothing. Early in his life, the actions of the youth and those around him are depicted as strongly constrained by material concerns. When first meditating in retreat, the length of time he can remain there is determined by the amount of food in his possession. As he deepens his asceticism, his clothing wears away and he dresses in empty flour sacks crudely tied together, eventually going about essentially naked. So as never to have to interact with the world, he resorts to foraging for wild nettles, the ingestion of which turns his skin green—his complexion ever after serving as a symbol of his absolute transcendence of the relationship to material things that most fundamentally defines human existence for the rest of us.

Although the didactic and hagiographic traditions may be in agreement regarding the ultimate goal of severing ties to clothing and food, the existence of the ideal of separation does not preclude a more nuanced and pragmatic discourse about how a retreatant is to navigate those relationships, but in fact necessitates it, in parallel to what we saw in chapter 3. To briefly address the less problematized of the two items, prescriptive texts for long-term individual retreat rarely refer to clothing in more than a passing way. Related to the view that clothing constitutes an object of attachment, authors may mention the ideal of making do with the bare minimum—wearing "only a cotton cloth, or torn clothing," or "the clothing of a mere servant."[5] Some have addressed whether or not a cleric must continue to wear the normative skirt, shirt, and shawl-style monastic robes during a retreat.[6] As described in chapter 2, Yangönpa problematized clothing for the way it can convey harmful taints or positive dependent connections to its wearer.

Although there is no sustained conversation about the clothing a meditator might wear, food has garnered consistent and detailed attention throughout the entire history of the Tibetan eremitic tradition. This chapter goes beyond the kind of categorical statement about the negative relationship to food cited above to look more closely at what retreat texts have had to say concerning how the ascetic should relate to food more pragmatically, constituting an essential part of the evolving Tibetan eremitic habitus and inculcating different self-understandings for the meditator. Mipam Püntsok Sherap writes that the ascetic should "survive on the barest sustenance" (*'tsho ba ngan ngon la brten*) and "assume the mentality of a beggar" (*blo rtse sprang po la gtod*).[7] What is living in such a manner actually understood to entail? This chapter examines treatments of food as articulated by exegetes of the eremitic tradition, focusing on what specific concerns are raised for consideration by the retreatant and what the author seems to understand their horizon of ascetic possibility to be. These ways of problematizing food give rise to different practical techniques that serve to constitute different forms of selfhood. We are interested in these authors' respective approaches, as well as the relative intensity or emphasis with which they invoke the various possible problematizations. Foucault convincingly shows that, owing to the dangers with which it was attributed, its potential cost to the individual, and its connection to the question of life and death, in ancient Greece *aphrodisia* "constituted a privileged domain for the ethical formation of the subject." This chapter will show that the most privileged domain for the ethical formation of the ascetic subject in the Himalaya was food, being one of the most important reference points for the stylization of the contemplative's eremitic lifestyle.[8] The tradition's understanding of the retreatant's proper relationship to food has also served as the basis for the attitude of lived deferential reverence, as latter-day exegetes have often deemed this relationship to be inflected by temporal conditions. In the course of this chapter, I will also highlight moments in these texts where sociological realities of anchoritic practice historically are denoted in relation to food.

As is the case with so many concerns, Yangönpa's problematization of food in the *Blazing Jewel* is distinctive within the broader sweep of Tibetan eremitism. Yangönpa prescribes that the beginning of a retreat should be marked by fiercely generating the resolution articulated as follows: "I have not achieved well-being and joy so far in this lifetime. In order to fulfill the intentions of my lama, and for the sake of other sentient beings, I will achieve buddhahood. Until such point as the final good quality has been achieved, no matter if I grow hungry or cold, or fall ill, or die of starvation, or get abducted by a demon with my eyes wide open, I will see my meditation through to the end." Shortly after this Yangönpa writes of how, as the root of the Dharmic life, a retreatant should reflect, "If tomorrow I die of starvation, then I shall die. I will not hold on to even a needle's worth in this world."⁹ In Yangönpa's presentation, when a meditator is erecting the mental architecture that will structure their time in retreat, hunger and even the possibility of dying from starvation are invoked as outcomes that they must recognize and accept. The fear of starving is to be directly confronted, playing a critical role in generating heroic resolve. Other authors refer to the possibility of starvation in a similar manner.[10]

Later in the *Blazing Jewel*, when discussing obstacles that may arise after the retreatant has begun to achieve *siddhi*s, Yangönpa mentions running out of food, along with experiencing a serious illness, an infestation of lice or bedbugs, and having others begin to speak about you in a denigrating fashion. On this point he quotes Kodrakpa, saying that "once you begin to obtain the supreme and ordinary *siddhi*s, you will have the experience of not acquiring the conducive circumstances, which is a sign" of spiritual progress.[11] Rather than signifying a deficiency of some kind, the experience of material lack is posited as an advantage. Characterizing such challenges as experiences to be "brought onto the path," a convention in Tibetan contemplative practice addressed in chapter 5, Yangönpa states that the meditator should understand them as resulting from the kindness of the lama, and as providing opportunities to learn and grow. Through this succession of statements, it seems that Yangönpa expects the meditator to embrace precarity by reconciling themselves to the likelihood of facing penury, and to frame this as a positive experience.

When it comes to the actual consumption of food, Yangönpa's primary concern is how it will affect the psychophysical continuum of the meditator. This makes food by and large an object of suspicion. In the section on dealing with obstacles that can arise within the body, Yangönpa refers to how a retreatant can contract a harmful taint by consuming impure food.[12] It is important that a practitioner of *tummo* clear their lungs before eating, that they not do *tummo* when overly hungry, and that they not eat food that weakens the yogic drops.[13] The yogic drops, which are a critical concern for those practicing sexual yoga, are thought of as being particularly affected by what a person ingests. The drops are "dried" by eating in general, and any food that causes their degeneration must be discarded. The consumption of certain powerful substances, however, can revivify the drops.[14] If the meditator's progress has stalled, necessitating "further improvement" measures, they should perhaps "eat some nutritious food," among other practical and ritual remedies.[15]

In keeping with Yangönpa's manner of problematizing food, he offers an intervention on the level of the practitioner's psychophysical continuum: the yoga of eating, presented as a necessary part of the retreatant's daily comportment. This is an internalized version of the fire pūjā or *homa* ritual, in which the food swallowed and ingested is purified by a fire visualized inside of the meditator and offered to the deities. You visualize yourself in the form of the tutelary deity, with spoon in hand. As you eat, the food travels down to satisfy the lama visualized at your throat, the tutelary deity in your belly, and the heroes and ḍākiṇīs that reside in the three channels. Yangönpa explains that through this practice, everything a person eats or drinks becomes the stuff of a feast offering (*tshogs*). The food is purified, to prevent it from becoming a cause of obscurations. As it is consumed, it is transmuted from a mundane object of desire into an offering to the deities. Yangönpa instructs the meditator to generate the thought that the food they are consuming will dispel the hunger of all sentient beings, about which he states, "Whether or not your disciples or patrons (*yon bdag*) get happiness and so on depends upon" maintaining this mindset. If the yoga of eating is done properly, consuming food becomes an act of compassion toward all beings. The *Great Appendix* describes the yoga of eating by saying something like the following: "Eating this food will sustain your life and nourish your body. Therefore, this is a critical moment in determining whether the outcome will be good qualities or faults."[16]

In Yangönpa's presentation, the very moment of consuming food is regarded as a decisive point of interface between the meditator and the material world, and the yoga of eating is a mechanism for preventing a negative outcome. Yangönpa's prescriptions concerning food are part of his distinctive treatment of the ascetic self, which regards the meditating subject as a kind of empty vessel constituted by various positive and negative forces flowing through it, from the outside in and the inside out. This leads Yangönpa to frame his treatment of many facets of life in retreat in terms of taints, obstacles, obscurations, dependent connections, positive qualities, and faults. The ascetic is not merely a passive observer, however: at the moment of ingestion, they have the potential to ensure the transmutation of bad into good through proper visualization practice.

The only other reference in the *Blazing Jewel* or the *Great Appendix* to how the retreatant is to be supported materially comes amid the instructions for generating a circle of protection through visualization—necessary because of our living in a degenerate time, when people tend toward nonvirtue and the power of the protector deities is limited—where the *Great Appendix* states that a meditator should do this practice "when moving about, such as when gathering wood or provisions" (*shing dang rgyags*).[17] Yangönpa's near silence on how to acquire food is consistent with his treatment of the meditator as a being who shuns all interpersonal interactions as potential causes of obstacles; he therefore does not see a need to elaborate on the proper and improper forms of such relations. Skirting the issue of how the ascetic will be supported materially makes Yangönpa an outlier in the eremitic intellectual tradition, for although other authors at times problematize food in terms of purity and pollution and provide instructions for its proper consumption, including the yoga of eating, the central concern in the tradition's discourse historically has been the matter of how to procure food without losing one's moral standing.[18] Whereas Yangönpa's understanding of the ascetic self leads him to locate the critical interface at the moment of contact between food and the ascetic's alimentary system, for other authors the critical interface would be found in the interpersonal realm (or less prominently, the interspiritual).

Creating a fundamental point of divergence from Yangönpa, authors of retreat texts tend overwhelmingly to espouse an opposite interpretation of the experience of food precarity, positing it as the ripening of past negative karma or an indication of insufficient good karma.[19] This gives a negative rather than a positive valence to having insufficient provisions. As for the question of how the ascetic is to acquire those provisions, in chapter 3 we saw suggestions of how important a concern food has been in the ascetic's negotiation of interpersonal relations, as meditator-authors have specifically commented upon contingencies related to returning home to gather provisions, or about family members or other faithful who arrive at the retreat bearing offerings of sustenance. Here we more fully direct our attention to the topic relating to food that has provoked the longest and most detailed elaboration by authors in the retreat tradition: how to go about acquiring it. This leads to questions of how to relate to patrons and sources of income in general. The central concern is how to secure the material things needed to survive without losing moral rectitude or spiritual progress. We will see how these authors weigh competing ideals relative to differently imagined horizons of possibility.

A hermit's access to provisions has at times been thought of as a question of their relationship with the spirit beings who have jurisdiction over the place where the retreat is located. Jikten Sumgön's early *Large Vase of Nectar* details how a retreatant's access to food, water, and firewood is attributable to relationships maintained with the local deities via the offering of ritual cakes, accompanied by supplications for assistance and protection, and the dedication of any merit gained to the liberation of all beings, including the local deities themselves. In general, Jikten Sumgön's prescriptions emphasize the role played by spirit beings in the course of a retreat. His teacher, Pakmodrupa, had offered similar instructions.[20]

Although other authors of retreat texts also mention the role of local deities, a far greater amount of care and attention is given to the question of how a retreatant is to acquire their sustenance from other people, which is seen as full of potential pitfalls. Chegom Sherap Dorjé writes in his *Lamp for Fortunate Mountain Hermits* that one staying in a mountain hermitage need not be unduly concerned about the "conducive circumstances," for they will be provided by local hunters, herdsmen, and wood collectors.[21] If this proves insufficient and the meditator becomes utterly without sustenance, then they may go begging among human settlements, sneaking off like a tantric departing to do the Secret Practice. Upon acquiring some provisions, the meditator should immediately hurry back to their retreat. Chegompa warns that if they become attached to the honors shown them in the village, which is "the noose of the Māra," they risk losing whatever spiritual progress they may have made. And so the anchorite should strive to be like the wind, unconcerned with acquisitiveness; should keep to their mountainous redoubt, like a deer; should not become prideful, even if they become as wealthy as the gods; should not become dejected, even if they find themselves as destitute as a hungry ghost.[22]

A far more detailed exposition on how to properly beg for provisions appears in Zurmang Lekshé Drayang's *Words on the Mountain Dharma,* dating from some three hundred years later. One of its eight chapters—titled "the means of obtaining the material things that are the conducive circumstances"—is devoted almost entirely to the issue of food, with clothing taken up only in the final few lines. Lekshé Drayang's treatment of food is organized around the question of how the ascetic acquires their sustenance, and the moral implications thereof. He presents three options: by using the yogic alchemical practice of "essence extraction," by begging from the laity, or by a third, unacceptable way, detailed below.

According to Lekshé Drayang, from one perspective the best of these three possibilities is essence extraction (*bcud len*). This refers to a category of practices by which a person is able to sustain themselves bodily by extracting (*len*) the essence (*bcud*) from certain material substances, ranging from the extremely mundane, like pebbles, air, and ordinary food, to the rare, like certain highly potent flowers and herbs. Lekshé Drayang presents this as an advanced technique reserved for the elite practitioner, characterizing such a person as follows: "There is a qualified individual possessed of faith who principally practices the yogas of the channels, winds, and drops, who has had achievement thanks to their experience in the practice of removing obstacles and in further improvement practices, and who has completely severed their appetite for the food of this world. In order to never descend to the village, one such as this sustains themselves by means of the esoteric instructions for essence extraction." One advantage of doing this practice, as presented here, is that having terminated any need for ordinary foodstuffs, the ascetic can cut the social ties that such reliance customarily entails. Lekshé Drayang mentions that there are more than twenty different ways of doing essence extraction, but limits his presentation to five, each based on the transmutation of an ordinary food: *tsampa*, alcohol, yogurt, tea, and molasses. For each of these starting materials he describes a specific process—of drying, boiling, grinding, and mixing with medicinal herbs—and the particular benefits that the resulting substance will produce. Consuming the empowered substance derived from *tsampa* (roasted barley flour, the staple food of Tibet) is beneficial to a practitioner's *samādhi*, while that produced from yogurt helps with problems of the phlegm, among other benefits.

Lekshé Drayang concludes this section on essence extraction by characterizing the enterprise as probably not realistic for his reader. He explains that in order to succeed, an individual must have achieved complete control over the psychophysical channels and winds, and must also have full knowledge of the practices of essence extraction, which is "rare these days." Moreover, it can be difficult to gather the right materials, and the process for producing the empowered substances must be done perfectly. Given these realities, attempting essence extraction is likely to become a distraction to the meditator. Therefore, it is probably best to settle for the second of the three options, to beg for one's food.[23] The question of essence extraction's place in the Tibetan eremitic tradition will be addressed more fully below.

Lekshé Drayang's instructions for how to go begging for provisions are extensive. Before breaking their retreat, the meditator must mentally don a certain "armor" (*go cha*), which creates a buffer between them and the world they are about to step into. Three times the retreatant is to generate the following thoughts:

> In going forth from my mountain hermitage, I do so in order to maintain this physical body, which practices the holy Dharma. Because I am not seeking fame or praise in this life, when I go into the village, even if there are unwise people pretending to be wise, or bad people pretending to be good, or unaccomplished people pretending to be accomplished, I will not engage in talkativeness. Nor will I talk about my dreams or extrasensory perceptions, or about my meditation or my religious practices, and so on. Once I have acquired alms from this village or these nomads in an amount sufficient to sustain me for half a year or half a month, I will come immediately back to this place of meditation. Forget about staying longer to serve as a chaplain, practice rituals, and so forth: I will not stay for even a few days.

He continues, "I will not have any enmity toward the households from whom I do not acquire alms. Nor will I have any attachment or praise for the patron households who treat me best." From here, Lekshé Drayang explains how the rigors of travel provide an opportunity to practice the Mahāmudrā, through which all experiences while outside of the retreat—fatigue, darkness, wind, rain, snow, dangerous passes—are rendered neutral through purposeful contemplation. The ascetic can also use these physical trials as an opportunity to improve their control over the channels and winds, or do illusory body or *bardo* meditations, or simply practice taking experiences onto the contemplative path.

Lekshé Drayang next offers a series of directives for how an anchorite should interact with the laity among whom they beg. While out begging, the individual, here assumed to be a monastic, is to keep their behavior in line with the dictates of the Vinaya, to preserve the faith of potential donors. They can beg from specific households, but should not engage them in conversation. They should bless each household, regardless of whether or not they give them anything. They may recite sutras and dedicatory prayers, but should not go so far as to make a feast offering or construct a mandala.

Lekshé Drayang closes his instructions on begging with some advice on how the retreatant should respond if their attempt at gathering sustenance is not successful. The hermit may find that beggars who are lowlier than them get more offerings, which should not cause them to become discouraged or jealous. They should take what little they were able to gather, return to their retreat, seal the door, and resume their meditation without giving it any further thought. Like Yangönpa, Lekshé Drayang mentions the importance of the meditator protecting themselves from potential defilement at the moment of eating through ritual and mental preparation.[24]

Next Lekshé Drayang describes what he regards as a third possible way of relating to foodstuffs during a retreat, which is to give no forethought to the matter. This will inevitably make the meditator reliant on other retreatants, to whom they become a significant burden. He quotes the famous yogin Orgyenpa Rinchen Pel's (1229/30–1309) description of a scene where a meditator who has made insufficient preparations runs out of provisions and must scurry to his guru for help. He quotes another passage from Orgyenpa as follows:

> There are some referred to as "having abandoned everything" (*kun spang*) or "mendicants" (*bya bral*), who, when they stay somewhere, have no clothing; who, when they sit down to meditate, have no cushion; who, when they go to collect alms, have neither the three [parts of the robe?] nor boots; who, when it

snows or rains, have no hat; who, when they are given provisions, have no sack [in which to carry them].... When a meal is being served, they have no bowl. When they inhabit a cave or a cabin, they have neither a pot nor a flint. Such a one will seek out their Dharma siblings in hope that the Dharma siblings will give the things that they lack. And so it is others who will take care of them. While their lama, Dharma siblings, and patrons take responsibility for their welfare, helping them, that kind of Dharma practitioner becomes ever more boastful about themselves.

This is an irresponsible and unacceptable manner of relating to one's material circumstances. Lekshé Drayang explains that because such an ascetic will inevitably be a distraction and an inconvenience to others, disrupting their contemplative pursuits, this is a moral failing—in spite of the tradition's rhetoric of abandoning (*spang*) concern for all material things (*kun*).[25]

Throughout his chapter dedicated to dealings with material things, Lekshé Drayang is highly pragmatic about how a retreatant should acquire food, dismissing out of hand any other attitude. Food is problematized not principally for the specific substance of the provisions or how its consumption may affect the meditator, but rather on the grounds of the interpersonal relationships that an ascetic's need for it necessarily creates. The difficulty of navigating these relationships means that the need to eat represents a slippery slope to moral ruination.

The question of how to go begging for provisions has been taken up by many authors of prescriptive retreat texts. The Third Karmapa, Rangjung Dorjé, devotes two folio sides of his early fourteenth-century *Quintessence of Nectar* to providing instruction on how properly to beg for food during a retreat. He writes about maintaining the necessary attitude of detachment, restraining the senses, and moving lightly like a bee among flowers. If the ascetic fails to acquire provisions, they should regard this as resulting from the ripening of their own negative karma, as the Buddha is recorded to have done. If you do acquire provisions, you should be prepared to donate them to any needy person you might encounter, giving from your own stock and keeping only the worst of it for yourself.[26] A few hundred years later, Karma Chakmé explains that we should trust that anchorites practicing legitimately have no reason to fear starvation, as taught by the Buddha. He then provides instructions similar to those given by Lekshé Drayang, using the analogy of a bee in an extended fashion. Later in the handbook Karma Chakmé addresses how to maintain the proper attitude of equanimity when away from your retreat for the purpose of begging, and how to bring onto the spiritual path whatever you experience in the process. Karma Chakmé mentions that hermits would traditionally go on their major begging rounds in the summer, when dairy products become plentiful, and in the autumn, around the time of the main grain harvest.[27]

Shabkar's nineteenth-century *Beneficial Moon* provides a rich source for tracking how the Tibetan eremitic tradition has problematized the retreatant's relationship with food. In an interesting dynamic, *Beneficial Moon* shows how persistent the concern about starvation has been within the yogic tradition (often mentioned twinned with the possibility of freezing to death) while simultaneously using that same record to argue that the reader need not worry about such an outcome. With the aim of normalizing such trials as part of the Buddhist ascetic endeavor, Shabkar quotes passages that refer to the hardships endured by the great masters of the past, going all the way back to the Buddha-to-be's surviving for six years on a drop of water and a grain of food per day. He cites the example of "the holy ones of the past," who renounced everything to meditate in isolated places—and about whom there is not a single story of an individual actually dying of starvation. He quotes the Kadampa master Geshé Kharakpa or Kharak Gomchung (tenth–eleventh century), who dismisses the perceived dangers of retreat as follows: "Until now, have you ever seen or heard of a great meditator who has died from cold or hunger, even though they neither farm nor amass material things? Nor will you ever see or hear of it in the future." (This passage is quoted by other authors as well.) Shabkar follows with what he presents as a well-known saying: "The [snow] lion does not get cold in the snow. The vulture does not fall from the sky. Dharma practitioners don't die from starvation." The reason, Shabkar argues, is that if a meditator goes into retreat and practices sincerely, they will be taken care of materially. Shabkar cites numerous textual passages that have made this point, running over many pages, including from sutras, tantras, Atīśa, Chenga Lodrö Gyeltsen (1402–1472), Milarepa, Lama Zhang, and the Kadampa master Potowa.[28] For Shabkar, fear of starvation is to be downplayed, even mentally removed from the horizon of possibility, so as not to make potential anchorites worry unnecessarily about their sustenance, which could frighten them away from the undertaking. This is a mental architecture very different from that erected by Yangönpa's imagined recluse, who was to be resigned to the possibility of starvation.

Shabkar also provides instruction for how to actually relate to sources of material support. In particular, he critiques certain improper attitudes that a meditator might harbor about how to gain provisions. Shabkar describes an individual who makes a mental list of what they believe they will need to sustain themselves during retreat. Even after receiving the minimum of what they need from their lama, they persist in seeking out a patron who will make a formal pledge to support them with additional materials, even attempting to get this promise in writing. Such a person has not abandoned the eight worldly concerns (pleasure and pain, loss and gain, fame and ignominy, praise and blame). Elsewhere, Shabkar observes that during his own day, there are many who lament, "I want to do religious practice in an isolated mountain hermitage as those others have in the past, but I don't have the conducive circumstances." To them he poses the question, "What is it that you lack?" He details how the Buddha and his disciples made do with the minimum in terms of food and clothing. Some retreatants wrongly spend their time acquiring nice foodstuffs and thereby end up acting like householders, with no time to actually practice the Dharma. In another place, after laying out critiques of the many wrong ways of sustaining oneself during retreat, Shabkar offers a more positive suggestion: echoing a directive that has been voiced throughout the history of the tradition, he prescribes striving to sustain oneself in a manner resembling that of birds and mice. With no fixed residence, permanent relations, or accumulated possessions, throughout their entire lives they consume whatever they find each day.[29]

Drakar Lozang Pelden's approach to the issue of food similarly includes an attempt to head off preemptive worry about provisions, stating that as long as a meditator practices sincerely, their basic needs will be met, and therefore they should not be concerned about whether they will be supported.[30] As for how to acquire the needed sustenance, Lozang Pelden states that the meditator must ask their lama's permission before going begging and be entirely truthful in explaining their purpose for leaving. Showing how the dictates of monasticism shaped his early twentieth-century vision of retreat practice, Lozang Pelden stipulates that if traveling alone or in a small group, the retreatant should not go away for more than thirteen days, to ensure that they can return to the community in time for the next fortnightly confession ceremony. If the region is poor in resources, requiring travel farther afield, perhaps taking a month or two, those going begging should travel in a group of five, so as to be able to perform the ceremony themselves. Lozang Pelden writes very negatively about ascetics who manipulate their patrons into giving them things, perhaps by complaining that their clothes have worn thin or claiming to have an illness for which butter and meat might provide relief. A meditator must not coddle, flatter, or deceive their patrons, and should treat this as a fleeting relation rather than a long-term one. To remain attached to a patron is to waste one's precious human life. He describes an ascetic who cannot sit in meditation for longer than the time it takes to drink a single cup of tea, saying, "I'm too tired!," but who, for the sake of acquiring the patron's inheritance, will do thread cross rituals day and night.[31]

As indicated already, an issue closely related to how an anchorite should beg for provisions and relate to patrons is the possibility of performing rituals or other religious services for payment, which is mentioned as a concern in a great many prescriptive retreat texts. Mipam Püntsok Sherap instructs, "Don't stay in the village for a long time in order to subdue demons, receive gifts, do village rituals, and so on, or for the sake of getting food." In characterizing modes of behavior that a retreatant should be sure to avoid, Lhatsün Namkha Jikmé describes an individual who "does rituals in the village for the sake of food." Such a one, he asserts, is "an oxymoron of a Dharma practitioner" (*gnam rdib kyi chos pa*). He states that in general the ascetic should make do with just enough food and clothing to survive. If they engage in any unnecessary striving for those things, then they will end up squandering the rare opportunity for spiritual advancement that is a human life.[32] We saw in chapter 3 that Karma Chakmé assumes that the retreatant will need to perform rituals to fulfill their obligations to patrons. There are nevertheless limits that they must observe. The fortieth chapter of his *Direct Advice on Retreat* addresses various aspects of "how to work for the benefit of other beings," including proper and improper behavior for an individual who, having completed their intensive meditative practice, departs from retreat in order to engage with the world. Here Karma Chakmé writes about the great evil of giving empowerments, transmissions, and teachings while harboring concern for the material considerations one will garner, which is "selling the Dharma." He seems to consider this as crossing over into a different classification from that of performing small-scale ritual favors for individual patrons that can be viewed as fulfilling genuine needs. Meanwhile Karma Chakmé refers to himself in a self-denigrating fashion as a "old village ritualist" (*grong chog rgan po*).[33]

Drakar Lozang Pelden regards the possibility of falling into the habit of performing ritual services for pay as a major concern, addressing it at length in the *Garland of Pearls*. He states that a retreatant should not resort to doing "divinations, astrology, medicine, or rituals," because "the path to their retreat cabin will become well traveled" due to people's constant coming and going. Moreover, such behavior constitutes a "wrong form of making one's livelihood" (*log pa'i 'tsho ba*), framing the matter in terms of the notion of the "right livelihood," one part of the Buddha's Noble Eightfold Path.[34] Other authors also invoke the notion of "wrong livelihood" in addressing how the retreatant should or should not be kept fed.[35]

Most prominent in the Tibetan retreat tradition's problematization of food is the question of how a meditator will acquire it. The prescriptions for acquiring provisions are similar in form to those for limiting interpersonal relationships, as they amount to attempts to maintain behavioral and conceptual boundaries that are always in the process of being tested. The need to eat threatens to drag the hermit into interpersonal relationships that could nullify whatever separation from the world they have managed to achieve, posing an existential threat to the retreat endeavor. Even worse, this most human of needs threatens to make the ascetic engage in immoral acts, potentially even despoiling their fundamental relationship to the Dharma itself.

In the latter centuries of the retreat traditions, discussions of how the retreatant should acquire sustenance began to feature a new category, *dkor* (pronounced "kor"), which refers to material wealth that has been offered to the *sangha* or community of legitimate monastics. As it is an essential means of maintaining the symbiotic relationship between the *sangha* and the lay society that supports them materially, the Tibetan Buddhist tradition has attached grave karmic implications to *dkor*: to accept and use such donated material while presenting oneself outwardly as a monk or nun but being imperfect in monastic comportment will have a very negative karmic effect on the individual. The fortnightly confession ceremony plays an indispensable role in sustaining this dynamic, as it ensures the purity of the vows of the monastic community. Improperly consuming *dkor* is similar to pursuing a "wrong form of making one's livelihood," but pertains specifically to monastics and the material things offered to them. In Tibet, relating improperly to *dkor* is often referred to as contracting a harmful taint due to misappropriated offerings (*dkor grib*). To discuss a retreatant's relationship to food in terms of *dkor* constitutes a variation on the treatment of how to properly acquire sustenance as reviewed in this chapter but invokes different parameters, and explicitly defines the retreatant as a celibate monastic.

Writing in the middle of the seventeenth century, Karma Chakmé mentions *dkor* as a concern for an ascetic trying to conduct themselves properly with respect to material things. Karma Chakmé describes rites that can remove the taint of misappropriated offerings. He also mentions that if a meditator's efforts at begging for food should prove fruitless, then at least they can take solace in knowing that they have not been exposed to the risk of improperly consuming monastic property. This suggests an ever-present anxiety over the matter. Karma Chakmé deprecatingly refers to himself as a "sack of *kor*" (*dkor sgye*), implying deficiencies in the purity of his monastic comportment.[36] His spiritual heir, Karma Ngedön Tenkyé, instructs the ascetic to think, "Whatever you acquire [from begging], be content with it, as it is the collective wealth of the clerical community." He describes how the wealth and livestock a meditator makes use of during a retreat should be thought of not as their own possessions but as the resources of the monastic community, to be used toward the benefit of the Teachings and of sentient beings. Later in the text, Karma Ngedön Tenkyé addresses *dkor* from a different angle: when presenting practical instructions on antidotes to the five basic afflictions (desire, aversion, ignorance, envy, and pride), he describes how to overcome excessive pride by thinking of one's own faults. He tells the meditator to think of the many facets of their own hypocrisy: wearing the maroon and yellow robes of virtue while harboring these afflictions on the inside; accumulating wealth like a thief while regarding yourself as a Dharma practitioner; pursuing deluded thoughts day and night while falsely claiming to be doing a retreat—and most important for our purposes here, "eating food donated to the *sangha* despite not having any of the three virtues of learning, nobility of bearing, and goodness."[37]

Shabkar thoroughly addresses the issue of improperly consuming material donated to the monastic community, emphasizing that this particular form of misconduct will result in negative consequences in both this life and the next. He quotes from the *Sūtra on Ending Lax Monastic Conduct*: "For one with worn-out monastic ethics to wrap himself in the victory banner of uprightness and to consume for one day that which has been donated out of faith—that is a greater nonvirtue than for a person endowed with all ten nonvirtues to accumulate sins uninterruptedly for a hundred years." This is followed by quotations from canonical Indian sources expressing a similar sentiment. He then relates the story of a Kadampa master who, when a small bird was flying overhead, moved to avoid being touched by the bird's shadow. When asked by his disciples why he did this, he answered that the bird was carrying a mouthful of grain that it had pilfered from the *sangha*'s inventory, explaining, "If its shadow (*grib*) should touch me, I fear that I would experience the harmful taint of improperly consuming monastic donations." This is based on a play on words, stemming from the fact that the word *grib* can mean a shadow or a harmful taint. Shabkar punctuates this example by asking his reader, "How much worse would it be if those improperly appropriated offerings were actually inside of you?"[38] He lists these examples in hope of compelling his reader into a deep and critical self-examination of their own status as a monastic. Other authors of the late nineteenth and early twentieth centuries would also see fit to frame the retreatant's relationship to sustenance in terms of its constituting *dkor*.[39]

To problematize food as *dkor* is to combine the concerns about consuming and acquiring. In some ways we have come full circle, back to an idiom of purity and pollution and a concern about food at the moment when it penetrates the physical boundary of the individual. But whereas Yangönpa's conception was based on how ingesting some bit of food might in its own right affect the meditator's psychophysical continuum positively or negatively, here it is a question of whether or not the individual is at the moment of consumption "pure," as defined by their adherence to the hundreds of rules that make up the monastic code. This makes the consumption of food a matter of perpetual moral self-scrutiny. The effects of being "polluted" will be registered in the karmic balance of the individual, producing consequences that can last for lifetimes. Referring to *dkor* as these authors do defines the retreatant not as a heroic loner but as a member of a collective: the food received or consumed is not their own but the property of the *sangha* as a whole, raising the moral stakes. The increasing prevalence of the category of *dkor* in discussions of how and how not to sustain oneself during a retreat is an indication of the normalization of the relationship between monasticism and long-term retreat that took place in the latter centuries of the tradition, as observed in chapter 3.

Working primarily with Tibetan hagiographic and autohagiographic accounts, in *Food of Sinful Demons: Meat, Vegetarianism, and the Limits of Buddhism in Tibet* Geoffrey Barstow draws attention to the fact that entering into a long-term retreat has for some meditators provided an occasion to abandon the consumption of meat, often paired with a vow to only eat one meal per day, which is part of the traditional monastic code but commonly ignored in Tibet.[40] Barstow presents this as an example of "partial vegetarianism," an attempt to find a "middle way" between consuming meat and renouncing it entirely. Here we can look at the matter from a different angle, by considering what prescriptive texts for individual retreat have had to say about avoiding meat consumption (which often accompanies the forgoing of alcohol, as Barstow points out), contextualized within the retreat tradition's discourse about food more generally.

When authors of retreat texts have occasion to refer to limiting or giving up meat consumption, it most often comes in one of two ways: when meat is brought up as an object of attachment that must be severed, or in connection to the monastic vow of not consuming the flesh of animals that have been killed specifically to be served to you. As an example of the former, amid his broader discussion of how to counteract obstacles that arise due to desire, Zurmang Lekshé Drayang mentions the possibility of "falling under the power of the sense pleasures of meat and beer." Lhatsün Namkha Jikmé similarly states, in a discussion of proper ascetic comportment, "While wandering in mountain hermitages, you must have an aversion to alcohol, meat, and so on—those sinful foods that cause distractions."[41] The human tendency to take particular pleasure in these consumables makes them especially dangerous to the anchoritic undertaking. As for the other most common way meat consumption gets brought up, Karma Chakmé and Karma Ngedön Tenkyé both write of how for monks, meat killed specifically for you and alcohol must be "abandoned as if they were poison," a key dictate for monastic comportment.[42]

A notable source for understanding the Tibetan eremitic tradition's attitude toward meat is Jikmé Lingpa's brief *Ocean of Wonders*, which is something of an outlier in its treatment of food, having three distinct features. First, Jikmé Lingpa presents food as being inherently problematic at all times. He encourages the meditator to reflect on how, given that any material support received from a person of power must ultimately be connected to sin in some way, such cannot be of benefit to your religious practice. Because food has the potential to be "the great stone that pulls you down to hell," you should subsist only on what is received as alms. Second, Jikmé Lingpa foregrounds the question of how much to eat. On one hand, eating too much gives rise to the afflictive emotions. On the other hand, the fact of not having enough can force the meditator into performing rituals for pay, thinking, "If I don't do this, I will have no food!" In keeping with the ideal of moderation, the meditator should never drink more than a single cupful of alcohol. Third, and most important for our purposes, Jikmé Lingpa writes, "If you are unable to abandon meat, eat it in moderation" (*sha spong ma nus na ran par bza'*). Later in the text he mentions that during his own retreat he would recite spells and mantras over the meat at his afternoon meal, along with practicing the yoga of eating.[43]

The category of meat is one among many avenues through which food is constituted as a privileged domain for the ethical formation of the Tibetan ascetic subject. Although it is mentioned in a number of prescriptive retreat texts, forgoing meat consumption is far less prominent a concern in the eremitic tradition than issues like begging properly, not performing rituals for pay, the improper consumption of *dkor*, or cutting attachment to food in general. Nor does it feature prominently—within this body of literature, at least—in references to the great ascetic accomplishments of past masters. By contrast, the practice of essence extraction is very commonly invoked in this way.

Some of the authors who have been most prominent in the Tibetan Buddhist discourse against consuming meat historically as chronicled by Barstow, like Karma Chakmé, Jikmé Lingpa, and Shabkar, also wrote prescriptive retreat texts.[44] Save for Jikmé Lingpa in his *Ocean of Wonders*, none of these authors puts any noted emphasis on limiting meat consumption. When it does come up, eating meat tends to be mentioned in ways that are in line with concerns in the life of a Buddhist practitioner that are not specific to the retreat endeavor. As

Barstow argues, throughout the history of Tibetan Buddhism, practicing some form of vegetarianism has very often been about taking the renunciatory ideal of monasticism a step further.[45] In the absence of any sustained discussion of vegetarianism in the prescriptive literature for individual long-term retreat, it seems that any overlap between vegetarianism and retreat may be attributable to the fact that they align with each other as supererogatory renunciatory measures.

Zurmang Lekshé Drayang presented essence extraction as a positive technique to make possible the ultimate negative relationship to food. The Tibetan science of essence extraction, which is related to the ancient Indian practice of *rasāyana*, is treated in the Nyingma tantras, the *Kālacakra Tantra*, and Tibet's foundational medical texts, knows as the *Four Treatises* or *Tantras (rgyud bzhi)*, among other places. These methods for nourishing and sustaining the body are related to the advanced tantric practices of manipulating the drops that circulate within the system of yogic channels and winds.[46] Charles Jamyang Oliphant has written a dissertation summarizing the corpus of Tibetan literature providing instruction on how to practice essence extraction, coupled with accounts from present-day practitioners. His summaries of sixty-seven such prescriptive texts offer some insight into how authors saw essence extraction as supportive of the retreat endeavor. For example, Lozang Jangchup Tenpé Drönmé's (1504/05–1565/66) *Instruction on Extracting the Essence of Flowers* presents itself as directions passed down from the primordial buddha Vajradhara for use specifically by those living in mountain hermitages. The text asserts that the very best practitioners can subsist without substantial food of any kind and therefore have no need for these instructions. But for those unable to cut the fetter of food absolutely, the technique involves collecting flowers, drying them in the sun, then mixing them with roasted barley, honey, and other substances. This mass would then be rolled into individual pills, which get empowered through ritual. The ascetic should eat these pills two or three times a day along with soup or tea, over time reducing the number of pills they consume. Similarly, a text on essence extraction by the Third Karmapa notes that it is "for mountain hermits."[47]

While the literature for the practice of essence extraction can in this way add to our understanding of the history of individual retreat, the literature for the practice of individual retreat can help us better understand essence extraction, by contextualizing it within the eremitic tradition's treatment of food more broadly. Essence extraction is presented as a solution to the moral problem of food, but one that is difficult, if not impossible, to enact—at least in what the author regards as the historical present.

In evaluating how essence extraction has been treated in prescriptive retreat literature, it is essential to differentiate between idealizing references to abiding via essence extraction and actual instructions conveyed to the reader. In the crucial sixteenth chapter of his *Direct Advice on Retreat*, Karma Chakmé mentions Milarepa's "doing the asceticism of subsisting on nettles" as an example of abiding with absolutely no desire for food, and therefore in a state in which one will never commit any form of nonvirtue for the sake of food. More than a prescription to be enacted, this is a hagiographic reference that draws attention to an ideal to be theoretically strived toward. Mentions of the actual practice of essence extraction are very limited in this most comprehensive of retreat texts. In a song at the beginning of the handbook, Karma Chakmé makes a passing reference, telling the reader to "make do with whatever food and clothing you possess. / Not accumulating things, do asceticism and essence extraction." Essence extraction is also mentioned as a means to strengthen the yogic drops, in the context of the "further improvement" practices related to the Perfection phase and the Path of Means (sexual yoga).[48] In all, although Karma Chakmé's mountainous handbook makes occasional reference to the ideal of sustaining oneself bodily through essence extraction, nowhere does it provide instructions for how to actually do so. There is no reference to essence extraction in Yangönpa's *Blazing Jewel*.[49]

When authors of prescriptive retreat texts directly address the prospect of a reader's abiding via essence extraction, they almost always suggest an unbridgeable divide between the retreatant and the possibility of sustaining oneself in this way. Lekshé Drayang described the amazing benefits of abiding via essence extraction, only to then downplay this outcome as a real possibility, portraying the pursuit as likely to cause more trouble than it is worth given the circumstances he imagines his reader to inhabit "these days." Typical in this regard is Sönam Chödzin, who writes:

> You go to meditate on the upper slope of a snow mountain, free of people.
> Wearing only a cotton cloth, with *tummo* to protect you from the cold, and having abandoned attachment to food, you do the asceticism of essence extraction—
> and thereby preserve the ways of the very kings of *siddha*s.

Sönam Chödzin here mentions abiding via essence extraction (along with *tummo*, taken up in chapter 5) as an extraordinary accomplishment that would place the ascetic in the highest echelons of the tradition. Although his reference to the "kings of *siddhas*" (*grub thob rgyal po*) is ambiguous, he likely intends to refer to the founding masters of earlier generations. Statements to such an effect are commonplace in the prescriptive retreat literature. The Third Karmapa mentions in his *Quintessence of Nectar* that essence extraction is for the "supremely fortunate" kind of practitioner. Shabkar mentions this practice only once in his *Beneficial Moon*, in a quotation by Jetsangpa Rinchen Peljor: "As for the food and clothing for sustaining one's life, the Victors of the past had countless essence extraction instructions, and could do the practice of essence extraction. However, it's also acceptable to support oneself through an asceticism of doing a little bit of begging. For clothing, one can wear things like scraps, garments taken from corpses, and dogs' hides."[50] These statements suggest that the horizon of possibility for ascetic practice has changed: in relating to food and clothing, the retreatant will most likely need to make concessions that were not necessary for more advanced beings who lived long ago.

This historically inflected thinking concerning the relative feasibility of abiding via essence extraction is exemplified with great clarity in the writings of Ngawang Tenzin Norbu of Dza Rongpu, whom we encountered at the end of chapter 3. In a short text, *Instructions on Extracting Essences from Flowers: An Ear Ornament for the Fortunate*, he extols essence extraction:

> The benefits of the practice are as follows: because you will not be defiled by an incorrect livelihood, it will be easy to give rise to the realizations of the Paths. You will have no need for patrons or any such. Extrasensory perception will arise. Tutelary deities and *ḍākiṇī*s will gather around you. People and foodstuffs will gather around you. Your body will not give off any odor. You will remain free of parasites. You will cease to defecate and produce snot. You will become free of white hair and wrinkles. You will live for as long as the sun and the moon. You will become as strong as an elephant. Your discernment and awareness will be clarified. Warmth will blaze within your body. You will be able to live without sleeping. And you will achieve the *siddhi* of "swift-footedness."[51]

To abide via essence extraction, then, is to acquire many wonderful and desirable religious and corporeal qualities, including transcending the need to pay any mind to questions of sustenance. However, in his 1914 *Charter: Direct Advice on the Mountain Dharma*, Ngawang Tenzin Norbu strikes an entirely different stance, readily acknowledging the difficulty, if not the impossibility, of achieving a life off the grid: "As for sustaining ourselves with food and clothing during the present lifetime, we may not be capable of using essence extraction and so on as the superior ones of the past did. But we can beg for just one meal at a time, as the Teacher [Śākyamuni Buddha] sought upkeep from his father, and we can be wise with respect to the way we eat."[52] This quotation is consonant with the prescriptive retreat literature as a whole: while essence extraction and other yogic techniques may theoretically make it possible to abide in perfect detachment from the world, annulling the need to make any comprises in one's asceticism, they are not presented as realistic options for the reader. Instead they are reserved for individuals who are more extraordinary than the imagined reader, or who lived long ago, or both. The fact that Ngawang Tenzin Norbu wrote about essence extraction in such different ways across these two texts highlights how different a picture may emerge if a particular practice is considered from the perspective of prescriptions for individual long-term retreat, or based on more specialized instructions. What Ngawang Tenzin Norbu wrote in his *Charter* suggests that what he wrote in his *Ear Ornament for the Fortunate* may be essentially theoretical.

The treatment of essence extraction across these instructions for individual long-term meditative retreat evinces the disposition of lived deferential reverence in the Tibetan eremitic habitus. In referring positively to the ideal of living from essence extraction, these authors uphold the Buddhist ideal of maintaining one's asceticism while completely disentangled from all social relations. This also reasserts the greatness of the past masters of the tradition, whose life stories form a common lore that is an orienting reference point for later generations of writers and practitioners. Referring to essence extraction in this way fosters a sense of historical consciousness in the reader, as the gap between what is and what was once possible creates a sense of how things have changed. All of these truths are then reinforced continually as the anchorite makes the compromises to their ascetic practice required on account of the moment they understand themselves to inhabit.

———

Properly relating to food during a long-term retreat emerges as an especially difficult needle to thread, as comporting oneself improperly with respect to food can result in squandering one's religious efforts, accumulating immense negative karma, completely wasting a precious human lifetime, or even perhaps dying of starvation—which in the logic of the tradition is not the gravest among these possible outcomes. Across this body of discourse, the most mundane of all human concerns has been problematized in dramatically different ways: for what its consumption may do to one's psychophysical being, as a critical object of attachment, for the interpersonal relationships it drags us into, in relation to the monastic status of the person who consumes it, or for its being the flesh of an animal that has been killed. These are not mutually exclusive, as many authors appeal to multiple different orientating ideals in the course of their prescriptions. Across nearly all of these permutations, food is treated in a way that makes it an axis of moral concern, as the retreatant's behaviors in relation to food determine their moral standing. Changes in what exegetes of the tradition have posited as being possible in that relationship reflect a growing historical consciousness, which then becomes instantiated through the ascetic's comportment relative to food.

The sources referred to in this chapter, both prescriptive and hagiographic, all convey idealized understandings of the relationship between the retreatant and comestibles. I would like to close with a different kind of depiction, both more intimate and more dire. In his capacity as head of the community of female Nyingma clerics at the famous hermitage of Drakar Taso—one of Milarepa's habitations, and one of the most renowned and powerful places of contemplative practice across the Himalaya—Drakarwa Chökyi Wangchuk (1775–1837) composed a charter providing behavioral guidelines for that community, titled the *Sunlight Illuminating the Darkness: The Charter Clarifying the Progression of What Is to Be Adopted or Rejected by the Renunciants of the Retreat Center at Drakar Taso, the Great Abode of Accomplishment*. In the introductory section, Chökyi Wangchuk offers an unvarnished depiction of the community's material circumstances, which he understands as a product of both geography and history, as he describes their existence in a mountainous locale far from villages and places of agricultural production, in a benighted age in which life and asceticism are becoming ever more difficult. In 1816 he wrote:

> In general, people who perform austerities and bear suffering out of their renunciation of this life for the sake of the Dharma are these days as rare as a star during daytime. Moreover, at our monastery here, we do not have the means to distribute payments to our members as they do at many other monasteries—not even a single cup of tea or soup. There are few people who arrive here from the outside to offer faithful service. And because of the times, the alms we manage to collect are becoming increasingly sparse. Not only that, but the little bit that we do manage to acquire [is subject to being lost to] the many thieving bandits out there. And so on. It is such that at this time, when even water and wood are becoming ever scarcer, seeking the food and clothing to sustain ourselves is difficult.[53]

The prescriptions for the comportment of the community in the charter that follows are explicitly qualified as having been given in view of these unfortunate circumstances. The contrast between what Milarepa is storied to have achieved and the crushing penury experienced by these hermitesses seven hundred years later could hardly be conveyed more starkly, with any hope of bridging the chasm between them seeming to have long since faded away.

CHAPTER 5

PRESERVING THE ASCETIC SELF

Texts offering instructions for individual long-term retreat typically portray the endeavor, if done properly, as a lonely, hazardous, even life-threatening affair. In his early eighteenth-century *Direct Advice That Is the Ship for Great Liberation*, Sönam Chödzin equates the potentially calamitous outcomes of life in retreat with the achievement of the Buddhist ascetic's highest aims. He writes that a meditator who wanders alone in the mountains is a person "who enjoys being sick, who is happy to die." To experience suffering while in a place of isolation is to be purified of sins and obscurations (*sdig sgrib*). To feel sad and lonely is to maintain one's vows purely. To feel pain is to fulfill one's intentions. If a genuine ascetic were to die in isolation, they would have no sadness or remorse. One's very life is to be viewed as like a drop of dew on a blade of grass: just another example of the impermanence of all phenomena.[1]

These texts commonly instruct the meditator to mark the beginning of the retreat by making a formal affirmation of the dangers and bodily hardships about to be braved, along with a commitment to persevere no matter what may come. As the Kagyu yogin Orgyen Namdröl Wangpo (also known as Chakbuk Rinpoché, born ca. 1808) describes in the ten-folio-side manual *Drop of Ambrosia: The Secret Quintessence of Direct Advice on How to Stay in Concealed Hermitages in Border Areas and Mix All Aspects of One's Continuum with the Dharma*, dated 1846: "You must ardently resolve yourself to the thought that, 'Although I may fall ill, become feverish, die, get cold, or be hungry, until such time as this promise I have made to the deity is fulfilled, I will not descend from this mountain hermitage, nor be compelled by circumstances to go to any other mountain.'"[2] Zurmang Lekshé Drayang enjoins the retreatant to develop the single-pointed determination, "While staying in this mountain hermitage, even if I am killed or destroyed by nonhuman spirits, predatory beasts, or bandits, I must endure it. Even if I should die with my eyes wide open from an illness, a demonic force, or from hunger, I will not waver." Yangönpa's version of this—about the ascetic's enduring in the face of hunger, starvation, cold, illness, and demonic attack—was quoted in chapter 4. Other similar examples abound.[3]

With the diverse potential causes of physical hardship and mortal peril placed in the fore of the meditator's mind from the outset, individual long-term retreat is framed as an uncomfortable and dangerous endeavor. Although the passage from Sönam Chödzin suggests that the ascetic should face these dire outcomes with absolute dispassion, prescriptive retreat texts tend to devote a great deal of space to practical techniques for averting or resolving this kind of threat to life and limb. The specific ways that exegetes of the retreat tradition have problematized these challenges are the subject of this chapter.

Abiding in retreat has not simply been a matter of delimiting interpersonal relations and meditating intensively for a certain number of months or years, but has entailed cultivating a distinctive manner of relating to one's own being, which figures centrally in the ways of seeing and behaving that are the Tibetan eremitic habitus. This chapter focuses on the range of prescriptions authors of retreat instructions have offered for dealing with three potential afflictions that are commonly featured in the kind of declaration quoted above: illness, cold conditions, and the harms that bandits might visit upon a retreatant. Some of what the tradition has had to say about dealing with dangerous animals and demonic forces will be addressed along the way. Looking at the pragmatic methods for preserving the anchorite in the face of these threats helps to clarify the kind of selfhood that these methods individually and collectively instantiate. In other words, we will be considering these exercises for self-preservation as technologies of self. In addition to providing discrete techniques for averting some particular peril, exegetes of the tradition have hierarchically ordered those possible interventions vis-à-vis one another, a discursive practice that is highly revealing of the guiding values in relation to which the meditator is being trained to understand their ascetic life. In all, the Tibetan eremitic tradition's prescriptions for avoiding or overcoming the diverse potential causes of harm are technologies for a kind of selfhood that I refer to as *imaginal*, which becomes instantiated and made a reality by the ascetic as they attempt to abide by these prescriptions. This chapter also offers a partial window onto the distinctive medical culture of self-healing that infuses Tibetan anchoritism, to the extent that it is known through the prescriptive literature that is the focus of this study.

The long-term retreat tradition has been entirely consistent in problematizing illness as posing a threat to a meditator's interpersonal isolation. Lhatsün Namkha Jikmé writes that if they happen to fall ill, a contemplative of the superior type, having overcome all attachment to this life, will take joy in the prospect of dying. A contemplative of middling capacities will embrace the experience of being ill as a means to improve their religious standing. Meanwhile, for a contemplative of the lowest capacities, "it is enough that they should not have to rely on anyone else for medical treatment or companionship."[4] For Namkha Jikmé, being able to face an illness without external assistance is a baseline expectation for any retreatant. This passage also introduces the discursive tendency of referring to a variety of approaches to dealing with illness, which are regarded as unequal in light of certain values espoused by the author.

Drakar Lozang Pelden's directions for sick meditators reflect his understanding of retreat as a communal monastic undertaking, while still seeing illness as a threat to the interpersonal boundaries that define the retreat. For a cleric to claim that they must maintain ties with their family to ensure that they have someone to look after them should they fall seriously ill or grow too old to care for themselves is "the statement of an unthinking person." Lozang Pelden continues that if a retreatant comes down with a severe illness, then it is the lama, the Dharma siblings, and other practitioners who should tend to them. For relief from more temporary and minor afflictions, the Dharma protectors and *yidam* deities can be relied on. To have a family member serve as one's nurse is contradictory to the Dharma and is the cause of accumulating faults. Moreover, Lozang Pelden reasons, if a practitioner's lama and fellow monastics cannot discern the specific means needed to cure their illness, then their family members certainly won't possess the wherewithal to do so. Ideally, rather than focusing on medical or ritual interventions, the practitioner will cultivate the attitude that the malady is the result of bad karma from past lives. As such, being ill becomes an opportunity to dispel sins and obscurations. Lozang Pelden also refers to this as being about the practitioner knowing how to "take [challenges] onto the religious path."[5]

In keeping with this view that sickness poses an existential threat to the retreat endeavor, the Tibetan anchoritic literature devotes a great deal of space to instructing a meditator in how to deal with an illness entirely on their own, without recourse to professional medical intervention or to rituals performed by someone else. This has led to the creation of a distinctive tradition of self-healing—one not of maintaining a healthy regimen of exercise or diet or proactively warding off ailments, but of being armed with an arsenal of contemplative solutions to physical ailments after they arise. This tradition of eremitic self-healing is defined both by discrete prescriptions for dealing with illness while constrained to interpersonal isolation and by how those possible interventions are ranked in terms of preferability. Here we will consider three basic approaches, from the most favored to the least. The inequality among them expresses the guiding values of this homespun anchoritic medical tradition.

The approach most widely and favorably prescribed in retreat discourse was referenced in both Namkha Jikmé's and Lozang Pelden's treatments of illness: to embrace the prospect of being sick, and even potentially dying, as itself constituting a means of or an opportunity for religious practice. The Third Karmapa's *Quintessence of Nectar* conveys this attitude explicitly. Regarding how a retreatant should think of the physical pain they feel when suffering from an illness, Rangjung Dorjé asserts that one should seize this chance to remind oneself of the nature of karma and its ripening: if even such a minor unwellness feels unbearable, then how horrifying is the prospect of being born in a hell realm? Having reasoned in this way, the meditator should increase their resolve to eschew the activities that cause sentient beings to have bad rebirths. They should also reflect upon the totality of the suffering experienced by all the sentient beings of the universe. The meditator then reasserts their willingness to personally take on the suffering of those countless beings, and to selflessly devote all accumulated merit to their future wellness. The Third Karmapa prescribes taking this basic approach to other kinds of bodily threat as well. He describes a scenario in which a predator such as a tiger arrives to do harm to a retreatant. For an ascetic who has renounced body and life, the proper reaction is to think of this creature as being in effect their own mother or father. Rangjung Dorjé states that even if the predator should eat the hermit, they should only feel sad that the animal is so controlled by the afflictive emotions. Cultivating the mindset of the bodhisattva, you should relish the opportunity to repay the kindness of your mother by offering up your own body in order to satisfy her hunger. Likewise, if the retreat dwelling is invaded by a demonic entity, you should use this as an occasion to remind yourself of the truth of the emptiness of the self, and thereby neutralize whatever fear such an encounter might otherwise provoke. In the Third Karmapa's presentation, encounters with sickness, dangerous animals, and demonic entities all provide occasions for the retreatant to improve themselves and put Buddhist values into action.[6]

One common way of framing illness as a positive opportunity, as already mentioned, is to use the terminology of the individual's being purified of "sins and obscurations" by suffering through the physical pain of being sick. The operative idea is that to experience this suffering is to be relieved of some part of one's negative karmic balance or of the obscurations that cloud one's vision of reality.[7] A different way of framing illness as a positive opportunity is to posit it as the occasion to do "further improvement" practice, or, more commonly, by invoking the notion of bringing the illness "onto the [religious] path." Exemplifying this approach, in response to the question, "If one staying in a mountain hermitage should experience the suffering of illness, what should they do?," Chegom Sherap Dorjé offers a few related points of instruction. He begins by stating that ideally, the ascetic will meditate on the esoteric instructions given by the lama, which should be sufficient to deal with any ailment, obviating the need for any other means. He writes of bringing the sickness "onto the path" and thinking of it as a boon, as a result of which the illness will "certainly just vanish." Should that not work, Chegompa continues, "then the suffering becomes the path. Even if their suffering from the illness should become grave, it nevertheless constitutes a method for casting away body and life. The death of the mountain dweller *is* the mountain hermitage, and so they should not leave their mountain hermitage to go down to the village."[8] In Chegompa's presentation, the genuine practitioner should regard falling ill as a gift, as the suffering it causes creates an opportunity to practice. If this results in death, that will be the culmination of one's asceticism. Falling ill becomes an inflection point in relation to which one's eremitic practice is defined. Chegompa offers these possible ways of working with infirmity in a hierarchical manner, with the unspecified esoteric instructions received from the lama occupying the highest position.

Zurmang Lekshé Drayang provides a detailed method for treating illness as a positive opportunity for Buddhist practice in a section of his *Words on the Mountain Dharma* titled "The Manner of Bringing Illness Onto the Path via the Wisdom of the Mahāmudrā, Animated by Ultimate *Bodhicitta*," which runs just under four pages, and which we will consider in some detail. Prior to this, Lekshé Drayang states explicitly that there is a hierarchy among possible types of self-healing: should this ideal method fail, the meditator can attempt to rectify the situation through working with the channels and winds. After that, in descending order of preferability, they should try using a specific object of visualization, and then the practice of Cutting. Lekshé Drayang states that actual physical medicine should be used only as a last resort.[9]

The best option, the process of bringing an illness onto the path via the Mahāmudrā, begins with generating the following thought: "I have set out to obtain precious unsurpassed enlightenment for the sake of all sentient beings. In order to achieve that, I must bring this sickness onto the path." Lekshé Drayang then outlines a form of mind training (*blo sbyong*) that entails conceiving of the pain one feels as subsuming all the illness experienced by all the beings in the universe. The meditator is to examine the pain they are experiencing and arrive at the conclusion that it has no essence, is not established based on any intrinsic nature. This gives way to an understanding of the true nature of the mind, as progenitor of all things in existence—and in relation to which there is no exterior perspective from which circumstances can be judged. The ailing meditator is to think, "The *siddha*s of the past brought sickness and other intolerable circumstances onto the path, by which they attained their *siddhi*s. I too need to bring this sickness onto the path." Now the meditator approaches their pain through the practice of "equalizing taste" (*ro snyoms*): because the meditator and the sickness cannot be established as two separate things, the sickness does not stand as an independent entity. It is evanescent, like a rainbow, or like a pleasant dream that disappears the moment you wake. Having mentally dispelled the sickness in this way, the meditator extends their thinking into the future, reasoning that even if the sickness should get worse, they will be able to resolve it. By practicing in this way, the sick person extends the temporal frame of reference for their own experience while simultaneously shortening that for the ailment, until the latter is so comparatively reduced that it disappears. Lekshé Drayang then adds a few contextualizing points. He affirms that by enduring sickness, a person undergoes a kind of purification, and karmic residues are erased. He also dispels the misconception that this technique might be too difficult for ordinary people to apply. He briefly casts this practice in a Mahāmudrā perspective: the illness is nonrecognition of awareness involving all-consuming labeling. Viewing it correctly through meditation on the *dharmakāya* or truth aspect of buddhahood can destroy this nonrecognition, which renders sickness a useful means of arriving at a better understanding of reality. Lastly, Lekshé Drayang adds that a retreatant can do this even while relatives and friends on the outside arrange for medical and ritual interventions, because the practice entails engaging with the illness on the level of ultimate truth, which is separate from what may take place on the level of the conventional.[10]

As reviewed here, the most highly venerated general approach to dealing with illness during an individual long-term retreat is to frame it as an opportunity or a positive experience in relation to the practitioner's higher religious goals. The tradition offers a few different contemplative practices and kinds of terminology through which to do this. It is a catch-all approach, placing all kinds of sickness and bodily pain in the same essential category, to be resolved in a way that advances the practitioner on their path toward enlightenment.

Occupying a middle place in the hierarchy of healing technologies are widely practiced visualization-based meditations that are attributed with the power to heal. Cutting, for example, is touted for its ability to dispel illness. As presented by Karma Chakmé, this can be either for the practitioner or for a client on whose behalf the practice is done.[11] Reflecting Karma Chakmé's interest in practical measures to create boundaries in interpersonal relations, he stipulates that if a retreatant who practices either Cutting or equalizing taste should become ill, they should limit themselves to sticking their arm out of the cell to present a medical professional with their wrist in order to have their pulse read, the principal means of diagnosis in mainstream Tibetan medicine. He instructs, "No matter how bad it gets, do not loosen your retreat. Even if you are going to die, you can die right there on your cushion." For one who is not practicing Cutting or equalizing taste, however, it is acceptable to consult a doctor, take medicine, and so on.[12] Occupying a similar position among the hierarchy of healing technologies is guru yoga. Yangönpa tells the reader to visualize the guru at any place in the body that may be ailing or hurting. The visualized lama is posited as having the power to eliminate obstacles both internal and external, and to improve the body and mind. Other authors also refer to the ability of guru worship to heal illness or remove pain.[13]

Continuing down to the third position in the hierarchy of approaches to dealing with illness, Yangönpa's *Blazing Jewel* explicitly states that if the retreatant should experience some kind of illness or pain, there are three possible options, clearly ranked: "The best is if you can put [the ailment] to rest. The middling is if you can neutralize it with a turning-back meditation (*bzlog bsgom gyis ro snyom*). The least is to fix it with an object of visualization."[14] The first of these aligns with the tradition's preferred approach, detailed above; the second is to render the pain neutral through a practice like those reviewed in the last paragraph. Failing in these, the ascetic may need to resort to resolving the problem in the third way: using an ailment-specific directed visualization. In three folio sides of the root text and eleven folio sides of commentary, Yangönpa details dozens of visualizations for dealing with specific bodily ailments, largely organized in terms of diagnostic categories used by the Tibetan medical tradition and grounded in the *Four Treatises*, composed in the twelfth century.[15] Yangönpa begins with the blanket statement that a person sufficiently adept in *tummo* can use that practice to counteract any kind of bodily hurt or sickness. *Tummo* is commonly mentioned as an essential tool in the yogic tradition of self-healing, being attributed with the power to remove a range of ailments, in particular those relating to the stomach and digestion.[16] Yangönpa continues by stating that every disease is either the "hot" or the "cold" type. As long as the practitioner can determine to which category their ailment belongs, they have a basic means of redress: if it is a cold disease, the meditator need only visualize the beloved lama in a warming red shade at the afflicted bodily location. If it is a hot disease, they need only visualize the lama in a cooling white shade. Visualizing the lama dissolving into the painful spot is said to be able to overcome anything. After presenting these semigeneralized healing techniques, Yangönpa provides specific visualizations that can be used to counteract particular maladies. For example, some hot illnesses are counteracted by visualizing a cool dew that accumulates on the lotus the meditator sits upon: the dew travels up through the body and pushes the illness out of the mouth. Other hot illnesses are counteracted by visualizing a block of ice at one's upper back. If a meditator's joints hurt, they can visualize the psychophysical winds passing out from them. If the meditator has an open wound, they can imagine over that spot a divine mansion, inside of which is the tutelary deity in sexual embrace with his consort: this visualized union causes the cut to be closed. Diarrhea can be counteracted by visualizing a vajra blocking off one's lower orifice. At the end of this section, at the very bottom of the hierarchy of possible interventions, Yangönpa mentions the use of physical yogic exercises.

Karma Chakmé similarly details how to use the technology of visualization to overcome a wide variety of physical ailments in a ten-folio-side section on "clearing away obstacles pertaining to sickness." The pain of a toothache, for example, can be quelled by visualizing the lama in the form of the medicine buddha, or a white syllable *vaṃ*, inside the tooth. For a headache, the retreatant can imagine their head as filled with a thousand-petaled lotus, then splitting open; garudas arrive to eat the brains that have spilled out, taking the headache away with them. If one's gall bladder hurts, the solution is to imagine a hundred thousand black dogs biting it and sucking out the bile. And so on.[17]

This least preferred among the three basic approaches to illness is a do-it-yourself medical practice specifically suited to the constraints of life in retreat, as it forgoes any reliance on physical medicine, professional diagnoses, or ritual interventions by other persons. In contrast to the literature for individual retreat, charter documents for Tibetan monastic communities describe how if a monk should fall ill, certain material resources (those of the monk himself, or the communal property of the monastery) should be put toward sponsoring rituals to counteract the ailment.[18] During an individual long-term retreat, however, the ascetic is expected to keep entirely to their own devices. This has resulted in the articulation of a litany of imaginative solutions to bodily afflictions, some of which are canonical, while others seem to be the product of this specific milieu of meditator-intellectuals searching for creative means of self-preservation while living in isolation. These visualizations rely on laws of resemblances, oppositions, and (imagined) contact, similar to those that undergird the logic of most Tibetan Buddhist ritual systems.

Not all interventions are regarded as equal in the Tibetan eremitic healing tradition. Again and again a general hierarchy of healing techniques (and nesting hierarchies within that hierarchy) is asserted. While authors within the tradition are not in lockstep agreement over what the precise ranking should be (for example, Lekshé Drayang's placing Cutting lower than most other authors), there is a clear consensus that when faced with an illness it is best to employ a universalizing practice that applies in the same way to all kinds of pain, and puts the unpleasant experience of an illness toward the achievement of higher Buddhist goals like increasing one's compassion toward other living beings or realizing one's own lack of a true self. Somewhat less preferred are common meditation practices with some capacity to counteract a range of ailments, such as *tummo*, Cutting, and visualizing the guru. If those should fail, the tradition has described specific visualizations each intended to counteract only a particular ailment. Should these prove ineffective, one might resort to performing body-manipulation exercises, or, in the worst possible case, ingesting actual medicine.

This hierarchy of potential healing techniques achieves two interrelated things. First, even when one must resort to a "lower" form of healing, the mere fact of knowing that there exist "higher," closer-to-ideal ones serves to reinforce broader Buddhist values and goals. Even when dealing with something as personal as an aching tooth, whatever intervention is relied upon occupies its place within a larger matrix of possibilities expressing Buddhism's highest ideals. This serves to maintain key religious values that might otherwise be lost in an ad hoc subculture of self-healing.

Second, built into this manner of asserting the superiority of certain kinds of intervention over others is the expression of a number of interrelated hierarchies: the universalizing over the specific, the abstract over the representational, a view that sees the whole of time rather than the present moment, striving toward higher Buddhist goals rather than mere personal rehabilitation and survival. At the root of all these distinctions is a devaluing of the conditions of gross materiality. This seems to derive from a conscious reversing of the dynamic that ordinarily defines human existence. In this way the hierarchy of technologies of self-healing recapitulates the ideal implicit in the various individually prescribed healing methods concerning the power of the mind to overcome external circumstances. Dealing with illness, no matter which approach is resorted to, reinforces the fact of an individual's mental ability to overcome any physical circumstance. The body, in its limited and gross materiality, is subordinate to the infinite potential of the mind to comprehend and shape reality. As we will see, the eremitic tradition's prescriptions for subverting other kinds of conditions that threaten a retreatant's physical well-being also rely on the technology of visualization and explicitly devalue reliance on anything material or external. In this way they all reinforce a particular manner of relating to oneself and the world.[19]

Although cold is almost always listed among the physical challenges that a retreatant must mentally steel themselves to endure, it is remarkably little discussed in the prescriptive literature, given the simplicity of the retreatant's material circumstances and how cold high-elevation Himalayan winters can be.[20] We saw in the last chapter how Shabkar took pains to downplay the cold as a concern by using the entire record of the Buddhist ascetic tradition as proof that one need not worry about dying from exposure to frigid conditions or starvation. Shabkar also argues, like Sönam Chödzin, that if an ascetic were to actually succumb to the dangers of life in retreat—including "hunger, freezing, dangerous animals, sickness, demonic attacks"—such would be a praiseworthy conclusion to their religious practice motivated by compassion for all sentient beings. Shabkar encourages his reader to seek out a place devoid of people, where no one will even find the corpse—"in that way you cast away your body and life for the sake of the Dharma, as if it were a blade of grass."[21] No matter what the ultimate outcome may be, Shabkar argues, the cold is not something the meditator need be preoccupied with.

When the prescriptive retreat literature does address what practical measures the meditator should take in order to better endure the cold, there is universal agreement that the solution is not to dress in warmer clothing or seek a more temperate locale but to generate warmth from the inside via *tummo*, Tibet's version of the yogic practice known as *caṇḍālī* in South Asia. These texts often explicitly mention the usefulness of *tummo* for enduring freezing conditions, including such statements as, "In general, if you have control over *tummo*, you can meditate amid the snow without experiencing any cold," and "Even if on the outside your body is cold, in your mind, because of the appearance of warmth, you will not feel cold."[22] Along with his being green, another distinctive feature of Milarepa's iconography is his wearing only a simple cotton cloth, which distinguishes him as a *repa* (*ras pa*) or "cotton-clad one," directly referencing his facility in *tummo*. This has become part of his very name.

Yangönpa's *Blazing Jewel* is the only prescriptive retreat text consulted in this study that describes actual *tummo* meditation, presented as the foundational practice among the Six Yogas of Naropa. Yangönpa writes that "by practicing in this way, first heat is produced. By producing heat, even if the body is cold on the outside, on the inside heat will continue to blaze." Eventually the meditator will lose all sense of difference between the interior and the exterior of their body, and will be without any feeling of coldness or warmth. Once an individual has achieved full stability in *tummo*, that warmth is maintained even when not consciously meditating. As preparation for the practice, Yangönpa describes exercises in breathing, physical movement, and visualization by which a meditator readies their gross body, the channels of the yogic body, and the psychophysical winds that circulate throughout. After spending some weeks training in this way, they can begin the main *tummo* meditation. This features the visualization of a blazing syllable just below the navel, which, when stoked with the psychophysical winds, produces a tongue of flame that climbs upward through the central channel of the yogic body, penetrating the cakras at the heart and throat, ultimately reaching the syllable at the top of the head. Warmed by this flame, the syllable begins to melt, releasing a viscous white fluid that further feeds the fire. The complementary processes of melting and blazing mutually feed each other and gain intensity. The *Great Appendix* describes how a practitioner can intensify this process with the arousal produced by the visualization of divine sexual intercourse.[23]

Tummo is one of the tantric Buddhist practices that Euro-American observers have most thoroughly documented and studied, from a wide range of perspectives. It received academic treatment in Graham Sandberg's 1906 *Tibet and the Tibetans*, and was brought to the attention of wider audiences through Alexandra David-Néel's *Mystiques et Magiciens du Tibet*, published in 1929.[24] The details of the practice have been broadly known since the 1935 publication of Lama Kazi Dawa Samdrup and W. Y. Evans-Wentz's translation of a manual for the practice of the Six Yogas of Naropa. There was a watershed moment in 1982, when a team of researchers led by Dr. Herbert Benson of Harvard published the first study of the medical effects of *tummo* on the human body, including the shocking conclusion that experienced practitioners can raise the surface temperature of their fingers and toes by more than eight degrees Celsius.[25] Western science's surprise with respect to this finding has catalyzed the field of contemplative studies. Since Benson's groundbreaking work, the physiological and psychological study of *tummo* has advanced greatly.[26] Approaching the phenomenon from a different perspective, Toni Huber's ethnographic and historical work has detailed how a yogic community in the area of the holy mountain of Tsari would traditionally spend an entire winter night out of doors once a year, to demonstrate to the local community their prowess in the technique.[27] Meanwhile popular figures like Wim Hof, "the Iceman," have spread awareness of the practice even more broadly, using such vehicles as YouTube and social media.

This study can perhaps advance our understanding of *tummo* by examining how it was thought of and practiced in the traditional Himalayan anchoritic milieu. I highlight evidence from the prescriptive literature for individual long-term retreat regarding how *tummo* was contextualized in three specific ways: in the everyday comportment and the career arc of the practitioner, and as a way of relating to the self.

As for how practicing *tummo* conditions an ascetic's regular comportment, Yangönpa informs that everything they eat, drink, or wear is "blessed by fire": "Paying no mind to the cold, it will be as if you are being hit by a thousand suns." An individual should not attempt to do *tummo* when feeling very cold or hungry, must continually exercise their body to maintain its suppleness, and should be careful to avoid wearing clothes that may be a vehicle for a harmful taint. A *tummo* practitioner should not sit in the sun or close to a fire, in order to avoid overheating; nor should they go barefoot or swim, which could sap their internal warmth. If an individual produces too much heat and finds themselves sweating continually, they should rub their body with butter that has been mixed with the three "hot" medicinal substances, then dust themselves with pea flour. The logic behind this seems to be that creating a burning sensation on the surface of the skin will draw out some of the body's excessive warmth. A *tummo* practitioner's behavior would be conditioned not only with respect to their own body but also relative to the dimensions of space and time: Yangönpa states that staying on a rocky mountain is conducive to the practice. A meditator doing *tummo* should not sleep with their head facing south; nor should the doorway to their retreat face southward. This is because the south is associated with the element of water. Lastly, Yangönpa states that one should not begin the practice of *tummo* during the summer or winter, when the weather is at an extreme, but only in spring or fall, and ideally when the moon is in an auspicious phase.[28] In *Direct Advice on Retreat,* Karma Chakmé mentions the great physical suffering one is likely to experience in the early stages of training in *tummo.* He adds that a person practicing *tummo* should not wear furs, because doing so will prevent them from being able to tell whether or not heat is being generated. As the practitioner makes progress, they should wear thinner clothing.[29] These details draw attention to the important fact that the aspects of ascetic comportment examined in this book—place, interpersonal relations, clothing, food, and so on—are always subject to reproblematization based on what specific practices have been taken on, adding further layers of complexity for the retreatant (and the historian of religion) to adjudicate.

As for how *tummo* was contextualized in the career arc of a practitioner, this body of literature is highly ambiguous about whether keeping warm via *tummo* should be regarded as an ordinary or an extraordinary yogic accomplishment. Karma Chakmé writes that if the ascetic can persevere in wearing nothing more than a simple cotton cloth for a period of three years, then "they will be regarded as among the very best of the realized ones" (*rtogs ldan rab*).³⁰ Sönam Chödzin, as quoted in chapter 4, expresses a similarly ambiguous sentiment, stating that by using *tummo* to keep warm and essence extraction to remain nourished, a meditator "preserve[s] the ways of the very kings of *siddha*s." Karma Ngedön Tenkyé similarly describes the ascetic trajectory:

> The fortunate person with superior faculties will request empowerments, transmissions, and oral instructions from a qualified lama. They generate a devotion that sees the lama as an actual buddha. They renounce all activities of this world. Abandoning all forms of pretense, they wander in empty valleys with no people. For clothing they have *tummo*, for food they have *samādhi*, and they thereby do asceticism and rightly protect their mental state. They pass their time in love and compassion for transmigrating beings. They do the yoga that can get a person buddhahood in one lifetime. Unnoticed by anyone, they die like a lion. Even the most supreme of glorious lamas is pleased by one like that.... These practices of fortunate people are those that appear to have been practiced by the ocean of the *siddha*s of the Kagyu.³¹

In passages like this one, keeping warm through *tummo* is mentioned alongside other yogic feats—such as abiding via essence extraction, paying no mind to one's sustenance, living free of any interpersonal interactions, having an unnoticed, heroic death—that latter-day authors commonly treat as all but impossible to achieve in the present moment, being confined to the earlier days of the great *siddha*s. Despite this, I have found no direct assertion of the impossibility of keeping warm through *tummo* during an author's present, as is often said about the other extraordinary ascetic abilities. In all, there seems to be a degree of ambivalence in the Tibetan ascetic tradition's treatment of *tummo*, such that it is presented as a reliable and accessible countermeasure to unpleasantly cold conditions while also being mentioned as an extraordinary accomplishment. Other genres of literature likely portray a different horizon of possibility when it comes to using *tummo* to survive the harshness of a Himalayan winter in a cave or a thatched hut.

As a way of relating to the self, *tummo* is a visualization practice that directs a meditator's attention to the space inside their own body. The discourse maintains that, if done properly, this practice can completely neutralize the external circumstance of cold temperatures: life-threatening cold is rendered bearable by means of a method that requires no material support whatsoever. The instructions offered by Yangönpa and Karma Chakmé regarding what the *tummo* practitioner should and should not wear, eat, and do further specify the bodily conditions in which this meditation should be performed, without altering the fundamental interiority of the practice.

Of a very different order than illness or cold conditions is the threat of bodily harm caused by lawless persons who may wander into sparsely populated areas and be tempted to rob or hurt a defenseless meditator. Central to the story of Milarepa's time in retreat is a series of interactions with hunters and thieves who arrive at his cave with the intention to steal and are shocked and disappointed to find, after manhandling him to see what he may be concealing under his rear end, that he indeed has no possessions whatsoever. A short play distilling Milarepa's encounters with these hunters is one of the most commonly staged popular entertainments in the Himalaya, reflecting the tale's foundational importance to the Tibetan national mythos.

Concern about this kind of dangerous ruffian is mentioned consistently throughout the prescriptive retreat literature. When discussing more and less ideal locations for a retreat, it is common to state that a meditator should avoid places where bandits are likely to pass through.[32] It is also sometimes said that more accomplished meditators should purposefully do their retreats in such intimidating places.[33] The literature maintains that the best protection against thieves is to impoverish oneself completely, and thereby cultivate the kind of natural protection Milarepa achieved. Chegom Sherap Dorjé expresses this in the form of a rhetorical question: "If you wear clothing that no one would want, what reason would there be for you to have fear of harm by unruly people?" Zurmang Lekshé Drayang writes of how prevalent such bandits are during the degenerate time in which we live, which makes wandering and staying in mountain hermitages especially difficult. He also reviews some of the misconceptions people have about what specific dangers those bandits pose. Karma Chakmé recommends that if a meditator staying in solitude is afraid of being harmed by thieves or dangerous animals, they can bang a drum while reciting their liturgies. This will prevent animals from approaching and will discourage thieves. However, if the meditator does not presently fear animals or bandits, they should refrain from drumming in this manner, lest it cause people to think they are doing black magic.[34]

These measures not being enough to ensure a hermit's safety, the tradition has offered a more proactive approach to the problem. Yangönpa prescribes doing a circle of protection ritual both when setting up the retreat and when roving about outside of it. He also mentions a "further improvement" practice that entails visualizing oneself as a wrathful deity, which has the side effect of warding off potential thieves.[35] Four centuries later, Karma Chakmé would dedicate the twenty-third chapter of his *Direct Advice on Retreat* to providing instructions for visualizations and recitations by which a meditator can "prevent harm from bandits while staying in a mountain hermitage." According to the text, Tsöndrü Gyatso had a particular fear of being harmed by lawless people while staying in retreat, which prompted Karma Chakmé to deliver these instructions. Over six folio sides he describes a handful of practices focused on the goddess Mārīcī. In the morning, visualize yourself as the goddess, with two arms, holding a needle and thread, and seated upon a boar, surrounded by whatever you would like to include in the sphere of protection, which is in turn surrounded by concentric circles of snarling wild yellow boars. In the afternoon, again visualize yourself as the goddess Mārīcī, with additional emanations of the deity issuing forth from your heart. Riding on yellow boars, the emanations swoop throughout the universe, using needle and thread to sew shut the eyes and mouths of all persons who might do you harm. One option is do a short-term retreat focused specifically on Mārīcī, in which the meditator recites her mantra six hundred thousand times while maintaining this visualization, thus ensuring her protection ever after. Alternatively, a meditator doing a long-term retreat can incorporate Mārīcī practices into their daily regimen, or do them only when they feel they face a particular danger.[36] Elsewhere in the handbook Karma Chakmé provides instruction for a similar protection rite based on visualizing oneself as Avalokiteśvara, which protects an individual from "fire, water, poison, weapons, tyrants, thieves" or any other frightening or harmful thing.[37] These diverse potential causes of peril are all subsumed under the same kind of intervention: using self-visualization and mantra recitation to harness the superhuman powers of the deity and remove oneself from harm's way. While the retreatant's normal, mundane self is defined by its very susceptibility to such dangers, these ritual technologies offer the possibility of a new self generated through a reordering of the basic relationship between the internal and the external, the envisioned and the material.

In spite of the Tibetan ascetic tradition's rhetoric about facing the perils of individual retreat with dauntless resolve and concluding one's life through a demonstration of the loftiest of Buddhist ideals, this literature shows a sustained and thorough concern with how to avert or undo threats to one's life or physical well-being. The prescribed methods for dealing with such different problems as illness, cold weather, and bandits are the same insofar as they rely on the same basic technology: the power of visualization centered within and around one's body. Implicit in this technology is the supremacy of the mind over the body: the mind is treated as having an almost unlimited capacity to overcome any circumstance, while the constraints of the material world are all ultimately mutable. These techniques of self-care promise the possibility of passing beyond ordinary existence as we know it, a longed-for ideal articulated in other aspects of eremitic abiding as well, such as by mentally transforming one's physical surroundings into a perfected realm, the fantasy of escaping from all interpersonal interaction, or ending all need for gross foodstuffs. By caring for one's body and life through the techniques described in this chapter, a particular version of selfhood is produced and maintained, based on an ideal of transcending the ordinary material bounds of human existence. This is the ideal that resides at the innermost core of the Tibetan ascetic self—a being instantiated through the efforts of countless individual meditators trying to put this ideal into practice, as well as through the combined efforts of exegetes of the tradition as they have strived without cease to articulate ever-better instructions for how to do so.

This form of selfhood is cultivated through techniques for dealing with more quotidian concerns as well. What the scourge of lice or bedbugs (*shig*) may lack in perilousness it more than makes up for with prevalence and peskiness. Yangönpa offers a technique for dealing with this affliction (the appearance of which is to be regarded as a sign of spiritual progress) that begins with visualizing in the space above your head the lama in sexual union with his consort. As a result of their congress, a white nectar drips down and pours into your body. Once your bodily vessel is completely full, the nectar seeps out of your pores, in the form of tiny white lotus flowers with vajras at the tips of their petals. You then imagine all the lice turning into flowers. If you do this at night, by the next morning all of your lice will have disappeared.[38] Whether or not this technique achieves its stated end, the mere fact of its being prescribed for and then taken up by the practitioner means that it will inculcate a particular way of conceiving of, relating to, and experiencing their own personhood. Similarly, as mentioned in chapter 1, the daily life of the ascetic as understood by Yangönpa includes a practice referred to as the "yoga of bathing." This begins with visualizing the guru in the form of the tutelary deity in the space before you, out of whose heart there emerges a goddess holding a vase filled with nectar, to whom you direct a request to be cleansed. Various buddhas and bodhisattvas make auspicious declarations, while the wrathful deities are engaged in removing obstacles. Other innumerable male and female gods cast down a rain of flowers. By reciting the specified mantra while washing up, the practitioner receives the equivalent of the vase empowerment, the first of the four empowerments of higher tantric practice. Repeating the process of washing, they receive the remaining three empowerments as well. The daily act of eating was subject to a similar kind of ritualization, as seen through Yangönpa's instructions for the "yoga of eating." Karma Chakmé takes the ritualization of ordinary behaviors even further. He describes how, for *kusali*-style practitioners of middling and superior capacities, when urinating they should imagine their body as a golden vase out of which a stream of nectar flows, satisfying the desires of all the hungry ghosts who would be satisfied with urine. The act of defecation can also produce feast offerings to satisfy members of a different class of hungry ghost.[39] Through practices such as these, visualization of and around one's body, often accompanied by the recitation of formulas, is used to transform the commonest of activities during retreat into practices of religious significance.

These techniques for dealing with mundane body-related concerns are based on the same fundamental technology as deity yoga via *sādhana*, the most pervasive form of meditation in Tibet's tantric tradition. This makes up the core of the Generation phase of tantric practice and is for many practitioners the primary focus of their formal meditation throughout the course of a retreat. The diverse forms of *sādhana* practice tend to follow the same basic progression, with the goal of fostering full self-identification of the practitioner with the deity, achieved through a multisensory program of reordering one's identity in order to align with the enlightened being that is the object of the practice. Out of emptiness, with your mind's eye you conjure the divine setting or mandala of the deity, and then the deity him- or herself, in full detail, possessing all of their enlightened qualities. After you offer forms of worship, a switch is enacted by which you place yourself in the position of the deity, effectively viewing yourself and the world around you as the deity does. This is to repeat the process of identification that was imparted at the moment of ritual empowerment. Personal assimilation with the deity is achieved through the choreographed, scripted (*sādhana* refers both to the practice and the text that provides its script) use of ritual technologies alongside this purposeful cultivation and manipulation of perspective, including the cultivation of certain images, feelings, and thoughts, bodily manipulation, and the recitation of mantras. The bulk of any practice session is taken up with the recitation of the mantra—the sonic form of the deity, by which you speak as and manifest it—as many times as possible while maintaining the visualization, after which the entire scene dissolves back into emptiness. The theory is that through this process, we can access our own true natures as already-enlightened beings, no different from the enlightened buddhas.[40] Many other tantric practices performed during retreat have this same technology of self-visualization at their core, even if they are not technically examples of deity yoga.

The ways of dealing with potential causes of peril reviewed in this chapter operate by the same fundamental dynamic that undergirds *sādhana* practice. Although the basic form of these interventions may seem to result from a spilling-over of deity yoga and *sādhana* practice into other facets of the ascetic undertaking, I propose that the practices of self-preservation based on this same technology would also bolster and support the process of self-identification meant to be achieved through *sādhana*—that the influence would go in both ways, mutually supportive, and break down the distinction between the more formal practices that are the ostensible purpose of the retreat and these less formal practices that might be seen as incidental to the retreat. In short, *sādhana*-based deity-centric practice and these techniques of self-maintenance are ways of instantiating the same fundamental manner of relating to the self, in- and outside of the four daily periods of formal meditation.

The significance of all this can be better understood when considered in comparison to other basic manners of relating to the self that have been found to predominate in Asian religious traditions historically. In his 1996 book, *The Alchemical Body*, David Gordon White details the centrality of the practices and ideals of alchemy to the *siddha* traditions of medieval India. This was in effect an ascetic subculture in the idiom of interaction with substances, through which life was preserved and liberation and immortality attained. In his 2014 book, *The Body Incantatory*, Paul Copp argues that in the religious culture of late medieval Chinese Buddhism, of central, organizing importance were practices in which individuals' bodies were adorned or infused with the stuff of a spell, and transformed into that spell, as the path to liberation. Copp writes of the "deep corporality of the person—and the modes of its salvation—[that are] central" to this kind of Buddhism, which he designates as "dharanic."[41] Meanwhile, in *Rethinking Meditation*, David McMahan highlights defining features of a modern, secular, post-European enlightenment, capitalistic selfhood, and the stripped-down version of Buddhist mindfulness meditation with which it is mutually constitutive.

In comparison to these basic modes of selfhood, I believe we can characterize the manner of relating to one's being that is central to Tibetan eremitism as that of an *imaginal* self. This is a self produced not out of unchecked fantasies but out of specific prescribed visualizations—whether done as the core formal meditative practice of the retreat or when attending to more mundane concerns in the gaps between formal meditation sessions. Although these visualizations center on the body, in fact that body is regarded as completely plastic, subject to the reality created by the mind. In contrast to the "deep corporality" observed in Chinese Buddhism by Copp, we have in this Tibetan ascetic subculture a mutable corporality and an envisioned, imaginal self. The dynamic underlying this imaginal version of selfhood does not claim so much as it instantiates the superiority of the mental over the physical and the embodied. Through diverse practices, the ascetic is inculcated into treating physical circumstances as always subject to reconfiguration by the reality of the mental. This is a central means by which the ascetic's personhood is positively defined and constituted in the course of their pursuit of the negative ascetic ideal of renunciation and withdrawal. As seen in Karma Chakmé's model of the retreatant as ritualist for hire in chapter 3, the meditator's capacity for imaginal self-reconstruction can provide the basis for a transactional relationship with others. Every indication is that this has been a stable part of the Tibetan ascetic self throughout the history of the eremitic tradition; the techniques for preserving the self reviewed in this chapter do not show evidence of significant change over time, as have other themes explored in the previous three chapters.

The imaginal form of selfhood that arises out of and orients this tradition of eremitic practice stands in a stark contrast to the modes of healing and personhood that undergird other kinds of medical thinking in Tibet. Janet Gyatso has written that the central texts of the mainstream Tibetan medical system "focus first and foremost on material, bodily conditions and material, bodily treatments—even in the case of illnesses caused by demons." This is an etiology in which maladies are primarily seen as resulting from imbalances in the three humors or *doṣas*: wind, bile, phlegm. The system's pervasive concern for how the doctor is to navigate physical and social situations "reflects the deep imbrication of medicine in the concrete realities of the world." This is a culture of healing in which techniques based primarily on visualization are the exception rather than the rule, "the preponderance of its therapies proceed[ing] through material means."[42] This highlights how distinctive the eremitic subculture of healing is, insofar as it effectively reverses the fundamental relationship between the material world and the self that defines mainstream Tibetan medicine.

In seeking to preserve oneself bodily in order to continue striving toward a realization of the ultimate Buddhist truth of the lack of a true self, the retreatant employs technologies that, on a conventional and discursive level, create and sustain them as a specific kind of being in the world. The imaginal self that is instantiated by following the prescriptions for eremitic practice is but one possibility among many distinctive forms of personhood that we can identify, within the culture of Tibetan religions and elsewhere. That the definition of personhood is so starkly variable can be seen as proving true the Buddha's foundational assertion about the lack of objectivity and the contingency of the human self. Maintaining sensitivity to the conventional and discursive forms of selfhood that come into being while in pursuit of that goal allows for new comparative insights into the history of religions, in Asia and beyond.

CHAPTER 6

FORMING THE ASCETIC SELF

As a religious tradition whose claims of authenticity and authority are always rooted in the past, Tibetan Buddhism regards transgenerational lineages of many types as being of vital importance. Reflecting the diversity of lineages and the roles they play in a practitioner's development, in *Direct Advice on Retreat* Karma Chakmé describes how an individual will have five different kinds of guru in the course of a full spiritual career: the teacher who gives the basic Buddhist refuge vow, the preceptor who imparts the monastic vows, the spiritual friend who conveys the bodhisattva vow, the guru who initiates one into tantra, and the realized teacher who transmits the ineffable Mahāmudrā. The key qualification for serving in any of these roles is the guru's having legitimate standing in the pertinent lineage—monastic ordination, tantric initiation, realization of the Mahāmudrā, and so on.[1] In such a religiocultural context, much attention is paid to instantiating the ideal form of the student–teacher relationship, since it is the guru or lama who incorporates the student into the lineage's present and connects them to its past. The rigor of this bond, and of whatever relationship may later be formed with the student's own disciples, will maintain the potency of the lineage into the future.

To better understand how practicing in individual long-term retreat affects and is affected by a meditator's relationship to the spiritual lineage, this chapter focuses on the prescriptions for how the meditator should conceive of and relate to earlier generations of masters of the tradition, their own tantric guru, and, should the meditator someday rise to the stature of having them, their own disciples. These are vertical relationships that define the position of the retreatant in a many-generational spiritual lineage. Our interest is in how the selfhood of the ascetic is shaped through techniques for relating to the lineage, both proximate and at a remove. Contiguous with the question of how the retreatant relates to their spiritual lineage, this chapter will close by considering what authors of prescriptive retreat texts have expressed regarding what they perceive as their own and their imagined readers' prospects for spiritual advancement. This reveals a palpable shift historically, as both authors and readers of prescriptive retreat texts are established as existing in a particular moment in historical time through their simultaneous deferential positioning relative to the forefathers of the spiritual lineage and to the prospect of enlightenment itself.

———

Across the full range of their religious practices, the long-term retreatant is oriented in many different dimensions of their being via direct reference to the past masters of the spiritual tradition. As shown in chapter 2, in the latter centuries of Tibetan anchoritism, it became widely held that an essential criterion for determining if a specific location was suitable for a retreat was whether enlightened beings had previously spent time there, orienting the meditator in space via reference to those masters. The retreatant is also oriented in the dimension of time through the observance of holidays commemorating those masters, both on a monthly cycle (such as the tenth day of each lunar month, dedicated to memorializing Padmasambhava) and on an annual one (such as the month of Sakadawa, which is associated with the Buddha, and annual memorials for figures like Milarepa and luminaries of other lineages). The history of the lineage and the meditator's position relative to it are continually reinforced through the visualization of the refuge tree, in which generation upon generation of lineage masters are arranged hierarchically among various buddhas, deities, and revered symbols, all arrayed on a multilimbed tree. The instructions for this practice given in Karma Chakmé's handbook explain that the meditator should visualize in the space before them a three-dimensional tree with five main limbs. The middle limb is occupied by the tantric guru, in the form of the buddha Vajradhara, immediately surrounded by the lamas of the lineage. On the branches to the guru/deity's right and left are a gathering of buddhas and representatives of the monastic community. The branches in the rear and front hold books of the holy Dharma and the tutelary deities of the tradition. Beneath are gatherings of *ḍākiṇīs* and Dharma protectors.[2] In doing this visualization, the practitioner actively fosters a sense of connection to and reverence for previous generations of past masters. Also reinforced is the status difference between the practitioner and those masters, expressed through their relative orientation in space: practitioner below, masters above. The members of the lineage are arranged vertically, such that to go upward is to go backward in time. Visualizing such a tree while reciting an associated ritual formula one hundred thousand times is included in all major versions of the "preliminary" practices that one must complete prior to advanced tantric initiation. Individuals would continue to do refuge tree practice throughout their tantric careers, including during retreat. Some texts prescribe spending the first month of a long retreat on the preliminary practices. Since at least one hundred thousand repetitions of each would have been completed prior to receiving tantric initiation, a week spent on each of these exercises at the outset of a retreat has traditionally served as a kind of refresher, making up for any faults or deficiencies in the preliminary practices completed prior.[3] Just as commonplace as refuge tree practice in Tibetan Buddhism is the recitation of prayers chronologically listing the members of one's spiritual lineage, stretching all the way back to its enlightened beginning, which fosters a sense of connection with the past while again making manifest the difference in status between the practitioner and their forbears, as well as the passage of time. In both the physical world and the mental one, in space and in time, the retreatant's being is oriented through references to the past masters of the tradition. These mechanisms continually reinforce the connection while never expunging the sense of the meditator's lesser status.

The ways of relating to the past masters just described are ubiquitous throughout Tibetan Buddhist tantra and are in no way unique to individual long-term retreat, although it may be that in the immersive religiosity of retreat, orienting references to the past masters are particularly omnipresent. Somewhat distinct from this issue and of greater interest here is the question of how the past masters are invoked with respect to the retreat endeavor as a whole (rather than specific aspects of life in retreat, such as where to do it, how to relate to food, and so on, as have been explored in previous chapters). What ongoing role do the past masters play in defining the eremitic endeavor in totality for later generations of practitioners?

We begin by considering a short poetic work penned by the Third Karmapa in 1296, at the age of about twelve, when he was in retreat above Tsurpu monastery, titled *Mountain Dharma: The Garland of Siddhis*. This first third of the text is a history of the Karmapa's direct spiritual lineage across ten generations, from Tilopa down to his own guru, Orgyenpa Rinchen Pel. This history focuses on how each member of the lineage achieved the greatest heights of religious accomplishment through years of "wandering in mountain hermitages." The Karmapa positions himself as the direct heir of this tradition, who, despite his being an "end-of-time yogi," as translated by Ruth Gamble, has achieved good qualities through the same kind of ascetic behavior. Having established his legitimacy in this way, Rangjung Dorjé spends the remainder of the text offering instructions intended to be useful to others pursuing a life of eremitism. For the Third Karmapa, there is value in retelling the history of the lineage to which he is directly and intimately connected, although by calling himself an "end-of-time yogi" he suggests a substantive difference between them and him.[4]

Far more commonly, an author of a prescriptive retreat text—typically possessing far less illustrious connections and status than the Karmapa—will refer generically to the "past masters," phrased in various ways, treating them as less proximate or individuated. Chegom Sherap Dorjé states that although residing in a mountain hermitage is rare during his own time—due to people's ignorance, grasping at self, and lack of merit—staying in retreat "was the path traversed by the Noble Ones who have already passed away." The "holy beings living in the present" are also found in retreat, and that will provide the way for fortunate beings to escape from samsara in the future as well. Chegompa here presents asceticism in undomesticated spaces as a timeless, uninterrupted enterprise that we can learn about from past exemplars. Seven hundred years later, Drakar Lozang Pelden would quote Chegompa on this point, and then amplify the statement by naming some of the past masters one might look to as role models: late Indian Buddhist figures, Tibetan Kadampas, and members of the New schools, including Tsongkhapa.[5] In the early eighteenth century, Mipam Püntsok Sherap tells the reader to "model your behavior on the life stories of the past masters of the Kagyu" through ascetic practice. Orgyen Namdröl Wangpo stated in 1846 that when beginning a retreat, a meditator should take joy in the thought that they are preserving the ways of the past masters of the tradition.[6] As quoted in chapters 4 and 5, Sönam Chödzin and Karma Ngedön Tenkyé declared that in practicing a pure form of asceticism, a retreatant can follow in the footsteps of the earlier *siddha*s of the tradition. Examples of this type abound, showing the enormous importance of the memory of the *siddha*s in erecting the conceptual architecture that structures the anchoritic pursuit as a whole.

Going beyond references to the past masters of the tradition that characterize the eremitic endeavor in a general way, authors also invoke these forbears' memories to specific ends. For example, Yangönpa prescribes that should a meditator experience difficulties early in a retreat, the solution is to "fiercely supplicate your guru, tighten your retreat, and think of the life stories of [famous, eminent] Kagyupas." In this instance, recollecting the life stories of the past masters is presented as a means to reestablish the footing on which the meditator's asceticism rests. More commonplace in retreat discourse are statements that one should make a point of remembering and drawing inspiration from the lives of the spiritual forefathers when feeling particularly daunted by the challenging circumstances of asceticism. At the end of his chapter on "further improvement" practices, Yangönpa implores the reader to "Look at the extent of the austerities (*dka' ba*) performed by the *siddha*s of the past. Milarepa meditated so much that his backside became like that of a monkey!" He concludes, "You must equate life with practice. You must meditate on these instructions for further improvement, without getting the critical points wrong, for a long time. Meditate for a long time! You are to meditate for a long time!"[7] In chapter 5, Lekshé Drayang was quoted as instructing an ill retreatant to persevere through the experience of sickness by bringing it onto the religious path, just as the *siddha*s of the past had done. When explaining methods for generating stronger renunciatory resolve, Karma Chakmé reminds the reader of how "all the Kadampas of the past" would abstain from feeding their fires before going to sleep, under the rationale that they could die during the night. Karma Chakmé then mentions how the early Kagyu masters like Pakmodrupa exemplified the renunciatory ideal by leaving their homelands and never going back.[8] These examples encourage the meditator not only to persist in their asceticism but also to always strive to take it further. Shabkar's nineteenth-century *Beneficial Moon* is above all else concerned to provide readers with the strength to endure by making them see connections to and draw inspiration from a succession of past masters stretching all the way back to the Buddha himself.

Although which particular "past masters" are meant may differ depending on the author's or reader's sectarian affiliations, the ubiquity of statements like these suggests that the entire prospect of retreat, with all its highs and lows, was commonly conceived of with these exemplars vividly in mind. Those past masters are proof positive that the challenges of eremitism can and should be endured. And yet the sense of a gap between one's own asceticism and that of those earlier masters is immutable. Many of the references given above convey a conviction that although we should strive to accomplish ascetically something resembling what the *siddha*s of the past had done, we cannot realistically hope to rise to their level.

At the beginning of the pivotal sixteenth chapter of his handbook, "Direct Advice on Retreat," Karma Chakmé expresses this explicitly. He writes, "Regarding the way the fully liberated Kagyupas wandered in mountain hermitages: although I may have an idea about it, because of the fact that I have not practiced it, even if I might know how to explain it, I would not dare to do so. But I will lay out what comes to my mind based on the extent to which I have practiced personally, as this could be beneficial to other beings of lesser merit like myself."[9] In spite of his massive erudition and many years already spent in retreat, Karma Chakmé is careful not to present himself as possessing any special authority.

Karma Chakmé is recorded as having addressed this issue in even greater detail in response to Tsöndrü Gyatso's initial request that he compose a "mountain

Dharma" text of his own. This passage from the second chapter of the handbook is significant for how it details both how Karma Chakmé understood the ideal form of asceticism and the specific ways he fell short of that goal.

> Haha, Tsöndrü Gyatso! The root meaning of the *Mountain Dharmas* as taught by the past masters of the Kagyu is this: after renouncing activities of this life, having abandoned your homeland and withdrawn to a mountainous place, disquieted by thoughts of impermanence and death, you make yourself destitute of food, clothing, and conversation. You drink water, chew on rocks, and wear garments from corpses.[10] Other than to preserve the nature of the mind, you have nothing whatsoever to do. Other than reciting a few verses of devotion toward your lama, you have nothing to recite or meditate upon. Other than waiting for the Lord of Death to arrive, you have nothing whatsoever to think about. If a patron should arrive, moved by faith in you, you flee unseen like an injured deer to an empty valley, where human voices are not to be heard. That is the "mountain Dharma" of the past masters of the Kagyu.
>
> As for being a Dharma practitioner ceaselessly blown about by the wind, I am not capable of that. I have stayed here in the place of my birth for a long time, such that even the name of the place has attached itself to me.[11] I am surrounded by family members, nobles, and monks, and have not experienced staying in solitude for even a single day. From the age of eight I have consumed donations offered to the monastic community (*dkor*). These days I even have a few horses and cattle. Death has not been staked to my heart, making my mountain hermitage in this great holy place nothing more than a house.
>
> For those reasons, I have no means (*thabs*) to compose a *Mountain Dharma*. If I were to compose such a text using certain teachings of the Kagyu as a model, it would be an embarrassment to all who are familiar with these things—like the nose being embarrassed by what the mouth is saying.[12] If I were to teach a Dharma that I had not myself practiced, who would trust in it? Therefore, I have no means for composing a *Mountain Dharma*.

This passage would be quoted in Shabkar's *Beneficial Moon* a century and a half later.[13] According to Karma Chakmé, the genuine "mountain Dharma" enacted by the past masters of the Kagyu and conveyed through earlier *Mountain Dharma* texts is characterized by the utter renunciation of all worldly entanglements and the greatest possible simplification of one's bearing—all motivated by a sincere reckoning with the reality of one's impermanence. Having in his own estimation achieved only a pale version of this, Karma Chakmé lacks the authority to compose a *Mountain Dharma* of his own. The more than eight hundred folio sides of text that follow—a record of teachings delivered only after further prodding from Tsöndrü Gyatso—are framed by this anxiety about Karma Chakmé's inadequacy in comparison to his accomplished spiritual forefathers. The theme of his own lack of accomplishment is brought up regularly throughout the remainder of the text in many self-disparaging remarks, particularly in the colophons to the individual chapters.[14] If a figure as learned and devoted to eremitism as Karma Chakmé is to be seen as so inferior, then for the reader just setting out, the anchoritic path ahead must have looked very long and steep indeed.

In ways both general and specific, formal and informal, the memory of the past masters of the tradition has provided orientation and inspiration for latter-day practitioners of long-term retreat. In addition to sharing a common purpose with those past masters, the meditator is reminded of their connection as members of a shared, unbroken lineage. While those predecessors are to be remembered and followed, they are just as clearly in a different category than oneself—they may be emulated, but they will not be equaled no matter how many years are devoted to the attempt.

———

Drakar Lozang Pelden writes, "For a Dharma practitioner, the basis of all good qualities, both provisional and ultimate, is the lama." The root guru represents the possibility of direct access to the enlightened origins of the tradition. In a tantric context, it is said that the guru becomes the embodiment of all three of the refuges or jewels: the Dharma, the *sangha*, and the buddhas themselves. Karma Chakmé states, "If you maintain conviction that the [tantric guru] is in fact your tutelary deity, you will quickly achieve the *siddhi*s of that deity."[15] A key means of doing so is the practice of guru yoga, which is a visualization of the guru as a representation of enlightenment. Although Yangönpa counts this as one of the Six Yogas of Naropa and includes it as part of every formal meditation session, it is more commonly counted as one of the preliminary practices. It is ubiquitous throughout Tibetan Buddhism, both in and outside of retreat.[16]

There are ways of relating to the guru that are specific to the practice of individual long-term retreat. For one, the guru plays both tangible and intangible roles in sustaining a meditator's eremitism. As highlighted in chapter 3, the guru may play a gatekeeping function in a meditator's interpersonal relations. In chapter 5 we saw how the conjured image of the guru was used for purposes of healing. As mentioned above, Yangönpa instructs the retreatant to "fiercely supplicate your guru" as a means of overcoming difficulties. In the meditator's ongoing spiritual development, Mipam Püntsok Sherap writes that the most important and powerful of all "further improvement" practices is to "supplicate from your heart the lama, whom you do not think of as being other than an actual buddha for a single second." This is the "universal panacea of devotion" (*mos gus dkar po chig thub*). He avers, "This is superior to any other form of further improvement practice. I have personally experienced how this can make you travel quickly through all the Paths." Other authors also write that maintaining this kind of devotion to the guru constitutes the "universal panacea."[17] In these diverse ways, the lama, whether present in physical form or merely envisioned or recollected by the meditator, is attributed with the ability to deliver an anchorite from all kinds of challenging circumstances that might otherwise prevent spiritual progress or force them to abandon their asceticism.

A central factor in how the retreatant's relationship with the guru has been problematized is the expectation that a disciple will spend some length of time in the presence of the guru, during which they render service and receive spiritual transmissions and instructions, to be put into practice more earnestly later. This period provides an opportunity for the disciple to show their devotion, to be purified through work that serves as payment for spiritual access, and to remain in intimate proximity to the lama while receiving instructions. The fact of being destined for retreat places an added pressure on the disciple during this training, making it a topic of particular concern in the texts used in this study. Orgyen Namdröl Wangpo emphasizes the necessity of persistently asking the guru for corrections to your understanding during this time, because "when you are practicing all on your own, you must not have doubts or be of two minds about anything." How to relate to the lama prior to the retreat is taken up in the first two chapters of Lekshé Drayang's *Words on the Mountain Dharma*. After describing how to find a lama who exemplifies the necessary qualities, the instructions turn how to properly serve, follow, and learn from them. They must be found to display the possession of *siddhi*s, knowledge of the Dharma, generosity, adherence to vows, detachment, compassion, and an overriding commitment to helping to liberate their trainees. Serving such a lama entails gladly making gifts of whatever material things one possesses, as well as physical labor. Lekshé Drayang states that a critical factor, as specified in numerous Buddhist texts, is that the lama be pleased with everything the student does: if the student ensures that the lama is never the slightest bit unhappy, then later when meditating in retreat, they will experience no obstacles in their practice. There seems to be a belief in a kind of isomorphism between this earlier period of training under the guru and the actual retreat. In the second chapter of his manual, Lekshé Drayang addresses the importance of receiving instructions from the lama with an attitude of faith and devotion. He criticizes those who insincerely accumulate reading transmissions and empowerments—perhaps while paying insufficient attention in the moment, improperly sharing with others what they have received, or merely increasing the number of instructions they possess, lacking the intention to really practice them.[18]

Drakar Lozang Pelden's early twentieth-century problematization of the relation between student and guru in the time before retreat brings some additional concerns above the threshold of consideration. While confirming the importance of serving the lama with body, speech, and mind, Lozang Pelden addresses some potential pitfalls. While living with the lama and serving him intimately, one must avoid slipping into casualness in the relationship. The student should not abuse their physical proximity to the lama to meet with them too often. The student should approach the lama with discernment and caution, as they would an actual buddha or a powerful lord of this world, and must maintain pure vision of the lama as an enlightened being; otherwise, there can be no spiritual progress later during retreat. If the lama scolds them, the student should view it as an esoteric oral instruction. If the lama hits them, this is the transmission of a blessing that can purify an obscuration. Lozang Pelden explains that later, when physically separated from the lama during retreat, the disciple remains connected by visualizing them at the crown of the head through guru yoga, and by continuing to maintain pure vision toward them. Even if the lama should pass away, the student should request their blessing and think of them as if still alive, regarding this as only a temporary separation and hoping to meet again in their next life. In general, one should reflect on one's good fortune to meet a qualified lama, after so many lifetimes of aimless wandering throughout samsara, as being "like a blind person catching their ox by the tail."[19]

Echoing the concern raised by Lekshé Drayang, Lozang Pelden addresses those who "attend to the lama for a year or a few months, request instructions, then go off on their own to practice Dharma," whom he likens to a crow absconding with a piece of meat. He asserts that receiving instructions from a lama is like taking on a debt, which, if not repaid through subsequent behavior, becomes a kind of theft. Failure to maintain this relationship properly will ensure that one's spiritual practice produces no benefit. Lozang Pelden specifically critiques those who employ Potowa's instruction to "Roam everywhere, like the sun and the moon" to justify, as he so colorfully puts it, "throwing away your lama and Dharma siblings as you would a rock used for wiping your rear end." He clarifies that Potawa's statement (quoted in a passage from the Fourth Panchen Lama in chapter 3) is meant to refer to practicing itinerancy while living in the mountains for retreat, remaining detached from sense pleasures—not to justify uncouth or thoughtless behavior.[20]

Prescriptive retreat texts therefore show a notable degree of anxiety about a meditator's relating improperly to the lama. Although the time of serving the lama and receiving instructions is finite because of the separation that individual retreat necessarily entails, the student must not regard this as a mere transaction but as an experience that will carry lasting significance and responsibility.[21] The great scrutiny to which this matter is subjected suggests that it was an issue of heightened concern. As Foucault observes, "Problematization and apprehension go hand in hand; inquiry is joined to vigilance."[22]

A resource that authors commonly call upon for how to navigate this fraught matter is the accumulated lore of previous generations of spiritual masters. As examples of how the disciple should relate to the guru, Drakar Lozang Pelden cites the stories of Dromtönpa and his lamas Setsünpa and Atīśa, Naropa and his teacher Tilopa, Marpa and Naropa, Milarepa and Marpa—the greatest luminaries of the Kadampa and Kagyu traditions. He concludes that the reader should model their behavior on "how those *mahāsiddha*s revered and served their gurus." Similarly, at the outset of his *Garland of Critical Points for the Precious Mountain Dharma*, Lhatsün Namkha Jikmé writes about the utter centrality of the qualified and holy lama, without whom there can be no hope of accomplishment on the tantric path. Relying on the lama in a proper fashion is of such critical importance that the meditator should take direction from the stories of the past masters: "Because it is so very difficult to reach perfection in the holy Dharma, you should think hard about the stories relating how the past great holy beings of your tradition served their own teachers. In the service of their lamas, they did whatever they were told, even to the point of throwing away their own lives." Kachö Wangpo likewise states that a meditator should model their behavior toward their lama on how past exemplars of the tradition followed their own gurus: just as the great and learned Naropa conducted himself without any regard for his own body or life, so should you relate to your lama while receiving all you can from him.[23] Naropa—the Indian scholar-monk turned tantric master—stands out as the most-cited example of the extreme lengths to which past masters went in serving and obeying their gurus, in order to prove themselves worthy recipients of tantric instruction.

The relationship between the student and the guru who in so many tangible and intangible ways makes the retreat possible is but a single link in a chain that continues all the way back to the early enlightened masters. Retreatants are instructed to look to those past generations as models for how to follow the lama in the present. Their endeavoring to follow the guru in this more perfect manner makes the remembered ways of the past masters manifest in the present, which will preserve the integrity of the tradition into the future. This creates a recursiveness that tries to close the loop among trainee, guru, and the enlightened *siddha*s of the past.

The retreat tradition provides other means of repairing weak or broken links in the chain that connects the practitioner with their enlightened forbears. Karma Chakmé instructs that if the practitioner should fail to find a teacher of Mahāmudrā who displays full realization, they can resort to imagining the lama they have settled on in the form of a renowned earlier master of the lineage, such as Gampopa or the First Karmapa, Düsum Khyenpa (1110–1193).[24] Here the image of a figure from the past is laid over the meditator's guru in the present, in order to subsume them—and oneself—into a tradition reaching back in time.

In a similar vein, Karma Chakmé's discussion of potentially adverse circumstances that a meditator must rectify "prior to the sealing of the retreat" is entirely concerned with the possibility of having received teachings or ritual empowerments through a lineage that is weakened or illegitimate, or of having lost connection to a legitimate lineage through improper thoughts or behavior. If either of these is the case, then the efforts the individual puts toward religious practice during retreat will yield no results. According to *Direct Advice on Retreat*, the method for removing such a potential obstacle is as follows: on an auspicious day, the meditator should lay out offerings, then visualize the guru in the form of the tutelary deity at the middle of the mandala. The meditator then performs the traditional feast offering while maintaining the mental association between the guru and the tutelary deity. Inside the guru/deity's head is a white *oṃ*, at the throat a red *āḥ*, and at the heart a blue *hūṃ*. Surrounding each of these is the hundred-syllable mantra of Vajrasattva, in white, red, and blue letters. From those strings of text identical copies are emanated, which enter the meditator's body and encircle the *oṃ*, *āḥ*, and *hūṃ* at their head, throat, and heart. From these descend white, red, and blue nectars that fill the meditator's body and purify them of any broken *samaya*s associated with the body, speech, and mind, respectively. This is followed by recitations. More important than the visualizations or the recitations in this rite, Karma Chakmé asserts, is maintaining the certainty that the guru *is* the tutelary deity, and vice versa. "If you achieve stability in the certainty that (*ngas* [sic] *shes brtan po thob*) the lama and the tutelary deity are inseparable [or undifferentiated, indistinguishable; *dbyer med*], then it makes no difference whether the lineage is a short one or a long"—in other words, the meditator's forming a connection with the source of the tradition is assured, rendering moot what may have happened among all the intervening generations, closing the gap between then and now. Performing a similar function, elsewhere in the text Karma Chakmé describes a few methods for getting the equivalent of a reading transmission for a specific religious text when it cannot be acquired through the ordinary means. One of these methods requires access to a painting bearing foot- or handprints of one of the forefathers of the Kagyu. The meditator is to regard the image as the actual physical presence of the great master, and as they read the text aloud, they are to imagine that they are receiving the text directly from him.[25]

The evidence provided by prescriptive texts for individual long-term retreat suggests that in this subculture of eremitism, a meditator's relationship with the lama was understood to present significant challenges. The physical and interpersonal isolation entailed by long-term retreat put a particular strain on that relationship during the preretreat period, deriving from concerns about the trainee's bodily closeness to the lama and the debt incurred in receiving initiations and transmissions from them. There is also the concern that the lama may not embody the full measure of spiritual accomplishment required to allow a disciple to subsequently progress on the spiritual path. The tradition has prescribed the invocation of past masters to overcome these challenges, whether through recalling the stories of their impressive lives to provide direction for how to behave now or through using visualization to invoke their presence and compensate for the present-day lama's shortcomings. These latter practices employ the technology of visualization of the guru/earlier master to form the meditator as a new and improved being in the world—the inheritor of a legitimate lineage rather than a broken one. These techniques are based on similar technologies and instantiate the same kind of imaginal selfhood reviewed in chapter 5, insofar as practicing them defines and forms the meditator as a being with the ability to effectively rewrite history and reconfigure external conditions (in this case, the actual facts of what the guru is) through visualization and the generation of a certain contemplative intention, supported by other ritual means.

This examination of what this body of literature says regarding an ascetic's relationship to the earlier masters of the lineage and to their guru shows the extent to which the two are inextricably related. The tradition provides numerous means of closing the loop among the trainee, the guru, and the enlightened *siddha*s of earlier generations, ensuring the latter-day practitioner's connection to a legitimate tradition stretching back across generations to its point of origin, which will be preserved for future generations to access as well. Many of these means rely on the power of the mind to regard the guru as a deity or an enlightened master and thereby make the guru functionally equivalent, which serves to overcome gaps in space, time, and degree of spiritual awakening. These creative means of reforming broken links to the enlightened past evince that the inherent conservatism of a lineage-based tradition does not mean being strictly bound to inherited forms and structures but invoking memories or images from the past to serve present, traditionally defined needs.

It is common for texts offering instructions for individual meditative retreat to include occasional statements like Yangönpa's "Take this to heart, my sons!," which serve as reminders of their pedagogical intent. Mipam Püntsok Sherap's *Refined Honey That Extracts the Essence of Accomplishment in the Profound Mountain Dharma*, written at Lapchi in 1715, provides a far richer sense of how the author imagined himself to teach and relate to his students through the text. While presenting the manual as something he wrote in response to repeated requests from his disciples, a common trope in this literature, Püntsok Sherap takes the further step of saying he was motivated to write out of a concern for the morality of his disciples' conduct.[26] This work also stands out among prescriptive retreat texts for the detail with which the author describes his own life of ascetic practice, in hope that it will inspire his students to follow suit. Over four folio sides, Püntsok Sherap describes twenty-eight years of ascetic practice, including three years of meditation each at Lapchi, Mount Kailash, and Tsari, and numerous shorter stints at sites from western Tibet to Kongpo in the east, from Reting in the north down to the Kathmandu Valley. He writes about wearing out the soles of his boots wandering from place to place, always returning to retreat after being disrupted by certain bad associates or the arrival of an invading army, and refraining from speaking to the many faithful who arrived at the portal to his retreat. The author claims to have carried himself unhypocritically throughout all of this, never wavering from the correct mindset and motivations. Having reviewed this past, Püntsok Sherap, the Mendicant of Taktsé, now invites his readers to "examine my behavior—external, internal, and secret. If you understand me to be without fault, then learn from me! Follow after me! Meditate like me! All my sons, you need to behave only in accordance with the Dharma! Understand this! Understand it and practice it! That is my instruction." This autobiographical stock-taking of a life of ascetic practice—written in sadness, his eyes welling with tears as he thinks about what the future holds for his disciples, and with his repeated references to his own old age (calling himself "your old father" throughout), all of which combined to compel him to write the text as quickly as possible—imbues the text with a pathos and an immediacy not often found in this kind of literature. Moved by his feeling of the nearness of death, Püntsok Sherap addresses his disciples with an urgency and candor that provide a sense of the intimacy of a long-time retreatant's relationship with their students. The sixty-folio-side text closes with the author declaring, "This is my direct advice. This is my rebuke. This is my heart instruction (*snying gtam*). This is the training. This is the clearing away of obstructions. This is the further improvement practice. This is the final testament at the time of my death. There is nothing more than this."[27] He would pass away less than a year later. Having given his entire life over to the Dharma, Mipam Püntsok Sherap can only hope that his example inspires his disciples to make good use of their opportunity to practice. As his final act, writing *Refined Honey* is intended to ensure some measure of this.

Beyond communicating with students through the composition of retreat instructions or using his own example to inspire them, Karma Chakmé's handbook is unique for its inclusion of details for how to properly serve as a guru to other retreatants. In this way Karma Chakmé offers the reader an opportunity to imagine themselves assuming the position of the revered teacher, becoming a figure of eremitic authority in their own right. Looking closely at what Karma Chakmé says about this will provide some revealing details about the practice of retreat historically. This will also allow us to transition into considering what Karma Chakmé seems to regard as the spiritual prospects for both himself and his reader, then to compare his statements to other authors' respective treatments of this issue. Although the meditator has been encouraged to at least attempt to do as the past masters of the tradition did, whether or not they should hope to achieve something comparable is a different matter entirely.

Karma Chakmé's brief treatment of serving as a lama to other retreatants is included in the fortieth chapter, on "how to work for the benefit of other beings." This is about pursuing a spiritual career after one's time in retreat that aligns with the bodhisattva ideal, which is largely a question of how to be generous in disseminating the precious Dharma without giving it away indiscriminately. Amid this discussion Karma Chakmé addresses how to prepare a disciple to enter retreat and then see them through it. Karma Chakmé details that if it is possible for the student to commit to a retreat of three years and three fortnights while residing in a cell near your own, then you can remain in communication via writing on a dust-covered slate during the first week of the retreat, providing what instructions may be necessary regarding details of the visualizations, daily schedule, and the objects of meditation. But if that is not possible and the student must do their retreat some distance away, an added pressure is placed on the period of training that precedes the retreat. In such a situation, the teacher may need to ensure that the disciple has explanations of the practices in a condensed written form. Then, during the course of the retreat, whether near or far away, the guru should every day perform visualizations and recitations to both remove obstacles for and impart blessings to the student. The guru may need to communicate with the student through writing letters. Karma Chakmé here states, "At the conclusion of the three years and three fortnights, when the approach–accomplishments have been completed and experiential realization has been produced, at that time one has become a 'lama.'"[28]

Of particular interest is what Karma Chakmé says one must have achieved before rightfully taking on the role of guru to an aspiring retreatant. Karma Chakmé states that the baseline requirement is "having found a degree of certainty in the Generation and Perfection phase practices" (*bskyed rdzogs nges pa cung zad rnyed*). Khenpo Karthar Rinpoché, as rendered by his interpreters, glosses this as meaning that in one's Generation phase practice there is "a spontaneously clear appearance of the deity's form, without fixation on its substantiality," and in Perfection phase practice, "it means some experience within the nonreferential practice of the unity of emptiness and wisdom of your mind's nature."[29] Karma Chakmé also writes that a more spiritually advanced individual can cease practicing for themselves and instead focus entirely on benefiting others. A person may do this in the style of a merchant, which entails traveling from place to place and giving empowerments and teachings, hopefully compelling people to practice; in the style of a ferryman, doling out instructions one at a time to individuals who seek you out at the retreat where you remain permanently; or in the style of a king, which concerns how to create Dharmic benefits from the material offerings received. A practitioner will know that they have reached the point when it is appropriate to end intensive meditation practice and devote themselves to working for the benefit of others based on what appears in the three kinds of dependent connections or signs: "If *externally* the local harvest is good, and there is no fighting in the area; if *internally*, your tent, clothing, and ritual materials have all been gathered; and if *in secret*, you have assuredness (*gdeng*) in your Generation and Perfection phase practices."[30] At such a time, a meditator can prioritize dispensing the Dharma over the pursuit of their own personal practice.

Karma Chakmé's treatment of the prerequisites for taking on these different teaching roles brings us to the question of what he seems to think regarding his and his reader's prospects for spiritual accomplishment in general. As shown earlier in this chapter, he characterized his own life of meditative practice with great humility. But what else does he say in the course of the handbook about his own spiritual accomplishments and the spiritual outlook for his imagined reader? For the remainder of this chapter we will focus on the question of how the Tibetan ascetic self has historically been defined in relationship to the matter of ultimate importance, the possibility of escape from this realm of suffering, which is the ostensible purpose of retreat practice. This question is key to defining the personhood of the meditator as existing in the dimension of time. We will begin with Karma Chakmé, then consider other authors who came both before and after. Taken individually, their statements are somewhat sparse and inconclusive, but together, and viewed in connection to the pattern of lived deferential reverence observed throughout this study, they form a clearly discernable trend.

Within *Direct Advice on Retreat*, Karma Chakmé refers to the endeavor of individual long-term meditative retreat somewhat poetically as "the white path to liberation" (*thar lam dkar po*).[31] In a passing way, he mentions that as the result of completing the accumulations of merit and wisdom via the practice of mandala offerings, "realization is naturally produced. Wisdom naturally increases. Your thoughts accord with the Dharma. You understand the meaning of all Dharma teachings. You cross the Grounds and Paths in stages. You achieve final enlightenment" (*mthar thug byang chub 'thob*). A gloss of an instruction given by Tilopa to Naropa, this is in line with canonical descriptions of mandala offering practice.[32]

More revealing of Karma Chakmé's own thoughts, the thirteenth chapter is devoted to a discussion of an individual's progression into deeper and deeper meditative states in the course of a retreat. The chapter begins with a reaffirmation of the need to cut off worldly distractions of all kinds (material things, reading, writing). As for the experiences a meditator is likely to have during a retreat, Karma Chakmé describes how early on it is natural to experience frustration due to hearing distracting sounds like birds chirping, water falling, or dogs barking. At this point a meditator might think, "This place is not isolated enough. If I went to an empty valley that was more isolated than this, then I would be happier." But if you cannot take control of your own mind, there is no place without some condition that can rob you of your *samādhi*. Instead, when you hear distracting sounds that assault your ears and give rise to conceptual thoughts, you should ask, "Where does this thought first arise from? In the middle, where does it reside? In the end, where does it go? What is the nature of this thing that bothers my mind?" By examining the sound in this way, "it disappears into the emptiness of its baselessness." What had been distracting become a means to realization. This is the first step in a process of deepening the meditative experience that Karma Chakmé describes in great detail over the next twenty-five folio sides. He talks of settling into a retreat, becoming less restless, and watching cravings subside. The meditator begins to see, on a conceptual level, the emptiness of all things. Here Karma Chakmé addresses in detail the traditionally recognized experiences of bliss, clarity, and nonconceptuality, focusing on how they arise and why they might fade. The meditator reaches a point where they are beginning to see the nature of the mind, arriving at an understanding that the entire realm of reality we experience is coterminous with knowing awareness. This is a moment of critical importance in a meditator's development, because it is unfortunately commonplace to become attached to this thought and therefore cease making progress. Karma Chakmé talks about this in terms of certain "places of deviation" a meditator may run across at this moment in their development, each being the pursuit of a specific understanding of the nature of things that diverges slightly from the ultimate view. At this stage the meditator will command various types of extrasensory perception, about which they must not become prideful. If able to navigate these pathways correctly, they can reach the point of "the dawning of realization of the Mahāmudrā." One who arrives at this state can rightfully be described as "possessing realization" (*rtogs ldan*). Karma Chakmé continues to elaborate, addressing the different possible levels of experiencing all things as being of "one taste."[33]

At this point Karma Chakmé's exposition takes a deferential turn. He declares that up to now, all that he has explained is in accordance with his own firsthand experience. But there are states of meditative accomplishment beyond what he has attained. For the sake of providing the reader with a comprehensive account, he will now shift to describing things as he has been able to glean from the teachings of Kagyu masters closer to enlightenment than himself. The final two folio sides of the chapter discuss the possibility of transcending the dualism of experiencing the binary states of "meditation" and "nonmeditation"; entering into the highest possible meditative state, the Vajra-Like Samādhi; reaching a state of needing no further meditation; and achieving buddhahood in one lifetime.[34] How any of this maps onto Karma Chakmé's understanding of the six categories of practitioner, as summarized in chapter 1, is not addressed. The issue of critical importance is that he disavows the higher echelons of spiritual advancement for himself: he can only write about those states of meditative experience academically, as it were, as he proclaims the limitations of his own spiritual development at this juncture within chapter 13.

Elsewhere in the handbook, regarding his readers' spiritual prospects, likely directly connected to how he thought of his own, Karma Chakmé offers detailed instructions for certain mechanisms that had developed in Tibetan Buddhism for bypassing the process of rebirth. These are more prominent in *Direct Advice on Retreat* than in any other retreat text consulted in this study. These options include achieving liberation for oneself via postdeath meditation, which entails entering the *bardo* and recognizing the luminosity found there (described in chapter 44), and gaining the grace of a buddha that sends a being's sentience to a Pure Land, whence release from samsara can be secured in the future (chapter 42). In a client-oriented mode, Karma Chakmé also provides the retreatant with methods to secure release for others after death—through his instructions on the *bardo*, which offers "liberation upon hearing" (chapter 22), and the funerary practice focused on the Sarvavid form of the buddha Vairocana (chapter 21).

Karma Chakmé understands his and his reader's spiritual trajectories to intersect with their place in historical time by virtue of our living in the "degenerate age," when the afflictive emotions are more powerful and we therefore ought to multiply any ritual recitation by a factor of four.[35] As Khenpo Karthar Rinpoché explains, in general Karma Chakmé sees us as living during the "time of the cause" (*rgyu dus*), which comes after the "time of fruition" (*'bras dus*) that immediately follows a buddha's arrival in the world. Because of this, we cannot aspire to true awakening in the present, but can only prepare for the arrival of the next buddha, Maitreya, when the positive karma we create can finally bear its proper fruits. As Khenpo Karthar Rinpoché explains, "the period of realization is over and we are involved in the period of scholarship." He distinguishes between "attempting to uphold realization" and a lesser option, to "merely uphold tradition." He states that the latter is in general more appropriate given our moment in time.[36]

Stepping back to view the seventeenth-century *Direct Advice on Retreat* in its entirety, we can observe that Karma Chakmé explicitly defines the ascetic in terms of the current historical age. He does not preclude reaching the higher echelons of attainment in our present but treats this as unlikely, his own circumscribed realization serving as a testament to the probable limits of the possible. His prescriptions for numerous alternative means of escaping from samsara speak to these conditions.

Other authors before and after Karma Chakmé have had something to say regarding the meditator's relative prospects for spiritual advancement, including both how far they might get in the present lifetime and the relative likelihood of such an outcome. At the end of Chegom Sherap Dorjé's twelfth-century retreat manual, the following question is posed: "If one practices in thought and deed in a mountain hermitage in that way [i.e., as has been taught in this text], what kind of fruit will be produced?" In response Chegompa asserts that if one practices as he has instructed, then "in this lifetime you will certainly (*nges*) have well-being, happiness, and renown. You will naturally achieve different kinds of benefit to other transmigrating beings. You will certainly obtain the ordinary and the extraordinary *siddhi*s. You will manifest the Ten Signs, the Eight Good Qualities, and so on." He then explains these signs and qualities, which are lists of classically recognized signs of accomplishment (including having perceptions of mirages, smoke, and fireflies) and bodily states (such as a softness of the body, fattiness of the body, brilliance to the body, moving quickly, and the mind's appearing as emptiness). Chegompa here does not talk of highest liberation, but says that these lesser spiritual accomplishments are "certain." Earlier in the text he mentions the fact of our living in a degenerate age, when people are in their basic nature ill aligned with the Dharma.[37] We saw how he nevertheless referred to "holy beings living in the present" who reside in retreat. For many other authors of prescriptive retreat texts, such spiritually advanced beings are only to be found in the past. Chegompa's ideas about these matters are not fully expressed in this short text, but we do not see him closing the door to the possibility of higher accomplishment.

The final two chapters of Yangönpa's *Blazing Jewel*, written a few decades after Chegompa's *Lamp*, consist of a detailed discussion of the full course of spiritual progress and the enlightenment in which it culminates. In the penultimate, sixth chapter, Yangönpa provides a comprehensive explanation of the various Paths through which an individual progresses while transforming from an ordinary person, mired in samsara, to a fully enlightened being. The facts about these Paths have been a mainstay of the canonical Buddhist tradition going all the way back to the sutras. In Yangönpa's presentation, after some changes in one's general bearing (finding no shortage of motivation for religious practice, achieving total renunciation of the concerns of this life), progress through these Paths is manifested through increasingly subtle and profound states of mind, described through the categories of *samādhi*s or specific meditative experiences. There are potential "places of deviation" that are likely to arise amid these mental transformations. Yangönpa discusses these outcomes so that the reader can be aware of and hopefully avoid them.

Up to this point, Yangönpa's exposition is similar to that given in Karma Chakmé's thirteenth chapter. But whereas Karma Chakmé signaled clearly that his own understanding reached a definitive limit, Yangönpa continues without interruption to the point of enlightenment. The climax of this spiritual transformation is described as follows:

> There is no meditation and no postmeditative state. There is no bringing to closure or not bringing to closure via mindfulness. There is no self or other. There is no this life or after. This is achieving a state of perfection in the Vajra-Like Samādhi. This is the Path of No More Learning [the last of the five Paths]. At this time, this is said to be "the empowerment of authentic great light" or "the authentic fourth [empowerment] of Secret Mantra." In truth, it is the Great Sealing [Mahāmudrā] in bliss and emptiness of all the phenomena of apparent

existence, samsara and the beyond. A perfect, unadulterated state in which emptiness and compassion are inseparable, without needing an object, self-appears and becomes manifest. There no longer existing any obscuration with respect to knowable things, the great wisdom self-appears—and in that instant, finality is attained. At that time, all obscurations concerning the knowable are completely abandoned, and through the workings of codependent origination, there is a dissolution, and like a snake shedding its skin, your body becomes a rainbow body. Your mind becomes the *dharmakāya*.

Yangönpa next describes the ontological status of the new kind of being that one has become, with the ability to appear in different physical forms in order to teach different kinds of sentient being. The section concludes, "That is the manner of achieving buddhahood in this very life." The remaining five lines of the sixth chapter address the achievement of buddhahood at various points in the death and rebirth process. Continuing on this trajectory, the seventh and final chapter is devoted to understanding what it means to be a buddha. This is approached in terms of physical state, the nature of the wisdom that is buddhahood, the different categories of action a buddha may perform, and the compassion that motivates such a being. With this discussion, the 125 folio sides of Yangönpa's *Blazing Jewel* come to a close.[38]

In his discussion of the steps culminating in complete liberation from samsara, there is no indication that Yangönpa intends to be taken as speaking from personal experience. But it is significant that he does not feel a need to deferentially distance himself from higher states of being in the same way Karma Chakmé would four hundred years later. Nor is there any suggestion in the *Blazing Jewel* that a practitioner's place in history should pose an obstacle to achieving these highest echelons of accomplishment. (It may be significant that the *Great Appendix* refers to our living in "here in the period of fruition," whereas Karma Chakmé would locate us in the "time of the cause," which comes after.)[39] For Yangönpa, it seems that enlightenment was a possibility the ins and outs of which are worth considering and knowing about. Misconceptions about spiritual accomplishment at the more advanced stages should therefore be cleared up for the reader.

In comparison with other retreat texts, Yangönpa's presentation can be seen as quite bullish, reflecting an understanding of the horizon of possibility for meditators that later authors would not share. Retreat texts written in the latter centuries express more modest conceptions of the individual's potential for spiritual accomplishment, and a correspondingly increased association between that potential and their positionality in the dimension of time. While Yangönpa's retreat manual ends with the loftiest possible discussion of liberation, creating a sense of unchecked possibility, Lekshé Drayang's circa sixteenth-century text closes with instructions for techniques for recognizing and removing obstacles to spiritual progress, which leaves the reader with a sense of a definite ceiling to their liberatory prospects. In the place of Yangönpa's description of the process of buddhahood, Lekshé Drayang details how a person might develop an *entirely wrong* sense of their meditative accomplishments. This is "the obstruction of becoming haughty on account of attaining some very modest good qualities, and pursuing the eight worldly concerns," described in Lekshé Drayang's final chapter as follows:

> After you have completed just a few years of good meditation, it may come about that your Dharma siblings and your lama praise you. Or maybe once a little bit of experiential realization has arisen, you are able to impart a good introduction [to the nature of reality], giving a person of lesser intelligence who has praised you some sense of bliss, clarity, and nonconceptuality. Perhaps your dreams become clear, or extrasensory perception begins to appear. Perhaps a patron requests a Dharma teaching from you and generates some merit for themselves by venerating you. On account of any of those things you begin to be proud and arrogant. You brag and have an elevated self-regard. You start disputes over being at the front of the line or about the height of your seat. You become vain and ostentatious. Some, out of a desire for more people requesting Dharma teachings from them and more disciples, will summon patrons and monks to them through various means. They will start giving empowerments, Dharma teachings, and esoteric instructions in exchange for material things. Or there are those who will talk of extrasensory perception and give prophecies, who will through various means make others think they are liberated. Some become so haughty on account of their experience that, paying no mind to the kindness showed in the past by the lama and the stewards of the Dharma, they think they have now obtained their own mandate for bestowing empowerments and Dharma, thinking they are allowed to do things even without the permission of the lama and the stewards of the Dharma. In that way one behaves as if one has but little faith in the lama, thinking, "In terms of good qualities, I myself am equal to the stewards of the Dharma and so on, my peers, and the past masters," and acts contemptuously toward their equals.
>
> Through any of those avenues, one can squander the religious practice that one has done. It's like mixing medicine with poison.

Lekshé Drayang continues, describing how a person who has fallen into such a state cannot recognize their own faults, and any steps their lama might take to provide a corrective will produce only more ill feeling. This is a very difficult situation to reverse. The method for removing this obstacle involves reconciling oneself with the lama's teachings, engaging in rigorous self-examination, actively visualizing oneself as below all other sentient beings, and abandoning thoughts relating to the eight worldly concerns.[40]

Earlier in the text, the question of a meditator's prospects for spiritual gain had been put in an explicitly historical framework. In his discussion of the proper locations for a retreat, Lekshé Drayang writes, "In general, if you attain mastery over *tummo*, you can meditate among the white snows without feeling any cold. If you attain mastery in illusory body, you can meditate in forests without being frightened. If you develop the ability of luminosity, you can meditate on a white rocky mountain without any relations or associates. As for beginners, they should meditate at the feet of their lamas." At this point a note is inserted in the text: "In the time before 'realization of retention' is manifested, a person is a beginner (*las dang po pa*). After it has manifested, a person has achieved stability (*brtan pa thob pa*). But these days, everyone—all the great meditators, the old and the young—are only beginners. There won't be any who have achieved stability."[41] There is no indication whether this note originated with Lekshé Drayang or with a later editor of the text, but the point it expresses could not be more certain: we live in a benighted moment of human history, on account of which our prospects for spiritual accomplishment are definitively curtailed. Because we are confined to the status of mere beginners, meditatively speaking, there may be no point in wasting precious paper or ink discussing what higher accomplishment looks like.

In the *Words on the Mountain Dharma* as a whole, Lekshé Drayang summarily cuts off conversation about genuine higher meditative accomplishment but writes at length about those who wrongheadedly believe they have achieved such a thing. The manual does not leave a reader much space to think or feel very positively about their spiritual prospects. Anyone who does so is likely to be misrecognizing their status, which is to show a grave disrespect to one's lama and the past masters of the tradition, not to mention potentially squandering all of one's prior religious efforts. If Lekshé Drayang believes that meditators of his and subsequent generations can rightfully aspire to join the elevated ranks of their forbears, his *Words on the Mountain Dharma* gives no indication. A retreatant's development has become very much delimited by their place in time. Indeed, Lekshé Drayang prefaces his manual by stating, "These days practicing the path to liberation is important. It is also difficult to understand." These facts prompt him to give the instructions to follow.[42]

The most explicit statement about a retreatant's place in historical time and the limitations of their spiritual prospects comes from Jamgön Kongtrül's late-nineteenth-century charter for the Tsadra retreat center. This text provides instruction specifically for communal retreat, and therefore has not been considered in this study. But on account of this text's enormous importance to long-term meditative retreat as practiced in global Tibetan Buddhism today, it figures prominently in chapter 7 and warrants some attention here. In the closing pages of the charter, Jamgön Kongtrül writes (as translated by Ngawang Zangpo, who also supplies the brackets), "These days, we can't really expect to achieve accomplishment or even the beginnings of [the signs of] heat. We're just ordinary individuals who must practice [toward the realization of] enlightenment in a simple manner."[43] The "signs of heat" (*drod rtags*) are an early marker of progress toward realization of emptiness, and Jamgön Kongtrül portrays them as extremely unlikely to occur. For Chegompa, both ordinary and extraordinary *siddhi*s were to be regarded as expected outcomes of the retreat endeavor. Seven hundred years later, Jamgön Kongtrül would explicitly deny the possibility of those accomplishments. This divergence is indicative of the larger reconceptualization of spiritual accomplishment and of the retreat endeavor that Jamgön Kongtrül was involved with, to be addressed in detail in the final chapter of this study.

Reviewing what prescriptive texts for individual long-term retreat have had to say about navigating vertical religious relationships has revealed the ideal forms of those relationships, the challenges that stand in the way of manifesting those ideal forms, and the mechanisms for reestablishing them once lost. These considerations provide some new perspectives on the workings of spiritual lineages in Tibetan Buddhism. Again we see the imaginal self's ability to alter surrounding circumstances, including the spiritual status of the guru from whom transmission is received.

Throughout the history of the Tibetan ascetic tradition it has been commonplace for authors of prescriptions for retreat to refer to their existing in a benighted epoch, such as the Third Karmapa's calling himself as an "end-of-time yogi" and the many scattered references to our living in a "degenerate age." Although this rhetoric and the humility it expresses have remained consistent throughout the history of the Tibetan eremitic tradition, we can nevertheless track the development of a sense of historical consciousness through an ever-increasing sense of a meditator's separation from the prospect of higher spiritual accomplishment. Chegom Sherap Dorjé asserted that one's retreat practice was "certain" to produce superhuman abilities; around the same time, Yangönpa found it necessary to equip his reader with an understanding of what happens as one reaches the highest possible levels of meditative accomplishment. Karma Chakmé would also write at length about high-level meditative experiences, while explicitly abjuring the possibility of his own attainment thereof. Later authors would forego even addressing these kinds of accomplishments, ascribing to everyone the status of a mere beginner on the contemplative path, more likely to have a false than a duly earned sense of accomplishment. These assertions about the rarity, if not the impossibility, of achieving enlightenment in one's current age must be considered alongside statements highlighted in the previous chapters about the impossibility of enacting the kind of asceticism performed by the earlier *siddha*s of the tradition, and the need, therefore, to adjust expectations for ascetic practice in the present historical moment. Whether we cannot aspire to enlightenment because we cannot practice the correct asceticism or vice versa is not clear. But these claims all fit together as part of a larger pattern in which, animated by an overriding attitude of deferential reverence, over the long course of the Tibetan ascetic tradition, a meditator's spiritual horizons have increasingly been thought of as inflected by their place in history and curtailed. The sense of position in history is established with respect to a horizon of possibility that is always in the process of receding, the reality of this being manifested through diminished expectations for individual ascetic comportment in the present. The ideal of enlightenment remains the same, but the ascetic's relationship to it is differently imagined, newly affixing the meditator in the dimension of time. As we have seen across the past five chapters, the gradual growth of thinking about the meditator as a being in time, having ever more limited realizational potential, is the most central, organizing development in the history of the Tibetan ascetic self, tying together many other observable changes over eight centuries of eremitic practice in the Himalaya.

CHAPTER 7

THE TIBETAN ASCETIC SELF IN TIME

The expectation that a long-term meditative retreat should last for three years and three months is recognized almost universally by observers of Tibetan Buddhism today. There are sundry cloisters attached to monasteries in Tibet where communal tantric retreats of this length are being undertaken. The practice has continued among the Tibetan exile community living in Bhutan, India, and Nepal. As Tibetan Buddhism has spread to other parts of the world, the three-year, three-month communal retreat has been taken up by converts with non-Himalayan ethnic and linguistic backgrounds living in places far from the tradition's origin. The first such retreat outside of Asia took place in a lightly adapted chateau in Burgundy between 1976 and 1979. Since that time, at least eight other Buddhist centers in France have also held communal tantric retreats lasting a minimum of three years and three months. The practice has spread to other places in Europe, the United States, Canada, Australia, and elsewhere. These institutions represent the traditional Tibetan sects, but also Shambhala and multi- and nonsectarian affiliations.

Variations on the standard model have also been created. Gampo Abbey in Nova Scotia has since 1990 hosted seven different groups of meditators, totaling sixty-four individuals, who have completed three-year, three-month retreats on a one-year-in, one-year-out schedule, the endeavor therefore taking more than five years from start to finish, with two separate groups on overlapping timelines. Some of these institutions offer the opportunity to follow along with the curriculum while living on the outside: individuals receive the tantric empowerments and instructions along with the retreatants via videoconference, and do their best to keep up with the prescribed amount of practice while carrying on with their careers and family life. It has also become increasingly normative over the last few decades for converts to Tibetan Buddhism to commit to completing a three-year, three-month retreat in a series of installments—one month, week, day, or hour of meditation at a time.[1] These periods of meditation may be done at a retreat center, a local Buddhist temple, or even one's own home.

The growing popularity of these different options—often called "hybrid," "parallel," or "virtual" retreats—indicates just how central a position the three-year, three-month retreat occupies in the way practitioners of present-day Tibetan Buddhism think about meditation: the ideal has become so normative that it has spawned alternative means of adhering to it. Put differently, the category of the three-year, three-month retreat itself has become a locus of elaboration. This chapter will leave aside the question of how these developments may relate to the present-day popular and academic trend of thinking about meditation instrumentally, as something to be quantified and calculated, as was discussed in the introduction. Instead we will look backward, to better understand how these developments relate to the history of retreat practice and the long evolution of the Tibetan ascetic self.

The central question is how this way of thinking about how long a retreat should last has come to be so ubiquitous across the Tibetan Buddhist world. To more fully understand the history of the three-year, three-month retreat, we will use the prescriptive literature for individual long-term retreat, supported by evidence from other kinds of sources like hagiography and historical chronicles, to track the ideal over time, along with a more general expectation of performing some undertaking for a period of three years that has historically had great currency in Tibet and neighboring cultures. From a present in which the ideal of three years and three months is pervasive, it is clear that the most important development bringing the tradition to this point was the communal retreat established in 1860 by the great polysectarian master Jamgön Kongtrül. This formulation provided the blueprint now followed, to varying degrees of exactitude, by retreat communities all over the world. Understanding Kongtrül's role in these developments requires departing from an exclusive focus on individual retreat to consider his particular version of communal retreat. Individual and communal forms of retreat can generally be seen as distinct long-standing phenomena with separate histories. This chapter will show that Kongtrül's communal retreat served as a culmination of developments that had been taking place in prior centuries of the individual retreat tradition, and that it concretized a model that would affect expectations for both communal and individual retreat ever after. To this end, the latter half will address how the communal retreat established by Kongtrül relates to how issues of place, interpersonal relations, food, potential causes of peril, and the spiritual lineage have historically factored into individual long-term retreat practice. Tracking the continuities and differences between individual retreat as traditionally practiced and Kongtrül's and by extension today's version of communal retreat clearly shows that we have entered a new phase in relation to the central, organizing question in the history of the Tibetan ascetic self: how the meditator exists in relation to the dimension of time.

———

The Tibetan term originally used to refer to this length of time is *lo gsum phyogs gsum* (pronounced "lo-soom, chok-soom"), meaning three years and three of something referred to as a *phyogs* ("chok"). Tibetans of recent decades have understood *lo gsum phyogs gsum* to mean three years and three fortnights; three years and three months; three years, three months, three weeks, and three days; or three years, three months, three days, and "the time of three meals."[2] These variations result from different interpretations of what is indicated by the word *phyogs*, which has a variety of meanings in both colloquial and literary Tibetan. One of its more technical uses is as a translation of the Sanskrit *vakṣa*, meaning "growth," which refers to one half of a lunar month, *vakṣa* being related to the English "wax."[3] In a sense the original and most technically correct definition of the length of time indicated by *lo gsum phyogs gsum* is three years and three fortnights. But over the many centuries that have passed since the association between the Sanskrit and Tibetan terms was made, variant understandings of "three *phyogs*" have come into circulation. These days when speaking of retreat practice, the term most often used is *lo gsum zla gsum* ("lo-soom, da-soom"), which means three years and three months. In the course of this chapter there will be some slippage between my references to an ideal of retreat lasting three years and three fortnights and an ideal of it lasting three years and three months, as there has long been significant overlap between or muddling of the two notions, especially outside of technical contexts. We are in fact talking about retreats that last for a *minimum* of three years and three fortnights or months: because of the expectation that an endeavor of such importance should begin and end on particularly auspicious days (such as a holiday associated with a major event in the life of Śākyamuni Buddha, or at the very least a full moon), a retreat will typically last a few weeks or months longer than the minimum prescribed time.

The primary explanation for how the ideal of practicing for a period of three years and three fortnights was established comes from the *Kālacakra*—"wheel of time"—*Tantra*, which dates from the early decades of the eleventh century.[4] This hugely influential scripture attempts to explain the relationships between the universe, the individual, and time, which are understood to be interconnected through a variety of micro- and macrocosmic relations. One way the individual is connected to both the universe and the dimension of time is through the act of respiration. To present a simplified account, the *Kālacakra Tantra* posits that one thirty-second part of each breath a person takes (or one out of every thirty-two breaths; understandings of this vary) carries the potential to be transformed into the "[psychophysical] wind of wisdom" (*jñānavāyu, ye shes kyi rlung*). The text also posits that we live in a cosmological age when a full human lifespan is 100 years. In this view, the minimum amount of time necessary to generate the amount of "wisdom wind" requisite for spiritual liberation is one thirty-second of 100 lunar years, which is 1,125 days—or three lunar years and forty-five days. (These matters have intricate connections to the *Kālacakra*'s highly detailed models of embryology, the human body, the universe's origins, structure, and eschatology, the movement of celestial bodies, language, the pantheon of divinities, and other important things beyond our interest here.) Over time, a slight distortion has set in owing to the fact that the original calculations are based on a lunar year of 360 days (twelve months of thirty days each), while latter-day observers are more likely to think in terms of solar years of 365 days. For our purposes, it suffices to note that the norm of the three-year, three-fortnight retreat derives from an understanding of the meditating self as existing in a very specific way in relation both to a particular conception of how enlightenment is achieved and to the dimension of time itself. The *Kālacakra Tantra*'s articulation of the standard of meditating for three years and three fortnights has been the most influential, but it was not the only one: elements of this same calculation can also be found in materials surrounding the *Hevajra* and other tantric texts.[5]

This explanation based on technical calculations deriving from tantric scripture has had a degree of currency throughout the entire history of Tibetan meditative practice. Another significant influence was the widespread Tibetan cultural notion of taking on an endeavor, such as an ascetic trial, for a period of three years. The *Blue Annals*, the encyclopedic Tibetan Buddhist history compiled by Gö Lotsawa Zhönnu Pel (1392–1481) in the 1470s, contains two references to a group or an individual meditating specifically for a period of three years and three fortnights, both of which are about members of the Jonang sect practicing the Kālacakra. Meanwhile the text contains dozens of references to people performing a certain practice, undergoing an ascetic trial, or maintaining a religious vow for a period of "three years," or a multiple thereof. The Kagyu-centric history by Pawo Tsuklak Trengwa (1504–1564/66), the *Scholar's Feast*, dating from about a hundred years later, contains no reference to anyone's meditating for three years and three fortnights or three years and three months.

It does, however, contain many mentions of individuals doing a wide of range of activities for periods of "three years."[6] Similarly, the hagiographic literature depicting eminent Kagyupas of the fifteenth and sixteenth centuries makes frequent mention of taking on meditative trials for a period of "three years," while almost never mentioning the categories of three years and three fortnights or three years and three months.[7]

An important caveat, in recognition of the limitations of the evidence, is that some of these references to "three years" could in fact pertain to periods of time lasting three years and three fortnights or months, the author not seeing fit to specify so precisely *lo gsum phyogs gsum* or *lo gsum zla gsum*, which could seem unnecessary or tedious. It is also possible that some of these literary references to "three years" were meant to express something less precise, "a few years," as in the phrase, common in eastern Tibetan dialects, *tshig gsum*—literally "three words," but meaning "a few words." But to my knowledge there is no Tibetan literary convention of using "three years" to mean "a few years."

The preponderance of references to ascetic undertakings of "three years" coming from Tibetan sources far from one another in both space and time suggests that this category has long had its own legitimacy. Orgyen Lingpa's (b. ca. 1323) *Testimonial Record on Kings* tells of meditators' practicing for a period of "three years" in the famous caves at Chimpu and elsewhere during the time of King Trisong Detsen (742–797/804) and Padmasambhava.[8] The act of sequestration for three years has been posited by Tibetans as part of their very origin story: the Tibetan royal chronicle known as the *Clear Mirror*, dating from 1368, tells of how the bodhisattva-monkey who united with the rock ogress—their descendants would become the people of Tibet—withdrew into a forest for "three years" with his family. There were six children at the beginning of this period and five hundred at its end.[9] Other examples from throughout Tibetan history and mythology, both Buddhist and Bönpo, abound.[10]

Also pertinent here is the ample evidence that Tibetans conceived of activities not at all connected to meditation or asceticism in terms of three-year periods. The historical record shows leadership positions being taken on for periods of three years, rituals being performed on three-year cycles, and individuals being expelled from a monastic community for three years, as punishment for an infraction.[11] In eastern Tibet in recent years, there has been a movement toward taking a vow to abstain from meat eating for a period of three years.[12] Significantly, this span of time also played an organizing role in the early centuries of Chan Buddhist practice in China. From the early centuries of religious Daoism into the present, certain ascetic endeavors—such as remaining in contemplation, performing a ritual, serving a master, abstaining from grain, or ingesting certain substances—have been undertaken for periods of three years.[13] There are examples from the religious traditions of South Asia as well.[14]

This tendency to think about an undertaking in terms of a three-year period may be connected to the use of a twelve-year calendrical cycle. Whatever its origins, in Tibet and neighboring cultures and religious formations there has long been a practice of thinking about human endeavors in terms of three-year periods. This has entered into and affected Tibet's culture of eremitism, such that at any moment in the tradition, the expectation of undertaking a retreat of three years or three years and three fortnights or months is probably just as much attributable to this general expectation as to the more technical explanation deriving from late Buddhist tantras. The two expectations—one coming from scriptural mandate, one coming from popular pan-Asian cultural practice—most likely had a complementary relationship over many centuries.

Given today's near-universal expectation that a retreat should last three years and months, along with the fact that this ideal derives from tantric scripture, it is surprising how minor a role it played in organizing individual retreat practice historically, as evidenced by the prescriptive literature. The expectation of practicing for a period of "three years" is only slightly more visible in this body of texts. Both categories seem to have gradually gained in currency until the nineteenth century. The writings of Yangönpa provide an example of this conspicuous absence early in the tradition. In the *Secret Explanation of the Vajra Body* (one of the three texts making up the "Mountain Dharma Trilogy"), Yangönpa discusses the theory of human ontology given in the *Kālacakra Tantra*, showing that essential parts of this explanation are also to be found in earlier canonical texts, such as the *Net of Magical Manifestations of Mañjuśrī*, the *Guhyasamāja Tantra*, and the *Prophetic Declaration of Intention*. He includes the pivotal detail that the "wisdom wind" flows for a total of three (lunar) years and one and a half months in the span of a hundred years of human life.[15] Although Yangönpa is clearly fully informed of these calculations, nowhere in the *Secret Explanation of the Vajra Body,* the *Blazing Jewel,* or the *Great Appendix* is there any suggestion that an ideal of three years and three fortnights or months (or even simply three years) should determine the length of a meditative retreat. As mentioned in chapter 1, in other contexts Yangönpa is recorded to have suggested an ideal of three, six, or nine years; whether this derives from to the kind of calculation given in the *Kālacakra Tantra* or from a more general cultural expectation is unclear. But the *Blazing Jewel* and the *Great Appendix* remain silent on this point.

In his seventeenth-century *Garland of Critical Points for the Precious Mountain Dharma*, Lhatsün Namkha Jikmé mentions the ideal of doing advanced tantric ascetic trials like the Practice of the Observance or the Public Practice for a period of "six months or three years," without suggesting anywhere that an individual meditative retreat should last that length of time. As mentioned in chapter 6, while relating his own history of ascetic practice in the 1815 *Refined Honey,* Mipam Püntsok Sherap mentions doing the Practice of the Observance for three years, as well as having completed a retreat of "three years" at each of Tibet's three holiest yogic destinations. The text itself was written while Mipam Püntsok Sherap was in the midst of "three years of strict seclusion."[16]

Of all the prescriptive texts for individual long-term retreat examined for this study, the only one to explicitly mention the ideal of practicing for a period of three years and three fortnights or months is Karma Chakmé's *Direct Advice on Retreat,* dating from 1665. The handbook makes numerous references to the category of *lo gsum phyogs gsum.* Karma Chakmé provides instruction on how to lead a disciple who has vowed to complete a three-year, three-fortnight retreat; having done so will earn that individual the title of "lama," a norm that predominates in the Tibetan Buddhist world to this day.[17] In this way Karma Chakmé's handbook clearly reflects an ascetic culture where the category of *lo gsum phyogs gsum* was recognized and used in organizing some people's contemplative activity. But there is no evidence that the handbook was formulated specifically for individuals doing retreats of three years or three years and three fortnights or months in duration. Nor is there such evidence for any other prescriptive text for individual retreat examined here.

Nowhere in the prescriptive literature for individual retreat used in this study is the length of the retreat subject to discussion or further elaboration. This is surprising, giving how foundational a concern this would seem to be (at least to a modern American observer like myself). The closest thing is Karma Chakmé telling his reader in the handbook's integral sixteenth chapter that vowing from the outset to do a long retreat will expose a person to demonic obstacles. Instead, it is better to plan on a shorter retreat and then extend it. Karma Chakmé was residing at the time in what he had vowed to be a permanent, lifelong retreat.[18]

Considering both the prescriptive literature for individual long-term retreat and the hagiographic and historical sources cited above, it seems that an ideal of undertaking an ascetic trial for a period of three years has been recognized throughout the entire history of eremitic practice in Tibet, over time coming to play an increasingly important role in dictating the form that individual retreat practice would take.[19] The ideal of three years and three fortnights or months seems to have had comparatively less impact. Until the nineteenth century, the practice of individual long-term retreat and the expectation that a meditative undertaking should last either three years or three years and three fortnights or months were on trajectories of gradual and partial convergence. The incremental merging of these expectations took place as an attitude of lived deferential reverence increasingly affected diverse aspects of the ascetic endeavor, such as the retreatant's relationships to place, other people, food, and the possibility of enlightenment itself. I suggest that as the meditator was conceived of as existing an unbridgeable distance away from both the forbears of the tradition and the possibility of enlightenment, as manifested through their enacting what were characterized as less ideal forms of ascetic abiding, the retreat endeavor itself slowly came to be understood in a different way. The gradual confluence of retreat practice and the ideal temporal duration ultimately served to formalize an understanding of the ascetic's place in the dimension of time. Although the moment when these two trajectories become inextricably entwined is clear in hindsight, during Kongtrül's time it merely represented one more exegete's attempt to provide solutions to the challenges of retreat, as so many of his forbears had done.

The remainder of this chapter considers the career of Jamgön Kongtrül Lodrö Tayé; how his communal retreat program came to be an integral part of globalized Tibetan Buddhism in 150 years' time; the details of this retreat program; and how this model of retreat relates to the prior history of individual retreat. Kongtrül is sometimes credited with having invented the very practice of the three-year, three-fortnight communal retreat. This is a misapprehension, given that such a communal retreat was being practiced during Kongtrül's own lifetime prior to the establishment of his retreat center, and had been practiced in earlier times by other Tibetan Buddhists, including Jonangpas many centuries earlier.[20] That he is believed to have invented this practice speaks to the outsized importance of his formulation of it within Tibetan Buddhism today. Kongtrül's communal retreat provides resolution to many of the persistent concerns whose perpetual renegotiation had defined the Tibetan ascetic self over centuries of individual retreat practice, and its success effected a major shift in thinking about meditation in Tibetan Buddhism, such that individual retreat would perhaps never be the same again. The present convention of piecing together a three-year, three-month retreat, one day at a time over a span of many years, represents a late point in a genealogy that can be traced backward into the venerable depths of the individual retreat tradition, running directly through Kongtrül.

A leader of the Rimé (*ris med*), a non- or polysectarian movement, Kongtrül revived a number of Tibetan Buddhist practice lineages that were on the brink of extinction. He was an incredible polymath: his *Collected Works* total more than ninety volumes (many essentially reprinting and systematizing the compositions of earlier masters). Kongtrül's spiritual charisma was so great that he was found to have more than five reincarnations.[21] Early in his career he received a transmission for Karma Chakmé's *Direct Advice on Retreat* from the fifth in the Karma Chakmé reincarnation lineage. The first Karma Chakmé would be one of the most prominent figures in Kongtrül's visionary life: he had numerous dream visions of Karma Chakmé, believed that he had been his disciple in a past life, and wrote of being inspired by his combining of the Kagyu and Nyingma traditions. Karma Ngedön Tenkyé, the Retreatant of Mendong, cited many times in this study, may have studied under Kongtrül.[22]

Jamgön Kongtrül established and oversaw a retreat community in Kham, known as Künzang Dechen Ösel Ling or Tsadra Rinchen Drak. Between the hermitage's formal opening in 1860 and Kongtrül's death in 1899, he oversaw nine three-year, three-fortnight retreats there, exclusively for men.[23] This specific form of retreat was brought out to the rest of the world by Kalu Rinpoché (1905–1989), who is sometimes considered to have been one of Kongtrül's reincarnations. Having done a three-year, three-fortnight retreat there as a teenager, Kalu Rinpoché took over as Tsadra's retreat master around 1940. After going into exile in 1955, he established a retreat center in Bhutan and three more in India. In the decades to follow, he would establish Dashang Kagyu Ling in France, where the first three-year, three-month retreat in the West was held, and a new Künzang Dechen Ösel Ling in British Columbia, Canada. By Alex Gardner's counting, over time Kalu Rinpoché created more than twenty centers in the West for long-term retreat or related teaching activity, including in Argentina, Brazil, Italy, Spain, Hawaii, and upstate New York. Thanks in large part to Kalu Rinpoché's decades of work, Kongtrül's version of retreat is now "the standard" in Kagyu and Nyingma institutions in Tibetan communities and throughout the entire Euro-American Tibetan Buddhist world.[24]

Our foremost source for understanding Kongtrül's version of retreat is the sixty-two-folio-side charter he composed in 1876—sixteen years after the start of the first retreat—titled *Guidelines for the Conduct of the Meditators at Künzang Dechen Ösel Ling, the Upper Hermitage of Pelpung, Clarifying What Is to Be Accepted and Rejected: The Source of Well-Being*. An English translation of this text, rendered as *Jamgon Kongtrul's Retreat Manual*, was published by Snow Lion in 1994. A French translation based on the English has been available since 1997. It is somewhat ironic that Kongtrül's version of retreat, which was meant to be instituted in one specific location at a particular moment in time, would provide the blueprint for retreat practice across today's entire Tibetan Buddhist world, including in places Kongtrül could never have dreamed of. Although these communities have modified Kongtrül's example to suit their respective contexts, it constitutes a norm off of which adaptations are made.

We now turn to consider the specific form of retreat instituted by Kongtrül, with an eye toward how it problematizes or circumvents what have traditionally been key concerns in the practice of individual long-term meditative retreat. This will give a sense of how Kongtrül's version relates to various trajectories in the history of the Tibetan ascetic self, and how understandings of retreat practice would be forever transformed due to his influence.

The available records allow us to trace in great detail the long process by which the location for the retreat, Künzang Dechen Ösel Ling—known more commonly as Tsadra, which references the site's equivalency to the great holy mountain of Tsari in central Tibet, itself associated with the powerful Devikoṭa in India—was discovered, ritually opened, and inscribed with significance. This is a potent example of how retreat provided an avenue for the millennium-long project of taming and mapping the Tibetan landscape, as discussed in chapter 2. The location is several hours' walk from Pelpung, the Kagyu monastery with which Kongtrül was affiliated, and the community with whom he had an uneasy relationship, largely owing to his multisectarian activities. Kongtrül had first meditated at the site between 1842 and 1846, among the ruins of a defunct hermitage. Later he requested the treasure revealer Chokgyur Dechen Lingpa (1829–1870) to write a gazetteer of sacred places in Kham, including a discussion of the wonders of this location. Chokgyur Lingpa revealed a treasure text fulfilling this purpose in 1857, unearthing it from a cliff at what would become Tsadra. *A Brief Inventory of the Great Sites of Tibet Composed by Padmasambhava, the Wise One of Oḍḍiyāna* explicitly and self-consciously maps eastern Tibet as part of the broader Tibetan landscape, including a history and a description of what would be the location of Kongtrül's retreat.[25] Then, on the tenth day of the monkey month of the sheep year of 1859, Chokgyur Lingpa unearthed from a cave at Tsadra a brief treasure text, the *Gazetteer of the Supreme Site of Enlightened Mind, Tsadra Rinchen Drak*. In the voice of Padmasambhava, it discusses features of the place and offers prophecies about the religious institution that would be established there. Kongtrül would later portray this event as marking the official "opening" (*'byed*) of Tsadra. The *Gazetteer* asserts that every duodecennial sheep year, and in particular the monkey month, will be the most empowered time at this location, as various supernatural beings descend upon the place at such times.[26]

Kongtrül expanded on the material revealed by Chokgyur Lingpa in his own 1864 text, *Music from the Ocean of the Mind: An Account of Devikoṭa Tsadra Rinchen Drak, the Supreme Abode of Enlightened Mind*. This sixty-eight-folio-side text (available in English translation thanks to Ngawang Zangpo, born Hugh Thompson, a disciple of Kalu Rinpoché who participated in the first three-year, three-month retreat in Burgundy) is a remarkable example of guidebook literature, making as comprehensive an argument for the sanctity of the place as I can imagine. In the course of its eight chapters, the text addresses the cosmological mechanisms that enable sacred places to exist; the different schemes for organizing the Tibetan landscape, based on the sacred places of tantric Buddhism; and the proof of the existence of such sacred places, quoted from authoritative sources. Its fourth chapter addresses Tsadra in particular, locating it within the information Kongtrül has already laid out, discussing its name and how its specific features appear to different kinds of people. The next three chapters respectively tell the story of how Tsadra came to be imbued with such sacredness over many successive generations of enlightened activity, and the ritual and visionary activity needed to "open" the site; provide another description of the locale's features, attuned to how a pilgrim will interact with them; and give full instructions on how to do pilgrimage there. The eighth and final chapter gives the payoff to all of this, in the form of grand promises about the amazing benefits of a pilgrimage to Tsadra. In composing this text, Kongtrül connected every possible dot, such that specific activities performed at the site by a nineteenth-century pilgrim link them to layer upon layer of Buddhist and world history through a landscape supersaturated with meaning. Kongtrül's strategy for establishing the holiness of Tsadra involves regularly drawing connections to Tsari and Devikoṭa, thereby tapping into the charisma of those older and better-established destinations. To make the strongest possible case, Kongtrül creates a mutually strengthening network of people, places, texts, and events by telling a history of the visionary activity tied to the locale, carried out both by members of his own circle in recent decades and by deities and great luminaries living many centuries earlier.

Kongtrül's argument for the potency of this location deploys both the geomantic and reverential modes of geospatial awareness. He states that Tsadra possesses every positive geomantic feature, according to both the Indian and the Chinese systems. The mountain behind it resembles a seated meditator and the lower meadow its crossed legs. The ground to the west slopes upward. It features forests, high areas, and hollows, conducive to different kinds of meditative practice. Dozens of past masters prophesized, visited, and left a presence in the place; individuals of clearer vision can see that they in fact continue to reside there. Kongtrül draws upon the logics of other modes of geospatial awareness—cosmological, Buddhological, cartographic—as well.

In 1871, in the twelfth year after the "opening" of Künzang Dechen Ösel Ling, a written proclamation was circulated throughout Kham, announcing an upcoming time of special pilgrimage to the site in the monkey month of the sheep year. The letter retells part of the history of the location, arguing for its power, and declares that normally at Tsadra the effect of any virtuous act is multiplied one hundred thousand times. But during this particularly holy month, when all the deities of Devikoṭa would descend upon the place, its transformative power would be increased dramatically: a single circumambulation of the outer walking path surrounding Tsadra would be equal to the merit gained by reciting Padmasambhava's mantra seven hundred million times. Three circumambulations would equal a full pilgrimage around Tsari itself. Kongtrül's own records show that the event was well attended. Similar letters were sent out concerning the special times of pilgrimage in 1883 and 1895.[27] Through these diverse means—visionary, expository, ritualistic—the significance of the location was thoroughly proclaimed and registered. It was then affirmed by those who came to reap its fruits via pilgrimage.

Kongtrül's 1876 charter for the practice of communal retreat in this location, *Guidelines for the Conduct of the Meditators at Künzang Dechen Ösel Ling*, makes no reference to the history of the place or the virtues of practicing there. Kongtrül merely provides the name of the retreat center in the text's colophon, refraining even from the expected listing of praiseful adjectives.[28] It seems that for the individual arriving at Tsadra to meditate, the questions of where to do a retreat and why had already been definitively answered. The modes of geospatial awareness that had for so long contoured the Tibetan ascetic tradition's treatment of space still had relevance, as shown in Kongtrül's *Music from the Ocean of the Mind,* but the extent to which any individual practitioner had to engage with them was greatly diminished. What had been a critical calculation for an ascetic doing a retreat on an individual basis would not be relevant to a meditator doing a communal retreat at an established location.

As described by the charter, the closed structure of the Tsadra retreat cloister protected meditators from outside influences, both environmental and interpersonal. This complex included the retreatants' individual rooms, a kitchen, some storerooms, and a series of temples, all of which opened onto a central courtyard. The expectation was that from the moment the *mtshams tho* or retreat signboard was put up until it was taken down three years and some months later, none but the retreatants, their guru, the small support staff, and a cadre of temporary ritual helpers would set foot inside the physical space of the retreat. The retreatants were expected not to see the faces of or have their own faces seen by anyone on the outside. They might write a short, practical letter to someone outside only if doing so was unavoidable.[29]

The retreatants would remain in their respective cells for the four main daily practice sessions, and to sleep at night. Their activities would be tightly regulated, it being forbidden to do anything other than meditate during the appointed times. The beginning and end of each individual practice session would be signaled by the ringing of a communal gong. Practitioners would also assemble in the temple twice daily to perform rituals as a group.

The behavior of all the meditators was regulated by the dictates of the Vinaya, it being expected that they were all celibate monks. The endeavors of long-term retreat and monasticism now being formally aligned in this way, an ambiguous issue throughout most of the history of the individual retreat tradition was definitively resolved. All the meditators would be constituted as Dharma siblings training under the same guru, the vajra master, who would come and go from the retreat precincts as duty compelled. The vajra master's responsibilities included giving the necessary empowerments, reading transmissions, and instructions for all the tantric traditions to be learned and practiced. The vajra master was also responsible for ensuring that all the participants were fully trained in the proper ways of doing recitations, making offerings, playing the musical instruments, and singing.[30] Having continued access to the vajra master during the retreat relieves much of the pressure that had earlier characterized the preretreat training period.

In this model of retreat the meditators are allowed to speak to one another during the times between the daily sessions, although Kongtrül cautions against becoming overly friendly, which is likely to end in discord.[31] Kongtrül's charter lays out clear rules for how the retreatants should interact, including what punishments the vajra master should mete out when infractions occur. In the event of a verbal altercation, the instigator may be forced to do one hundred prostrations; the other involved party should do fifty. A physical altercation will lead to canings and fines, in the form of measures of dry tea leaves paid to the community. Leaving one's room during a meditation session is punishable with twenty-five prostrations.[32] The text states expectations for faithfully obeying the vajra master; failure to do so will lead to illness among the retreatants. The forefathers of the Kagyu—especially Naropa and Milarepa—are said to provide the ultimate guides for how to follow the guru during the retreat.[33]

The ecosystem of the retreat was designed based on clear divisions of both spiritual and worldly labor. To accomplish spiritual labor in the absence of the vajra master, the retreatants with better voices would take turns leading the communal recitations.[34] One of them would be appointed chant leader, while others would play the necessary instruments during communal prayer sessions. Clear guidelines are given for how all the members of the group are to participate equally in tasks like making ritual cakes and preparing offerings.

Meanwhile, in parallel to the activities of the four people following the main retreat (expanded to around two dozen after the 1940s), one practitioner would remain in a separate temple doing activities dedicated to the protector deities. This position was referred to as the "meditator of the protector [deity] temple" (*mgon khang sgrub pa po*). Over the three years and three fortnights, this person would follow their own course of ritual practice, supplicating those deities with many hundreds of thousands of mantra recitations, adhering to a daily, monthly, and annual schedule. (Ngawang Zangpo supplies the detail that this role was usually filled by someone who had already completed the standard retreat.[35]) The central deity enshrined in the protector deity temple was a six-armed form of Mahākāla associated with the Shangpa Kagyu. The inhabitant of the protector deity temple would join the rest of the group for certain rituals occurring on monthly or annual cycles. Twice a year the meditator of the protector deity temple would be compelled to leave the confines of the retreat. One occasion was in order to propitiate the local *nāga*s, following a script composed by the first Karma Chakmé, to ensure good weather and prevent disease. The other was to mark the anniversary of Chokgyur Lingpa's 1859 unearthing of the *Gazetteer* treasure and the "opening" of Tsadra. This would entail performing extensive rituals in six caves in the area, including the one in which the *Gazetteer* was found. This annual observance would serve to keep alive the story of the site's discovery and opening, so important to authenticating the holiness of the place. The meditator of the protector deity temple would be assisted in both endeavors by another practitioner residing within the retreat who was devoted to long-life practices (referred to as the *zhabs brtan mtshams pa*). Little is said in the charter about this individual, who may have been a long-term resident of the retreat center. It may be that this individual's ritual activities were devoted to the preservation of Kongtrül's own life.[36]

On a more worldly plane, a small staff would support the meditators throughout the duration of the retreat. The most essential position was that of the cook-attendant (referred to in the text as *sgrub gnyer* or *ma chen*), who provided food, tea, and water, and was responsible for tasks like sweeping, shoveling snow, and the upkeep of the buildings and facilities. The other permanent support position was that of the woodcutter, who maintained the community's supply of fuel. The cook-attendant and the woodcutter would come and go from the confines of the retreat as necessary.

The delegating of these ritual and worldly responsibilities to specific individuals freed the meditators following the main meditation program from such concerns, minimizing potential disruptions to their practice and preserving the sanctity of the retreat. While a meditator would remain interpersonally connected to the others inside the retreat, the ideal of not seeing or being seen by anyone outside for more than three years seems to have been a realistic possibility. The closed structure of the retreat center, its back turned to the world on all four sides, would help keep family members and well-wishers at bay. Clearly articulated rules and punishments would govern relationships between the retreatants themselves, on an explicitly monastic basis.

Kongtrül's charter outlines how a common fund was relied on to supply the retreatants with their sustenance. Whether given as general donations to the institution or as payment for ritual services, all monies or materials were held in the fund, then distributed equally to all the retreatants. The cook-attendant would draw from this stock to prepare communal meals twice daily. Materials needed for ritual purposes, which could be quite costly, would also be taken from this fund. An account book listing all the material belongings of the retreat center—including statues, texts, musical instruments, ritual items, even the silk offering scarves—was maintained, against which the actual inventory would be checked. Anything found missing or broken would need to be replaced. Each year, the retreatants had to pool their personal resources to come up with a donation equal to two bricks of tea. One would be put toward the purchase of whitewash for the buildings of the retreat complex. The other would be used to buy juniper to be prepared as incense, burned daily to propitiate the local spirits.[37]

Further details regarding how Tsadra was supported materially are supplied by Kongtrül's biography. As compensation for his performance of ritual services, Kongtrül was given some nomadic pastureland down the valley from Pelpung, which would be dedicated to the support of the retreat center in perpetuity. Another plot of land was dedicated to Tsadra as payment for his performing a successful rainmaking ritual. Smaller one-time donations were also made. It is recorded that the seventh three-year, three-fortnight retreat overseen by Kongtrül at Tsadra was sponsored by his niece.[38] A concern about a retreatant's relationship to material wealth nevertheless remains: Kongtrül writes in his charter, "If your mind is not pure and your practice not authentic, that is to defraud (*bslus*) the patrons who have sponsored you."[39] It is clear that the settled, corporate structure of the retreat at Tsadra shifted the issue of sustenance to the institution's administrators and the surrounding community, away from the individual retreatants. Many of the traditional concerns relating to begging and maintaining proper relations with donors were now moot. Despite these profound changes, food nevertheless remained a moral issue of heightened importance for the individual practitioner.

Safe within the confines of the retreat complex, no worry about bandits or predatory beasts need be harbored. The charter says that a retreatant may perform a "circle of protection" if having bad dreams. The local demons had also been subdued long before, through the activities of Kongtrül and his circle of charismatic friends. According to the charter, if a retreatant should fall ill, then it becomes the responsibility of the retreat attendant to care for him. The vajra master also bears some responsibility for the health of the retreatants.[40]

Once a year, on the holiday memorializing the life of Milarepa, the retreatants who had succeeded in generating bodily warmth via *tummo* were expected to perform the "offering of the cloth" ceremony, which typically entails using *tummo* to dry wet sheets wrapped around the meditator's body, as a way of demonstrating their yogic prowess.[41] No longer required for survival amid dangerous conditions, *tummo* has become a benchmark for yogic development and a means of commemorating past masters. In these ways, with many of the challenges inherent to the endeavor of individual long-term retreat resolved, some of the traditional avenues of cultivating the imaginal self have been eliminated or have significantly less of a place in the retreatant's conduct. It would seem that these changes would allow the individual to pour their imaginal capacities more completely into the central practices of the retreat.

To understand how Kongtrül's version of retreat positions the individual meditator vis-à-vis the spiritual lineage requires consideration of the specific meditations and rituals to be studied and practiced, which brings into relief what may be the most distinctive aspect of Kongtrül's program relative to the practice of individual retreat historically. This comes up in each of the three chapters of Kongtrül's charter, which address the period of preparation before the retreat; the curriculum for and the conditions adhered to during the retreat (taking up four-fifths of the document); and how to go about living after the retreat.

Kongtrül's presentation of how to prepare for retreat is similar to that found in many other prescriptive retreat texts insofar as he discusses the proper motivation, the required qualifications, and the kinds of merit-making activities an individual should do. Kongtrül appeals to tradition to make the case concerning correct and incorrect mindsets motivating one to do retreat, in the form of a two-folio-side quotation from Jikten Sumgön's *Large Vase of Nectar*, the writings of the early masters of the Kagyu evidently still being the go-to authority on this pivotal question.[42] Kongtrül's charter diverges dramatically from the norms of individual retreat by listing dozens of texts of which each meditator must procure a physical copy, to be read and studied during the retreat. The charter includes the detail that most of the texts are available in woodblock prints; the few that are not must be copied manually.[43] The fact that each retreatant was expected to possess physical copies of the texts and to spend significant amounts of time reading and studying signals that Kongtrül's version of retreat is drastically different from earlier centuries of individual long-term retreat, where textual study was discouraged and very little such material would be brought into the retreat.

As for the main curriculum of the retreat, the first five months are to be spent on the preliminary practices. This resolves what had been a matter of ambiguity throughout the individual retreat tradition: whether one should do the preliminary practices prior to or during the retreat. Many prescriptive texts had straddled both possibilities by suggesting the meditator dedicate some time at the beginning of the retreat to the preliminaries without doing a full hundred thousand of each. This aspect of Kongtrül's retreat program formalizes the position of the meditator as a newcomer to serious tantric practice. After completing the preliminaries, the retreatants (excepting the meditator of the protector deity temple and the one dedicated to long-life practices) progress through a curriculum of rituals and meditations deriving from three different Tibetan Buddhist traditions: the Shangpa Kagyu, an endangered lineage that Kongtrül succeeded in re-forming, to which fifteen months of the retreat are dedicated; the Kālacakra, as preserved by the Jonang sect, practiced for six months; and the Nyingma, which takes up most of the final year of the retreat. This diversity reflects the value Kongtrül saw in engaging with religious traditions outside of his root tradition, the Kagyu, and his goal of preserving these lineages for later generations.

The ecumenism built into Kongtrül's retreat program was not well received by all whose opinions mattered during his lifetime. Indeed, this basic orientation was a cause of friction with other Kagyupas throughout Kongtrül's entire life. In defense of the specific form of his program, Kongtrül wrote in his 1864 catalogue (*dkar chag*) of Künzang Dechen Ösel Ling, the *All-Pervading Melody of the Pure Lands: A Catalogue of the Buildings and Contents of Künzang Dechen Ösel Ling, the Upper Hermitage of Pelpung* (as translated by Gardner), "It might seem that putting one's efforts into the creation and completion [Generation and Perfection] phases of a single tradition during a three years and three fortnights period is the way to zero in on the essentials. But then, it might also seem that not having so many elaborate prayers and recitations would be easier for dullards and lazies." Kongtrül here refers to the existence of other institutions where the communal three-year, three-fortnight retreat was being practiced, but whose programs were devoted to a single sectarian tradition. Kongtrül suggests that the unwillingness to do more may be an issue of effort and mental capacity. He writes that certain people, "by force of the time in which we live," are strictly limited in what they have been able to achieve religiously. He writes negatively of those who "only concern themselves with the study, meditation, teaching, and propagation of their own traditions, without endeavoring to learn from others. Even if they dabble in another tradition, they do not involve themselves in the maintenance or spread of its lineage, and so while their own established traditions flourish like an excellent harvest, superior and distinguished practice lineages are disappearing."[44] Like his activities in compiling the eighteen volumes of the *Treasury of Instructions*, Kongtrül's retreat program was intended to stem this tide of decline and loss by producing individuals legitimately initiated and fully trained in these tantric practices. Instead of creating enlightened masters, the retreat serves as a period of initial training in tantric practice, seminary-like, to produce qualified individuals who can pass on the lineage to others, making them bulwarks against the possibility that these spiritual lineages might be lost—as necessitated by Kongtrül's understanding of the historical moment in which he lived. The individual retreatant is conceived of as a vessel who can carry the teachings and the lineage forward into the future.[45] This is a version of retreat structured from start to finish around an intent not indicated in other prescriptive retreat texts consulted for this study. Moreover, with the group of retreatants receiving fully legitimate transmissions and empowerments from a qualified vajra master inside the confines of the retreat, the imaginal methods for repairing their connection to the many spiritual lineages are obviated.

While meditators progressed through the main training curriculum, other practices would remain part of the daily schedule for the duration of the retreat, such as certain offerings and supplications, Cutting, and practices deriving from Chokgyur Lingpa's *Secret Essence*. There would be communal and individual practices on monthly and annual cycles as well. The charter details the additional rituals to be performed on certain days of each month, devoted to the ninth Tai Situ, Pema Nyingjé Wangpo (1774/75–1853), who was a teacher of Kongtrül (the seventh day of the month); the goddess Tara (the eighth); treasure revealers (the tenth); the deity Kālacakra (the fifteenth); the Shangpa Kagyu lineage (the twenty-fifth); and the deity Yangdak Heruka (the last day of the month). Liturgies from multiple traditions are practiced on these days. Specific days are set aside each year for doing rituals to commemorate figures like Marpa; the treasure revealer Terdak Lingpa (1646–1714); the Third Karmapa; Gampopa; Khyungpo Neljor, a founder of the Shangpa Kagyu (1002–1064); and Dolpopa Sherap Gyeltsen, the famous Jonangpa (1292–1361/62).[46] Around each New Year a major "approach" ritual was performed, requiring seven days of uninterrupted recitation, devoted to the six-armed protector deity. Eight ritual helpers could be brought in from the outside to assist (because their names were listed on the retreat signboard from the beginning).[47] These ritual practices performed on monthly and annual bases formalized the retreatants' deferential and reverential positioning relative to the past masters of the various spiritual lineages for which they were in the process of becoming living vessels.

Of central importance to Kongtrül's retreat program is his defining the retreat as an endeavor that should last specifically for three lunar years and three fortnights. Defining retreat in this way affects the daily bodily comportment of the meditator, unambiguously positions the retreat within the career arc of the practitioner, and positions the meditator in relationship to the dimension of time and the possibility of enlightenment.

Although it is not mentioned in the charter for the retreat community at Tsadra, Kongtrül's model of retreat carried the expectation that the meditator would sleep sitting up, in the cross-legged posture. This is to bring the practitioner closer to the ideal of directing the entirety of the three years and three fortnights to actual meditation practice, toward accumulating the minimum number of hours required for enlightenment as assumed by this particular way of thinking about the personhood of the meditator, derived from the *Kālacakra* and other tantric scriptures. The retreatant's room would be furnished with a wooden box, with a high back and low sides to support the legs, to foster remaining upright both day and night.[48] A review of the more expansive record of prescriptive texts for individual long-term retreat suggests that the expectation of sleeping sitting up gained force over a long period of time. Yangönpa explicitly mentions assuming the lion's pose when beginning one's nighttime yogas, but also mentions going to sleep while sitting upright while practicing *tummo* specifically.[49] By the middle of the seventeenth century, the practice of sleeping upright had been further established: Karma Chakmé specifies that "you can sleep sitting upright or lying down in the lion's posture—whichever is pleasant for you." Karma Chakmé would also discuss the benefits and drawbacks of sleeping in the lion's posture or upright in relation to the practice of dream yoga, and the possibility of alternating between the two as a means of "further improvement."[50] Two hundred years later when Kongtrül formulated a retreat explicitly defined as lasting three years and three fortnights, the expectation of sleeping in the meditation posture was total.[51] Sleeping upright during a Kongtrül-style retreat continues to be a common practice the world over. It seems that the ideal of sleeping sitting upright spilled over from being directly connected to the practice of *tummo* to being a general expectation for retreatants, as part of redefining the Tibetan ascetic self through changes in the technologies of self-constitution.

Much is conveyed about how Kongtrül imagined his form of retreat to fit within the career arc of the practitioner in the charter's chapter on life after the retreat, which he offers "so that the fruit you have produced does not go to waste." When discussing life after the three-year, three-fortnight retreat, Kongtrül gives the comments quoted in chapter 6 expressing his view that these days retreatants should not conceive of themselves as being able to achieve *siddhi*s or even the first signs of "heat." Nevertheless, completing the full-length retreat earns a person the title of "lama," the significance of which Kongtrül pointedly undercuts. He addresses the one having completed the retreat as follows: "If you imagine this to be sufficient for you to carelessly accept offerings from the faithful or on behalf of the deceased, and you feel content with the meditation practice you have done, this is more repugnant than [if you were to support yourself with] the profit from the sale of animals you slaughter." Although an individual may now technically be a lama, they should never bank on this fact or feel content with the relatively little practice they have completed. Moreover, Kongtrül portrays the completion of the three-year, three-fortnight retreat as being just a step in the spiritual journey, and not the final one. He describes an individual retreat that the meditator should set out to do after completing the three-year, three-fortnight communal one. This individual retreat will last around eleven months and features meditations focused on the buddhas Vairocana and Akṣobhya and rituals connected to Amitābha, derived from the Sky Dharma treasures, which Karma Chakmé played so key a role in propagating. In the closing pages of the charter, Kongtrül directly addresses the individual who has completed the three-year, three-month retreat:

> You have now found the path to liberation. You should recognize and acknowledge that this is thanks to the kindness of the spiritual master and [to your own] virtuous good fortune. In order to not waste these good karmic propensities [you possess], you should not apathetically abandon the creation and completion [Generation and Perfection phase] meditations you have done here for as long as you live.
>
> The best [thing for you to do] is to sever all worldly bonds of attachment and to do a retreat alone to take [your practice] to its fruition. Second-best is to promise yourself to never support yourself in ways that are contradictory to spiritual life, and then to practice meditation for the full extent of your life, serving the spiritual master and Buddhism and doing whatever is beneficial for others or meaningful to your own spiritual life. The least [you can do] is to never barter your three years of retreat for food or clothing, thus irreparably harming yourself in this life and the next.[52]

Here Kongtrül prevails upon the meditator to maintain an attitude of great humility: rather than the achievement of some lofty goal, the retreat is but an early step in one's journey. The tools having been acquired, they are now to be put into use over the rest of one's meditative life, including, Kongtrül hopes, in an individual long-term retreat. Positioned vis-à-vis individual retreat in this way, the entire endeavor of the three-year, three-month communal retreat becomes an expression of lived deferential reverence, as individual retreat is aspirationally preserved as primarily being the purview of other, more perfected beings, including one's own future self.

As for how Kongtrül situates his version of the retreat endeavor relative to historical time and the possibility of enlightenment, late in the text he quotes a long passage from the Third Karmapa, about how because we live in a "dark and troubled time," retreat practitioners are rare, people have short and unpredictable lives, and we have too little time to educate ourselves. Despite these adverse conditions, we can nevertheless meditate. Kongtrül concludes, "You should keep this advice as if it were divine heart nectar." In the charter's colophon he mentions our living in an "inestimably bad degenerate age." The text closes with Kongtrül's signature, in which he refers to himself as "the mere reflection of a holder of the Practice Tradition during the degenerate age."[53]

In comparison to a retreat manual like Yangönpa's *Blazing Jewel*, in which the reader is presented with a discussion of the highest echelons of the enlightened state, Kongtrül's charter for communal retreat presents a far more modest horizon of possibility. The very form of the retreat derives from a diminished notion of what the meditator can hope to achieve. Despite how it may sit in tension with the technical explanation for why a retreat should last specifically for three years and three fortnights, the three years and three fortnights of meditation in Kongtrül's retreat is offered as the means to achieve not liberation but rather a kind of competency, turning the individual into a vessel for the transmissions received, capable of ensuring their continuance into the future. In this way, although completing the retreat earns one the title of "lama," a person so qualified remains deferentially positioned vis-à-vis the early solitary practitioners who were the fountainheads of these lineages, and who are memorialized in so many ways. This redefining of the retreat endeavor itself—from an individual ascetic trial that could potentially result in enlightenment to a time-delimited period of training intended to instill basic tantric competency, so as to preserve traditions under threat due to the realities of the current moment—may be the most impactful and enduring instance of lived deferential reverence noted in this study. Now we all meditate and live in a world as understood by Jamgön Kongtrül.

Communal retreat existed long before Kongtrül, and both individual and non-time-delimited retreat practice continue into the present. Nevertheless, because of the massive impact it has had on how meditation and retreat are conceived of in Tibetan Buddhism the world over, the specific model of retreat instituted by Kongtrül stands out as a watershed moment in the history of the Tibetan ascetic self. As this book has demonstrated, the Tibetan ascetic self, understood as being constituted in relationship to a variety of concerns, has always been multiple and in the midst of a process of change. The establishment of Kongtrül's version of retreat amounted to a complete redrawing of the threshold of consideration in many facets of the ascetic's being, and the formalizing of a specific understanding of the purpose of meditative practice.

The moderate, middle-way asceticism adhered to in Kongtrül's version of retreat provides resolution to many persistent issues in ascetic life, as many of the kinds of relations problematized by authors of instructions for individual retreat are rendered obsolescent and fall almost completely out of consideration. Under Kongtrül's model, the meditator need no longer be concerned with the question of place, as the value of the location has already been long established—through Kongtrül's and his peers' visionary activity, and through the place's hosting numerous successful classes of retreatants previously. Defining the meditator as part of a specific, codified retreat community allows structures to be put into place to keep them strictly cut off from the world outside—more strictly, it would seem, than can be achieved during an individual retreat, when the ascetic's need for food or the outside world's need for ritual performance continually threatens to destroy that boundary. The retreatant's access to sustenance is regulated thanks to the institution's communal wealth and mechanisms to maintain it. The practice of *tummo* continues but is no longer relied on for survival; a meditator's facility in the yogic exercise gets demonstrated in the specific ritual context of an annual commemoration of Milarepa. Successful completion of the retreat makes the meditator a worthy vessel for the Teachings and earns them the title of lama, which Kongtrül is certain to downplay, stressing the need for humility in our present world age. The codification of this model of retreat as lasting for a specific amount of time formalizes and instantiates a specific understanding of the meditator's relationship to enlightenment and to time, both historical and cosmological, providing a basis for myriad other adjustments to ascetic expectations.

The great success of Kongtrül's model of retreat must be seen as an indication of the ever-increasing disposition of lived deferential reverence in the Tibetan Buddhist world. This model allows a meditator to participate in the same activity as the past masters, while preserving a deferential distance from them through the form that activity takes. This revolution in the basic parameters of long-term retreat practice can be seen as a shift in assumptions about the fundamental relationship between meditative practice and life amid ascetic circumstances. Many of the texts reviewed in this study talk explicitly about the inevitability of having to endure such challenging circumstances during an individual long-term retreat, whether as a necessary condition for meditation or a natural consequence of staying in isolation. As the tradition has shifted, putting the question of temporal duration in a position of greater prominence in defining what a meditative retreat should be, the ascetic aspects of retreat have declined in importance. The present-day viability of doing a virtual retreat from the comfort of home or the tendency to organize meditation around the goal of accumulating three years and three months of contemplation represent the victory of meditation over all thoughts of the necessity of living amid ascetic conditions. We have thus entered a new phase in the history of the Tibetan Buddhist ascetic self, defined by an attitude of lived deferential reverence that has been growing over centuries. For latter-day practitioners, long-term retreat may be above all else an act of homage to those who came before.

There is evidence suggesting that the heirs of Kongtrül's retreat tradition have not preserved the ecumenism that was so important a part of his program: of the communal three-year, three-month retreat programs currently running outside of Tibet that I have reviewed, the overwhelming tendency is to convey only teachings from a single sectarian tradition. I know of none that preserves Kongtrül's full array of lineages. Although Kongtrül specifically formulated his retreat program to save multiple lineages from extinction, it seems that Tibetan religious communities of various stripes have adapted the retreat to suit their own individual needs, to create new generations of qualified tantric practitioners in the wake of the disruption of traditional religious networks. Although Kongtrül's retreat model may not have succeeded in spreading or maintaining his ecumenical vision for Tibetan Buddhism, it is helping maintain lineages that might otherwise be lost. Viewed from a different perspective, we could say that what Kongtrül's program has ended up achieving is the continuance of the retreat tradition itself, employed by individual traditions to preserve themselves in the face of the challenging realities of the historical moment in which we live.

CONCLUSION

L'enfer, c'est les autres.

Jean-Paul Sartre

The pages of this book have grown out of an attempt to identify what authors of Tibetan-language instructions for practicing individual long-term retreat have been most concerned about in relation to the pragmatic aspects of living and meditating in seclusion—*what* the Himalayan anchoritic tradition has problematized—and the specific prescriptions offered for relating to those concerns—*how* it has problematized them. Studies of other ascetic traditions, Buddhist or otherwise, will reveal a different configuration of major concerns and different manners of adjudicating them, as the contours of any tradition of religious asceticism will be determined by its own goals, ideals, and entailments. Each ascetic tradition problematizes the world in its own way, in other words. In this study we have seen the profound degree to which Buddhism's injunction against clerics' engaging in productive labor (or what the Buddhist clerical estate has maintained amounts to such an injunction) has determined the contours of ascetic concern. This stands in almost polar contrast to the Christian monastic tradition, which has taken the need to be materially self-sufficient as a starting point, incorporating labor as one of its primary tenets, as enshrined in Benedict of Nursia's *Rule*, from around 530. Each ascetic tradition is defined by the places where it is compelled to draw an unbreachable boundary. Beyond the issue of material support, ascetic traditions also diverge on points related to celibacy, self-mortification (in active or passive forms), ritual and contemplative exercises, dietetic regimes and fasting, silence, sleep deprivation, the donning of visible markers of ascetic status, including nudity, and the attainability of deliverance and how it is arrived at. The question of where the ascetic's vigilance is directed can be divined in part by paying attention to the nature of the "demons" that must be combated. Employing the hermeneutical category of an "ascetic self" enables us to systematically explore these matters in a way that keeps the practitioner as the focal point. Existing in both synchronic and diachronic dimensions, the ascetic self can be studied genealogically, allowing for new perspectives on the histories of religiocultural traditions. As shown across the discrete areas of concern addressed in chapters 2 through 7, the history of eremitism in Tibet has been defined by the various means by which an individual attempting to live according to these prescribed ascetic dictates will cultivate a form of selfhood that can be described as imaginal; by the increasing prevalence over centuries of a disposition of lived deferential reverence; and, directly related to this, by a developmental arc that culminates in an understanding of Buddhist contemplative practice as profoundly influenced—perhaps even defined—by the practitioner's positionality in historical time. The Tibetan eremitic tradition has intersected with other major historical developments in Tibetan religious culture, such as the expansion of the monastic ideal and the civilization-wide project of ordering the Himalayan landscape.

There has also been a deeper, all-pervading concern about materiality itself. The ideals of abiding without reliance on food, being able to survive without warm clothes or medicine, possessing a self capable of reconfiguring most any aspect of one's circumstances through the powers of visualization—from head-lice to the threat of bandits—all speak to the same goal of existing in a way that subverts absolutely the most basic and universal defining quality of existence in the world for the rest of us. The Tibetan Buddhist eremitic tradition has been so invested in problematizing existence in this way not because the material world is itself the problem—is not in itself "evil," as another tradition might put it—but because the relationship to materiality that defines our unenlightened existence entails a reliance upon and a need to interact with other people. The ultimate problem is not materiality but sociality. To abide via essence extraction, to never need an expert's medical diagnosis, to never be impeded by the shortcomings of your guru, indeed, to never interact directly with another person—these goals share in the fantasy of existing in a pure self-sufficient solitude. The mountain of the "mountain Dharma" expresses the dreamed-for isolation that is the ultimate goal, never realized, toward which the other domains of anchoritic comportment are all marshaled. The cultivation of interpersonal isolation as detailed in chapter 3 sets the agenda for all of the other aspects of ascetic comportment examined in this study. Separation from the mundane world is therefore not asceticism's starting point but rather its never-realized goal. Foucault's insight about techniques of self-care in fact being technologies of self-fashioning allows us to see that at root the Tibetan Buddhist eremitic endeavor has been motivated by the goal of instantiating a self that has the capacity to abide in a way that entails no reliance upon material things or, more importantly, other people. Jean-Paul Sartre's famous statement, "Hell is other people," may succinctly express why the tradition has been so profoundly oriented around this goal: it is through the objectifying gaze of others that we are constituted as what we are in this world. In light of this, the Tibetan eremitic injunction against letting your face be seen by others—or worse, seeing someone else's face—is not merely about limiting interpersonal interaction but about maintaining a space that makes possible a break with the ordinary modes of constituting our own personhood, as a precondition for the possibility of becoming something different.

One reader of this book thoughtfully pointed out that nowhere amid the exploration of Tibet's tradition of individual long-term meditative retreat do I address the foundational question: Why? What have been Tibetans' motivations for going into retreat? I think the most feasible way of addressing this is by reframing the question: Among all the Buddhist cultures and all the religious traditions of Asia and elsewhere, why is it that in Tibet the eremitic imperative has historically been felt, expressed, and pursued more than anywhere else? Relatedly, why have so many highly learned individuals taken pains over nearly a thousand years to devote so much thought and energy to composing new and improved instructions for the eremitic endeavor?

In response, I would point to Tibetan geographic conditions conducive to isolation: a tiny population occupying an enormous territory, with a vertiginous geography that has produced a great number of habitable caves. More substantively, I would point to Buddhism's millennium-long near-monopolistic position in the religion and culture of the plateau, which has meant that the tradition's creative energies have not been directed toward defining themselves against an *other*, but toward internal competitiveness and differentiation. This has led to the development of strong sectarian and lineage-based identities but also divergent paths to holiness, all to a degree being in competition for legitimacy and finite resources. These paths to holiness and religious standing include ascetic trials and meditative and ritual practice, sometimes taken to extreme degrees, but also the vow-based discipline of monasticism, impressive philosophical and textual learning demonstrated through the drama of debate, the charisma accrued through treasure text revelation, the identification of reincarnations of past masters, place- and object-based modes of worship, modes of communion with the divine, and supremacy over adverse spirit beings. The humble material conditions of life in premodern Tibet supported this competitive dynamic and clericalism in general, as well as eremitism specifically. Also pertinent is the lack of centralized political and religious power in Tibet, especially in the earlier centuries under consideration.

In *Apparitions of the Self*, Janet Gyatso has argued that this very same environment of competitiveness and the need for individual validation led to the rise and prevalence of another distinctive feature of Buddhist Tibet: autobiographical writing. Seeing that individual long-term retreat and Tibetan autobiographical (or as may be more accurate here, autohagiographical) writing grew out of the same pressures, it may be instructive to reflect on what the two have had to do with each other. As portrayed by Gyatso based on her case studies, they are symbiotically related, insofar as proving the enlightenment of the text's subject through the narrative of their heightened spiritual experiences and visions is the ultimate purpose of Tibetan Buddhist life writing, and individual long-term retreat provides the context in which those experiences can occur. There is nevertheless a chasm between Tibetan autobiography and the prescriptive literature for retreat, owing to the differences in how they respectively portray the possibility of enlightenment. While Tibetan life writing is very much invested in, even predicated upon, the possibility of achieving enlightenment in its subject's present, the prescriptive literature for retreat has been far more circumspect on this matter, over time evolving away from viewing enlightenment as a realistic possibility. However, enlightenment is to be found quite readily in the prescriptive retreat literature in the distant past, during the time of the great masters who came long before. While the [auto]biographical literature portrays enlightenment with such zeal, it seems that the prescriptive literature giving actual instruction for retreat must be far more careful about making such a promise. In light of this difference, based on this body of prescriptive literature, it seems that historically individual long-term meditative retreat has served primarily as a vehicle for paying homage to the earlier exemplars of one's tradition, building them up and arguing their greatness through the deferentially lesser asceticism performed in later generations, rather than as an arena for a self-aggrandizing manner of personal striving. In this way, practicing in retreat like the past masters—but with a greatly reduced horizon of possibility and an ascetic comportment that is but a pale reflection of theirs—may itself be viewed as a kind of life writing, as the latter-day practitioner's eremitic activity is a means of retelling and adding to the metastory of those earlier figures and their direct spiritual descendants—*the* story—on which the entire legitimacy of the lineage or tradition depends.

The geographic, economic, political, sociological, and religiocultural factors that I have suggested as supporting conditions provide only a partial explanation for the unique and enduring potency of the eremitism found in Tibetan religious culture. Nor does the existence of a prior tradition in South Asia or the Himalayas suffice to explain it, for as this study itself has made clear, traditions change. At this point we must recognize the inaccessibility and the irreducibility of the individual minds of the countless men and women who have had the bravery and fortitude to abandon everything they know of this world in the pursuit of something more through the practice of reclusion. After more than two decades of studying this tradition from a variety of angles, I feel I have no better understanding of this irreducible element. Nor do I find it any less intriguing or inspiring.

APPENDIX

Prescriptive Texts for Individual Retreat

AUTHOR	AUTHOR DATES	TEXT TITLE	LENGTH (PAGES OR FOLIO SIDES)
Pakmodrupa Dorjé Gyelpo	1110–1170	*Mountain Dharma: The Vase of Nectar*	7
Chegom Sherap Dorjé	1124–1204	*Lamp for Fortunate Mountain Hermits*	12
Jikten Sumgön	1143–1217	*Mountain Dharma: The Vase of Nectar*	2
		Mountain Dharma: The Large Vase of Nectar	16
		Wandering Alone in Mountain Hermitages for the Sake of Sentient Beings	3
Yangönpa Gyeltsen Pel	1213–1258	*Blazing Jewel: The Mountain Dharma That Is the Source of All Good Qualities*	125
		Great Appendix to the Mountain Dharma That Is the Source of All Good Qualities	175
Third Karmapa, Rangjung Dorjé	1284–1339	*Mountain Dharma: The Quintessence of Nectar*	23
		Mountain Dharma: The Garland of Siddhis (1296)	8
Longchenpa Drimé Özer	1308–1364	*Words of Joy in a Forest Grove*	13
Second Red Hat, Kachö Wangpo	1350–1405	*Heart of the Esoteric Instruction That Completely Untangles the Mountain Dharma*	34
Zurmang Lekshé Drayang	b. 16th cent.	*Words on the Mountain Dharma: The Melody Producing Nothing but Good*	108
Fourth Trungpa, Künga Namgyel	1567–1629	*Necklace for Those Wanting Liberation, Called "Mountain Dharma: The Garland of Beryl"*	8
Fourth Panchen Lama, Lozang Chökyi Gyeltsen	1567/68/70–1662	*Beryl Ladder for Ascending to the Palace of the Three Bodies: Guidelines for Earnest Mountain Hermits*	13
		Words on Taking Joy in Isolation, Composed Based on the Thirty Letters of the Alphabet	2

Lhatsün Namkha Jikmé	1597–1650	*Garland of Critical Points for the Precious Mountain Dharma*	60
Karma Chakmé	1608/10/13–1678	*Mountain Dharma: Direct Advice on Retreat* (1665)	840
Mipam Püntsok Sherap, Reincarnation of Taktsé	1654–1715	*Refined Honey That Extracts the Essence of Accomplishment in the Profound Mountain Dharma* (1715)	60
Ngawang Lozang Samten	1687–1748/49	*Song of Taking Joy in Isolation*	2
		Song of Taking Joy in Isolation: Exhorting My Own Mind Toward Virtue	5
Sönam Chödzin	b. 1688	*Reminder for Those Who Wander in Isolated Mountain Hermitages: Direct Advice That Is the Ship for Great Liberation*	11
Third Changkya, Rölpé Dorjé	1717–1786	*Long Dharmic Song About Taking Joy in Isolation*	5
Jikmé Lingpa	1729/30–1798	*Direct Advice on the Mountain Dharma: The Ocean of Wonders*	9
Shabkar Tsokdruk Rangdröl	1781–1851	*Beneficial Moon: A Dharma Address* (1812)	283
Orgyen Namdröl Wangpo	b. ca. 1808	*Drop of Ambrosia: The Secret Quintessence of Direct Advice on How to Stay in Concealed Hermitages in Border Areas and Mix All Aspects of One's Continuum with the Dharma* (1846)	10
Drakar Lozang Pelden Tenzin Nyendrak	1866–1928	*Garland of Pearls: The Mountain Dharma Requisite for All Dharma Practitioners Staying in Isolated Places*	280
		Guidelines for Renunciant Meditators: The Beautiful Garland of Flowers, the Mountain Dharma of Esoteric Instruction That Is Easy to Grasp	15
Ngawang Tenzin Norbu	1867–1940/49?	*Charter: Direct Advice on the Mountain Dharma* (1914)	73
Karma Ngedön Tenkyé, Mendong Tsampa	b. late 19th cent.	*Instruction Pointing Out the Mountain Dharma, the Path to Liberation*	44

NOTES

INTRODUCTION

1. Émile Durkheim, *The Elementary Forms of Religious Life,* trans. Karen Fields (New York: The Free Press, 1995 [1912]), 315–16.
2. Lindsay Jones, ed., *Encyclopedia of Religion (Second Edition)*, 15 vols. (Detroit: Macmillan Reference USA, 2005), 11: 7768–73, 5: 2822–2830. Both of these entries were written by Juan Manuel Lozano in 1987, who notes, "Very little, if anything, of a general nature has been published on the topic of retreat. References to retreats, seclusion, and the like can be found in any general survey on Hindu, Muslim, and Christian mysticism, as well as in works dealing with phenomenology of religion" (11: 7773). Note the absence of Buddhism from Lozano's list.
3. Roger Jackson, "A Fasting Ritual," in *Religions of Tibet in Practice,* ed. Donald Lopez Jr. (Princeton, NJ: Princeton University Press, 1997), 271–92; Geoffrey Barstow, *Food of Sinful Demons: Meat, Vegetarianism, and the Limits of Buddhism in Tibet* (New York: Columbia University Press, 2019), 107–11.
4. Christopher Hatchell, *Naked Seeing: The Great Perfection, the Wheel of Time, and Visionary Buddhism in Renaissance Tibet* (New York: Oxford University Press, 2014). One practitioner recorded as having practiced the dark retreat for periods far longer than forty-nine days is A yu mkha' 'gro (1839–1953), whose biography is related in Tsultrim Allione, *Women of Wisdom* (Ithaca, NY: Snow Lion, 2000), 137–64.
5. Elio Guarisco, trans., *Secret Map of the Body: Visions of the Human Energy Structure* (Merigar, Italy: Shang Shung Publications, 2015), 198–99; Rgod tshang ras pa sna tshogs rang grol, *Gtsang smyon he ru ka phyogs thams cad las rnam par rgyal ba'i rnam thar rdo rje theg pa'i gsal byed nyi ma'i snying po* (New Delhi: Sharada Rani, 1969; BDRC W1KG9090), 269.7–275.1; David DiValerio, *The Holy Madmen of Tibet* (New York: Oxford University Press, 2015), 37.
6. Georges Dreyfus, *The Sound of Two Hands Clapping: The Education of a Tibetan Buddhist Monk* (Berkeley: University of California Press, 2003), 249, 374n34. A tradition specific to the three Lha sa-area Dge lugs monasteries was that of monks' convening in a separate location for one or two months of intensive study and debate relating to Dharmakīrti's *Pramāṇavārttika,* during which time they would endure more ascetic conditions than usual; 234–6.
7. Michael Aris, *Bhutan: The Early History of a Himalayan Kingdom* (Warminster, England: Aris and Phillips, 1979), 235. See also Aris, *Hidden Treasures and Secret Lives: A Study of Pemalingpa (1450–1521) and the Sixth Dalai Lama (1683–1706)* (London and New York: Kegan Paul

International, 1989), 110, 123–24; Tsepon W. D. Shakabpa, *Tibet: A Political History* (New Haven, CT, and London: Yale University Press, 1967), 125–28; Matthew Kapstein, *The Tibetans* (Malden, MA: Blackwell, 2006), 142; Karma Phuntsho, *The History of Bhutan* (Noida: Random House India, 2013), 249–50; Yoshiro IMAEDA, *The Successors of Zhabdrung Ngawang Namgyel: Hereditary Heirs and Reincarnations* (Thimphu: Riyang Books, 2013), 15–23; Dagmar Schwerk, *A Timely Message from the Cave: The Mahāmudrā and Intellectual Agenda of dGe bshes Brag phug pa dGe 'dun rin chen (1926–1997), the Sixty-Ninth rJe mkhan po of Bhutan* (University of Hamburg, Department of Indian and Tibetan Studies, 2020), 35, 37.

8. Decline an invitation: Biographies of Dol po pa shes rab rgyal mtshan relate that upon receiving an invitation from Yuan Emperor Toghon Temür in 1344, he went into a *bsnyen sgrub* retreat so as to avoid having to go; Matthew Kapstein, *The 'Dzam thang Edition of the Collected Works of Kun mkhyen Dol po pa Shes rab Rgyal mtshan: Introduction and Catalogue* (Majnu-Ka-Tilla, Delhi: Sherup Books, 1992), 16–17; Cyrus Stearns, *The Buddha from Dolpo: A Study of the Life and Thought of the Tibetan Master Dolpopa Sherab Gyaltsen* (Albany: State University of New York Press, 1999), 28–30.

   Avoid embarrassment: There is a famous example of this from 1941, when Rwa sgreng rin po che, 'Jam dpal ye shes rgyal mtshan (1912–1947), was faced with the dilemma of being expected to impart the monastic vows to the young Fourteenth Dalai Lama although it was widely known that his own vow of celibacy was not intact. He claimed to have had dreams foretelling that he must go into retreat to avert a threat to his life; Melvyn Goldstein, *A History of Modern Tibet, 1913–1951* (Berkeley: University of California Press, 1989), 353–63.

   Avoid danger: Alexander Gardner, *The Life of Jamgon Kongtrul the Great* (Boulder, CO: Snow Lion, 2019), 244, 309; Jörg Heimbel, *Vajradhara in Human Form: The Life and Times of Ngor chen Kun dga' bzang po* (Lumbini: Lumbini International Research Institute, 2017), 226.

   Healing: Guarisco, trans., *Secret Map of the Body*, 188; Gardner, 94, 157. *The Blue Annals*, trans. George Roerich (Delhi: Motilal Banarsidass, 1996 [1949]), contains numerous mentions of individuals' using religious practice in seclusion to heal themselves of leprosy: 678, 709, 942, 986, 989, 1050–51.

   Death of parent: Rgod tshang ras pa, *Gtsang smyon he ru ka phyogs thams cad las rnam par rgyal ba'i rnam thar*, 198.7; David Jackson, *A Saint in Seattle: The Life of the Tibetan Mystic Dezhung Rinpoche* (Boston: Wisdom, 2004), 16.

9. Berthe Jansen, *The Monastery Rules: Buddhist Monastic Organization in Pre-Modern Tibet* (Berkeley: University of California Press, 2018), 38. One major example of this is the position of *rje mkhan po* or "Chief Abbot" of Bhutan, the qualifications for which are outlined in the Bhutanese constitution of 2008 (art. 3, sec. 4). Dagmar Schwerk, *A Timely Message from the Cave*, 38–41; Schwerk, "Drawing Lines in a Maṇḍala: A Sketch of Boundaries Between Religion and Politics in Bhutan," *Working Paper Series of the HCAS "Multiple Secularities—Beyond the West, Beyond Modernities,"* no. 12 (Leipzig University, 2019), 28–29; C. T. Dorji, *A Concise Religious History of Bhutan* (Delhi: Prominent Publishers, 2008), 112–45. I thank Dagmar for further information on this provided by email, April 2022.

10. For descriptions of caves in central Tibet purported to have been occupied by King Srong btsan sgam po (seventh cent.), founder of the Tibetan empire, see Keith Dowman, *The Power-Places of Central Tibet: The Pilgrim's Guide* (London and New York: Routledge and Kegan Paul, 1988), 50, 52, 55–56, 62, 65, 73–79.

11. Examples of such traditions are documented in Patrick Sutherland and Tashi Tsering, *Disciples of a Crazy Saint: The Buchen of Spiti* (Oxford: Pitt Rivers Museum, 2011).

12. 'Brug pa kun legs, *'Brug pa kun legs kyi rnam thar* (Beijing: Bod ljongs mi dmangs dpe skrun khang, 2005; BDRC W29517), 106.14–16; R. A. Stein, trans., *Vie et chants de 'Brug pa Kun legs le yogin* (Paris: G.-P. Maisonneuve et Larose, 1972), 182–83.

In the more popular lore depicting the exploits of 'Brug pa kun legs, he frequently criticizes these meditators for their lack of education, or for their concealed avarice or lust; Keith Dowman, trans., *The Divine Madman: The Sublime Life and Songs of Drukpa Kunley* (Varanasi and Kathmandu: Pilgrims Press, 2000 [1982]), 54, 74–75, 105, 107, 111, 140. The passage given on 111 is derived from a longer passage in 'Brug pa kun legs's own writings: *'Brug pa kun legs kyi rnam thar*, 309.21–311.12.

13. Herman Melville, *Moby-Dick; Or, The Whale* (New York: Penguin, 2013 [1851]), 506. See instances on 133, 136, 166, and 217 where Melville employs similar rhetoric and imagery.

14. Based on the first two episodes of season 1 of the spinoff series *Acolyte*, which began streaming in 2024, it seems the *Star Wars* franchise will continue to embrace this subject matter.

    Dates separated by slashes indicate possible years in which the individual may have been born or died. In many instances, the uncertainty is tied to Tibetans' use of a twelve-year calendrical cycle.

15. *Sera Monastery* (Somerville, MA: Wisdom, 2019), 330–48, quoting 339, 341.

16. Pierre Bourdieu, *Outline of a Theory of Practice*, trans. Richard Nice (Cambridge: Cambridge University Press, 1977), 86; *The Logic of Practice*, trans. Nice (Stanford, CA: Stanford University Press, 1990), 52.

17. The question was: "Do you still think that understanding sexuality is central for understanding who we are?" The full response reads: "I must confess that I am much more interested in problems about techniques of the self and things like that rather than sex ... sex is boring"; Foucault, "On the Genealogy of Ethics: An Overview of Work in Progress," in *Ethics: Subjectivity and Truth*, ed. Paul Rabinow, trans. Robert Hurley et al. (New York: Penguin, 1997), 253.

18. Michel Foucault, *About the Beginning of the Hermeneutics of the Self; Lectures at Dartmouth College, 1980*, trans. Graham Burchell (Chicago and London: University of Chicago Press, 2016), 25. See also Steven Collins, "Some Remarks on Hadot, Foucault, and Comparisons within Buddhism," in *Buddhist Spiritual Practices: Thinking with Pierre Hadot on Buddhism, Philosophy, and the Path*, ed. David Fiordalis (Berkeley, CA: Mangalam Press, 2018), 30. Compare with the oft-quoted passage in Foucault, "Technologies of the Self," in *Technologies of the Self: A Seminar with Michel Foucault*, ed. Martin, Gutman, and Hutton (Amherst: University of Massachusetts Press, 1988), 18.

    I follow Collins in his argument that it should be "technologies of self," rather than "technologies of the self," as it is more commonly rendered in English; 22–28.

    Mark Jordan has pointed out that in many instances where it appears Foucault is offering a definition of something, he in fact is creating a list of somewhat disparate things that the reader must do the work of placing in relationship to one another, and thereby arrive at some understanding of the phenomenon being described; *Convulsing Bodies: Religion and Resistance in Foucault* (Stanford, CA: Stanford University Press, 2015), 49, 112. The passage quoted here exemplifies this tendency in Foucault's exposition.

19. Foucault, "Technologies of the Self," 22.

20. Michel Foucault, *The Use of Pleasure: Volume 2 of the History of Sexuality,* trans. Robert Hurley (New York: Vintage, 1990), 91.

21. Collins, "Some Remarks," 43.

22. Daud Ali, "Technologies of the Self: Courtly Artifice and Monastic Discipline in Early India," *Journal of the Economic and Social History of the Orient* 41, no. 2 (1998): 159–84; Ali, *Courtly Culture and Political Life in Early Medieval India* (Cambridge: Cambridge University Press, 2004). Although it precedes Foucault's work by several decades, Norbert Elias's *The Civilizing Process,* which contains two separate works, *The History of Manners* and *State Formation and Civilization,* trans. Edmund Jephcott (Oxford: Blackwell, 1994 [1939]), has been highlighted as taking a similar fundamental approach; Collins, "Some Remarks," 43; Dennis Smith, "*The Civilizing Process* and *The History of Sexuality*: Comparing Norbert Elias and Michel Foucault," *Theory and Society* 28, no. 1 (1999): 79–100.

23. In "The Ascetic and the Domestic in Brahmanical Religiosity," Patrick Olivelle offers a different tripartite manner of conceptualizing the wide array of things that can be described as "asceticism," having some points in common with what I offer here; in *Asceticism and Its Critics: Historical Accounts and Comparative Perspectives*, ed. Oliver Freiberger (New York: Oxford University Press, 2006), 25–42. Also very useful is Freiberger's summary of Olivelle's schema; "Introduction," 6.
24. Collins, "Some Remarks," 28–33. Examples of work in this area include Matthew Kapstein, "*gDams ngag*: Tibetan Technologies of the Self," in *Tibetan Literature: Studies in Genre*, ed. José Ignacio Cabezón and Roger Jackson (Ithaca, NY: Snow Lion, 1996), 275–89; Kapstein, "Tibetan Technologies of the Self, Part II: The Teachings of the Eight Great Conveyances," in *The Pandita and the Siddha: Tibetan Studies in Honour of E. Gene Smith*, ed. Ramon Prats (Dharamsala: Amnye Machen Research Institute, 2007), 110–29; and David Fiordalis, ed., *Buddhist Spiritual Practices: Thinking with Pierre Hadot on Buddhism, Philosophy, and the Path*, which contains further references to work done in this area.
25. Foucault, *The Use of Pleasure*, 23–24.
26. Foucault, *The Use of Pleasure*, 115. Foucault briefly compares this manner of thinking about sexual activity with that of ancient China, 137; and of Christianity in Late Antiquity, 115–16, 138.
27. Such structures may be referred to using terms like *spyil po, spyil bu, khang chung, sgrub khang, mtshams khang, sbra gur*, and *cog bu*. Karma nges don bstan skyes mentions that one may reside in "a cave that is built, a cave of rock, a [large] yak-hair tent, a [smaller] tent, and so on," *rtsigs phug brag phug sbra gur cog pu sogs*; *Ri chos thar lam mdzub ston*, in *The Collected Works of Sman sdong mtshams pa rin po che Karma nges don bstan rgyas*, 3 vols. (Bir, H.P.: D. Tsondu Senghe, 1975; BDRC W10982), 3: 161–204, citing 168.5.
28. Yang dgon pa rgyal mtshan dpal, *Ri chos yon tan kun 'byung gi lhan thabs chen mo*, in *The Collected Works (gsung 'bum) of Yang dgon pa*, 3 vols. (Thimpu: Kunsang Topgey, 1976; BDRC W1KG17449), 2: 1–175, citing 10.1; Lha btsun nam mkha' 'jigs med, *Ri chos rin chen gnad kyi phreng ba*, in *Rdo rje snying po sprin gyi thol glu*, 2 vols. (n.p.; BDRC W13780), 2: 609–68, citing 621.5–622.5.

    On Lha btsun nam mkha' 'jigs med, who is credited with spreading the Karma bka' brgyud and the Great Perfection traditions to Sikkim, see Franz-Karl Ehrhard, "'Turning the Wheel of the Dharma in Zhing sa va lung': The Dpal ri sprul skus (17th to 20th centuries)," *Bulletin of Tibetology* 44, nos. 1–2 (2008): 5–29; Gardner, *Life of Jamgon Kongtrul*, 85; and James Gentry, *Power Objects in Tibetan Buddhism: The Life, Writings, and Legacy of Sokdokpa Lodrö Gyeltsen* (Leiden: Brill, 2017).

    Brag dkar blo bzang dpal ldan bstan 'dzin snyan grags also writes of the importance of not harboring any feeling of ownership over the structure in which one does a retreat, whether cottage or cave; *Gnas dben par sdod pa'i chos mdzad mtha' dag la nye bar mkho ba'i ri chos mu tig gi phreng ba* (Gser rta rdzong: Gser thang bla rung lnga rig nang bstan slob gling, n.d.; BDRC W3CN4732), 125.7–130.14; *Spong ba bsam gtan pa rnams la bslab pa'i khrims su bca' ba man ngag lag tu bcangs bde ba'i ri chos me tog phreng mdzes*, in *Collected Works*, 20 vols. (compiled in Chengdu; BDRC W23608), 3: 633–48, citing 637.1–6. These texts will be introduced in chapter 1.
29. Niki Kasumi Clements, *Sites of the Ascetic Self: John Cassian and Christian Ethical Formation* (Notre Dame, IN: University of Notre Dame Press, 2020), 102–3. The approach that Clements and I have taken also aligns with that suggested by Richard Valantasis in "Is the Gospel of Thomas Ascetical? Revisiting an Old Problem with a New Theory," *Journal of Early Christian Studies* 7, no. 1 (1999): 55–81.
30. The thesis of Flood's *Ascetic Self* is presented as follows: "My general claim is that asceticism can be understood as the internalisation of tradition, the shaping of the narrative of a life in accordance with the narrative of tradition that might be seen as the performance of the memory of

tradition," *The Ascetic Self: Subjectivity, Memory and Tradition* (Cambridge: Cambridge University Press, 2004), ix. See also 8–9, 12, 80. My argument about the role of lived deferential reverence in the Tibetan eremitic tradition may be seen as the description of a more specific process that fits within the broader proposition made here by Flood. As my own study focuses on a single tradition to capture elements of its evolution over centuries, it tracks changes internal to that ascetic tradition in a way that Flood's study does not.

31. Andrew Quintman, trans., *The Life of Milarepa* (New York: Penguin, 2010 [1488]), 177–97; DiValerio, *The Holy Madmen of Tibet*, 104–12.
32. David McMahan, *Rethinking Meditation: Buddhist Meditative Practices in Ancient and Modern Worlds* (New York: Oxford University Press, 2023), 48.
33. Harold Roth, "Against Cognitive Imperialism: A Call for a Non-Ethnocentric Approach to Cognitive Science and Religious Studies," in *The Contemplative Foundations of Classical Daoism* (Albany: State University of New York Press, 2021), 405–29; first published in *Religion East and West* 8 (2008): 1–23. *Contemplative Foundations*, which contains a series of articles published by Roth over the past thirty years, provides an excellent record of one strain of the kind of work that has been done within contemplative studies. This essay in particular offers something of a manifesto for the field.
34. Kate Crosby, *Esoteric Theravada: The Story of the Forgotten Meditation Tradition of Southeast Asia* (Boulder, CO: Shambhala, 2020).

1. THE PRESCRIPTIVE LITERATURE FOR INDIVIDUAL RETREAT

1. This literature remains as yet little-studied. Exceptions include Eric Haynie's 2013 M.A. thesis at the University of Colorado, "Karma chags med's *Mountain Dharma*: Tibetan Advice on Sociologies of Retreat"; and Marta Sernesi, "The *History of the Mountain Teachings*: 13th century Practice Lineages at rTsib ri," *Revue d'Études Tibétaines* 64 (2022): 479–515. The existence of this body of literature is nowhere addressed in *Tibetan Literature: Studies in Genre*, ed. José Ignacio Cabezón and Roger Jackson (Ithaca, NY: Snow Lion, 1996).
2. Elio Guarisco, trans., *Secret Map of the Body: Visions of the Human Energy Structure* (Merigar, Italy: Shang Shung Publications, 2015) is an excellent resource for all things relating to Yang gdon pa, containing a summary of Yang gdon pa's life and times, 5–27; a full translation of Yang gdon pa's main biography, the *Me long chen mo*, by his disciple Spyan snga rin chen ldan, 113–216; and a full translation of Yang gdon pa's *Rdo rje lus kyi sbas bshad*. Guarisco, *Secret Map of the Body*, 2–3, lists other textual sources for the life of Yang dgon pa.

    Other sources include Willa Blythe Miller's PhD dissertation, "Secrets of the Vajra Body: Dngos po'i gnas lugs and the Apotheosis of the Body in the Work of Rgyal ba Yang dgon pa," Harvard University, 2013; Miller's synopsis of Yang dgon pa's life for the Treasury of Lives (https://treasuryoflives.org/biographies/view/Yanggonpa-Gyeltsen-Pel/7775); *The Blue Annals*, trans. George Roerich (Delhi: Motilal Banarsidass, 1996 [1949]), 688–91; and Cyrus Stearns, *Hermit of Go Cliffs: Timeless Instructions from a Tibetan Mystic* (Boston: Wisdom, 2000), which focuses on Yang gdon pa's master, Ko brag pa.
3. Spyan snga rin chen ldan, *Ri chos bskor gsum du grags pa zab chos brgyan bzhi'i dkar chag*, in *The Collected Works (gsung 'bum) of Yang dgon pa*, 3 vols. (Thimpu: Kunsang Topgey, 1976; BDRC W1KG17449), 1: 155–66, citing 158.1–5.

    Spyan snga rin chen ldan also wrote a history of the *Ri chos skor gsum*, which is mainly dedicated to relating the various teaching lineages Yang dgon pa possessed and how the *Trilogy* was transmitted to Yang dgon pa's disciples: Spyan snga rin chen ldan, *Ri chos brgyud tshul gyi lo rgyus*, in Yang dgon pa, *Collected Works*, 1: 1–9. This text is discussed and translated in Sernesi, "The History of the Mountain Teachings." Among other instructions for how to practice retreat, Yang dgon pa received texts attributed to Phag mo gru pa and 'Jig rten gsum mgon bearing some variation on the title *Ri chos bdud rtsi['i] [']bum*, or *Mountain Dharma: The Vase of Nectar*, which are discussed in the present study: Sernesi, 481–82, 491, 497, 501, 506.

For a brief biography of Spyan snga rin chen ldan, see Roerich, trans., *The Blue Annals*, 691–92. See also Miller, "Secrets of the Vajra Body," 39–40.

4. Yang dgon pa rgyal mtshan dpal, *Ri chos yon tan kun 'byung gi lhan thabs chen mo*, Collected Works, 2: 1–175, citing 174.4–175.1. At the beginning of the *Lhan thabs*, another statement is made regarding how it relates to the main text of the *Rin po che 'bar ba*; 2.2.

5. I have come across one instance of the two texts being referred to as *ri chos rtsa 'grel*; Zur mang legs bshad sgra dbyangs, *Ri yi chos gtam kun tu bzang po'i sgra dbyang* (Mtshur phu dgon gtsug lag dpe tshogs, n.d.; BDRC W3CN5072), 18.17.

6. There are a number of places in the *Ri chos yon tan kun 'byung [ba] rin po che 'bar ba* where a quotation is described as having originated from *rje ratna*. An interlinear note identifies this with [S]ko brag pa; Collected Works, 1: 447–570, citing 450.5. I understand the text's mentions of *rje rin po che* to refer to Ko brag pa as well.

Regarding the interlinear notes preserved throughout the Pha jo ldings versions of Yang dgon pa's writings that I use for this study, Miller concludes that "the authorship of the interlinear notes is uncertain, but it is not impossible that Yang dgon pa or Spyan snga ba [Rin chen ldan] may have written some of them"; "Secrets of the Vajra Body," 49. Guarisco addresses these notes in *Secret Map of the Body*, 3–4.

7. Yang dgon pa, *Rin po che 'bar ba*, Collected Works, 1: 448.4–5; 490.6, 498.2, 499.1. Spyan snga rin chen ldan's *Ri chos bskor gsum du grags pa zab chos brgyan bzhi'i dkar chag* mentions that the retreat manual was composed at the request of one Seng ge rgyal mtshan, along with many other *sgom chen*; Yang dgon pa, Collected Works, 1: 157.5. More detail on Yang dgon pa's circle at the time of composing these texts is given in Sernesi, "The *History of the Mountain Dharma Teachings*."

8. Yang dgon pa, *Rin po che 'bar ba*, Collected Works, 1: 450.2–5.

9. The month devoted to the preliminary practices is mentioned, Yang dgon pa, *Rin po che 'bar ba*, Collected Works, 1: 455.3; the month dedicated to *gtum mo*, which comes after a period of a few weeks spent focusing on the channels, is mentioned at 469.6–470.1.

10. Yang dgon pa, *Lha gdong pa'i zhal chems bka' shog ma*, Collected Works, 1: 113–20, citing 117.5 (translated in Guarisco, *Secret Map of the Body*, 213); *Ri chos kyi phyag len gsal ba'i sgron me*, Collected Works, 1: 11–19, citing 12.3–4. Compare with William Gorvine, "The Life of a Bönpo Luminary: Sainthood, Partisanship and Literary Representation in a 20th Century Tibetan Biography" (PhD diss., University of Virginia, 2006), 449, 452.

11. Yang dgon pa, *Rin po che 'bar ba*, Collected Works, 1: 453.6–454.1.

12. This paragraph paraphrases the third part of the third chapter, which runs 506.3–514.1 in the *Rin po che 'bar ba*, Yang dgon pa, Collected Works, vol. 1; the corresponding section of the *Lhan thabs chen mo* runs Collected Works, 2: 89.2–97.1. Some additional details concerning Yang dgon pa's presentation of sleep yoga are drawn from an earlier section of the chapter, running 482.3–486.2 in the *Rin po che 'bar ba*. The *Lhan thabs chen mo* reminds us that it was at the break of dawn that Śākyamuni achieved buddhahood, 90.1.

13. For references to the four daily meditation sessions (*thun bzhi*), see *Rin po che 'bar ba*, Yan dgon pa, Collected Works, 1: 506.3, 511.6. Reference is made to practicing in either four or six daily sessions in the *Lhan thabs chen mo*, Collected Works, 2: 82.3. Lha btsun nam mkha' 'jigs med refers to six sessions, *Ri chos rin chen gnad kyi phreng ba*, in *Rdo rje snying po sprin gyi thol glu*, 2 vols. (n.p.; BDRC W13780), 2: 609–68, citing 626.2.

1. THE PRESCRIPTIVE LITERATURE FOR INDIVIDUAL RETREAT 199

Karma chags med provides the details that the four sessions occur at something like "morning, forenoon, afternoon, and night," and that when expanded to six, the additional sessions are at "dusk and dawn" (*zhogs pa snga dro nyin gung dgongs ka bzhi/ srod dang tho rangs thun drug bya ba*); Karma chags med, *Ri chos mtshams kyi zhal gdams* (Brag dkar dgon pa, 1970; BRDC W23259), 381.3–5. For commentary on this passage, see Khenpo Karthar Rinpoché, *Karma Chakme's Mountain Dharma*, 4 vols. (Woodstock, NY: Karma Triyana Dharmachakra Publications, 2004), 3: 110–11. Karma Chags med refers to starting off with four sessions but potentially reducing down to two at 253.2 (Karthar 2: 163).

14. The meaning of *kuśala* is from Sir Monier Monier-Williams, *A Sanskrit-English Dictionary* (Springfield, VA: Nataraj Books, 2004 [1899]), 297. The practice is described by Karma chags med, *Ri chos mtshams kyi zhal gdams*, chapter 17, which runs 260.1–271.2 (Karthar 2: 195–221).

15. For examples, see David DiValerio, trans., *The Life of the Madman of Ü* (New York: Oxford University Press, 2016), 62, 69; these references correspond to 391.6 and 406.1–2 in *Dpal ldan bla ma dam pa grub pa'i khyu mchog phyogs thams cad las rnam par rgyal ba'i spyod pa can rje btsun kun dga' bzang po'i rnam par thar pa ris med dad pa'i spu long g.yo byed*, by Smyug la paN chen ngag dbang grags pa and Lha mthong lo tsA ba bshes gnyen rnam rgyal, in *Bka' brgyud pa Hagiographies: A Collection of Rnam Thar of the Eminent Masters of Tibetan Buddhism*, ed. Khams sprul don brgyud nyi ma, 4 vols. (Palampur, H.P.: Sungrab Nyamso Gyunphel Parkhang, Tibetan Craft Community, 1972; BDRC W20499), 2: 383–660. See also Rgod tshang ras pa sna tshogs rang grol, *Gtsang smyon he ru ka phyogs thams cad las rnam par rgyal ba'i rnam thar rdo rje theg pa'i gsal byed nyi ma'i snying po* (New Delhi: Sharada Rani, 1969; BDRC W1KG9090), 22.2; and Roerich, trans., *The Blue Annals*, 200, 549–50, 690, 752, 996.

16. Appended to the end of Karma chags med's handbook is an [auto]biography in which this detail is related: Karma chags med, *Ri chos mtshams kyi zhal gdams*, 824.4–5 (Karthar 1: 8). The full biography runs 821.5–831.4, which is summarized in Karthar 1: 5–15. The editors of Khenpo Karthar Rinpoché's commentary also include a biography of Karma chags med, 1: xix–xx, based on that contained in Tsering Lama Jampal Zangpo, *A Garland of Immortal Wish-fulfilling Trees: The Palyul Tradition of Nyingmapa*, trans. Sangye Khandro (Ithaca, NY: Snow Lion, 1988), 35–44. Details about Karma chags med's life are also supplied from Haynie, "Karma chags med's *Mountain Dharma*," 5–10; and Georgios Halkias, "Heavenly Ascents after Death: Karma Chags med's Commentary on Mind Transference," *Revue d'Études Tibétaines* 52 (2019): 70–89.

17. Many of the biographical sources listed in the previous note contain discussion of Karma chags med's relationship with Mi 'gyur rdo rje. For a biography of the latter, see Tsering Lama Jampal Zangpo, *Garland of Immortal Wish-fulfilling Trees*, 45–52. See also Alexander Gardner, *The Life of Jamgon Kongtrul the Great* (Boulder, CO: Snow Lion, 2019), 61. A translation of the biography of Mi 'gyur rdo rje by Karma chags med has been published: Karma Chagme and Rigdzin Kunzang Sherab, *Sky Dharma: The Foundations of the Namchö Treasure Teachings (The Life of Tertön Migyur Dorje and the Great Commentary to the Preliminary Practices)*, trans. Khenpo Sonam Tsewang and Judith Amtzis (Boulder, CO: Snow Lion, 2022).

18. The single exception is chapter 11, on how to perform mandala offerings, which is addressed to one Pad+ma thabs mkhas; Karma chags med, *Ri chos mtshams kyi zhal gdams*, 129.4 (Karthar 1: 275), 134.6.

19. See, for example, chapter 15, which runs Karma chags med, *Ri chos mtshams kyi zhal gdams*, 205.4–222.5, citing 222.1–2 (Karthar 2: 108); and chapter 49, which runs 768.1–779.4, citing 768.3–4.

Despite the text's having been composed in a somewhat piecemeal fashion (albeit during a relatively condensed period of time), Karma chags med regarded all of this content as composing a single text: in the colophon he makes a clear interdiction that in the future only complete copies of the handbook should be made, specifically forbidding the copying and circulating of individual chapters: 821.1–3 (Karthar 4: 412–13).

20. Karma chags med, *Ri chos mtshams kyi zhal gdams*, 599.3–4 (Karthar 4: 82).
21. Gardner describes this text as "a lengthy survey of the Buddhist path from the Karma Kagyu perspective," *Life of Jamgon Kongtrul*, 51.
22. For three examples regarding differences in *sādhana* practice, see Karma chags med, *Ri chos mtshams kyi zhal gdams*, 245.4–5 (Karthar 2: 155); 247.5–6 (Karthar 2: 158); and 381.5–382.6 (Karthar 3: 107–11). For an example regarding different ways of doing guru yoga, see 144.5–147.6 (Karthar 1: 297–301).
23. Karma chags med, *Ri chos mtshams kyi zhal gdams*, 820.5–6 (Karthar 4: 412).
24. The gloss is provided in the colophon to chapter 17; Karma chags med, *Ri chos mtshams kyi zhal gdams*, 270.3–271.2 (Karthar 2: 211).
25. Categorizing trainees as being more moved by faith or by their intellect and reason has a long precedent in the Indo-Tibetan Buddhist tradition, going back at least to the eighth-century philosopher Haribhadra; Georges Dreyfus, *The Sound of Two Hands Clapping: The Education of a Tibetan Buddhist Monk* (Berkeley: University of California Press, 2003), 179–80.
26. The quotation is from Karma chags med, *Ri chos mtshams kyi zhal gdams*, 244.1–2 (Karthar 2: 153). The reference to sleeping positions is at 243.6 (Karthar 2: 153). The section concerning this first kind of *kusali*-style practitioner runs 240.1–244.2 (Karthar 2: 148–53).
27. The section concerning the second and third kinds of *kusali*-style practitioners runs Karma chags med, *Ri chos mtshams kyi zhal gdams*, 244.2–252.4 (Karthar 2: 153–62).
28. On the practices of *sgrub chen*, *sgrub chung*, and *sgrub mchod* see Janet Gyatso, *Apparitions of the Self: The Secret Autobiographies of a Tibetan Visionary* (Princeton, NJ: Princeton University Press, 1998), 74; James Gentry, *Power Objects in Tibetan Buddhism: The Life, Writings, and Legacy of Sokdokpa Lodrö Gyeltsen* (Leiden: Brill, 2017), 58–59, 303–5, 420; Khenpo Karthar Rinpoché 2: 358; Gardner, *Life of Jamgon Kongtrul*, 89, 91–92.
29. Karma chags med, *Ri chos mtshams kyi zhal gdams*, 253.6. The section on the three kinds of *paṇḍita*-style practitioner runs 252.4–256.3 (Karthar 2: 162–69).
30. See chapter 7, note 17.
31. See note 13 above.
32. Chapter 42 runs Karma chags med, *Ri chos mtshams kyi zhal gdams*, 660.5–685.2 (Karthar 4: 245–95). Halkias, "Heavenly Ascents after Death," conveys some of what is distinctive in Karma chags med's religiosity in relation to this.
33. He was known as Brag dkar blo bzang dpal ldan bstan 'dzin snyan grags, Brag dkar dge bshes, Brag dkar rin po che, Brag dkar bla ma, Tre hor brag dkar sprul sku, and Mchog sprul blo bzang bstan 'dzin, among other appellations. On his life and works, see Nicola Schneider, "The Third Dragkar Lama: An Important Figure for Female Monasticism in the Beginning of Twentieth Century Kham," *Revue d'Études Tibétaines* 21 (2011): 45–60. On his contacts with Shar rdza bkra shis rgyal mtshan, see William Gorvine, *Envisioning a Tibetan Luminary: The Life of a Modern Bönpo Saint* (New York: Oxford University Press, 2019). On his debate with 'Ju mi pham, see John Whitney Pettit, *Mipham's Beacon of Certainty: Illuminating the View of Dzogchen, the Great Perfection* (Boston: Wisdom, 1999), 10, 21, 467n54.
34. Brag dkar blo bzang dpal ldan bstan 'dzin snyan grags, *Gnas dben par sdod pa'i chos mdzad mtha' dag la nye bar mkho ba'i ri chos mu tig gi phreng ba* (Gser rta rdzong: Gser thang bla rung lnga rig nang bstan slob gling, n.d.; BDRC W3CN4732), 54.15–57.2. See a very similar passage in *Spong ba bsam gtan pa rnams la bslab pa'i khrims su bca' ba man ngag lag tu bcangs bde ba'i ri chos me tog phreng mdzes*, in *Collected Works*, 20 vols. (compiled in Chengdu; BDRC W23608), 3: 633–48, citing 637.6–638.5.

The *Mu tig gi phreng ba* and *Me tog phreng mdzes* are clearly related, with the far lengthier *Mu tig gi phreng ba* providing longer expositions on passages that can be identified in the *Me tog phreng mdzes*. It is unclear which was written first, as the *Me tog phreng mdzes* is undated. A statement at 645.3–4 in the *Me tog phreng mdzes* may suggest that it was written after the *Mu tig gi phreng ba*.

The shorter *Me tog phreng mdzes* comes just before the *Mu tig gi phreng ba* in vol. 3 of the *Collected Works*. His text offering instructions to nuns, *Rab byung ma rnams la bslab khrims su bcas pa thar pa'i them skas*, comes directly after the *Mu tig gi phreng ba*, 3: 927–41.

35. Productive labor, Brag dkar blo bzang dpal ldan, *Mu tig gi phreng ba*, 156.3–15; servants and retinues, 147.13–149.14; illness, old age, and death, 110.1–116.4.
36. Brag dkar blo bzang dpal ldan, *Mu tig gi phreng ba*, 202.15–210.3.
37. Brag dkar blo bzang dpal ldan, *Mu tig gi phreng ba*, 174.2–187.1. The critique of those who do not pay sufficient attention to meditation runs 178.2–183.7.
38. Brag dkar blo bzang dpal ldan, *Mu tig gi phreng ba*, 83.16–84.1. This analogy is also mentioned at 86.4, and is given fuller discussion 218.16–220.3.
39. Brag dkar blo bzang dpal ldan, *Mu tig gi phreng ba*, 86.1–87.2, 214.4–235.11.
40. Brag dkar blo bzang dpal ldan, *Mu tig gi phreng ba*, 241.10–255.16. Yang dgon pa is quoted twice in this discussion, although neither quotation is from the *Rin po che 'bar ba* or the *Lhan thabs chen mo*; 246.14–247.1, 248.10–13.
41. Roerich translates *ri chos* as "Hermit Doctrine," *The Blue Annals*, 200; Sernesi renders it as "Mountain Teachings," "The *History of the Mountain Teachings*"; Gardner translates it as "Mountain Doctrine," *Life of Jamgon Kongtrul*, 458; Per Sørensen glosses *ri chos* as referring to "solitary or seclusion teachings," "The Prolific Ascetic Lce sgom Shes rab rdo rje *alias* Lce sgom Zhig po: Allusive, but Elusive," *Journal of the Nepal Research Centre* 11 (1999): 175–200; Kurtis Schaeffer renders it as "mountain spirituality," *Buddhist Meditation: Classic Teachings from Tibet* (New York: Penguin, 2024), 172–74.

To provide a sense of the charisma this term has traditionally conveyed, one of the most famous texts in the Tibetan Buddhist canon is the massive *Ri chos nges don rgya mtsho*, or *Mountain Dharma: An Ocean of Definitive Meaning*, by Dol po pa shes rab rgyal mtshan, a seminal thinker of the Jo nang, who spent a great deal of time in retreat (including as a means to decline an invitation from the Yuan emperor; see note 8 from the introduction). Dol po pa's text is a systematic work of philosophy, laying out and defending the Jo nang school's "other-emptiness" (*gzhan stong*) position. The text provides no instructions on how to actually conduct a retreat. At the end Dol po pa explains why he has titled the text in this way (trans. Jeffrey Hopkins): "This final *definitive meaning* thus of all the excellent profound scriptures of the conqueror— / Realized through the kindness of foremost venerable lamas from being illuminated / By profound instructional counsel from the mouths of conqueror-children such as the protectors of the three lineages and so forth— / Is the *mountain doctrine* of profound yogic practitioners in isolated mountain retreats." Jeffrey Hopkins, trans., *Mountain Doctrine: Tibet's Fundamental Treatise on Other-Emptiness and the Buddha-Matrix*, ed. Kevin Vose (Ithaca, NY, and Boulder, CO: Snow Lion, 2006), 547 (repeated 730–31). Hopkins provides an alternative translation of the last line on 252–53 (footnote a). The essential final line reads *ri khrod dben par zab mo'i rnal 'byor spyod pa rnams kyi ri chos*. Hopkins explains this statement: "[Dolpopa's] text is aimed at presenting not what is tentative, provisional, and requiring interpretation in the Indian source texts but the definitive meaning of ultimate reality itself, so profound and difficult to realize that it is a doctrine practiced in mountain retreats by yogis," 5–6.

The Tibetan is supplied from Dol po pa shes rab rgya mtsho, *Ri chos nges don rgya mtsho zhes bya ba mthar thug thun mong ma yin pa'i man ngag* (Dharamsala: Library of Tibetan Works and Archives; undated *dbu med* manuscript, in 922 pages; BDRC W23709), 704.2.

42. Drung pa IV Kun dga' rnam rgyal, *Ri chos bai dUrya'i phreng ba zhes bya ba thar 'dod kyi mgul rgyan,* in *Gdams ngag mdzod*, ed. 'Jam mgon kong sprul blo gros mtha' yas, 18 vols. (Paro: Lama Ngodrup and Sherab Drimey, 1979–1981; BDRC W20877), 9: 315–23.

43. Lha btsun nam mkha' 'jigs med, *Ri chos rin chen gnad kyi phreng ba*, 655.6–656.1.
44. Karma chags med, *Ri chos mtshams kyi zhal gdams*, 595.3–5 (Karthar 4: 76–77). The device is referred to as a *rdul byang*, meaning a "dust slate" or a "dust signboard."
45. Karma chags med, *Ri chos mtshams kyi zhal gdams*, 245.1–2 (Karthar 2: 154). See also 250.6 (Karthar 2: 160). Karma chags med also mentions possessing written instructions, 236.3–4 (Karthar 2: 144); and makes the case that retreat is not a time for study, 169.4–170.3 (Karthar 2: 7–8). There is also a critical moment in the deepening of an individual's meditative practice when they should absolutely not read any texts, because doing so would be harmful, 172.6 (Karthar 2: 13). Nor is retreat a time for writing, 170.3 (Karthar 2: 8–9).
46. Karma nges don bstan rgyas, *Ri chos thar lam mdzub ston*, in *The Collected Works of Sman sdong mtshams pa rin po che Karma nges don bstan rgyas*, 3 vols. (Bir, H.P.: D. Tsondu Senghe, 1975; BDRC W10982), 3: 161–204, citing 195.1. Karma chags med mentions the possibility of writing to one's disciple during the morning meal break; *Ri chos mtshams kyi zhal gdams*, 250.6 (Karthar 2: 160). On writing during a retreat, see Gyatso, *Apparitions of the Self*, 103.

    Karma nges don bstan rgyas's dates remain a mystery, with the dates of his birth and death variously proposed as 1849/1867/1879 and 1921/1942/1960. He is also known as 'Jam dbyangs dpal ldan, and founded the monastery Sman sdong thub bstan dar rgyas gling, in the Sman sdong area of western Tibet.
47. Monastic charters, for example, "were often compilations of new and previously existing rules and were even sometimes taken from the guidelines of other institutions"; Berthe Jansen, *The Monastery Rules: Buddhist Monastic Organization in Pre-Modern Tibet* (Berkeley: University of California Press, 2018), 22. Tibetan hagiography is another genre in which direct or indirect borrowing is commonplace. Additionally, Tibetan Buddhist monastic scholasticism is built upon sustained debates playing out over centuries, in which composing a direct refutation of another scholar's presentation is normative.
48. Brag dkar blo bzang dpal ldan, *Rab byung ma rnams la bslab khrims su bcas pa thar pa'i them skas*, *Collected Works*, 3: 927–41. This text is discussed in Schneider, "The Third Dragkar Lama"; see especially 55–56.
49. Yang dgon pa, *Lha gdong pa'i zhal chems bka' shog ma*, *Collected Works*, 1: 118.1–2 (Guarisco, trans., *Secret Map of the Body*, 213).
50. Brag dkar blo bzang dpal ldan addresses how to avoid or properly navigate relationships with women, both lay and clerical; *Mu tig gi phreng ba*, 60.8–73.12. Phag mo gru pa rdo rje rgyal po addresses how to interpret having a dream about a woman during a retreat; *Ri chos bdud rtsi bum pa'i gdams ngag*, in *'Bri gung bka' brgyud chos mdzod chen mo*, compiled by A mgon rin po che and Ra se dkon mchog rgya mtsho, 151 vols. (Lhasa: Bri gung mthil dgon, 2004; BDRC W00JW501203), 16: 277–83, citing 281.3–4.
51. Brag dkar ba chos kyi dbang phyug, *Grub pa'i gnas chen brag dkar rta so'i sgrub sde spong ba pa rnams kyi blang dor gyi rim pa gsal bar ston pa'i bca' yig mun sel nyin mor byed pa'i 'od snang*, in *Collected Works*, 12 vols. (Swayambhunath, Kathmandu: Khenpo Shedup Tenzin, 2011), 12: 645–92. The date of the composition of the text, *me byi lo*, is given at 691.5. This text will be quoted at the end of chapter 4.
52. The groundbreaking fifty-three-volume collection of texts and excerpts by, about, and for female Tibetan Buddhist practitioners titled *Mkha' 'gro'i chos mdzod chen mo*, ed. Bla rung ar+ya tA re'i dpe tshogs rtsom sgrig khang (Bod ljongs bod yig dpe rnying dpe skrun khang, 2017; BDRC W3CN2459), which became partially available to me late in the research for this book thanks to the BDRC, will provide a means to further explore women's participation in and contributions to the tradition of long-term retreat, both communal and individual. This collection includes texts by women identified as practicing lifelong retreat (*tshe mtshams ma*; 52: 325–31, 332–37); instructions for women practicing in communal retreat, written by a man (52: 343–44); advice for a hermitess,

1. THE PRESCRIPTIVE LITERATURE FOR INDIVIDUAL RETREAT 203

written by a man (52: 359–62); and instructions for an approach–accomplishment retreat by a female treasure revealer (35: 303–23). Through my limited work with this collection, I have not been able to identify any instructions specifically directed toward women practicing individual long-term retreat, nor instructions for long-term individual retreat written by a woman.

There is a three-page passage labeled *Jo mo ri khrod gsar du bzung ba la go bde'i ngo sprod cig* (52: 246–48), which would appear to be "An easy-to-understand introduction for nuns newly taking up a mountain hermitage." The text is identified in its colophon as having been given spontaneously ('*phral du*) to two female practitioners by RA ga a sya, which was how Karma chags med typically referred to himself. The title is not included in the passage, so may have been formulated by the collection's editors. The text, in verse, seems to be a record of meditation instructions, with some references to retreat in its latter parts. It is labeled as being excerpted from a text referred to as *Jo mo ri chos*, "A mountain Dharma for nuns." I have been unable to identify the larger work, which could prove revelatory for our understanding of the history of the tradition.

53. Dylan Esler, *The Lamp for the Eye of Contemplation: The* Samten Migdron *by Nubchen Sangye Yeshe, a 10th-Century Tibetan Buddhist Text on Meditation* (Oxford: Oxford University Press, 2022), 43–48, 68–75; Gnubs chen sangs rgyas ye shes, *Rnal 'byor mig gi bsam gtan or Bsam gtan mig sgron: A treatise on bhāvanā and dhyāna and the relationships between the various approaches to Buddhist contemplative practice* (Leh: Tashigangpa, 1974; BDRC W00EGS1016286), 5.5–10.5, 30.1–36.2.

54. Rdor 'dzin nam mkha' rdo rje's receiving Yang dgon pa's works is mentioned in his biography by Chos rgyal lhun po, *ShAkya'i dge slong rdo rje 'dzin pa chen po/ nam mkha' rdo rje'i rnam par thar pa ngo mtshar gsal ba'i me long* (undated woodblock print, in 103 folio sides; BDRC W3CN18491; NGMPP L18/5), 15a1–7, 16b7; transmitting Yang dgon pa's works is mentioned at 26a4, 36b5.

On the life of Nam mkha' rdo rje, see Franz-Karl Ehrhard, *Early Buddhist Block Prints from Mang yul Gung thang* (Lumbini: Lumbini International Research Institute, 2000), 51–66.

At the behest of Karma pa VII Chos grags rgya mtsho (1454–1506), in the early sixteenth century, Rdor 'dzin nam mkha' rdo rje's main teacher, Nam mkha' rgyal mtshan dpal bzang (1475–1530), established an institution dedicated to the study and practice of Yang dgon pa's instructions, referred to as the *yang dgon gyi sgrub sde*, in Gtsang, where he taught from the *Ri chos skor gsum*. Nam mkha' rdo rje, *Dpal ldan bla ma dam pa sprul sku nam mkha' rgyal mtshan dpal bzang po'i rnam par thar pa/ dgos 'dod kun 'byung nor bu'i 'phreng ba*, in *'Ba' ra bka' brgyud gser 'phreng chen mo*, 4 vols. (Dehra Dun: Ngawang Gyaltsen and Ngawang Lungtok, 1970; BDRC W19231), 2: 394–521, citing 457.1–462.3. See Ehrhard, *Early Buddhist Block Prints*, 55.

55. Nam mkha' rdo rje, *ShAkya'i dge slong rdo rje 'dzin pa nam mkha' rdo rje'i mgur 'bum yid bzhin nor bu'i bang mdzod* (undated woodblock print, in 47 folio sides; BDRC W3CN18491), 18a1–5, 19b7–21a1. For other instances where in the course of a song Rdor 'dzin nam mkha' rdo rje prescribes staying in retreat, see 5b4, 22a2–3.

56. For an example of a master–disciple dialogue about retreat, see 'Jig rten gsum mgon, *Gcig pu ri khrod du gnas tshe ji ltar dgos pa rom po 'gar ston gyi zhus lan*, in *Khams gsum chos kyi rgyal po thub dbang rat+na shrI'i phyi yi bka' 'bum nor bu'i bang mdzod*, ed. Drikung Kyabgon Chetsang VII, 12 vols. (Delhi: Drikung Kagyu Ratna Shri Sungrab Nyamso Khang, 2001; BDRC W23743), 6: 514–32.

Schaeffer's recent volume *Buddhist Meditation* contains translations of many such songs. See in particular the compositions by Mi la ras pa, 201–11, and by Zhabs dkar tshogs drug rang grol, 1–10, 171–200. The last of these, which is presented as a dialogue between Zhabs dkar and one of his disciples asking questions about retreat, is plagiaristically similar to Lce sgom shes rab rdo rje's *Ri khrod skal ldan sgron me*, to be introduced in chapter 2.

57. Yang dgon pa, *Lhan thabs chen mo, Collected Works*, 2: 8.3, 9.1.

2. LOCATING THE ASCETIC SELF

1. Yang dgon pa rgyal mtshan dpal, *Ri chos yon tan kun 'byung [ba] rin po che 'bar ba*, in *The Collected Works (gsung 'bum) of Yang dgon pa*, 3 vols. (Thimpu: Kunsang Topgey, 1976; BDRC W1KG17449), 1: 447–570, citing 453.6.

    Karma chags med stipulates that the larder for the retreatant's consumables ("tea, butter, grain, and so on") should be in the northern part of the dwelling, since the north is the home of the *yakṣa*s, who are responsible for material abundance; *Ri chos mtshams kyi zhal gdams* (Brag dkar dgon pa, 1970; BRDC W23259), 219.3–4 (Khenpo Karthar Rinpoché, *Karma Chakme's Mountain Dharma*, 4 vols. [Woodstock, NY: Karma Triyana Dharmachakra Publications, 2004], 2: 104).

2. Yang dgon pa, *Rin po che 'bar ba*, *Collected Works*, 1: 454.1–2; Lha btsun nam mkha' 'jigs med, *Ri chos rin chen gnad kyi phreng ba*, in *Rdo rje snying po sprin gyi thol glu*, 2 vols. (n.p.; BDRC W13780), 2: 609–68, citing 623.5–6; Karma chags med, *Ri chos mtshams kyi zhal gdams*, 238.1–2 (Karthar 2: 146).

3. Karma chags med, *Ri chos mtshams kyi zhal gdams*, 242.6–243.2 (Karthar 2: 152); also mentioned in Karthar 3: 355.

4. Karma chags med, *Ri chos mtshams kyi zhal gdams*, 528.3–5 (Karthar 3: 291). The wording here suggests that this convention was not normative in Karma chags med's native eastern Tibet.

5. Phag mo gru pa rdo rje rgyal po, *Ri chos bdud rtsi bum pa'i gdams ngag*, in *'Bri gung bka' brgyud chos mdzod chen mo*, compiled by A mgon rin po che and Ra se dkon mchog rgya mtsho, 151 vols. (Lhasa: Bri gung mthil dgon, 2004; BDRC W00JW501203), 16: 277–83, citing 278.1–6; 'Jig rten gsum mgon, *Ri chos bdud rtsi'i bum pa*, in *'Bri gung bka' brgyud chos mdzod chen mo*, 26: 383–84, citing 383.1–384.1; Yang dgon pa, *Rin po che 'bar ba*, *Collected Works*, 1: 453.3–6, 454.6–455.2; Lha btsun nam mkha' 'jigs med, *Ri chos rin chen gnad kyi phreng ba*, 623.4–624.1; Mi pham phun tshogs shes rab, *Ri chos zab mo grub pa'i bcud len sbrang rtsi'i snying po*, in *Collected Works*, 2 vols. (Darjeeling: Thub bstan gsang sngags chos gling 'brug sgar dpe mdzod khang, 2008; BDRC W2KG200924), 1: 377–435, citing 391.2–3.

6. Karma chags med, *Ri chos mtshams kyi zhal gdams*, 237.1–3 (Karthar 2: 145).

7. Mi pham phun tshogs shes rab, *Ri chos zab mo grub pa'i bcud len sbrang rtsi'i snying po*, 391.2. For more on this individual, see Kurtis Schaeffer, *Himalayan Hermitess: The Life of a Tibetan Buddhist Nun* (New York: Oxford University Press, 2004), 43.

8. Kazi Ashraf, *The Hermit's Hut: Architecture and Asceticism in India* (Honolulu: University of Hawai'i Press, 2013), 152. The thatched hut of Phag mo gru pa rdo rje rgyal po became a potent center of worship activity. A temple was constructed around it, and it continued to be venerated for hundreds of years. George Roerich, trans., *The Blue Annals* (Delhi: Motilal Banarsidass, 1996 [1949]), 560–62, 569–70; Olaf Czaja, *Medieval Rule in Tibet: The Rlangs Clan and the Political and Religious History of the Ruling House of Phag mo gru pa* (Vienna: Verlag der Österreichischen Akademie der Wissenschaften, 2013), 77, 347, 353–57, 362, 368–70. It may be that at this early moment in the history of Buddhism in Tibet, the hut held a greater significance in eremitic practice, perhaps showing a debt to the Indic tradition as described by Ashraf.

9. The *Bod rgya tshig mdzod chen mo* (Mi rigs dpe skrun khang, 1985) offers three glosses of *dben pa*: as a verb meaning "without or empty of" (*med pa'am stong pa*); as an adjective, indicating the states of being "outlying, remote" and "without distractions" (*bas mtha' dang / 'du 'dzi med pa*); and as a noun meaning "a place that is without distractions" (*du 'dzi med pa'i sa cha*); 1948.

    Dung dkar blo bzang 'phrin las glosses *dben pa* as follows: "In general, *dben pa*, as a verb, is to be understood as 'without,' 'free from,' 'not having,' 'reduced by,' and so on. In instances where it is a noun, it is understood as a location that is without a lot of people or activities that disturb"; *Dung dkar tshig mdzod chen mo* (Beijing: Krung go'i bod rig pa dpe skrun khang, 2002), 1537.

2. LOCATING THE ASCETIC SELF 205

In the *Scholar's Feast*, Dpa' bo gtsug lag phreng ba (1504–1564/66) uses the honorific phrase *dben pa mdzad*, as meaning to "live" or "remain in isolation," more than a dozen times (in one instance formulated as *dben par mdzad*); for examples, see *Chos 'byung mkhas pa'i dga' ston* (Beijing: Mi rigs dpe skrun khang, 2006; BDRC W8LS19006), 473.29, 501.11, 547.9, 548.4, 554.11, 558.9.

10. Karmapa III Rang byung rdo rje, *Ri chos bdud rtsi'i nying khu*, in *Collected Works*, 13 vols. (Lhasa: Dpal brtsegs bod yig dpe rnying zhib 'jug khang, 2013; BDRC W3PD1288), 4: 479–503, citing 493.6–494.1.

    Brag dkar blo bzang dpal ldan bstan 'dzin snyan grags, *Gnas dben par sdod pa'i chos mdzad mtha' dag la nye bar mkho ba'i ri chos mu tig gi phreng ba* (Gser rta rdzong: Gser thang bla rung lnga rig nang bstan slob gling, n.d.; BDRC W3CN4732), 131.10. My translation follows Dung dkar blo bzang 'phrin las, who glosses *rgyu 'grul* as meaning *phar 'gro tshur 'ong*; *Dung dkar tshig mdzod chen mo*, 707.

    The final reference here is to Ngag dbang blo bzang bsam gtan, *Dben par dga' ba'i glu*, in *Collected Works*, 4 vols. (Lan kru'u: Kan su'u mi rigs dpe skrun khang, 2005; BDRC W29486), 4: 22–23, citing 22.10.

    Note a similar statement from the *Life of Milarepa*, concerning a *mtshams dam po mi med khyi med*, in Gtsang smyon he ru ka, *Rnal 'byor gyi dbang phyug chen po mi la ras pa'i rnam mgur* (Zi ling: Mtsho sngon mi rigs dpe skrun khang, 2005), 125.16–17, which Andrew Quintman translates as "In strict retreat without human or dog"; *Life of Milarepa* (New York: Penguin, 2010), 113.

11. See Anne-Marie Blondeau and Ernst Steinkellner, eds., *Reflections of the Mountain: Essays on the History and Social Meaning of the Mountain Cult in Tibet and the Himalaya* (Vienna: Verlag der Österreichischen Akademie der Wissenschaft, 1996); and Jared Lindahl, "The Ritual Veneration of Mongolia's Mountains," in *Tibetan Ritual*, ed. José Ignacio Cabezón (New York: Oxford University Press, 2010), 225–48.

12. In Tibetan culture, the vertically differentiated parts of a mountain can be referred to as parts of a metaphor expressive of social hierarchies, the human socialization and aging process, and so on; Geoff Childs, *Tibetan Diary: From Birth to Death and Beyond in a Himalayan Valley of Nepal* (Berkeley: University of California Press, 2004), 101–3.

13. Zhabs dkar tshogs drug rang grol, *Chos bshad gzhan phan zla ba*, in *Collected Works*, 10 vols. (Zi ling: Mtsho sngon mi rigs dpe skrun khang, 2002; BDRC W1PD45150), 8: 1–283, citing 211.9–10.

14. The term appears as some variant of *ri mi 'babs pa* or *ri ma 'babs pa*; Roerich, trans., *The Blue Annals*, 544, 546, 860, 865, 991.

15. Lce sgom shes rab rdo rje, *Ri khrod skal ldan sgron me*, in *Blo sbyong nyer mkho phyogs bsgrigs*, ed. Cha ris skal bzang thogs med and Ngag dbang sbyin pa (Lan kru'u: Kan su'u mi rigs dpe skrun khang, 2003; BDRC W25275), 675–88, citing 683.3–4; O rgyan rnam grol dbang po, *Sbas mtha'i ri khrod du 'dug tshul dang rnams [=rnam] kun rang brgyud [=rgyud] chos dang bsre tshul gyi bslab bya zhal gyi gdams pa'i nying khu gsang ba bdud rtsi thig le* (undated *dbu med* manuscript, in 10 folio sides; NGMPP AT82/7), citing 2b4–5; Brag dkar blo bzang dpal ldan, *Mu tig gi phreng ba*, 132.1–3.

    Offering a snapshot of how eremitic activity was understood around the turn of the sixteenth century, the biography of Nam mkha' rgyal mtshan dpal bzang mentions how, after he imparted a series of teachings, certain of his students made vows to remain in retreat for the rest of their lives or to "not descend from the mountain"; to do retreat for the summer or the winter; or to do a retreat for a month or two (*la la tshe 'tshams* [sic] *dang / ri mi 'bab kyi dam bca'/ la las dbyar 'tshams dgun 'tshams/ zla re zla gnyis*); Nam mkha' rdo rje, *Dpal ldan bla ma dam pa sprul sku nam mkha' rgyal mtshan dpal bzang po'i rnam par thar pa/ dgos 'dod kun 'byung nor bu'i 'phreng ba*, in *'Ba' ra bka' brgyud gser 'phreng chen mo* (Dehra Dun: Ngawang Gyaltsen and Ngawang Lungtok, 1970; BDRC W19231), 462.1–2.

16. Karma chags med, *Ri chos mtshams kyi zhal gdams*, 24.3 (Karthar 1: 37; Eric Haynie, "Karma chags med's *Mountain Dharma*: Tibetan Advice on Sociologies of Retreat" [M.A. thesis, University of Colorado, 2013], 53–54, 84–85), 573.2–3 (Karthar 4: 24–25); Lcang skya III Rol pa'i rdo rje, *Dben par dga' ba'i gtam chos glu ring mo*, in *Collected Works*, 7 vols. (Beijing: Krung go bod brgyud mtho rim nang bstan slob gling nang bstan zhib 'jug khang, 1995; BDRC W28833), 4: 393–96, citing 394.1; Brag dkar blo bzang dpal ldan, *Mu tig gi phreng ba*, 10.2–6, 17.6–11, 32.1–4, 241.10–13.

    Although *ri dwags* is most often used to refer to deer, it can also refer to other wilderness-dwelling, herbivorous animals. There are also references to lions (or perhaps snow lions), who wander alone in the mountains with a more heroic aspect than that of deer: Brag dkar blo bzang dpal ldan, *Mu tig gi phreng ba*, 44.9–11, 168.15–169.11; *Spong ba bsam gtan pa rnams la bslab pa'i khrims su bca' ba man ngag lag tu bcangs bde ba'i ri chos me tog phreng mdzes*, in *Collected Works*, 20 vols. (compiled in Chengdu; BDRC W23608), 3: 633–48, citing 648.1–2. The deer would largely replace the older image from South Asian Buddhism of remaining in solitude "like a rhinoceros."

17. Ashraf, *The Hermit's Hut*, 31, 33, 34–37; Georges Dreyfus, *The Sound of Two Hands Clapping: The Education of a Tibetan Buddhist Monk* (Berkeley: University of California Press, 2003), 37.

    As Ruth Gamble has written with respect to Karma pa III's *Ri chos dngos grub phreng ba*, "In this work, and throughout his writing, mountains are a synonym for isolation and wilderness; they represent an otherworldly space into which those seeking transformation must travel"; *The Third Karmapa Rangjung Dorje: Master of Mahāmudrā* (Boulder, CO: Shambhala, 2020), 157. This is the case not just for Karmapa III, but for the entire Tibetan Buddhist tradition. See 240n372, on the term *ri khrod*. Gamble observes how the Tibetan "mountain" often slips into actually conveying the sense of "wilderness."

18. Lindsay Jones, ed., *Encyclopedia of Religion (Second Edition)*, 15 vols. (Detroit: Macmillan Reference USA, 2005), 5: 2822; Ashraf, *The Hermit's Hut*, 38.

    Émile Durkheim observes that in the aboriginal societies of Australia, where a young man's initiation would be preceded by a months-long period of asceticism in the wilderness away from home, "So much is the forest considered his natural milieu that, in quite a few tribes, the word for initiation means 'that which is of the forest.'" When such a novice attends a ceremony during this period, he may be decorated with leaves, thereby maintaining his association with the forest even when moving into a different kind of space; *The Elementary Forms of Religious Life*, trans. Karen Fields (New York: The Free Press, 1995 [1912]), 314–15.

19. 'Jig rten gsum mgon, *Sems can gyi don du gcig pur ri khrod 'grims pa*, in *Khams gsum chos kyi rgyal po thub dbang rat+na shrI'i phyi yi bka' 'bum nor bu'i bang mdzod*, ed. Drikung Kyabgon Chetsang VII, 12 vols. (Delhi: Drikung Kagyu Ratna Shri Sungrab Nyamso Khang, 2001; BDRC W23743), 1: 464–66, citing 465.3.

    Klong chen pa dri med 'od zer, *Nags tshal kun tu dga' ba'i gtam*, in *Miscellaneous Writings (gsung thor bu)*, 2 vols. (Gangtok: Pema Thinley, Sikkim National Press, n.d.; BDRC W23555) 1: 137–49, quoting 137.4–5, 142.3–4, 144.3–4.

    There exist at minimum three translations of this text: that by Timothy Hinkle from 2016, "Song of the Enchanting Wildwoods," distributed by Lotsawa House (https://www.lotsawahouse.org/tibetan-masters/longchen-rabjam/enchanting-wildwoods); "The Story of Wildwood Delights," in Herbert Guenther, *A Visionary Journey* (Boston and Shaftesbury: Shambhala, 1989); and a partial translation by Kurtis Schaeffer, whose rendering of the title I have borrowed, in *Sources of Tibetan Tradition*, ed. Schaeffer, Matthew Kapstein, and Gray Tuttle (New York: Columbia University Press, 2013), 433–35.

20. Ngag dbang blo bzang bsam gtan, *Dben par dga' ba'i glu rang sems dge bskul*, *Collected Works*, 4: 26–30, citing 27.4–6. On the author, see his entry in the Treasury of Lives: https://treasuryoflives.org/biographies/view/Tewo-Lungzang-Nangwa-Lobzang-Samten/2926.

21. Lcang skya III Rol pa'i rdo rje, *Dben par dga' ba'i gtam chos glu ring mo, Collected Works*, 4: 393–96.

   Other examples from the genre include PaN chen bla ma IV Blo bzang chos kyi rgyal mtshan, *Ka li sum cu las brtsams pa'i dben par dga' ba'i gtam*, in *Collected Works*, 5 vols. (Gzhis ka rtse: Bkra shis lhun po par khang, n.d.; BDRC W9848), 5: 562–63; Rong tha che tshang blo bzang dam chos rgya mtsho, *Ka li sum cu las brtsams pa'i bslab bya dbyangs kyi nges pa bya dka' bas spras pa dben par dga' ba'i gtam rab snyan dri za'i glu dbyangs*, in *Collected Works*, 6 vols. (Delhi: Ngawang Sopa, 1975; BDRC W13528), 3: 131–39; and *Dben par dga' ba'i gtam rab snyan dri za'i 'phang 'gro*, 6: 29–36.

22. Zhabs dkar, *Chos bshad gzhan phan zla ba*, 216.8–11. This is verse 26.10 in the translation provided by the 84000 project (https://read.84000.co/translation/toh127.html). See also Zhabs dkar 173.11–14, which is verse 30.62. There is a similar section late in Brag dkar blo bzang dpal ldan's *Mu tig gi phreng ba* featuring quotations from sutras regarding the necessity of removing oneself to an unpeopled locale for practice; 241.10–246.11.

   Zhabs dkar briefly describes how he came to compose this text, and his intentions in doing so, in his autobiography, which he wrote in 1837: Shabkar Tsokdruk Rangdrol, *The Life of Shabkar: The Autobiography of a Tibetan Yogin*, trans. Matthieu Ricard et al. (Ithaca, NY: Snow Lion, 2001), 249. For more information on *Chos bshad gzhan phan zla ba*, see *The Life of Shabkar*, 580–81, 590.

23. See the *Khaggavisāṇa Sutta*, preserved in the Pāli Canon as Sutta Nipata 1.3 (https://www.accesstoinsight.org/tipitaka/kn/snp/snp.1.03.than.html).

24. On Lce sgom shes rab rdo rje, see Per Sørensen, "The Prolific Ascetic Lce sgom Shes rab rdo rje *alias* Lce sgom Zhig po: Allusive, but Elusive," *Journal of the Nepal Research Centre* 11 (1999): 175–200; Yael Bentor, "The Tibetan Practice of the Mantra Path According to Lce sgom pa," in *Tantra in Practice*, ed. David Gordon White (Princeton, NJ: Princeton University Press, 2000), 326–46; Matthew Kapstein, *The Tibetan Assimilation of Buddhism* (New York: Oxford University Press, 2000), 77; Dan Martin, "The Woman Illusion? Research into the Lives of Spiritually Accomplished Women Leaders of the 11th and 12th Centuries," in *Women in Tibet*, ed. Janet Gyatso and Hanna Havnevik (New York: Columbia University Press, 2005), 49–82, citing 69–70.

   Many of these references came to my attention thanks to the bibliography included with Dan Martin's entry on Lce sgom pa in the Treasury of Lives (https://treasuryoflives.org/biographies/view/Chegompa-Sherab-Dorje/7373).

25. I am uncertain how best to translate the title, *Ri khrod skal ldan sgron me*, as a few different readings of this terse phrase are possible. In the printing colophon, the text is referred to, perhaps mistakenly, as *Ri chos sgron me*; Lce sgom shes rab rdo rje, 687.16. This is neither the first nor the last time the similar but not typically homophonic terms *ri khrod* and *ri chos* would be mistaken for each other. The mistake occurs regularly in the central dialect of Tibetan as spoken today.

26. Lce sgom shes rab rdo rje, *Ri khrod skal ldan sgron me*, 679.2–680.4.

27. Lce sgom shes rab rdo rje, *Ri khrod skal ldan sgron me*, 681.4–17, 680.4–14.

28. Klong chen pa dri med 'od zer, *Nags tshal kun tu dga' ba'i gtam*, 144.6–145.6. This corresponds to the section of Hinkle's translation beginning, "There, inspired by the turning of the leaves . . ." and ending six verses later, at "What is called 'empty of true existence.'"

29. Bhikku Ñāṇamoli, trans., *The Path of Purification (Visuddhimagga)* (Onalaska, WA: BPS Pariyatti Editions, 1999), citing 70–73 within the chapter that runs 58–81. See Ashraf, *The Hermit's Hut*, 42, 68; Gavin Flood, *The Ascetic Self: Subjectivity, Memory and Tradition* (Cambridge: Cambridge University Press, 2004), 128–33; Oliver Freiberger, "Early Buddhism, Asceticism, and the Politics of the Middle Way," in *Asceticism and Its Critics: Historical Accounts and Comparative Perspectives*, ed. Freiberger (New York: Oxford University Press, 2006), 235–58; Reginald Ray,

Buddhist Saints in India: A Study in Buddhist Values and Orientations (New York: Oxford University Press, 1994), 293–323. Brag dkar blo bzang dpal ldan, *Mu tig gi phreng ba*, 130.1–131.9.

30. Yang dgon pa's chapter on choosing a location for a retreat runs *Rin po che 'bar ba, Collected Works,* 1: 450.5–452.5. In this paragraph I have paraphrased up to 451.4.

    The term *mi rgod,* at 451.3, is ambiguous and can be used to refer to unruly or dangerous (*rgod*) persons (*mi*), or to the oversized and furry biped known as the yeti or abominable snowman. For other references to *mi rgod* in this body of literature, see Phag mo gru pa, *Ri chos bdud rtsi bum pa'i gdams ngag,* in *'Bri gung bka' brgyud chos mdzod chen mo,* 16: 281.5–282.1; Lce sgom shes rab rdo rje, *Ri khrod skal ldan sgron me,* 677.18–19; Zur mang legs bshad sgra dbyangs, *Ri yi chos gtam kun tu bzang po'i sgra dbyangs* (Mtshur phu dgon gtsug lag dpe tshogs, n.d.; 113 pages; BDRC W3CN5072), 18.9–12.

31. This paragraph paraphrases Yang dgon pa, *Rin po che 'bar ba, Collected Works,* 1: 451.4–452.5. In the subsequent chapter, in the context of describing how to begin a retreat, Yang dgon pa provides a very limited glimpse of what he understands this process to entail: "Then you go to the location and examine its characteristics. If it possesses [the correct] characteristics, then obstacles will not arise"; 453.3.

32. Yang dgon pa, *Ri chos yon tan kun 'byung gi lhan thabs chen mo,* in *The Collected Works (gsung 'bum) of Yang dgon pa,* 3 vols. (Thimpu: Kunsang Topgey, 1976; BDRC W1KG17449), 2: 1–175, citing 4.4–10.2.

    Showing a continuity with this general way of thinking about how the hermit relates to their physical surroundings, elsewhere in the *Lhan thabs chen mo* Yang dgon pa instructs that if a retreatant should experience an obstacle to religious progress, they can attempt to root it out by examining a number of specific factors: if they can determine there is no mistake being made in their yogic practices, their motivations, their adherence to *samaya*s, or obeying the word of their lama, then they should reexamine their dwelling and how it is oriented geomantically. The meditator should also examine their clothing, bedding, and the offering substances used in rituals. "The seed of the problem" (*skyon gyi sa bon*) may lie in any of these, from which the meditator may therefore need to separate themselves; 119.1–3. Clothing is discussed as a potential carrier of a harmful taint, 129.4–130.1.

    In his instructions on how to perform *gtum mo,* Yang dgon pa mentions that wearing clothing that carries a harmful taint can cause the loss of internal heat; *Rin po che 'bar ba, Collected Works,* 1: 473.6–474.1.

33. Yang dgon pa, *Lhan thabs chen mo, Collected Works,* 2: 4.4–5.

    In his *Rdo rje lus kyi sbas bshad,* Yang dgon pa gives a similar statement—in this case, concerning how the cycles of the movements of an individual's psychophysical winds are related to the cycles of years, months, and days—which Guarisco translates as "As it is externally, so it is internally," which is presented by Yang dgon pa as a quotation, most likely from the *Kālacakra Tantra* (*de thams cad phyi rol ji bzhin nang de bzhin zhal las shes par bya'o*); *Rdo rje lus kyi sbas bshad,* in *Collected Works,* 2: 421–97, citing 466.3 (Elio Guarisco, trans., *Secret Map of the Body: Visions of the Human Energy Structure* [Merigar, Italy: Shang Shung Publications, 2015], 279). On the *Sbas bshad's* place in the history of medical thinking in Tibet, see Janet Gyatso, *Being Human in a Buddhist World: An Intellectual History of Medicine in Early Modern Tibet* (New York: Columbia University Press, 2015).

    On the phrase "As it is outside so it is within the body" (*yathā bāhye tathā dehe*) in the *Kālacakra* literature, see Vesna Wallace, *The Inner Kālacakratantra: A Buddhist Tantric View of the Individual* (New York: Oxford University Press, 2001), 65, 85. See also note 54, below.

34. Charles Taylor, *A Secular Age* (Cambridge, MA: Harvard University Press, 2007).

35. Yang dgon pa's treatment of place would be discussed by Zur mang legs bshad sgra dbyangs, *Ri yi chos gtam kun tu bzang po'i sgra dbyangs,* 18.15–19.16. After Legs bshad sgra dbyangs refers to *rje*

2. LOCATING THE ASCETIC SELF 209

yang dgon pa'i ri chos at the beginning of this passage, I understand the subsequent references to *rje* to indicate Yang dgon pa. He also directs the reader to Yang dgon pa's teachings at 22.11–12, 64.4–16 (here specifically referring to the retreat manual), and 96.18–97.1. At 54.9–11, he references Yang dgon pa's instructions on *gsang spyod*.

Yang dgon pa's treatment of geomancy would be briefly discussed in Sde srid Sangs rgyas rgya mtsho's 1688 work, *Bstan bcos Bai dūr Dkar po las Dri lan 'Khrul snang G.ya' sel Don gyi Bzhin ras Ston byed* (*The 18th Century Sde dge Redaction of the Sde srid Sangs rgyas rgya mtsho's Vai dūrya G.ya' sel with the Snyan sgron Nyis brgya brgyad pa*), 2 vols. (Dehra Dun, 1976; BDRC W1KG12689), 1: 96.3–4. This text is a follow-up to Sangs rgyas rgya mtsho's treatise on astronomy, astrology, and geomancy, the *Baidūrya dkar po* or *White Beryl*.

36. Karma pa III Rang byung rdo rje, *Ri chos bdud rtsi'i nying khu*, Collected Works (2013), 4: 494.3–495.2.

    Zur mang legs bshad sgra dbyangs gives what is either a quotation or a paraphrase of Karma pa III on how the meditator will be affected by their circumstances, very reminiscent of Yang dgon pa's presentation; *Ri yi chos gtam kun tu bzang po'i sgra dbyangs*, 19.17–20.5. He also quotes Phag mo gru pa saying something similar, 20.13–16.

37. Bsod nams chos 'dzin, *Dben pa ri khrod 'grims pa'i gsal 'debs/ zhal gdam thar pa chen po'i gru sding* (undated *dbu med* manuscript, in 11 folio sides; NGMPP AT146/3), 3b4–4a3.

38. Karma chags med, *Ri chos mtshams kyi zhal gdams*, 22.5–6 (Karthar 1: 36; Haynie, "Karma chags med's *Mountain Dharma*," 83).

39. In the table of contents, this chapter (which runs 205.4–222.5) is referred to as "a brief presentation of geomancy: the compendium of jewels," *sa dpyad nyung ngu rin chen kun 'dus*; Karma chags med, *Ri chos mtshams kyi zhal gdams*, 7.3. Haynie translates this as "The Inclusion of All Jewels: A Snippet on Geomancy"; "Karma chags med's *Mountain Dharma*," 79.

    This chapter is presented as a free-standing text on geomancy, labeled *Sa dpyad rin chen kun 'dus*, in *Bka' brgyud pa'i gsung rab*, 19 vols. (Mtsho sngon mi rigs dpe skrun khang, 2004; BDRC W30023), 4: 789–800.

    Karma chags med also wrote a shorter, more general text on geomancy, called *Sa dpyad rin chen gter mdzod*, in Collected Works, 60 vols. (Nang chen rdzong: Gnas mdo gsang sngags chos 'phel gling gi dpe rnying nyams gso khang, 2010; BDRC W1KG8321), 58: 175–86.

    At the request of the Karma pa XVI, between 1999 and 2003 Khenpo Karthar Rinpoché—then serving as abbot of the North American seat of the Karmapa in Woodstock, New York, and the retreat master at Karmé Ling, in Delhi, New York—delivered over a series of occasions an extensive oral commentary on Karma chags med's *Ri chos mtshams kyi zhal gdams*. In 2004, an English translation of that commentary by Lama Yeshe Gyamtso, Chojor Radha, and Namgyal Khorko was published, in four volumes. My understanding of Karma chags med's handbook has been improved enormously thanks to this valuable resource.

    These four volumes have since been published in Chinese translation as well, released between 2009 and 2015. Audio recordings of Khenpo Karthar Rinpoché's teachings on the *Ri chos mtshams kyi zhal gdams*, in 29 compact discs, are also available.

    Because they were deemed secret, chapters 27 through 33 of the handbook were omitted from Khenpo Karthar Rinpoché's initial teachings and from the four-volume translation of his commentary. He returned to give instruction on those chapters in 2007. The transcripts are said to be available to members of the Karma Triyana Dharmachakra community (Karthar 4: 405, 420).

40. Karma chags med, *Ri chos mtshams kyi zhal gdams*, 208.2 (Karthar 2: 90).

41. On this final point, see Karma chags med, *Ri chos mtshams kyi zhal gdams*, 216.4–217.2 (Karthar 2: 10–12). In a similar fashion, Lha btsun nam mkha' 'jigs med mentions (among other considerations) that a location may prove conducive to taming, expanding, empowering, or fierce activity

depending on whether it resembles, respectively, a white circle, a yellow square, a red half-moon, or a black triangle; *Ri chos rin chen gnad kyi phreng ba,* 620.5–6.

42. Karma chags med, *Ri chos mtshams kyi zhal gdams,* 219.5–220.1 (Karthar 2: 105). The origins of this ideal are discussed in Ashraf, *The Hermit's Hut,* 108. Something that may be related to this is mentioned in Yang dgon pa, *Rin po che 'bar ba, Collected Works,* 1: 452.4; *Lhan thabs chen mo,* 2: 4.4, 10.1–2.

43. Karma chags med, *Ri chos mtshams kyi zhal gdams,* 208.1–2 (Karthar 2: 90).

44. Karma chags med, *Ri chos mtshams kyi zhal gdams,* 208.6–210.1 (Karthar 2: 91–93).

45. Zur mang legs bshad sgra dbyangs, *Ri yi chos gtam kun tu bzang po'i sgra dbyangs,* 19.5–10.

When giving oral commentary on Karma chags med's chapter on geomancy, Khenpo Karthar Rinpoché offered the following assessment: "It is very hard to find places to live that actually fulfill all of these criteria. Even if you find something that is good in general, there is still the effect on specific people because of the year of their birth. If you have a family of four people, what may be good for one person may be terrible for the other three. You really have to accept whatever dwelling you find yourself in based upon your own merit and karma, and you cannot necessarily expect to find a dwelling that has all of the criteria presented in the texts. The more you know about geomancy the more difficult it is to choose a dwelling," 2: 94–95. He also said, "Geomancy is very difficult because you can have everything you want, then one thing will throw it all off; or you can have everything you do not want, but one thing can make it all work," 2: 116.

I have not found any dates for Legs bshad sgra dbyangs's birth or death. He is noted as having been a disciple of Karma pa IX Dbang phyug rdo rje (1556–1601/1603) and a teacher of Drung pa IV Kun dga' rnam rgyal (1567–1629), from which we can deduce with some confidence that he was born in the sixteenth century.

46. Karma chags med, *Ri chos mtshams kyi zhal gdams,* 228.1–229.6 (Karthar 2: 134–36), quoting 228.5.

47. Zur mang legs bshad sgra dbyangs, *Ri yi chos gtam kun tu bzang po'i sgra dbyangs,* 18.2–7; Lha btsun nam mkha' 'jigs med, *Ri chos rin chen gnad kyi phreng ba,* 621.3–4.

48. Lha btsun nam mkha' 'jigs med, *Ri chos rin chen gnad kyi phreng ba,* 620.3–621.3, quoting 620.5. He also mentions the geomantic consideration that a place may prove conducive to the four types of tantric behavior (on which see note 41), the supremacy of "hidden valleys" (*sbas yul*), and other factors.

49. Zur mang legs bshad sgra dbyangs, *Ri yi chos gtam kun tu bzang po'i sgra dbyangs,* 18.2–12, quoting 18.9.

50. Mi pham phun tshogs shes rab, *Ri chos zab mo grub pa'i bcud len sbrang rtsi'i snying po,* 388.1–389.4.

51. Karma nges don bstan rgyas, *Ri chos thar lam mdzub ston,* in *The Collected Works of Sman sdong mtshams pa rin po che Karma nges don bstan rgyas,* 3 vols. (Bir, H.P.: D. Tsondu Senghe, 1975; BDRC W10982), 3: 161–204, citing 168.1–6.

Bsod nams chos 'dzin remarks that the meditator should reflect positively that the place where they are meditating had been "occupied by the *siddha*s of the past"; *Dben pa ri khrod 'grims pa'i gsal 'debs,* 5a1–2.

52. Andrew Quintman, "Toward a Geographic Biography: Mi la ras pa in the Tibetan Landscape," *Numen* 55, no. 4 (2008): 366, 370. Here I also refer to Rachel Pang, *Singer of the Land of Snows: Shabkar, Buddhism, and Tibetan National Identity* (Charlottesville: University of Virginia Press, 2024), especially chapter 2. Quintman's piece contains references to much of the earlier scholarship in this area.

For a few representative examples of research on Tibetan narrative construction and conceptions of space, see Janet Gyatso, "Down with the Demoness: Reflections on a Feminine Ground in Tibet," in *Feminine Ground: Essays on Women and Tibet,* ed. Janice Willis (Ithaca, NY: Snow Lion, 1987), 33–51; Toni Huber, "Where Exactly are Cārita, Devikoṭa, and Himavat? A Sacred Geography Controversy and the Development of Tantric Buddhist Pilgrimage Sites in Tibet," *Kailash* 14, nos. 3–4 (1990): 121–64; and Huber, "A Guide to the La Phyi Maṇḍala: History, Landscape and Ritual in South-Western Tibet," in *Maṇḍala and Landscape,* ed. A. W. Macdonald (Delhi: D. K. Printworld, 1997), 233–86.

53. Phag mo gru pa, *Ri chos bdud rtsi bum pa'i gdams ngag*, in *'Bri gung bka' brgyud chos mdzod chen mo*, 16: 281.6–282.1; 'Jig rten gsum mgon, *Ri chos bdud rtsi'i bum chen*, in *'Bri gung bka' brgyud chos mdzod chen mo*, 26: 384–99, citing 384.2–3, 386.6–388.3.

    The *Collected Works* of 'Jig rten gsum mgon contain a handful of other texts with *Ri chos* in their titles and seemingly offering instructions for retreat, which I have not read closely or integrated into my research. Some of these texts would later be received by Yang dgon pa; see chapter 1, note 3.

54. Longchenpa, *Finding Rest in Meditation (The Trilogy of Rest, Volume 2)*, trans. Padmakara Translation Group (Boulder, CO: Shambhala, 2018), 3–9; with autocommentary, 45–54; Kurtis Schaeffer, *Buddhist Meditation: Classic Teachings from Tibet* (New York: Penguin, 2024), 160–69; Klong chen pa dri med 'od zer, *Rdzogs pa chen po ngal gso skor gsum* (Zhang kang then ma dpe skrun khang, 2005; BDRC W1GS60877), 1.6–2.21. Like the *Bsam gtan mig sgron* by Gnubs chen sangs rgyas ye shes, it may not be fitting to describe this text as having the primary purpose of imparting prescriptions for individual long-term retreat, being more centrally devoted to meditative practice in general.

    In this passage, Klong chen pa makes statements similar to Yang dgon pa's regarding the relationship between the internal and the external that explains the basic principle behind his prescriptions: "the external and internal cycles of dependence coincide" and "in dependence on your dwelling place / Your inner mind is changed"; Longchenpa, *Finding Rest*, 5, 7. The Tibetan for these two passages reads *phyi nang rten 'brel gcig pas de yi phyir*, and *gnas la brten nas nang gi sems 'gyur*; *Rdzogs pa chen po ngal gso skor gsum*, 1.17, 2.3.

55. Yang dgon pa, *Rin po che 'bar ba*, *Collected Works*, 1: 466.3–468.1, quoting 466.3; *Lhan thabs chen mo*, 2: 41.3–43.5.

56. 'Jig rten gsum mgon, *Ri chos bdud rtsi'i bum chen*, in *'Bri gung bka' brgyud chos mdzod chen mo*, 26: 393.2–394.2.

57. Zhwa dmar II Mkha' spyod dbang po, *Ri chos gcig shes kun grol man ngag gi snying po* (Mtshur phu gdon gtsug lag dpe rnying phyogs sgrig khang; undated modern reprint, in 36 pages; BDRC W3CN5081), 1.5–6.2; 31.12–34.6, quoting 34.3–4. This text also prescribes the practice of *dag snang*, 27.11–28.10.

    This text would be quoted at least three separate times by Zur mang legs bshad sgra dbyangs, about ensuring that one has the correct mindset and understanding about the ascetic endeavor, without which all of one's efforts may be for naught: *Ri yi chos gtam kun tu bzang po'i sgra dbyangs*, 40.8–11 (which is Mkha' spyod dbang po, 32.14–33.1), 41.1–6 (Mkha' spyod dbang po, 33.1–7), and 65.2–5 (Mkha' spyod dbang po, 33.7–10). Zur mang quotes Mkha' spyod dbang po a fourth time, 11.4–8, the source of which I have not determined.

    Also pertinent to the Tibetan contemplative tradition's broader discourse about space is the practice of "dark retreat," in which spatiality is rendered moot via the meditator's being confined to a chamber of complete and utter darkness. Inhabiting such a no-place opens up the possibility of more deeply experiencing the worlds imaginally cultivated through meditation. As mentioned in the introduction, because it is generally practiced on a short- or medium-term basis, the dark retreat is not examined in this study.

3. ISOLATING THE ASCETIC SELF

1. The practice of *tshe mtshams* is mentioned in Karma chags med, *Ri chos mtshams kyi zhal gdams* (Brag dkar dgon pa, 1970; BDRC W23259), 20.5; 22.1 (Khenpo Karthar Rinpoché, *Karma Chakme's Mountain Dharma*, 4 vols. [Woodstock, NY: Karma Triyana Dharmachakra Publications, 2004], 1: 35; Eric Haynie, "Karma chags med's *Mountain Dharma*: Tibetan Advice on Sociologies of Retreat" [MA thesis, University of Colorado, 2013], 83); 25.6 (Karthar 1: 38; Haynie, 85).

For other references to this kind of permanent retreat, see Karthar 1: xi, 4: 121; 'Brug pa kun legs, *'Brug pa kun legs kyi rnam thar* (Beijing: Bod ljongs mi dmangs dpe skrun khang, 2005; BDRC W29517), 106.14–15 (R. A. Stein, trans., *Vie et chants de 'Brug pa Kun legs le yogin* [Paris: G.-P. Maisonneuve et Larose, 1972], 182–83); Nam mkha' rdo rje, *Dpal ldan bla ma dam pa sprul sku nam mkha' rgyal mtshan dpal bzang po'i rnam par thar pa/ dgos 'dod kun 'byung nor bu'i 'phreng ba*, in *'Ba' ra bka' brgyud gser 'phreng chen mo*, 4 vols. (Dehra Dun: Ngawang Gyaltsen and Ngawang Lungtok, 1970; BDRC W19231), 2: 394–521, citing 462.1–2; and Brag dkar ba chos kyi dbang phyug, *Grub pa'i gnas chen brag dkar rta so'i sgrub sde spong ba pa rnams kyi blang dor gyi rim pa gsal bar ston pa'i bca' yig mun sel nyin mor byed pa'i 'od snang*, in *Collected Works*, 12 vols. (Swayambhunath, Kathmandu: Khenpo Shedup Tenzin, 2011; BDRC W1KG14557); 12: 645–92, citing 650.3.

The circumstances of the text's composition are referred to in Karma chags med, 3.1–4.1; 20.4–27.4 (Karthar 1: 35–39; Haynie, 83–86). Haynie (9) and the editors of the four-volume translation of the commentary by Khenpo Karthar Rinpoché (1: ix, xx, 27) date the composition of the text as 1659. Almost all of the colophons to the individual chapters give *shing sbrul* or *me rta* as their year of composition, which I take as referring to 1665 and 1666, respectively. For many chapters of the handbook, the month, day, and time of day are given as well, allowing us to establish a remarkably detailed chronology of when the individual parts of the text were delivered orally by Karma chags med.

A brief account of the compiling of the text is given at Karma chags med, 20.6–21.2, where it is stated that the process began in *me pho rta* (1666) and ended in *me mo phag*; because the *me phag* years nearest to this time are 1647 and 1707, this reference should probably be understood as a mistake for *me lug* (1667). The gap between when the teachings were given in 1665–1666 and when the final version of the text was compiled in 1666–1667 likely reflects time spent by Brtson 'grus rgya mtsho to put together and finalize the instructions that Karma chags med had delivered to him orally, this editing process being referred to as *ri chos kyi glegs bam yongs su rdzogs par grub pa*, 21.2.

The biography of Karma chags med contained within Khenpo Karthar Rinpoché's commentary states that it was while doing a thirteen-year retreat that Karma chags med delivered the teachings that would be contained in the *Ri chos mtshams kyi zhal gdams*, which may be consistent with the view that the date of composition was 1659 (1: xx). However, the description of the text's composition makes clear that Karma chags med began delivering these teachings after having completed the thirteen-year retreat and having entered into a permanent retreat; 20.4–27.4 (Karthar 1: 35–39; Haynie, 83–86).

2. See Berthe Jansen, *The Monastery Rules: Buddhist Monastic Organization in Pre-Modern Tibet* (Berkeley: University of California Press, 2018), 8–9, 117–18; and Petra Kieffer-Pülz, "Rules for the *Sīmā* Regulation in the *Vinaya* and Its Commentaries and Their Application in Thailand," *Journal of the International Association of Buddhist Studies* 20, no. 2 (1997): 141–53.

3. The practice of *'dag 'byar* or *'dag sbyar* is referenced in Yang dgon pa rgyal mtshan dpal, *Ri chos kyi phyag len gsal ba'i sgron me*, in *The Collected Works (gsung 'bum) of Yang dgon pa*, 3 vols. (Thimpu: Kunsang Topgey, 1976; BDRC W1KG17449), 1: 11–19, citing 12.3–4; Lha btsun nam mkha' 'jigs med, *Ri chos rin po che gnad kyi phreng ba*, in *Rdo rje snying po sprin gyi thol glu*, 2 vols. (n.p.; BDRC W13780), 2: 609–68, citing 639.5; Mi pham phun tshogs shes rab, *Ri chos zab mo grub pa'i bcud len sbrang rtsi'i snying po*, in *Collected Works*, 2 vols. (Darjeeling: Thub bstan gsang sngags chos gling 'brug sgar dpe mdzod khang, 2008; BDRC W2KG200924), 1: 377–437, citing 389.3–4, in the context of quoting Rgod tshang pa mgon po rdo rje's assertion that "performing the Secret Practice (*gsang spyod*) for three days in a haunted place is more enhancing [to one's spiritual standing] than meditating for three years in a sealed retreat in an isolated place or some other ordinary kind of locale"; Zhabs dkar tshogs drug rang grol, *Chos bshad gzhan phan zla ba*, in *Collected Works*, 10 vols. (Zi ling: Mtsho sngon mi rigs dpe skrun khang, 2002; BDRC W1PD45150),

8: 1–283, citing 157.12–13, 245.2–3; Ngag dbang bstan 'dzin nor bu, *Bca' yig ri chos zhal gdams* (Rewalsar, H.P.: Zigar Drukpa Kargyud Institute, 1985; BDRC W9674), 18.2; and in a short biography of Karma nges don bstan rgyas, referred to as *Mdzad pa po'i rnam thar mdor bsdus*, in *Collected Works*, 2 vols. (Si khron bod yig dpe rnying bsdu sgrig khang, n.d.; BDRC W3CN3402), 1: 1–3, citing 2.8–9.

    The irony that doing a sealed retreat guarantees the meditator's dependence on other people, who become indispensable for the procuring of food and water and the removal of waste from the cell, has gone unremarked upon in this body of literature.

4. This difference in understanding of the term *mtshams [m]tho* results in part from the fact that the syllable *[m]tho* can refer to a pile of stones or cairn, or to a note, register, list, or sign.

    For some contextual examples, Yang dgon pa instructs the reader to *sgo drung du mtho dkar po rtsigs, Ri chos yon tan kun 'byung [ba] rin po che 'bar ba*, in *Collected Works*, 1: 447–570, citing 454.1; Lha btsun nam mkha' 'jigs med says to *mdun du tho dkar po gcig brtsigs, Ri chos rin po che gnad kyi phreng ba*, 623.6–624.1; 'Jigs med gling pa says to *sgo drung du tho brtsigs, Ri chos zhal gdams ngo mtshar rgya mtsho*, in *Collected Works*, 9 vols. (Sde dge: Sde dge dpar khang; BDRC W27300), 8: 699–708, citing 706.3; in the translation, this is rendered as "put a sign by your door," Jikmé Lingpa, "A Wonderous Ocean of Advice (For the Practice of Solitary Retreat)," anonymous translation, no publication information, 5.

    Karma chags med gives the instruction *sgo rtsar tho ni dkar po brtsegs, Ri chos mtshams kyi zhal gdams*, 237.1–2; Khenpo Karthar Rinpoché explains this as "making a pile of earth or stones and planting the sign on top," 2: 145. The passage continues, with Karma chags med describing a procedure by which the meditator writes on a piece of paper the name of any person who might need to come inside the confines after the retreat has been initiated; that piece of paper should then be wrapped around a rock (*shog gur ming bris rde'u gtums*) and placed somewhere inside the boundary of the retreat. The meditator performs a circle of protection rite while visualizing the person as being present. In this way the individual is represented as being inside at the time of setting up that retreat, so that the embodied person's arrival later on will not be a violation of the boundary (237.4–6; Karthar 2: 145–46). Setting up the cairn or sign is also mentioned at 233.4–5 (using the phrase *sgo rtsar tho brtsegs*), which Khenpo Karthar Rinpoché describes as a sign with writing on it (Karthar 2: 140).

    Throughout Karma chags med's text are a series of references to a *rgyal tho sgo byang*—a sign to be placed outside of the retreat (atop the cairn? somewhere else?) bearing depictions and ritual material relating to the four guardian kings, which are associated with the four cardinal directions. Reference is made to not taking down the *rgyal tho sgo byang* at the completion of one round of intensive ritual practice and before starting the next one (253.3; Karthar 2: 163–64); to staying within the boundary of the retreat as marked by the *rgyal tho* while doing a *sgrub chen* ritual (256.3; Karthar 2: 169); and to taking down the *rgyal tho sgo byang* on which the length of the retreat committed to had been written, once the retreat has been completed (259.2; Karthar 2: 172–73). Placing representations of the four guardian kings outside the doorway to a cloister housing a communal three-year, three-month retreat is common practice today.

    References for Brag dkar blo bzang dpal ldan's treatment of the retreat cairn will be given in note 24.

5. Tsong kha pa blo bzang grags pa's charter for the monastic community of Byams pa gling, in Lha zhol, where Dge lugs pa monks would do short- or medium-term retreats during the summer and winter, provides some colorful examples of how the retreat boundary was maintained; *Byams pa gling na bzhugs pa'i dge 'dun rnams kyi spyi'i khrims su bya ba'i bca' yig chung ngu*, in *Collected Works*, 18 vols. (New Delhi: Mongolian Lama Guru Deva, 1978–1979; BDRC W635), 2: 698–713. See in particular 698.4–702.6. This text's treatment of the retreat boundary is discussed in Jansen, *The Monastery Rules*, 89.

6. Yang dgon pa, *Rin po che 'bar ba, Collected Works*, 1: 454.4–5. Offering a further clue about the eremitic conditions to be adhered to, the *Lhan thabs chen mo*'s commentary on this part of the text mentions going out to gather wood and food, *Collected Works*, 2: 14.3. Unfortunately the commentary does not help clarify the passage that I have quoted, which itself may be significant: these are rather ordinary, taken-for-granted aspects of the eremitic endeavor, not generally being subject to further thought and elaboration.

7. An exception is the lone reference made to a patron's gaining benefit from the retreatant's consumption of food that has been offered; Yang dgon pa, *Rin po che 'bar ba, Collected Works*, 1: 509.2. This will be discussed in chapter 4.

8. Yang dgon pa, *Rin po che 'bar ba, Collected Works*, 1: 515.5–6, 534.3–5. Yang dgon pa also discusses the maintenance of interpersonal boundaries at 513.2–5.

9. Karma chags med, *Ri chos mtshams kyi zhal gdams*, 496.1–2 (Karthar 3: 224), 257.6–258.1 (Karthar 2: 171),

    In August 2024, I was in a multinational group meeting over digital videoconference that included a monk in Kathmandu who was in retreat at the time. He was allowed to listen and speak during the call but was not allowed to show his face on camera.

10. While performing these three "special practices," *khyad par gyi spyod pa* (consisting of *gsang ba'i spyod pa*, *tshogs kyi spyod pa*, and *rig pa brtul shugs* [sic] *kyi spyod pa*), the retreatant might interact with other advanced meditators, the public, or a sexual consort; Yang dgon pa, *Rin po che 'bar ba, Collected Works*, 1: 501.3–502.6; *Lhan thabs chen mo*, 2: 81.6–84.5.

    Other prescriptive retreat texts that reference these practices include Lce sgom shes rab rdo rje, *Ri khrod skal ldan sgron me*, in *Blo sbyong nyer mkho phyogs bsgrigs*, ed. Cha ris skal bzang thogs med and Ngag dbang sbyin pa (Lan kru'u: Kan su'u mi rigs dpe skrun khang, 2003; BDRC W25275), 675–88, citing 681.20–682.3, 684.11–685.4; Karma chags med, who offers instructions on doing *gsang spyod* tailored specifically to the funerary practices of the pastoralists of eastern Tibet, *Ri chos mtshams kyi zhal gdams*, 611.2–613.4 (Karthar 4: 103–6); Zur mang legs bshad sgra dbyangs, *Ri yi chos gtam kun tu bzang po'i sgra dbyangs* (Mtshur phu dgon gtsug lag dpe tshogs, n.d., 113 pages; BDRC W3CN5072), 54.9–11 (referencing the instructions on *gsang spyod* by Yang dgon pa [see chapter 2, note 35]); and Mi pham phun tshogs shes rab, *Ri chos zab mo grub pa'i bcud len sbrang rtsi'i snying po*, 389.3–4, quoting Rgod tshang pa.

11. Michel Foucault, *The Use of Pleasure: Volume 2 of the History of Sexuality*, trans. Robert Hurley (New York: Vintage, 1990), 106.

12. *de khyed rnams la drang por gleng na/ yul dang nor rdzas la sred pa gting nas spangs pa zhig byung na chos phyed tshar ba yin*, 'Jigs med gling pa, *Ri chos zhal gdams ngo mtshar rgya mtsho*, 702.1–2 (Jikmé Lingpa, "A Wonderous Ocean of Advice," 2).

    I thank Michael Sheehy for bringing this moment from the Mi la ras pa lore to my attention. The original Tibetan is given as *pha yul spangs pas chos phyed 'grub*, Gtsang smyon he ru ka, *Rnal 'byor gyi dbang phyug chen po mi la ras pa'i rnam mgur* (Zi ling: Mtsho sngon mi rigs dpe skrun khang, 2005), 691.6; translated in Christopher Stagg, *The Hundred Thousand Songs of Milarepa* (Boulder, CO: Shambhala, 2017), 587; and Garma C. C. Chang, *The Hundred Thousand Songs of Milarepa* (Boulder, CO: Shambhala, 1977), 563.

    This line, without attribution to Mi la ras pa, is quoted in Mi pham phun tshogs shes rab, *Ri chos zab mo grub pa'i bcud len sbrang rtsi'i snying po*, 383.1; and in Bdud 'joms rin po che 'jigs bral ye shes rdo rje, *Ri chos bslab bya nyams len dmar khrid go bder brjod pa grub pa'i bcud len*, in *Collected Works*, 25 vols. (Kalimpong: Dupjung Lama, 1979–1985; BDRC W20869), 13: 443–67, citing 447.5–6 (Dudjom Rinpoché, *Mountain Dharma: The Alchemy of Realization [Dudjom Rinpoche's Richo]*, trans. Keith Dowman [Dzogchen Now! Books, 2017], 28). This text has received considerable attention from Euro-American practitioners of Tibetan Buddhism, having been translated into English at least four separate times.

A similar line is attributed to Pha dam pa sangs rgyas: *pha yul rgyab tu bor dgos par gda' gsung / byes su bsdad pas chos phyed grub/ dge sbyor ngang gis 'phel*; Pha dam pa sangs rgyas, *Phyag rgya chen po brda'i sgor gsum and Zhal chems ding ri'i skor* (Thimpu: National Library of Bhutan, 1985; BDRC W23993), 220.1. David Molk translates this as "you must put your homeland behind you! By staying away, half the Dharma is already accomplished!"; *Lion of Siddhas: The Life and Teachings of Padampa Sangye* (Ithaca, NY: Snow Lion, 2008), 292.

See also Lama Surya Das, *The Snow Lion's Turquoise Mane: Wisdom Tales from Tibet* (New York: HarperCollins, 1992), 73.

13. Karma chags med, *Ri chos mtshams kyi zhal gdams*, 224.1–4 (Karthar 2: 127; Haynie, "Karma chags med's *Mountain Dharma*," 84). See also Karma nges don bstan rgyas, *Ri chos thar lam mdzub ston*, in *The Collected Works of Sman sdong mtshams pa rin po che Karma nges don bstan rgyas*, 3 vols. (Bir, H.P.: D. Tsondu Senghe, 1975; BDRC W10982), 3: 161–204, citing 168.2–4.
14. Zhabs dkar, *Chos bshad gzhan phan zla ba*, 53.2–54.5, 124.15–162.10; the quotation is at 126.3–5.
15. Brag dkar blo bzang dpal ldan bstan 'dzin snyan rags, *Spong ba bsam gtan pa rnams la bslab pa'i khrims su bca' ba man ngag lag tu bcangs bde ba'i ri chos me tog phreng mdzes*, in *Collected Works*, 20 vols. (compiled in Chengdu; BDRC W23608), 3: 633–48, citing 634.2–635.4, 639.1–4, 643.6–645.1.
16. Lce sgom shes rab rdo rje, *Ri khrod skal ldan sgron me*, 684.3–11.
17. Zhabs dkar, *Chos bshad gzhan phan zla ba*, 144.14–154.10.
18. Karma chags med, *Ri chos mtshams kyi zhal gdams*, 239.1–2 (Karthar 2: 146–47); 256.3–259.2 (Karthar 2: 170–71).
19. Karma chags med, *Ri chos mtshams kyi zhal gdams*, 258.4–6 (Karthar 2: 171–72). See also 379.5–6 (Karthar 3: 108).
20. Karma nges don bstan rgyas, *Ri chos thar lam mdzub ston*, 172.2–4. Biographical details are supplied from the *Mdzad pa po'i rnam thar mdor bsdus* in Karma nges don bstan rgyas, *Collected Works*, 2 vols. (Si khron bod yig dpe rnying bsdu sgrig khang, n.d.; BDRC W3CN3402), 1: 1–3, citing 2.8–9. His disciples included both *mtshams pa* and *sgrub dpon*, which typically means a "retreat master"; 2.19–3.4.
21. Drung pa IV Kun dga' rnam rgyal, *Ri chos bai dUrya'i phreng ba zhes bya ba thar 'dod kyi mgul rgyan*, in *Gdams ngag mdzod*, ed. 'Jam mgon kong sprul blo gros mtha' yas, 18 vols. (Paro: Lama Ngodrup and Sherab Drimey, 1979–1981; BDRC W20877), 9: 315–23, citing 319.2.
22. Yang dgon pa, *Rin po che 'bar ba, Collected Works*, 1: 542.6–543.1.
    Maintaining silence during retreat is mentioned in Ngag dbang bstan 'dzin nor bu, *Bca' yig ri chos zhal gdams*, 18.2, 65.3–5.
23. Brag dkar blo bzang dpal ldan, *Me tog phreng mdzes, Collected Works*, 3: 635.4. There is a similar passage in the longer *Gnas dben par sdod pa'i chos mdzad mtha' dag la nye bar mkho ba'i ri chos mu tig gi phreng ba* (Gser rta rdzong: Gser thang bla rung lnga rig nang bstan slob gling, n.d.; BDRC W3CN4732), beginning at 8.12.
24. Brag dkar blo bzang dpal ldan, *Mu tig gi phreng ba*, 10.15–11.9, 58.5–62.8. See also *Me tog phreng mdzes, Collected Works*, 3: 639.1–640.3.
25. Karma nges don bstan rgyas, *Ri chos thar lam mdzub ston*, 170.1–3.
26. Karma chags med, *Ri chos mtshams kyi zhal gdams*, 573.2–4 (Karthar 4: 24–25).
27. Haynie, "Karma chags med's *Mountain Dharma*," iii.
28. Karma chags med, *Ri chos mtshams kyi zhal gdams*, 496.2–4 (Karthar 3: 224).
29. Karma chags med, *Ri chos mtshams kyi zhal gdams*, 110.1–115.2 (Karthar 1: 227–34).
30. Karma chags med, *Ri chos mtshams kyi zhal gdams*, 271.2–285.2 (Karthar 2: 223–39), quoting 271.3 (Karthar 2: 223). See also chapter 24, which runs 358.4–368.5 (Karthar 3: 47–79).
31. Karma chags med, *Ri chos mtshams kyi zhal gdams*, 502.5–514.1 (Karthar 3: 230–44). Karma chags med mentions that these techniques apply to "you or someone else" at 502.5, 510.6, 511.3.

32. *Gcod* is the subject of chapter 17, which runs Karma chags med, *Ri chos mtshams kyi zhal gdams*, 260.1–271.2 (Karthar 2: 195–221). Its use to affect the weather is addressed in chapter 40, 606.3–611.2 (Karthar 4: 97–103). The reference to the degenerate age is at 606.6.
33. Dying process: chapter 25, Karma chags med, *Ri chos mtshams kyi zhal gdams*, 368.5–379.1 (Karthar 3: 81–105). Funerary rites: chapter 21, 327.3–346.4 (Karthar 2: 305–33). Also making dedications to the deceased, 817.1–818.4 (Karthar 4: 411–12). Funerary geomancy (*dur gyi sa dpyad*): 211.2–214.2 (Karthar 2: 95–100).
34. Brag dkar blo bzang dpal ldan, *Mu tig gi phreng ba*, 147.8–149.14. The author also comments on retinues and attendants (primarily regarding doing without them), at 90.15–91.3, 163.3–5, 194.2, 204.15–205.2, 251.15–252.10, 272.1–2.
35. Brag dkar blo bzang dpal ldan, *Me tog phreng mdzes*, Collected Works, 3: 638.6. See also 645.3.
36. 'Jigs med gling pa, *Ri chos zhal gdams ngo mtshar rgya mtsho*, 706.2 (Jikmé Lingpa, "A Wonderous Ocean of Advice," 4–5); Janet Gyatso, *Apparitions of the Self: The Secret Autobiographies of a Tibetan Visionary* (Princeton, NJ: Princeton University Press, 1998), 132–34.
37. Karma chags med, *Ri chos mtshams kyi zhal gdams*, 233.1–234.3 (Karthar 2: 139–40); 573.2–3 (Karthar 4: 24–25); 258.1–4 (Karthar 2: 171); quoting 234.2–3.

    Karma nges don bstan rgyas focuses on the importance of the retreat attendant's not being of the same sex as the retreatant; *Ri chos thar lam mdzub ston*, 168.6–169.5. He repeats Karma chags med's statement about the supreme kind of practitioner being those capable of caring for themselves. Mi pham phun tshogs shes rab's treatment focuses on the benefits accrued by the attendant, and the mindset they should maintain; *Ri chos zab mo grub pa'i bcud len sbrang rtsi'i snying po*, 430.2–5.
38. Karma chags med, *Ri chos mtshams kyi zhal gdams*, 237.4–5 (Karthar 2: 145–46). See note 4.
39. Zhwa dmar II Mkha' spyod dbang po, *Ri chos gcig shes kun grol man ngag gi snying po* (Mtshur phu gdon gtsug lag dpe rnying phyogs sgrig khang; undated modern reprint, in 36 pages; BDRC W3CN5081), 18.10–11; Karma chags med, *Ri chos mtshams kyi zhal gdams*, 168.6–169.1 (Karthar 2: 6); Karma nges don bstan rgyas, *Ri chos thar lam mdzub ston*, 168.5–6.
40. The entire chapter runs Zur mang legs bshad sgra dbyangs, *Ri yi chos gtam kun tu bzang po'i sgra dbyangs*, 25.11–30.13. The name of the chapter is given as *chos grogs brten pa* at 5.14, and as *chos grogs ji ltar bstan pa* at 25.11–12. The quotations are from 25.15–17 and 26.9.
41. Zur mang legs bshad sgra dbyangs, *Ri yi chos gtam kun tu bzang po'i sgra dbyangs*, 26.9–27.8; the quotations are from 26.14–18 and 27.4–6.
42. Zur mang legs bshad sgra dbyangs, *Ri yi chos gtam kun tu bzang po'i sgra dbyangs*, 28.1–29.6, quoting 28.6–7. This is the *Adhyāśayasaṃcodana Sūtra, Lhag pa'i bsam pa bskul ba'i mdo*.
43. Zur mang legs bshad sgra dbyangs, *Ri yi chos gtam kun tu bzang po'i sgra dbyangs*, 29.16–30.5. See also O rgyan rnam grol dbang po, *Sbas mtha'i ri khrod du 'dug tshul dang rnams [=rnam] kun rang brgyud [=rgyud] chos dang bsre tshul gyi bslab bya zhal gyi gdams pa'i nying khu gsang ba bdud rtsi thig le* (undated *dbu med* manuscript, in 10 folio sides; NGMPP AT82/7), 5a5–6; Mi pham phun tshogs shes rab, *Ri chos zab mo grub pa'i bcud len sbrang rtsi'i snying po*, 422.4–423.5.
44. Lha btsun nam mkha' 'jigs med, *Ri chos rin po che gnad kyi phreng ba*, 639.5, 627.1–628.5, 656.1–6.
45. Pan chen bla ma IV Blo bzang chos kyi rgyal mtshan, *Don du gnyer ba'i ri khrod pa rnams la khrims su bca' ba sku gsum gzhal med khang du 'dzeg pa baidUrya'i them skas*, in Collected Works, 5 vols. (Gzhis ka rtse: Bkra shis lhun po par khang, n.d.; BDRC W9848), 4: 501–16, quoting 502.3–4 and 508.5–509.3. Referenced in Brenton Sullivan, *Building a Religious Empire: Tibetan Buddhism, Bureaucracy, and the Rise of the Gelukpa* (Philadelphia: University of Pennsylvania Press, 2021), 113, 179, 222n4, 237n32.

    The early Bka' gdams pa master Po to ba rin chen gsal is quoted frequently in retreat literature. See, for example, Brag dkar blo bzang dpal ldan, *Mu tig gi phreng ba*, where this same line from Po to ba is quoted, 18.1–4.

46. William Gorvine, *Envisioning a Tibetan Luminary: The Life of a Modern Bönpo Saint* (New York: Oxford University Press, 2019), 135–36; Bskal bzang bstan pa'i rgyal mtshan, *Shar rdza bkra shis rgyal mtshan gyi rnam thar* (Beijing: Krung go'i bod kyi shes rig dpe skrun khang, 1990; BDRC W14023), 410.11–411.14.

    On Shar rdza bkra shis rgyal mtshan, see also Geoffrey Barstow, *Food of Sinful Demons: Meat, Vegetarianism, and the Limits of Buddhism in Tibet* (New York: Columbia University Press, 2019), 39; Barstow, ed., *The Faults of Meat: Tibetan Buddhist Writings on Vegetarianism* (Somerville, MA: Wisdom, 2019), 235–45.

47. Brag dkar blo bzang dpal ldan, *Me tog phreng mdzes*, Collected Works, 3: 645.5–646.6. This passage comes amid a broader conversation about relating to other practitioners, including other comments about the role of the community in ensuring a monk's behavior, such as at that found at 643.3–6. Another passage, about the necessity of making one's day-to-day behavior conform to that of the community, is at 637.5–638.6; much of the contents are revisited in the longer *Mu tig gi phreng ba*, in a discussion of how to relate to other practitioners, running 49.8–58.6.

48. The section on *tshul khrims* runs Yang dgon pa, *Rin po che 'bar ba*, Collected Works, 1: 455.5–459.6, quoting from 459.3–5. This theory of the three sets of vows is expanded upon in the *Lhan thabs chen mo*, 2: 16.2–25.3.

    Yang dgon pa's instructions on tantric sex show a concern for doing so without losing one's status as a celibate, *Rin po che 'bar ba*, Collected Works, 1: 528.3–531.3; *Lhan thabs chen mo*, 2: 122.5–127.1.

    In the early sixteenth century, Yang dgon pa's spiritual descendent Rdor 'dzin nam mkha' rdo rje, introduced in chapter 1, would only take full monastic ordination after completing his first three-year retreat. The three-year retreat is mentioned in Chos rgyal lhun po, *ShAkya'i dge slong rdo rje 'dzin pa chen po/ nam mkha' rdo rje'i rnam par thar pa ngo mtshar gsal ba'i me long* (undated woodblock print, in 103 folio sides; BDRC W3CN18491; NGMPP L18/5), 16a2, 17b2–21a7; he also did a further two years of concerted practice in retreat-like conditions, 23b5. Nam mkha' rdo rje is recorded to have taken the Buddhist *upāsaka* or layman's vows (*dge bsnyen gyi sdom pa*) at the age of eleven (6a6–7); monastic ordination (*dge tshul gyi sdom pa*) at the age of seventeen, after which he wore the clothing of a monk (*rab byung gi rtags rnams*) (7a2–3); and then full ordination (21b2–22b2) when in his thirties. See Franz-Karl Ehrhard, *Early Buddhist Block Prints from Mang yul Gung thang* (Lumbini: Lumbini International Research Institute, 2000), 56–58.

    Waiting until later in life to take full ordination seems to have been normal in this circle, as Rdor 'dzin nam mkha' rdo rje's main teacher, Nam mkha' rgyal mtshan, did not take full ordination until the age of thirty-six; Nam mkha' rdo rje, *Dpal ldan bla ma dam pa sprul sku nam mkha' rgyal mtshan dpal bzang po'i rnam par thar pa*, 462.5–464.5; Ehrhard, *Early Buddhist Block Prints*, 55.

49. Zhwa dmar II Mkha' spyod dbang po, *Ri chos gcig shes kun grol man ngag gi snying po*, 10.15–14.7; see in particular 12.12–15.

50. The chapter runs Karma chags med, *Ri chos mtshams kyi zhal gdams*, 72.2–88.5 (Karthar 1: 151–80). This paragraph also quotes 576.5–577.1 (Karthar 4: 29–30) and cites 55.6–57.3 (Karthar 1: 116–18).

51. Ngag dbang bstan 'dzin nor bu, *Bca' yig ri chos zhal gdams*, 14.4–16.6, quoting 14.4–6 and 16.4–6. The final quotation is from 64.1–3, amid a discussion that runs 53.1–65.1. On the Buddhist notion of inevitable decline in the Dharma and in the world, see Jan Nattier, *Once Upon a Future Time: Studies in a Buddhist Prophecy of Decline* (Berkeley, CA: Asian Humanities Press, 1991).

4. NOURISHING THE ASCETIC SELF

1. Bsod nams chos 'dzin, *Dben pa ri khrod 'grims pa'i gsal 'debs/ zhal gdam thar pa chen po'i gru sding* (undated *dbu med* manuscript, in 11 folio sides; NGMPP AT146/3), 4a4–5.

2. The term *nyer mkho*, "requisites," is also sometimes used in this way. In addition to food and clothing, *mthun rkyen* has been used to refer to drinking water and firewood as well; Lha btsun nam mkha' 'jigs med, *Ri chos rin po che gnad kyi phreng ba*, in *Rdo rje snying po sprin gyi thol glu*, 2 vols. (n.p.; BDRC W13780), 2: 609–68, citing 621.1; Karma Chags med, *Ri chos mtshams kyi zhal gdams* (Brag dkar dgon pa, 1970; BRDC W23259), 236.2 (Khenpo Karthar Rinpoché, *Karma Chakme's Mountain Dharma*, 4 vols. [Woodstock, NY: Karma Triyana Dharmachakra Publications, 2004], 2: 144). Karma chags med instructs that if the retreatant must go out to collect water, they should do so "in the manner of a thief," at night, when people have retired to their homes, 245.3–4 (Karthar 2: 155). Mi pham phun tshogs shes rab refers to the *'tsho ba'i yo byad* as consisting of *shing bu sogs*; *Ri chos zab mo grub pa'i bcud len sbrang rtsi'i snying po*, in *Collected Works*, 2 vols. (Darjeeling: Thub bstan gsang sngags chos gling 'brug sgar dpe mdzod khang, 2008; BDRC W2KG200924), 1: 377–435, citing 390.5–391.1.

Just before his discussion of *mthun rkyen*, Lce sgom shes rab rdo rje discusses its opposite, *'gal rkyen*, "adverse circumstances"; *Ri khrod skal ldan sgron me*, in *Blo sbyong nyer mkho phyogs bsgrigs*, ed. Cha ris skal bzang thogs med and Ngag dbang sbyin pa (Lan kru'u: Kan su'u mi rigs dpe skrun khang, 2003; BDRC W25275), 675–88, citing 677.15–20. The term *'gal rkyen* appears infrequently in this genre of literature.

3. Karma nges don bstan rgyas, *Ri chos thar lam mdzub ston*, in *The Collected Works of Sman sdong mtshams pa rin po che Karma nges don bstan rgyas*, 3 vols. (Bir, H.P.: D. Tsondu Senghe, 1975; BDRC W10982), 3: 161–204, citing 167.3–5. The word *dka' thub* derives from the phrase *dka' ba thub pa*, meaning "to withstand difficulty." This is used to translate the Sanskrit *tapas*, and can mean something like asceticism, austerity, hardship, trial.

For other examples of this kind of statement, see 'Jig rten gsum mgon, *Ri chos bdud rtsi'i bum chen*, in *'Bri gung bka' brgyud chos mdzod chen mo*, ed. A mgon rin po che and Ra se dkon mchog rgya mtsho, 151 vols. (Lhasa: Bri gung mthil dgon, 2004; BDRC W00JW501203), 26: 384–99, citing 385.1–3; Yang dgon pa rgyal mtshan dpal, *Ri chos yon tan kun 'byung [ba] rin po che 'bar ba*, in *The Collected Works (gsung 'bum) of Yang dgon pa*, 3 vols. (Thimpu: Kunsang Topgey, 1976; BDRC W1KG17449), 1: 447–570, citing 514.3–4; Mi pham phun tshogs shes rab, *Ri chos zab mo grub pa'i bcud len sbrang rtsi'i snying po*, 389.4–390.4.

In the chapter outlining the experiences a meditator is likely to have during the full arc of a retreat, Karma chags med instructs that one begins by making a commitment not to think about food, clothing, or wealth for the duration. Then, as the retreat and meditative experience begin to deepen, one's "cravings (*sred pa*) for food and clothing will naturally decrease." As one progresses further, the mind will at some point become scattered and wild (*'phro rgod*), at which time attachment to food and clothing will be greater than ever before; *Ri chos mtshams kyi zhal gdams*, 169.1–4 (Karthar 2: 6–7), 172.3–5 (Karthar 2: 12), 174.1–2 (Karthar 2: 15).

Elsewhere Karma chags med writes at length about the major potential "place of deviation" (*gol sa*) from the correct spiritual path that is constituted by being in any way motivated by material concerns or a desire for fame; 474.3–478.1 (Karthar 3: 170–77).

Karma chags med derides those who enter the monkhood "for the sake of food" (*lto phyir*), and those who take higher ordination for the sake of having a higher status than other monks, 30.2–3 (Karthar 1: 43). A basic attitude of acquisitiveness toward food and wealth defines the existence of a householder, 568.1–3 (Karthar 4: 17–18).

But one should not fall to the opposite extreme either: when discussing the mistaken views and practices of South Asian religions other than Buddhism, Karma chags med mentions those who do away with food and clothing entirely—subsisting only on water and going about naked—as being just as wrong-minded as those who carry out animal sacrifices, hold the view of nihilism, or believe in an all-pervading God; 49.6–50.2 (Karthar 1: 102).

4. NOURISHING THE ASCETIC SELF

4. Andrew Quintman, trans., *The Life of Milarepa* (New York: Penguin, 2010 [1488]), 199; Gtsang smyon he ru ka, *Rnal 'byor gyi dbang phyug chen po mi la ras pa'i rnam mgur* (Zi ling: Mtsho sngon mi rigs dpe skrun khang, 2005), 813.15–17. The Tibetan is *gyong lto gos gtam gsum la thongs*. Brag dkar blo bzang dpal ldan bstan 'dzin snyan rags attributes a similar phrase, *lto gos gtam gsum blos gtong dgos*, to the early masters of the Bka' gdams pa tradition; *Gnas dben par sdod pa'i chos mdzad mtha' dag la nye bar mkho ba'i ri chos mu tig gi phreng ba* (Gser rta rdzong: Gser thang bla rung lnga rig nang bstan slob gling, n.d.; BDRC W3CN4732), 91.6–8.

5. The lines quoted here are *ras rkyang ma gtogs hrul po'i gos gyon*, Mi pham phun tshogs shes rab, *Ri chos zab mo grub pa'i bcud len sbrang rtsi'i snying po*, 432.2; and *ched du lus sogs brgyan mi bya/ lus g.yog tsam gyi gos dang . . .* , Karma pa III Rang byung rdo rje, *Ri chos bdud rtsi'i nying khu*, in *Collected Works*, 13 vols. (Lhasa: Dpal brtsegs bod yig dpe rnying zhib 'jug khang, 2013; BDRC W3PD1288), 4: 479–503, citing 497.3–4.

    A similar line, *lto gos kha 'gro rgyab gros rtsam ma gtogs*, appears in Karma nges don bstan rgyas, *Ri chos thar lam mdzub ston*, 171.1; see also 198.5.

6. Karma chags med seems to say that one must continue to adhere to traditional monastic garb no matter the circumstances (*Ri chos mtshams kyi zhal gdams*, 226.2–227.3; Karthar 2: 131–33), while elsewhere suggesting that there is some flexibility on this matter during retreat (486.3–5; Karthar 3: 195–96). Karma nges don bstan rgyas seems to be aligned with the first of these two positions; *Ri chos thar lam mdzub ston*, 176.6–177.1. On this issue see also Zur mang legs bshad sgra dbyangs, *Ri yi chos gtam kun tu bzang po'i sgra dbyangs* (Mtshur phu dgon gtsug lag dpe tshogs, n.d., 113 pages; BDRC W3CN5072), 39.9–16; and Ngag dbang bstan 'dzin nor bu, *Bca' yig ri chos zhal gdams* (Rewalsar, H.P.: Zigar Drukpa Kargyud Institute, 1985; BDRC W9674), 10.2–11.3.

    An issue quite separate from these is the fact that a successful practitioner of *gtum mo* will wear less and less clothing, as will be addressed in chapter 5.

7. Mi pham phun tshogs shes rab, *Ri chos zab mo grub pa'i bcud len sbrang rtsi'i snying po*, 432.2–3.

8. Michel Foucault, *The Use of Pleasure: Volume 2 of the History of Sexuality*, trans. Robert Hurley (New York: Vintage, 1990), 139.

    As a point of comparison, about asceticism in a South Asian context, Kazi Ashraf writes: "Food and clothing are also two critical existential categories that define the parameters and practice of asceticism, but neither receives the wide range of discursive and conceptual treatment as the plain hut. The ascetic hut becomes critical because it is no mere object of reflection but a metonym of that reflection; the hut stands for how asceticism structures its intentions and practices"; *The Hermit's Hut: Architecture and Asceticism in India* (Honolulu: University of Hawai'i Press, 2013), 3.

9. Yang dgon pa, *Rin po che 'bar ba, Collected Works*, 1: 454.2–3, 455.6.

10. Zur mang legs bshad sgra dbyangs, *Ri yi chos gtam kun tu bzang po'i sgra dbyangs*, 22.3–9; Karma chags med, *Ri chos mtshams kyi zhal gdams*, 169.3–4 (Karthar 2: 7). Similar examples will be cited at the beginning of chapter 5.

11. The word I here translate as "sign" is *rten 'brel*; Yang dgon pa, *Rin po che 'bar ba, Collected Works*, 1: 537.2–6. This is discussed in the *Lhan thabs chen mo*, 2: 133.4–135.2.

12. Yang dgon pa, *Rin po che 'bar ba, Collected Works*, 1: 534.2.

13. Yang dgon pa, *Rin po che 'bar ba, Collected Works*, 1: 473.2–3.

14. Yang dgon pa, *Rin po che 'bar ba, Collected Works*, 1: 529.2–4; *Lhan thabs chen mo*, 2: 123.4–124.6.

15. Yang dgon pa, *Rin po che 'bar ba, Collected Works*, 1: 543.2.

16. The passage on *zas kyi rnal 'byor* runs Yang dgon pa, *Rin po che 'bar ba, Collected Works*, 1: 508.5–510.4, quoting 509.2. The commentary on this practice runs *Lhan thabs chen mo*, 2: 93.6–95.2, quoting 94.6–95.1.

17. Yang dgon pa, *Lhan thabs chen mo, Collected Works*, 2: 14.3. The reference to our living in a degenerate age is at 10.3–4.

18. The practice of *zas kyi rnal 'byor* is prescribed: Mi pham phun tshogs shes rab, *Ri chos zab mo grub pa'i bcud len sbrang rtsi'i snying po*, 432.4; 'Jigs med gling pa, *Ri chos zhal gdams ngo mtshar rgya mtsho*, in *Collected Works*, 9 vols. (Sde dge: Sde dge dpar khang; BDRC W27300), 8: 699–708, citing 704.2 (where he mentions a specific version of the practice contained in his own *Spyod yul lam khyer*), and 705.4 (Jikmé Lingpa, "A Wonderful Ocean of Advice [For the Practice of Solitary Retreat]," anonymous translation, no publication information, 4–5).

    Karma chags med prescribes this practice in a general way for those in retreat, *Ri chos mtshams kyi zhal gdams*, 225.6 (Karthar 2: 130); but also mentions it among his prescriptions for the *kusali*-style retreatant possessing superior faculties, whose daily comportment is highly ritualized, 251.2–6 (Karthar 2: 161). Also mentioned at 486.5 (Karthar 3: 196) and 578.6 (Karthar 4: 32). Karma chags med tends to refer to this practice as *nang gi sbyin sreg*.

    Karma chags med discusses food as a medium for transmitting a harmful taint, 496.4 (Karthar 3: 224–25).

    In his charter for the community of retreatants at TsA 'dra rin chen brag, 'Jam mgon kong sprul prescribes the use of a text on *zas kyi rnal 'byor* by Klong chen pa, titled *Padma'i zhal gdams grol thig mthong ba rang grol las/ rang lus a nu'i tshogs mchod*; 'Jam mgon kong sprul, *Dpal spungs yang khrod kun bzang bde chen 'od gsal gling gi sgrub pa rnams kyi kun spyod bca' khrims blang dor rab gsal phan bde'i 'byung gnas*, in *Collected Works*, 13 vols. (New Delhi: Shechen, 2002; BDRC W23723), 6: 1091–152, citing 1119.2; Jamgon Kongtrül, *Jamgon Kongtrul's Retreat Manual*, trans. Ngawang Zangpo (Boston: Snow Lion, 1994 [1876]), 125, 192.

19. 'Jig rten gsum mgon, *Ri chos bdud rtsi'i bum chen*, in *'Bri gung bka' brgyud chos mdzod chen mo*, 26: 392.2–393.1; Karma pa III Rang byung rdo rje, *Ri chos bdud rtsi'i nying khu*, *Collected Works* (2013), 4: 497.5; Lha btsun nam mkha' 'jigs med, *Ri chos rin po che gnad kyi phreng ba*, 628.3–5; Karma chags med, *Ri chos mtshams kyi zhal gdams*, 235.3–5 (Karthar 2: 142). Perhaps related to this question, Karma chags med asserts that to not feel hunger despite not having eaten is a sign of success in one's spiritual practice, 132.4–6 (Karthar 1: 279–80), 469.2 (Karthar 3: 149).

20. 'Jig rten gsum mgon, *Ri chos bdud rtsi'i bum chen*, in *'Bri gung bka' brgyud chos mdzod chen mo*, 26: 395.5–397.1; Phag mo gru pa rdo rje rgyal po, *Ri chos bdud rtsi bum pa'i gdams ngag*, in *'Bri gung bka' brgyud chos mdzod chen mo*, 16: 277–83, citing 278.1–6.

21. Lce sgom shes rab rdo rje, *Ri khrod skal ldan sgron me*, 677.20–678.9.

22. Lce sgom shes rab rdo rje, *Ri khrod skal ldan sgron me*, 681.17–682.12.

23. The introduction to the chapter and the instructions and comments regarding *bcud len* run Zur mang legs bshad sgra dbyangs, *Ri yi chos gtam kun tu bzang po'i sgra dbyangs*, 30.13–33.11, quoting 30.16–31.3.

24. The instructions on begging run Zur mang legs bshad sgra dbyangs, *Ri yi chos gtam kun tu bzang po'i sgra dbyangs*, 33.11–36.3. The block quotation represents the passage running 33.13–34.8.

25. The section on this improper way of sustaining oneself runs Zur mang legs bshad sgra dbyangs, *Ri yi chos gtam kun tu bzang po'i sgra dbyangs*, 36.3–39.9. The block quotation represents the passage running 38.13–39.5.

26. Karma pa III Rang byung rdo rje, *Ri chos bdud rtsi'i nying khu*, *Collected Works* (2013), 4: 497.3–499.5.

27. Karma chags med, *Ri chos mtshams kyi zhal gdams*, 234.3–235.5 (Karthar 2: 140–42), 625.4–632.1 (Karthar 4: 120–27). Ngag dbang bstan 'dzin nor bu also references the "summer and autumn begging rounds," *dbyar ston bsod snyom gyi dus*; *Bca' yig ri chos zhal gdams*, 66.1.

28. Zhabs dkar tshogs drug rang grol, *Chos bshad gzhan phan zla ba*, in *Collected Works*, 10 vols. (Zi ling: Mtsho sngon mi rigs dpe skrun khang, 2002; BDRC W1PD45150), 8: 1–283, citing 257.9–261.9, and quoting 261.3–9.

    The quotation from Kha rag pa, with slightly different wording, is also found in Pan chen bla ma IV Blo bzang chos kyi rgyal mtshan, *Don du gnyer ba'i ri khrod pa rnams la khrims su bca' ba*

4. NOURISHING THE ASCETIC SELF   221

sku gsum gzhal med khang du 'dzeg pa baidUrya'i them skas, in *Collected Works*, 5 vols. (Gzhis ka rtse: Bkra shis lhun po par khang, n.d.; BDRC W9848), 4: 501–16, citing 506.4–5.

The statement attributed to Po to ba, which runs Zhabs dkar 258.14–18, is quoted on two occasions in Brag dkar blo bzang dpal ldan's *Mu tig gi phreng ba*, 12.15–13.4, 101.6–11.

29. Zhabs dkar, *Chos bshad gzhan phan zla ba*, 155.2–10; 243.1–14, quoting 243.1–4; 245.12–16. Brag dkar blo bzang dpal ldan also mentions birds and mice in this connection, *Mu tig gi phreng ba*, 17.7, and birds and deer, 131.9–132.1.
30. Brag dkar blo bzang dpal ldan, *Mu tig gi phreng ba*, 11.16–13.12.
31. Brag dkar blo bzang dpal ldan, *Spong ba bsam gtan pa rnams la bslab pa'i khrims su bca' ba man ngag lag tu bcangs bde ba'i ri chos me tog phreng mdzes*, in *Collected Works*, 20 vols. (compiled in Chengdu; BDRC W13780), 3: 633–48, citing 643.6–645.1; *Mu tig gi phreng ba*, 19.14–22.12, 45.13–49.10, 187.1–196.13, quoting 187.10–11.
32. Mi pham phun tshogs shes rab, *Ri chos zab mo grub pa'i bcud len sbrang rtsi'i snying po*, 431.1–2; Lha btsun nam mkha' 'jigs med, *Ri chos rin po che gnad kyi phreng ba*, 653.6–654.1, quoting 654.1; 656.5–657.2.
33. Karma chags med, *Ri chos mtshams kyi zhal gdams*, 584.4–5 (Karthar 4: 60–61); 312.1 (Karthar 2: 286–87).

    In the second decade of the thirteenth century, 'Jig rten gsum mgon wrote a brief charter for a community of renunciants who were experiencing dire penury. Nevertheless, he discourages them from resorting to activities like drawing deities or working as scribes for payment, and says that a meditator should only go begging when they possess less than three *zho* of wealth. *Gdan sa nyams dmas su gyur skabs mdzad pa'i bca' yig*, in *Khams gsum chos kyi rgyal po thub dbang rat+na shrI'i phyi yi bka' 'bum nor bu'i bang mdzod*, ed. Drikung Kyabgon Chetsang VII, 12 vols. (Delhi: Drikung Kagyu Ratna Shri Sungrab Nyamso Khang, 2001; BDRC W23745), 4: 126–28, citing 127.3–4. On this text, see Brenton Sullivan, *Building a Religious Empire: Tibetan Buddhism, Bureaucracy, and the Rise of the Gelukpa* (Philadelphia: University of Pennsylvania Press, 2021), 236n2; and Berthe Jansen, *The Monastery Rules: Buddhist Monastic Organization in Pre-Modern Tibet* (Berkeley: University of California Press, 2018), 107.

34. Brag dkar blo bzang dpal ldan, *Mu tig gi phreng ba*, 16.7–19.14, quoting 17.3–4. See also 235.12–237.16, and less directly related, 98.16–101.11, 187.1–196.13.
35. Lce sgom shes rab rdo rje, *Ri khrod skal ldan sgron me*, 682.2; Mi pham phun tshogs shes rab, *Ri chos zab mo grub pa'i bcud len sbrang rtsi'i snying po*, 431.3; Ngag dbang bstan 'dzin nor bu, *Bca' yig ri chos zhal gdams*, 66.4–6; Karma nges don bstan rgyas, *Ri chos thar lam mdzub ston*, 171.2.
36. Chapter 24, on the *gson shog* ritual, runs Karma chags med, *Ri chos mtshams kyi zhal gdams*, 358.4–368.5 (Karthar 3: 47–79); that the ritual serves the purpose of *dkor sbyong* is mentioned at 362.6. A rite by which the most capable *kusali*-style practitioner can avoid the fault of improperly consuming monastic property is described 248.4–6 (Karthar 2: 158–59). See also 600.5 (Karthar 4: 82–83).

    Taking solace: 627.2–3 (Karthar 4: 122–23), 630.1–2 (Karthar 4: 125).

    Sack of *dkor*: 351.5. See also 24.5 (Karthar 1: 37; Eric Haynie, "Karma chags med's *Mountain Dharma*: Tibetan Advice on Sociologies of Retreat" [MA thesis, University of Colorado, 2013], 85), where Karma chags med mentions living off *dkor* among a list of his moral failings. This can be contrasted with 620.1–3 (Karthar 4: 114), the story of Bkra shis dpal 'byor, horse keeper of Zhwa dmar IV Chos grags ye shes (1453–1524), who was so afraid of being contaminated by consuming *dkor* that he would only eat used tea leaves, his skin turning blue as a result. This Bkra shis dpal 'byor (1457–1525) is the first of the Sangs rgyas mnyan pa incarnation lineage.

    The issue of *dkor* comes up many times in the section running 580.4–593.4 (Karthar 4: 53–72).
37. Karma nges don bstan rgyas, *Ri chos thar lam mdzub ston*, 170.3–172.5, quoting 171.4; 188.3–190.3, quoting 189.1–2.

38. Zhabs dkar, *Chos bshad gzhan phan zla ba*, 99.9–101.8. The sutra quoted is the *Duḥśīlanigrahī*, *Tshul khrims 'chal ba tshar gcod pa*.
39. Brag dkar blo bzang dpal ldan, *Mu tig gi phreng ba*, 138.15–139.14, 191.16–192.14, 230.1–231.12, 269.15–270.1; Ngag dbang bstan 'dzin nor bu, *Bca' yig ri chos zhal gdams*, 59.4–63.1, 66.5–67.2.
40. Geoffrey Barstow, *Food of Sinful Demons: Meat, Vegetarianism, and the Limits of Buddhism in Tibet* (New York: Columbia University Press, 2019), 3, 8–9, 171–72.
41. Zur mang legs bshad sgra dbyang, *Ri yi chos gtam kun tu bzang po'i sgra dbyangs*, 97.2–5. See also 26.4–6, where meat and beer are mentioned as a potential cause of ill feeling between retreatants. Lha btsun nam mkha' 'jigs med, *Ri chos rin po che gnad kyi phreng ba*, 653.3–4.
42. Karma chags med, *Ri chos mtshams kyi zhal gdams*, 225.6 (Karthar 2: 130–31); see also 86.5 (Karthar 1: 161), 575.2–5 (Karthar 4: 27–28). Karma nges don bstan rgyas, *Ri chos thar lam mdzub ston*, 176.4; see also 182.2–3. Karma chags med's handbook also mentions eating only nonmeat food (*dkar gro*) during one's preparation for initiation in Cārya and Yoga tantra systems, which is about adhering to ancient conceptions of preserving a ritual sense of bodily purity: 301.1–302.6 (Karthar 2: 259), 308.5–309.1 (Karthar 2: 283).

    Both of these authors specifically mention that the practitioner should not neglect to consume the small amounts of meat and alcohol that may make up part of the initiation ritual for the "higher" forms of tantra: Karma chags med, 252.1–3 (Karthar 2: 161–62), 483.6–484.5 (Karthar 3: 188–92), 575.2–5 (Karthar 4: 27–28); Karma nges don bstan rgyas, 176.5.
43. 'Jigs med gling pa, *Ri chos zhal gdams ngo mtshar rgya mtsho*, 703.5–704.2, 705.4 (Jikmé Lingpa, "A Wonderous Ocean of Advice," 3–5).
44. The only mention of the fault of meat consumption in Zhabs dkar's *Chos bshad gzhan phan zla ba* is a quotation of the *Laṅkāvatāra Sūtra* (66.18–67.3), which, as Barstow has shown, is the canonical text most frequently cited by Tibetan Buddhist authors making a case for vegetarianism; *Food of Sinful Demons*, 25–26.

    The volume of translations, *The Faults of Meat: Tibetan Buddhist Writings on Vegetarianism* (Somerville, MA: Wisdom, 2019), ed. Barstow, contains translations of two texts by Karma chags med regarding meat eating and its avoidance, as well as autobiographical comments and songs from Zhabs dkar, 181–221.
45. Barstow, *Food of Sinful Demons*, 64, 86, 131.
46. On essence extraction, see Cathy Cantwell, "Reflections on Rasāyana, Bcud len, and Related Practices in Nyingma (Rnying ma) Tantric Ritual," *History of Science in South Asia* 5, no. 2 (2017): 181–203; Barbara Gerke, "'Treating The Aged' and 'Maintaining Health': Locating bcud len Practices in the four Medical Tantras," *Journal of the International Association of Buddhist Studies* 35, nos. 1–2 (2012): 329–62; and David Germano, "Food, Clothes, Dreams, and Karmic Propensities," in *Religions of Tibet in Practice*, ed. Donald Lopez Jr. (Princeton, NJ: Princeton University Press, 1997), 293–312.
47. Charles Jamyang Oliphant, "'Extracting the Essence': *Bcud len* in the Tibetan literary tradition" (PhD diss., Faculty of Oriental Studies, Wolfson College, UK, 2015), 144–49.

    Karmapa III Rang byung rdo rje, *Ra mo shag gi bcud len*, in *Collected Works*, 16 vols. (Zi ling: Mtshur phu mkhan po lo yag bkra shis, 2006; BDRC W30541), 11: 635–41, citing 641.1–2 (Ruth Gamble, *The Third Karmapa Rangjung Dorje: Master of Mahāmudrā*. Lives of the Masters [Boulder, CO: Shambhala, 2020], 205). Gamble translates this text in its entirety, 201–5.
48. Karma chags med, *Ri chos tshams kyi zhal gdams*, 225.3–6 (Karthar 2: 130), 29.3 (Karthar 1: 42), 518.1–2 (Karthar 3: 271–72).
49. Yang dgon pa's *Lhan thabs chen mo* contains a single reference to Mi la ras pa's having sustained himself with nettles; *Collected Works*, 2: 94.6.
50. Bsod nams chos 'dzin, *Dben pa ri khrod 'grims pa'i gsal 'debs*, 3a3–4; Karma pa III Rang byung rdo rje, *Ri chos bdud rtsi'i nying khu*, *Collected Works* (2013), 4: 502.2–3; Zhabs dkar, *Chos bshad gzhan phan zla ba*, 246.7–13.

51. Ngag dbang bstan 'dzin nor bu, *Me tog bcud len gyi gdam pa skal bzang sna rgyan* (woodblock print, in 11 folio sides; NGMPP L318/2), 4b3–6. This text is addressed in Oliphant, "'Extracting the Essence,'" including a paraphrase of this passage, 275–80.
52. Ngag dbang bstan 'dzin nor bu, *Bca' yig ri chos zhal gdams*, 10.2–4.
53. Brag dkar ba chos kyi dbang phyug, *Grub pa'i gnas chen brag dkar rta so'i sgrub sde spong ba pa rnams kyi blang dor gyi rim pa gsal bar ston pa'i bca'yig mun sel nyin mor byed pa'i 'od snang*, in *Collected Works*, 12 vols. (Swayambhunath, Kathmandu: Khenpo Shedup Tenzin, 2011), 12: 645–92, quoting 653.3–654.1. The author asserts that life for the lay community is affected by the changing times as well: "These days, worldly households are burdened by corvée labor (*khral 'u lag*) and the needs of food and clothing, which only get more difficult each year," 686.3.

    On the history of Brag dkar rta so and the life of Chos kyi dbang phyug, see Marta Sernesi, "Writing Local Religious History: The *Abbatial History of Brag dkar rta so*," in *Unearthing Himalayan Treasures: Festschrift for Franz-Karl Ehrhard*, ed. Volker Caumanns, Sernesi, and Nicolai Solmsdorf (Marburg: Indica et Tibetica Verlag, 2019), 387–415.

5. PRESERVING THE ASCETIC SELF

1. I have changed the order in which these statements are given by Bsod nams chos 'dzin, *Dben pa ri khrod 'grims pa'i gsal 'debs/ zhal gdam thar pa chen po'i gru sding* (undated *dbu med* manuscript, in 11 folio sides; NGMPP AT146/3), 4b3–5a1, 3a5–3b1.
2. O rgyan rnam grol dbang po, *Sbas mtha'i ri khrod du 'dug tshul dang rnams [=rnam] kun rang brgyud [=rgyud] chos dang bsre tshul gyi bslab bya zhal gyi gdams pa'i nying khu gsang ba bdud rtsi thig le* (undated *dbu med* manuscript, in 10 folio sides; NGMPP AT82/7), 2b4–5.

    I follow Franz-Karl Ehrhard's reading and reconstruction of title of this text; "'Turning the Wheel of the Dharma in Zhing sa va lung': The Dpal ri sprul skus (17th to 20th centuries)," *Bulletin of Tibetology* 44, nos. 1–2 (2008): 5–29, citing 26. Still, my translation remains tentative and incomplete. This title is given on the NGMPP's metadata card for this text, but the version of the text to which I have access does not include a title page, and this title does not appear in the body of the text. The title as given may have been supplied based on some other source of information or created by the cataloguer. The text contains fragments of this title at 2a1–2, 5b6–6a1. At 1b4, the text is described as a *bcud dril ri chos man ngag*.

    In this article Ehrhard identifies O rgyan rnam grol dbang po as a disciple of Rig 'dzin padma dbang rgyal rdo rje (1779–1841), the fourth Dpal ri incarnation.

    The colophon to the text mentions Rig 'dzin padma dbang rgyal. Additionally, the author, here styling himself Smyon pa o rgyan rnam grol dbang po, states that he wrote the text in a *me rta* year, which was his thirty-eighth year; 6a1–2. This most likely places the date of composition at 1846, and the birth of its author at around 1808. This is far more likely than the date of composition's being 1786, which would place O rgyan rnam grol dbang po's birth at around 1748, making him some thirty-one years older than his teacher—possible, but less likely than what I have proposed.
3. Zur mang legs bshad sgra dbyangs, *Ri yi chos gtam kun tu bzang po'i sgra dbyangs* (Mtshur phu dgon gtsug lag dpe tshogs, n.d., 113 pages; BDRC W3CN5072), 22.3–6.

    See also Karma chags med, *Ri chos mtshams kyi zhal gdams* (Brag dkar dgon pa, 1970; BRDC W23259), 169.1–4 (Khenpo Karthar Rinpoché, *Karma Chakme's Mountain Dharma*, 4 vols. [Woodstock, NY: Karma Triyana Dharmachakra Publications, 2004], 2: 6–7); Mi pham phun tshogs shes rab, *Ri chos zab mo grub pa'i bcud len sbrang rtsi'i snying po*, in *Collected Works*, 2 vols. (Darjeeling: Thub bstan gsang sngags chos gling 'brug sgar dpe mdzod khang, 2008; BDRC W2KG200924), 1: 377–435, citing 391.3–4; Brag dkar blo bzang dpal ldan bstan 'dzin snyan grags, *Gnas dben par sdod pa'i chos mdzad mtha' dag la nye bar mkho ba'i ri chos mu tig gi phreng ba* (Gser rta rdzong: Gser thang bla rung lnga rig nang bstan slob gling, n.d.; BDRC W3CN4732), 197.12–14; and Pan chen bla ma IV Blo bzang chos kyi rgyal mtshan, *Don du gnyer ba'i ri khrod pa rnams la khrims su bca' ba sku gsum gzhal med khang du 'dzeg pa baidUrya'i them skas*, in *Collected Works*, 5 vols. (Gzhis ka rtse: Bkra shis lhun po par khang, n.d.; BDRC W9848), 4: 501–16, citing 503.3–504.2.

Here Pan chen bla ma IV quotes, without identifying the source, from the *Life* of Mi la ras pa, where the yogin sings a song with the refrain *ri khrod 'di ru 'chi nus na/ rnal 'byor bsam pa rdzogs pa yin*; Gtsang smyon he ru ka, *Rnal 'byor gyi dbang phyug chen po mi la ras pa'i rnam mgur* (Zi ling: Mtsho sngon mi rigs dpe skrun khang, 2005), 158.15–159.11, which Andrew Quintman translates as, "If thus I can die in this mountain retreat / The aims of this yogin will be complete," *Life of Milarepa* (New York: Penguin, 2010 [1488]) 145.

In the standard version of his *Life*, Mi la ras pa is recorded as having made a declaration about remaining in meditation and not descending to the village in the face of possible starvation, exposure to the elements, falling ill, etc.; Quintman, *The Life of Milarepa*, 133–34. This passage is missing from the 2005 Mtsho sngon mi rigs dpe skrun khang version of the text; it should appear beginning on 146.

4. Lha btsun nam mkha' 'jigs med, *Ri chos rin po che gnad kyi phreng ba*, in *Rdo rje snying po sprin gyi thol glu*, 2 vols. (n.p.; BDRC W13780), 2: 609–68, citing 626.5–6. Earlier in the text, the author mentions bringing medicine into one's retreat; 619.3–6.

5. This paragraph paraphrases three different passages by Brag dkar blo bzang dpal ldan: two similar passages in *Mu tig gi phreng ba*, running 11.16–14.15 and 112.5–115.10; and one in *Spong ba bsam gtan pa rnams la bslab pa'i khrims su bca' ba man ngag lag tu bcangs bde ba'i ri chos me tog phreng mdzes*, in *Collected Works*, 20 vols. (compiled in Chengdu; BDRC W23608), 3: 633–48, citing 641.5–642.5. Here I quote *Mu tig*, 12.5, and *Me tog*, 642.5.

Perhaps providing a counterpoint, when offering prescriptions for comportment during a retreat, Karma nges don bstan rgyas states on a few different occasions that the expectations are different for "the sick and the elderly," *na dang rgas pa rnams* (or some permutation thereof); *Ri chos thar lam mdzub ston*, in *The Collected Works of Sman sdong mtshams pa rin po che Karma nges don bstan rgyas*, 3 vols. (Bir, H.P.: D. Tsondu Senghe, 1975; BDRC W10982), 3: 161–204, citing 170.2–3, 175.5, 176.5.

6. Karma pa III Rang byung rdo rje, *Ri chos bdud rtsi'i nying khu*, in *Collected Works*, 13 vols. (Lhasa: Dpal brtsegs bod yig dpe rnying zhib 'jug khang, 2013; BDRC W3PD1288), 4: 479–503, citing 499.5–502.1. Rang byung rdo rje writes in a similar manner about facing and accepting physical threats, and rendering them neutral with compassion, in his *Ri chos dngos grub phreng ba*, *Collected Works*, 16 vols. (Zi ling: Mtshur phu mkhan po lo yag bkra shis, 2006; BDRC W30541), 5: 55–62, citing 58.1–5 (Ruth Gamble, *The Third Karmapa Rangjung Dorje: Master of Mahāmudrā*. Lives of the Masters [Boulder, CO: Shambhala, 2020], 161).

7. Karma chags med, *Ri chos mtshams kyi zhal gdams*, 520.4–5 (Karthar 3: 274); Bsod nams chos 'dzin, *Dben pa ri khrod 'grims pa'i gsal 'debs*, 4b5; Brag dkar blo bzang dpal ldan, *Me tog phreng mdzes*, *Collected Works*, 3: 642.4.

8. Lce sgom shes rab rdo rje, *Ri khrod skal ldan sgron me*, in *Blo sbyong nyer mkho phyogs bsgrigs*, ed. Cha ris skal bzang thogs med and Ngag dbang sbyin pa (Lan kru'u: Kan su'u mi rigs dpe skrun khang, 2003; BDRC W25275), 675–88, citing 682.12–683.4. Similarly, see Karma chags med, *Ri chos mtshams kyi zhal gdams*, 520.4–522.2 (Karthar 3: 274–77).

9. Zur mang legs bshad sgra dbyangs, *Ri yi chos gtam kun tu bzang po'i sgra dbyangs*, 82.17–83.3. The title of the practice is supplied from 90.13–14.

10. Paraphrasing Zur mang legs bshad sgra dbyangs, *Ri yi chos gtam kun tu bzang po'i sgra dbyangs*, 90.13–94.3; quoting 90.17–18 and 91.10–13.

11. The chapter on *gcod* runs Karma chags med, *Ri chos mtshams kyi zhal gdams*, 259.6–271.2 (Karthar 2: 195–221). *Gcod*'s abilities to heal self or others is described 265.5–266.4 (Karthar 2: 204–6) and 269.1–270.3 (Karthar 2: 209–10).

12. Karma chags med, *Ri chos mtshams kyi zhal gdams*, 239.2–4 (Karthar 2: 147–48).

5. PRESERVING THE ASCETIC SELF

13. Yang dgon pa rgyal mtshan dpal, *Ri chos yon tan kun 'byung [ba] rin po che 'bar ba*, in *The Collected Works (gsung 'bum) of Yang dgon pa*, 3 vols. (Thimpu: Kunsang Topgey, 1976; BDRC W1KG17449), 1: 447–570, citing 487.5–488.2; *Ri chos yon tan kun 'byung gi lhan thabs chen mo*, in *Collected Works*, 2: 1–175, citing 62.4–63.2. See also Phag mo gru pa rdo rje rgyal po, *Ri chos bdud rtsi bum pa'i gdams ngag*, in *'Bri gung bka' brgyud chos mdzod chen mo*, compiled by A mgon rin po che and Ra se dkon mchog rgya mtsho, 151 vols. (Lhasa: Bri gung mthil dgon, 2004; BDRC W00JW501203), 16: 277–83, citing 282.4–283.1; Karma chags med, *Ri chos mtshams kyi zhal gdams*, 164.4–166.2 (Karthar 1: 317–19), 503.1–3 (Karthar 3: 231).
14. Yang dgon pa, *Rin po che 'bar ba*, *Collected Works*, 1: 522.4–5.
15. The date for the composition of these texts comes from Janet Gyatso, *Being Human in a Buddhist World: An Intellectual History of Medicine in Early Modern Tibet* (New York: Columbia University Press, 2015), 4.
16. This paragraph paraphrases from Yang dgon pa, *Rin po che 'bar ba*, *Collected Works*, 1: 522.3–526.5; *Lhan thabs chen mo*, 2: 101.4–116.5.

    For additional comments on the healing powers of *gtum mo*, see *Rin po che 'bar ba*, 1: 476.2; and Karma chags med, *Ri chos mtshams kyi zhal gdams*, 247.3–4 (Karthar 2: 157), 464.3–5 (Karthar 3: 142), 506.2–3 (Karthar 3: 233).
17. Karma chags med, *Ri chos mtshams kyi zhal gdams*, 502.5–513.6 (Karthar 3: 230–44). Visualizing the lama to quell a toothache is also mentioned at 166.1–2 (Karthar 1: 319).
18. Brenton Sullivan, *Building a Religious Empire: Tibetan Buddhism, Bureaucracy, and the Rise of the Gelukpa* (Philadelphia: University of Pennsylvania Press, 2021), 36–37, 56–57; Berthe Jansen, *The Monastery Rules: Buddhist Monastic Organization in Pre-Modern Tibet* (Berkeley: University of California Press, 2018), 141–44.
19. Andrew Crislip's article, "'I Have Chosen Sickness': The Controversial Function of Sickness in Early Christian Ascetic Practice," in Oliver Freiberger, ed., *Asceticism and Its Critics: Historical Accounts and Comparative Perspectives* (New York: Oxford University Press, 2006), 179–209, contains many details about the contours of sickness in early Christian asceticism, an excellent starting point for a comparison with the tradition described here.
20. In the introductory chapter and the colophons to subsequent chapters of Karma chags med's *Ri chos mtshams kyi zhal gdams*, numerous mentions are made to how Brtson 'grus rgya mtsho endured wintry conditions while receiving the great master's dictations. For examples, see 26.3–5 (Karthar 1: 39; Eric Haynie, "Karma chags med's *Mountain Dharma*: Tibetan Advice on Sociologies of Retreat" [MA thesis, University of Colorado, 2013], 86), 114.5–6 (Karthar 1: 232–33), 534.6 (Karthar 3: 307–8). These frank statements, intended to increase appreciation for Brtson 'grus rgya mtsho's efforts and forming part of the metadata surrounding the text rather than its actual contents, stand out as exceptions that prove the rule that authors in the Tibetan ascetic tradition tend overwhelmingly to downplay the cold.
21. Zhabs dkar tshogs drug rang grol, *Chos bshad gzhan phan zla ba*, in *Collected Works*, 10 vols. (Ziling: Mtsho sngon mi rigs dpe skrun khang, 2002; BDRC W1PD45150), 8: 1–283, paraphrasing the argument made 250.12–252.3, quoting 251.1–2 and 252.2–3. The author continues with this topic until 280.10, quoting and citing many dozens of exemplars of the Indo-Tibetan Buddhist tradition regarding the need to endure hardships during ascetic practice.
22. Zur mang legs bshad sgra dbyangs, *Ri yi chos gtam kun tu bzang po'i sgra dbyangs*, 20.5–6; Karma chags med, *Ri chos mtshams kyi zhal gdams*, 464.5–6 (Karthar 3: 142).
23. The instructions on *gtum mo* run Yang dgon pa, *Rin po che 'bar ba*, *Collected Works*, 1: 468.3–477.1, quoting 474.1–2. Also addressed in the *Lhan thabs chen mo*, 2: 43.5–51.2.
24. Graham Sandberg, *Tibet and the Tibetans* (London: Society for Promoting Christian Knowledge, 1906), mentioning *gtum mo*, 251, 280–81. I highlight this text in part to draw attention to useful details about how long-term meditative retreat was practiced in premodern Tibet: 104–5, 276–78.

    David-Néel's book was published in English translation in 1932.

25. H. Benson, J. W. Lehmann, M. S. Malhotra, R. F. Goldman, J. Hopkins, and M. D. Epstein, "Body Temperature Changes During the Practice of gTum mo Yoga," *Nature* 295 (1982): 234–36.
26. See, for example, Maria Kozhevnikov, James Elliott, Jennifer Shephard, and Klaus Gramann, "Neurocognitive and Somatic Components of Temperature Increases during g-Tummo Meditation: Legend and Reality," *PLoS ONE* 8, no. 3 (March 2013); and Maria Kozhevnikov, Alina Veronika Irene Strasser, Elizabeth McDougal, Rupali Dhond, and Geoffrey Samuel, "Beyond Mindfulness: Arousal-Driven Modulation of Attentional Control During Arousal-Based Practices," *Current Research in Neurobiology* 3 (2022).
27. Toni Huber, *The Cult of Pure Crystal Mountain: Popular Pilgrimage and Visionary Landscape in Southeast Tibet* (New York: Oxford University Press, 1999). This tradition is described in Zhabs dkar's autobiography; Shabkar Tsokdruk Rangdrol, *The Life of Shabkar: The Autobiography of a Tibetan Yogin*, trans. Matthieu Ricard et al. (Ithaca, NY: Snow Lion, 2001), 249. See also David Germano, "Food, Clothes, Dreams, and Karmic Propensities," in *Religions of Tibet in Practice*, ed. Donald Lopez Jr. (Princeton, NJ: Princeton University Press, 1997), 293–312.
28. Paraphrasing Yang dgon pa's instructions on *gtum mo* in the *Rin po che 'bar ba, Collected Works*, 1: 468.3–477.1, quoting 473.1–2. The instruction about seeking out a snowy or rocky mountain comes from 450.6–451.1; that regarding how one sleeps is from 454.2; and the direction a retreat's doorway faces, *Lhan thabs chen mo*, 2: 8.5.
29. Karma chags med, *Ri chos mtshams kyi zhal gdams*, 464.3–466.2 (Karthar 3: 141–44).
30. Karma chags med, *Ri chos mtshams kyi zhal gdams*, 465.1–2 (Karthar 3: 143).
31. Karma nges don bstan rgyas, *Ri chos thar lam mdzub ston*, 199.5–200.4. There is a similar statement by Karma pa III Rang byung rdo rje, *Ri chos bdud rtsi'i nying khu, Collected Works* (2013), 4: 502.2–4.
32. Karma pa III Rang byung rdo rje, *Ri chos bdud rtsi'i nying khu, Collected Works* (2013), 4: 495.4–5; Zur mang legs bshad sgra dbyangs, *Ri yi chos gtam kun tu bzang po'i sgra dbyangs*, 18.11–12; Lha btsun nam mkha' 'jigs med, *Ri chos rin po che gnad kyi phreng ba*, 621.1–3.
33. Phag mo gru pa, *Ri chos bdud rtsi bum pa'i gdams ngag*, in *'Bri gung bka' brgyud chos mdzod chen mo*, 16: 282.1–3.
34. Lce sgom shes rab rdo rje, *Ri khrod skal ldan sgron me*, 677.18–19. On the term *mi rgod*, here translated as "unruly people," see chapter 2, note 30. Zur mang legs bshad sgra dbyangs, *Ri yi chos gtam kun tu bzang po'i sgra dbyangs*, 24.4–14. Karma chags med, *Ri chos mtshams kyi zhal gdams*, 245.5–246.1 (Karthar 2: 155–56). The danger posed by bandits is also mentioned by Yang dgon pa, *Lhan thabs chen mo, Collected Works*, 2: 145.1; Mi pham phun tshogs shes rab, *Ri chos zab mo grub pa'i bcud len sbrang rtsi'i snying po*, 426.3; and Brag dkar ba chos kyi dbang phyug, *Grub pa'i gnas chen brag dkar rta so'i sgrub sde spong ba pa rnams kyi blang dor gyi rim pa gsal bar ston pa'i bca' yig mun sel nyin mor byed pa'i 'od snang*, in *Collected Works*, 12 vols. (Swayambhunath, Kathmandu: Khenpo Shedup Tenzin, 2011), 12: 645–92, citing 653.5.
35. Circle of protection: Yang dgon pa, *Rin po che 'bar ba, Collected Works*, 1: 454.6; *Lhan thabs chen mo*, 2: 10.2–14.4.
    Further improvement: *Lhan thabs chen mo*, 2: 144.6–145.1.
36. The chapter paraphrased here runs Karma chags med, *Ri chos mtshams kyi zhal gdams*, 351.5–358.4 (Karthar 3: 27–45); it is translated in Haynie, "Karma chags med's *Mountain Dharma*," 89–92. The quotation characterizing the rite is from 8.2–3 (Karthar 1: 32).
37. Karma chags med, *Ri chos mtshams kyi zhal gdams*, 201.6–203.1, quoting 201.6–202.1 (Karthar 2: 77–78).
38. Yang dgon pa, *Rin po che 'bar ba, Collected Works*, 1: 538.2–4; *Lhan thabs chen mo*, 2: 133.4–5.
    Karma chags med mentions the disappearance of *shig* as a sign of spiritual progress for individuals of the highest faculties, *Ri chos mtshams kyi zhal gdams*, 454.4–5 (Karthar 3: 126). See also

Janet Gyatso, *Apparitions of the Self: The Secret Autobiographies of a Tibetan Visionary* (Princeton, NJ: Princeton University Press, 1998), 19, 66, 226.

39. Yang dgon pa, *Rin po che 'bar ba, Collected Works*, 1: 507.3–508.1; Karma chags med, *Ri chos mtshams kyi zhal gdams*, 250.1–4 (Karthar 2: 159–60).

40. For descriptions of these practices more detailed and eloquent than what I have given here, see James Gentry, *Power Objects in Tibetan Buddhism: The Life, Writings, and Legacy of Sokdokpa Lodrö Gyeltsen* (Leiden: Brill, 2017), 30–59; and Gyatso, *Apparitions of the Self*, 188–90.

41. Paul Copp, *The Body Incantatory: Spells and the Ritual Imagination in Medieval Chinese Buddhism* (New York: Columbia University Press, 2014), 143–45.

42. Gyatso, *Being Human in a Buddhist World*, 101, 377, 393. Each of these quotations comes from a larger passage on the fundamental materiality of Tibetan medicine. On 361–62, Gyatso describes a practice prescribed by the *Four Treatises* in which while making medical preparations, the physician is to imagine himself in the form of the Medicine Buddha, his medical instruments as those of the Medicine Buddha, and so on. This is a cultivation that sits inside the pervasively material grounding of medical practice in Tibet.

6. FORMING THE ASCETIC SELF

1. Karma chags med, *Ri chos mtshams kyi zhal gdams* (Brag dkar dgon pa, 1970; BRDC W23259), 135.1–139.1 (Khenpo Karthar Rinpoché, *Karma Chakme's Mountain Dharma*, 4 vols. [Woodstock, NY: Karma Triyana Dharmachakra Publications, 2004], 1: 285–90).

2. Karma chags med, *Ri chos mtshams kyi zhal gdams*, 94.2–5 (Karthar 1: 189).

3. Yang dgon pa rgyal mtshan dpal, *Ri chos yon tan kun 'byung [ba] rin po che 'bar ba*, in *The Collected Works (gsung 'bum) of Yang dgon pa*, 3 vols. (Thimpu: Kunsang Topgey, 1976; BDRC W1KG17449), 1: 447–570, citing 455.3; Karma chags med, *Ri chos mtshams kyi zhal gdams*, 236.5–6 (Karthar 2: 144).

4. The phrase is *dus mtha' rnal 'byor*; Karma pa III Rang byung rdo rje, *Ri chos dngos grub phreng ba*, in *Collected Works*, 16 vols. (Zi ling: Mtshur phu mkhan po lo yag bkra shis, 2006; BDRC W30541), 5: 55–62, citing 57.4. Ruth Gamble translates the text in full in *The Third Karmapa Rangjung Dorje: Master of Mahāmudrā*. Lives of the Masters (Boulder, CO: Shambhala, 2020), 157–66.

   'Jam mgon kong sprul would meditate in this same cave; Alexander Gardner, *The Life of Jamgon Kongtrul the Great* (Boulder, CO: Snow Lion, 2019), 192.

5. Lce sgom shes rab rdo rje, *Ri khrod skal ldan sgron me*, in *Blo sbyong nyer mkho phyogs bsgrigs*, ed. Cha ris skal bzang thogs med and Ngag dbang sbyin pa (Lan kru'u: Kan su'u mi rigs dpe skrun khang, 2003; BDRC W25275), 675–88, citing 678.9–679.2. See also 677.7–10, where he again praises empty mountain hermitages using similar terms. This latter passage would be quoted by Brag dkar blo bzang dpal ldan bstan 'dzin snyan rags, *Gnas dben par sdod pa'i chos mdzad mtha' dag la nye bar mkho ba'i ri chos mu tig gi phreng ba* (Gser rta rdzong: Gser thang bla rung lnga rig nang bstan slob gling, n.d.; BDRC W3CN4732), 137.11–16.

6. Mi pham phun tshogs shes rab, *Ri chos zab mo grub pa'i bcud len sbrang rtsi'i snying po*, in *Collected Works*, 2 vols. (Darjeeling: Thub bstan gsang sngags chos gling 'brug sgar dpe mdzod khang, 2008; BDRC W2KG200924), 1: 377–435, citing 432.2–3; see a similar statement by Brag dkar ba chos kyi dbang phyug, *Grub pa'i gnas chen brag dkar rta so'i sgrub sde spong ba pa rnams kyi blang dor gyi rim pa gsal bar ston pa'i bca' yig mun sel nyin mor byed pa'i 'od snang*, in *Collected Works*, 12 vols. (Swayambhunath, Kathmandu: Khenpo Shedup Tenzin, 2011; BDRC W1KG14557), 12: 645–92, citing 683.5–684.1. O rgyan rnam grol dbang po, *Sbas mtha'i ri khrod du 'dug tshul dang rnams*

[=rnam] kun rang brgyud [=rgyud] chos dang bsre tshul gyi bslab bya zhal gyi gdams pa'i nying khu gsang ba bdud rtsi thig le (undated dbu med manuscript, in 10 folio sides; NGMPP AT82/7), 3a2.

7. Yang dgon pa, Rin po che 'bar ba, Collected Works, 1: 518.5, 545.2–3. Commentary connected to the latter passage relates stories of how Mi la ras pa, Padmasambhava, Phag mo gru pa, 'Jig rten gsum mgon, Virūpa, and others overcame conceptual thoughts, demonic afflictions, and illnesses; Ri chos yon tan kun 'byung gi lhan thabs chen mo, in Collected Works, 2: 1–175, citing 135.2–161.2.

8. Zur mang legs bshad sgra dbyangs, Ri yi chos gtam kun tu bzang po'i sgra dbyangs (Mtshur phu dgon gtsug lag dpe tshogs, n.d., 113 pages; BDRC W3CN5072), 91.9–14. See also 78.2.

Karma chags med, Ri chos mtshams kyi zhal gdams, 223.5–224.3 (Karthar 2: 126–27). Karma chags med mentions reading from the writings of the earlier siddhas of one's tradition during a retreat, 245.1–2 (Karthar 2: 154). He refers to stories from the lives of many past masters to demonstrate the value and necessity of practicing humility, 616.6–623.2 (Karthar 4: 110–17).

9. Karma chags med, Ri chos mtshams kyi zhal gdams, 222.6–223.2 (Karthar 2: 125). This passage could be understood somewhat differently depending on how one takes the word rnam thar.

10. Karma chags med again refers to an asceticism of "drinking water and chewing rocks," using slightly different language, Ri chos mtshams kyi zhal gdams, 104.1–2 (Karthar 1: 209–10). The passage quoted here runs Karma chags med, 23.5–25.2 (Karthar 1: 37–38); translated and discussed in Eric Haynie, "Karma chags med's Mountain Dharma: Tibetan Advice on Sociologies of Retreat" (MA thesis, University of Colorado, 2013), 53–54, 84–85.

11. Khenpo Karthar Rinpoché explains, "During his lifetime Chakme Rinpoche was commonly referred to as the Yogi of Bari [dpal ri], which was the name of the place where he lived. He uses this as proof that he had not moved around very much," 1: 37; see also 27. Another possibility is that Karma chags med is here referring to the fact that he was called gnas mdo karma chags med, "Karma Chakmé of Nedo."

12. Khenpo Karthar Rinpoché explains, "This is a Tibetan expression that refers to the fact that when someone says something inappropriate, those around them will be embarrassed. What [Karma Chakmé] means is that if he were to teach the Dharma that he has not practiced himself, no one would have any confidence in that" (1: 38).

13. Zhabs dkar tshogs drug rang grol, Chos bshad gzhan phan zla ba, in Collected Works, 10 vols. (Zi ling: Mtsho sngon mi rigs dpe skrun khang, 2002; BDRC W1PD45150), 8: 1–283, citing 141.10–16.

14. For example, see Karma chags med, Ri chos mtshams kyi zhal gdams, 533.4–535.1 (Karthar 3: 305–8).

15. Brag dkar blo bzang dpal ldan, Mu tig gi phreng ba, 31.3–4; Karma chags med, Ri chos mtshams kyi zhal gdams, 91.6–92.3 (Karthar 1: 186–87). The quotation is from Karma chags med, 136.6–137.1 (Karthar 1: 287).

16. Yang dgon pa's description of how to do guru yoga is given in Rin po che 'bar ba, Collected Works, 1: 486.5–488.5; Lhan thabs chen mo, 2: 57.3–64.4. See also Rin po che 'bar ba, 506.6, 512.1.

The twelfth chapter of Karma chags med's handbook includes instructions on various ways of practicing guru yoga, from exoteric to highly esoteric versions; Ri chos mtshams kyi zhal gdams, 134.6–168.3 (Karthar 1: 285–333).

17. Mi pham phun tshogs shes rab, Ri chos zab mo grub pa'i bcud len sbrang rtsi'i snying po, 398.2–4; O rgyan rnam grol dbang po, Bdud rtsi thig le, 3b5–4a1.

18. O rgyan rnam grol dbang po, Bdud rtsi thig le, 2b6–3a1; Zur mang legs bshad sgra dbyangs, Ri yi chos gtam kun tu bzang po'i sgra dbyangs, 6.1–14.18.

19. Brag dkar blo bzang dpal ldan, Mu tig gi phreng ba, 31.3–45.13, quoting 39.14–40.2. See also 146.8–147.13, on how to serve the lama; and 255.16–263.16, on the importance of remaining devoted to a single lama.

20. Brag dkar blo bzang dpal ldan, Mu tig gi phreng ba, 41.1–6, 44.11–16. He attributes this statement to Po to ba at 18.1–4. The phrase 'phongs phyis pa'i rdo is also used by Lcang skya III Rol pa'i rdo rje, Dben par dga' ba'i gtam chos glu ring mo, in Collected Works, 7 vols. (Beijing: Krung go bod brgyud

6. FORMING THE ASCETIC SELF

mtho rim nang bstan slob gling nang bstan zhib 'jug khang, 1995; BDRC W28833), 4: 393–96, citing 393.4.

21. Somewhat at odds with what I have presented here is Karma chags med's prescription for assuming the comportment of a bee (*bung ba lta bu'i spyod pa*), where he emphasizes the necessity of merely getting what one needs from the guru, maintaining an attitude of impartiality, without forming a long-standing relationship; Karma chags med, *Ri chos mtshams kyi zhal gdams*, 565.4–568.1 (Karthar 4: 7–9).

22. Michel Foucault, *The Care of the Self: Volume 3 of the History of Sexuality*, trans. Robert Hurley (New York: Vintage, 1986), 239.

23. Brag dkar blo bzang dpal ldan, *Mu tig gi phreng ba*, 41.6–42.1, quoting 41.15–16; Lha btsun nam mkha' 'jigs med, *Ri chos rin po che gnad kyi phreng ba*, in *Rdo rje snying po sprin gyi thol glu*, 2 vols. (n.p.; BDRC W13780), 2: 609–68, citing 613.1–3; Zhwa dmar II Mkha' spyod dbang po, *Ri chos gcig shes kun grol man ngag gi snying po* (Mtshur phu gdon gtsug lag dpe rnying phyogs sgrig khang; undated modern reprint, in 36 pages; BDRC W3CN5081), 17.11–18.2.

Zhabs dkar devotes a significant portion of his *Chos bshad gzhan phan zla ba* to expounding upon the centrality of the lama to one's spiritual development and thus the necessity of adhering to him in a proper fashion, 162.11–170.11. This section is studded with quotations from past masters.

24. Karma chags med, *Ri chos mtshams kyi zhal gdams*, 137.5–139.1 (Karthar 1: 288–90).

25. Karma chags med, *Ri chos mtshams kyi zhal gdams*, 488.5–492.3 (Karthar 3: 212–18), quoting 491.2–3; 560.6–565.4 (Karthar 4: 10–14).

26. Mi pham phun tshogs shes rab, *Ri chos zab mo grub pa'i bcud len sbrang rtsi'i snying po*, 435.4–436.2. See also 381.2–5, 421.5–422.4.

27. Mi pham phun tshogs shes rab, *Ri chos zab mo grub pa'i bcud len sbrang rtsi'i snying po*, 404.2–408.2, quoting 407.5–408.2; 434.3–5. That he was sixty-one years old (in the Tibetan manner of calculating ages) when writing this text is mentioned at 406.3.

28. Karma chags med, *Ri chos mtshams kyi zhal gdams*, 594.3–596.3 (Karthar 4: 74–77), quoting 595.3–4. See also Karma chags med, 250.6 (Karthar 2: 160).

29. Karma chags med, *Ri chos mtshams kyi zhal gdams*, 593.5 (Karthar 4: 72).

30. Karma chags med, *Ri chos mtshams kyi zhal gdams*, 597.2–606.3 (Karthar 4: 78–84), quoting 597.2–3.

31. Karma chags med, *Ri chos mtshams kyi zhal gdams*, 7.4 (Karthar 1: 31), 222.5 (Karthar 2: 125). This would be echoed in the title, *Ri chos thar lam mdzub ston*, by Karma chags med's spiritual heir, Karma nges don bstan rgyas; *The Collected Works of Sman sdong mtshams pa rin po che Karma nges don bstan rgyas*, 3 vols. (Bir, H.P.: D. Tsondu Senghe, 1975; BDRC W10982), 3: 161–204.

32. Karma chags med, *Ri chos mtshams kyi zhal gdams*, 134.3–5 (Karthar 1: 282).

33. Karma chags med, *Ri chos mtshams kyi zhal gdams*, 168.3–194.5 (Karthar 2: 5–39), quoting 171.2–5 and 186.1–2.

34. Karma chags med, *Ri chos mtshams kyi zhal gdams*, 194.5–197.1 (Karthar 2: 39–43).

35. Karma chags med, *Ri chos mtshams kyi zhal gdams*, 118.1–4 (Karthar 1: 239–40).

36. Quoting Karthar 4: 58–59. Karma chags med also refers to this using the terminology of a "time of fruition" and a "time of practice" or "meditation" (*'bras bu'i dus, sgrub pa'i dus*); *Ri chos mtshams kyi zhal gdams*, 288.6–290.5 (Karthar 2: 246–48).

37. Lce sgom shes rab rdo rje, *Ri khrod skal ldan sgron me*, 686.7–687.10, 683.8–16. The "five degenerations" are also mentioned in the printing colophon, 688.2.

38. The sixth chapter runs Yang dgon pa, *Rin po che 'bar ba*, Collected Works, 1: 545.4–557.4, here quoting 556.2–5 and 556.7. The seventh chapter runs 557.4–567.4.

39. Yang dgon pa, *Lhan thabs chen mo*, Collected Works, 2: 174.2.

40. Zur mang legs bshad sgra dbyangs, *Ri yi chos gtam kun tu bzang po'i sgra dbyangs*, 102.7–104.10, quoting 102.7–103.7.

41. Zur mang legs bshad sgra dbyangs, *Ri yi chos gtam kun tu bzang po'i sgra dbyangs*, 20.5–12. I am not certain what is meant by *gzungs kyi rtogs pa*, which I have translated rather mechanically as "realization of retention." This may be related to Buddhist ritual spells or *dhāraṇī*, or could mean something like achieving perfect recall. *Gzungs* could be a mistake for *gzung*.
42. Zur mang legs bshad sgra dbyangs, *Ri yi chos gtam kun tu bzang po'i sgra dbyangs*, 5.12–13.
43. Jamgön Kongtrül, *Jamgon Kongtrul's Retreat Manual*, trans. Ngawang Zangpo (Boston: Snow Lion, 1994 [1876]), 175; 'Jam mgon kong sprul, *Dpal spungs yang khrod kun bzang bde chen 'od gsal gling gi sgrub pa rnams kyi kun spyod bca' khrims blang dor rab gsal phan bde'i 'byung gnas*, in *Collected Works*, 13 vols. (New Delhi: Shechen, 2002; BDRC W23723), 6: 1091–153, citing 1148.4–5. See also Kong sprul's statement about the prospect of not attaining some kind of confidence or assuredness (*gding* [sic] *khel*) in one's Generation and Perfection phase practices (*Jamgon Kongtrul's Retreat Manual*, 84; *Phan bde'i 'byung gnas*, *Collected Works*, 6: 1101.6–1102.1) in comparison to the two statements from Karma chags med (and Khenpo Karthar Rinpoché's glosses of them) about one's relative prospects for attaining "certainty" (*nges pa*) or "assuredness" (*gdeng*) in these same practices, discussed above. For a translation of an extended passage in which Kong sprul mentions numerous times his views about the low level of spiritual attainment that characterized the time in which he lived (touching upon how his own three-year, three-month retreat program fit into this state of affairs, to be addressed in chapter 7), see *Jamgon Kongtrul's Retreat Manual*, 26–31; 'Jam mgon kong sprul, *Dpal spungs yang khrod kun bzang bde chen 'od gsal gling rten dang brten par bcas pa'i dkar chag zhing khams kun tu khyab pa'i sgra snyan*, *Collected Works*, 6: 697–949, citing 884.1–890.4.

7. THE TIBETAN ASCETIC SELF IN TIME

1. Some details can be found in Reginald Ray, *Secret of the Vajra World: The Tantric Buddhism of Tibet (The World of Tibetan Buddhism, Volume Two)* (Boston and London: Shambhala, 2001), 448–59. Other details derive from my ongoing research among retreat communities globally.
2. The last of these is attested to by Dung dkar blo bzang 'phrin las, who glosses *lo gsum phyogs gsum bsgrub pa* as: *lo gsum/ zla ba gsum/ zhag gsum/ za ma gsum gyi dus yun nang mtshams bcad de sgom bsgrub byed pa*; *Dung dkar tshig mdzod chen mo* (Beijing: Krung go'i bod rig pa dpe skrun khang, 2002), 1975.
3. Sir Monier Monier-Williams, *A Sanskrit-English Dictionary* (Springfield, VA: Nataraj Books, 2004 [1899]), 911.
4. The dating of the text is established in John Newman, "The Epoch of the Kālacakra Tantra," *Indo-Iranian Journal* 41, no. 4 (1998): 319–49.
5. Jamgön Kongtrül, *Jamgon Kongtrul's Retreat Manual*, trans. Ngawang Zangpo (Boston: Snow Lion, 1994 [1876]), 18–20; Jamgön Kongtrül, *The Treasury of Knowledge, Book One: Myriad Worlds*, trans. Kalu Rinpoché Translation Group (Boston: Snow Lion, 1995), 158–59, 164–65; Jamgön Kongtrül, *The Treasury of Knowledge, Book Six, Part Four: Systems of Buddhist Tantra (The Indestructible Way of Secret Mantra)*, trans. Elio Guarisco and Ingrid McLeod (Ithaca, NY, and Boulder, CO: Snow Lion, 2005), 179–80, 445n66; Alexander Gardner, *The Life of Jamgon Kongtrul the Great* (Boulder, CO: Snow Lion, 2019), 212, 437n10; Yang dgon pa rgyal mtshan dpal, *Rdo rje lus kyi sbas bshad*, in *The Collected Works (gsung 'bum) of Yang dgon pa*, 3 vols. (Thimpu: Kunsang Topgey, 1976; BDRC W1KG17449), 2: 421–97, citing 461.4–462.3 (Elio Guarisco, trans., *Secret Map of the Body: Visions of the Human Energy Structure* [Merigar, Italy: Shang Shung Publications, 2015], 272–74).

On the Kālacakra system's understanding of the human person, their relationship to the various dimensions of being, and the process of transformation, see Vesna Wallace, *The Inner Kālacakratantra: A Buddhist Tantric View of the Individual* (New York: Oxford University Press, 2001).

6. Kālacakra practitioners doing *lo gsum phyogs gsum* are mentioned in 'Gos lo tsA ba, *Deb ther sngon po* (Chengdu: Si khron mi rigs dpe skrun khang, 1984), 910.18–911.1, 935.3–5 (George Roerich, trans., *The Blue Annals* [Delhi: Motilal Banarsidass, 1996 (1949)], 777, 798). At the former instance, 'Gos lo tsA ba states that it seemed this practice was active in eastern Tibet at the time of his writing: *ding sang yang rma chu'i 'gram na lo gsum phyogs gsum gyi dam bca' ba la gnas pa'i sgrub pa po mang du yod par snang ngo*. The fact that 'Gos lo tsA ba specifically notes this suggests that the practice was not widespread throughout the Himalaya.

Ascetic or religious trials of "three years" or multiples thereof are mentioned in Roerich, trans., *The Blue Annals*, 201, 235, 457, 482, 543, 572, 605, 683, 684, 686, 712, 743, 848, 916, 936, 944, 954, 1016, 1017, 1032. Some include multiple examples on the same page. In one instance an ascetic trial lasting three years is mentioned alongside trials of four, five, six, seven, ten, and fifteen years (869). Gling ras pa (1128–1188) is said to have at one point planned to spend seven years, seven months, and seven days in retreat; Roerich, trans., *The Blue Annals*, 662; *Deb ther sngon po*, 776.19–777.3.

There is mention of an early Bka' brgyud pa named Kha rag grags rgyal ba (1186–1271) who remained in meditation for two successive *ri thebs*: *ri thebs gnyis kyi bar du bzhugs nas phyir byon te dgon rin chen gling du lo skor cig tsam bzhugs*; *Deb ther sngon po*, 805.1–2. The translators take *thebs* as referring to a period of time, calling this a "mountain period," which they gloss this as meaning three years, three months, and three days; Roerich, trans., *The Blue Annals*, 687. I have found no other reference by which to corroborate this interpretation of the term *ri thebs*. *Ri thebs* appears in two other places in the Tibetan text; *Deb ther sngon po*, 682.14–16, 710.9. In both, the translators understand *thebs* to mean a donation to a clerical community, referring to funds donated to support hermits; Roerich, trans., *The Blue Annals*, 579, 603.

Neither *lo gsum phyogs gsum* nor *lo gsum zla gsum* nor any spelling variants thereof appears in Dpa' bo gtsug lag phreng ba's *Scholar's Feast*. The term *ri thebs*, however, appears seven times. Each instance is followed by a verb meaning to send, give, or furnish (*brdzangs, gnang, bsos*), which suggests that the second reading offered by the translators of the *Blue Annals* is the more prevalent usage. For examples from the life of Zhwa dmar IV Chos grags ye shes, see *Chos 'byung mkhas pa'i dga' ston* (Beijing: Mi rigs dpe skrun khang, 2006; BDRC W8LS19006), 580.28, 581.19, 581.24, 583.24, 583.25, 585.5.

7. Smyug la paN chen ngag dbang grags pa and Lha mthong lo tsA ba bshes gnyen rnam rgyal, *Dpal ldan bla ma dam pa grub pa'i khyu mchog phyogs thams cad las rnam par rgyal ba'i spyod pa can rje btsun kun dga' bzang po'i rnam par thar pa ris med dad pa'i spu long g.yo byed*, in *Bka' brgyud pa Hagiographies: A Collection of Rnam Thar of the Eminent Masters of Tibetan Buddhism*, ed. Khams sprul don brgyud nyi ma, 4 vols. (Palampur, H.P.: Sungrab Nyamso Gyunphel Parkhang, Tibetan Craft Community, 1972; BDRC W20499), 2: 383–660, citing 599.5 (David DiValerio, trans., *The Life of the Madman of Ü* [New York: Oxford University Press, 2016], 155), 600.2 (156), 631.2 (170).

Dngos grub dpal 'bar, *Rje btsun gtsang pa he ru ka'i thun mong gi rnam thar yon tan gyi gangs ri la dad pa'i seng ge rnam par rtse ba* (1508 woodblock print, in sixty-one folio sides; BDRC W2CZ6647), 17a3, 19a5.

Lha btsun rin chen rnam rgyal, *Grub thob gtsang pa smyon pa'i rnam thar dad pa'i spu slong g.yo ba*, in *Bde mchog mkha' 'gro snyan rgyud (Ras chung snyan rgyud): Two Manuscript Collections of Texts from the Yig cha of Gtsang smyon He ru ka*, ed. Gtsang smyon he ru ka, 2 vols. (Leh: Smanrtsis shesrig spendzod, 1971; BDRC W30124), 1: 1–129, citing 19.4, 30.1, 60.2, 104.7, 124.1. At 123.5–6 it is described how certain of Gtsang smyon he ru ka's students made vows to practice for "three years, four years, six years," or for the rest of their lives.

Rgod tshang ras pa sna tshogs rang grol, *Gtsang smyon he ru ka phyogs thams cad las rnam par rgyal ba'i rnam thar rdo rje theg pa'i gsal byed nyi ma'i snying po*, ed. Lokesh Chandra (New Delhi: Sharada Rani, 1969; BDRC W1KG9090), 35.1–2, 107.7, 140.5, 158.4, 164.7, 189.4, 197.7, 198.7, 204.7, 235.4.

'Brug pa kun legs, *'Brug pa kun legs kyi rnam thar* (Beijing: Bod ljongs mi dmangs dpe skrun khang, 2005; BDRC W29517), 523.2.

Chos rgyal lhun po, *ShAkya'i dge slong rdo rje 'dzin pa chen po/ nam mkha' rdo rje'i rnam par thar pa ngo mtshar gsal ba'i me long* (undated woodblock print, in 103 folio sides; BDRC W3CN18491; NGMPP L18/5), 16a2, 17b2–21a7; Franz-Karl Ehrhard, *Early Buddhist Block Prints from Mang yul Gung thang* (Lumbini: Lumbini International Research Institute, 2000), 58.

As an example deriving from an earlier period in time, Mi pham phun tshogs shes rab quotes Rgod tshang pa mgon po rdo rje (1189–1258) as referring to doing "three years" of sealed retreat; *Ri chos zab mo grub pa'i bcud len sbrang rtsi'i snying po*, in *Collected Works*, 2 vols. (Darjeeling: Thub bstan gsang sngags chos gling 'brug sgar dpe mdzod khang, 2008; BDRC W2KG200924), 1: 377–435, citing 389.3–4.

8. O rgyan gling pa, *Rgyal po'i thang yig*, in *Bka' thang sde lnga*, Dga' ldan phun tshogs gling edition, ed. Lokesh Chandra (New Delhi: International Academy of Indian Culture, 1982; BDRC W30450), 105–287, citing 163.5–164.1 (Helmut Hoffmann, *The Religions of Tibet*, trans. Edward Fitzgerald [New York: Macmillan, 1961], 60). I thank Brandon Dotson for his assistance in locating the original passage via email correspondence, August 2024.

9. Sonam Gyaltsen (1312–1375), *The Clear Mirror: A Traditional Account of Tibet's Golden Age; Sakyapa Sonam Gyaltsen's "Clear Mirror on Royal Genealogy,"* trans. McComas Taylor and Lama Choedak Yuthok (Ithaca, NY: Snow Lion, 1996), 77.

10. For examples from the Bön tradition, see Hoffmann, *The Religions of Tibet*, 96; William Gorvine, "The Life of a Bönpo Luminary: Sainthood, Partisanship and Literary Representation in a 20th Century Tibetan Biography" (PhD diss., University of Virginia, 2006), 14, 446, 449, 452.

11. Nam mkha' rdo rje, who was introduced in chapter 1, served for three years in a position that Franz-Karl Ehrhard calls the "rector" (*rdor 'dzin*) of the holy mountain and locus of meditative practice, La phyi; Chos rgyal lhun po, *ShAkya'i dge slong rdo rje 'dzin pa chen po/ nam mkha' rdo rje'i rnam par thar pa ngo mtshar gsal ba'i me long*, 37a5–38a2; Ehrhard, *Early Buddhist Block Prints*, 63.

Positions in the Tibetan secular government were also filled in three-year terms: Tsepon W. D. Shakabpa, *Tibet: A Political History* (New Haven, CT, and London: Yale University Press, 1967), 266; Matthew Kapstein, *The Tibetans* (Malden, MA: Blackwell, 2006), 118, 189; R. A. Stein, *Tibetan Civilization*, trans. J. E. Stapleton Driver (Stanford, CA: Stanford University Press, 1972), 126. Certain rituals connected to the earliest kings of Tibet, dating from the pre-Buddhist period, were performed on a three-year cycle; *Tibetan Civilization*, 132–33.

In his charter for the community of female meditators at Brag dkar rta so, Brag dkar ba chos kyi dbang phyug details that an individual could be expelled from the community for a period of three years if found guilty of an infraction; *Grub pa'i gnas chen brag dkar rta so'i sgrub sde spong ba pa rnams kyi blang dor gyi rim pa gsal bar ston pa'i bca' yig mun sel nyin mor byed pa'i 'od snang*, in *Collected Works*, 12 vols. (Swayambhunath, Kathmandu: Khenpo Shedup Tenzin, 2011; BDRC W1KG14557), 12: 645–92, citing 668.4.

12. Elizabeth McDougal, "Coming Down the Mountain: Transformations of Contemplative Culture in Eastern Tibet" (M.A. thesis, University of Sydney, 2016), 52.

13. Eric Greene, *Chan Before Chan: Meditation, Repentance, and Visionary Experience in Chinese Buddhism* (Honolulu: University of Hawai'i Press, 2021), 111–12; Robert Ford Campany, *To Live*

as Long as Heaven and Earth: A Translation and Study of Ge Hong's "Traditions of Divine Transcendents" (Berkeley: University of California Press, 2002), 36, 77, 135, 190, 200, 239, 267, 290, 298, 304, 311, 388, 512; Michael Thomas, "Mountains and Early Daoism in the Writings of Ge Hong," *History of Religions* 56, no. 1 (2016): 23–54, citing 49–50; Bill Porter, *Road to Heaven: Encounters with Chinese Hermits* (Berkeley, CA: Counterpoint, 1993), 41, 52, 56, 64, 66, 90, 127, 134, 152, 196; Dominic Steavu, *The Writ of the Three Sovereigns: From Local Lore to Institutional Daoism* (Honolulu: University of Hawai'i Press, 2019), 24–25, 28, 86, 104, 210. Perhaps pertinent to this issue, Steavu observes, "In and of itself, the number three was evocative of time (past, present, and future) just as five (representing the five directions) elicited notions of governed space" (100).

14. Carl Olson, *Indian Asceticism: Power, Violence, and Play* (New York: Oxford University Press, 2015), 47, 94; Shakabpa, *Tibet: A Political History*, 58.

15. Yang dgon pa, *Rdo rje lus kyi sbas bshad, Collected Works*, 2: 461.4–462.3 (Guarisco, trans., *Secret Map of the Body*, 272–74). The three texts mentioned here are *'Jam dpal sgyu 'phrul dra ba, Gsang ba 'dus pa*, and *Dgongs pa lung ston pa*; my translations of these text titles follow Guarisco.

16. Lha btsun nam mkha' 'jigs med, *Ri chos rin po che gnad kyi phreng ba*, in *Rdo rje snying po sprin gyi thol glu*, 2 vols. (n.p.; BDRC W13780), 2: 609–68, citing 648.1; Mi pham phun tshogs shes rab, *Ri chos zab mo grub pa'i bcud len sbrang rtsi'i snying po*, 404.2–405.1, 405.4–5, 436.3–4.

    Zur mang legs bshad sgra dbyangs mentions people who have passed "three or four years in meditation," *Ri yi chos gtam kun tu bzang po'i sgra dbyangs* (Mtshur phu dgon gtsug lag dpe tshogs, n.d.; BDRC W3CN5072), 104.12–13.

    In his short semiautobiographical guide to retreat written in the eighteenth century, 'Jigs med gling pa would describe his own practices during a retreat lasting "three years and five months," also referring to the same retreat (?) as lasting "three years," *Ri chos zhal gdams ngo mtshar rgya mtsho*, in *Collected Works*, 9 vols. (Sde dge: Sde dge dpar khang; BDRC W27300), 8: 699–708, citing 704.3 and 706.1 (Jikmé Lingpa, "A Wonderous Ocean of Advice [For the Practice of Solitary Retreat]," anonymous translation, no publication information, 4, 5); Janet Gyatso, *Apparitions of the Self: The Secret Autobiographies of a Tibetan Visionary* (Princeton, NJ: Princeton University Press, 1998), 131–34.

17. Karma chags med, *Ri chos mtshams kyi zhal gdams* (Brag dkar dgon pa, 1970; BRDC W23259), 595.2–4 (Khenpo Karthar Rinpoché, *Karma Chakme's Mountain Dharma*, 4 vols. [Woodstock, NY: Karma Triyana Dharmachakra Publications, 2004], 4: 75–76). Other references to *lo gsum phyogs gsum*: Karma chags med, 286.6 (Karthar 2: 243), 485.4 (Karthar 3: 193). References to *lo gsum*: 11.6–12.1; 465.1–2 (Karthar 3: 143).

    In the record of how Brtson 'grus rgya mtsho requested Karma chags med to compose this handbook, it is mentioned that Karma chags med had done retreats of both thirteen and seven years; 25.4–6 (Karthar 1: 38; Eric Haynie, "Karma chags med's *Mountain Dharma*: Tibetan Advice on Sociologies of Retreat" [MA thesis, University of Colorado, 2013], 85).

18. Karma chags med, *Ri chos mtshams kyi zhal gdams*, 238.3–4 (Karthar 2: 146).

19. The Thirteenth Dalai Lama is recorded as having been in the middle of a three-year meditation retreat when the British invasion of Tibet under Colonel Younghusband took place, 1903–1904; Shakabpa, *Tibet: A Political History*, 215.

20. Gardner, *Life of Jamgon Kongtrul*, 210.

    An account of the history of the three-year communal retreat on the website of Kagyu Thubten Chöling monastery, in Wappingers Falls, New York, states that "The three-year retreat was formally instituted in the nineteenth century by the great master Jamgon Kongtrul Lodrö Taye" (http://www.kagyu.com/index.php?option=com_content&view=article&layout=edit&id=605). The formation of the three-year, three-month retreat is also sometimes directly attributed to Kong sprul's teacher, the ninth Tai Situ, Padma snying rje dbang po (1774/75–1853), who was based at Dpal spungs. One account splits responsibility between the two: a page on the website of the Tsadra Foundation states, "It was Tai Situ Rinpoche and Jamgon Kongtrul Rinpoche of Palpung Monastery and Tsa'dra Rinchen Drak Hermitage who in the 19th Century initiated the first 'group' three-year retreat programs" (https://www.tsadra.org/2020/05/05/just-out-of-retreat/).

References to the Jo nang pas' practice of three-year, three-month retreat centuries earlier are given in note 6.

21. Gardner, *Life of Jamgon Kongtrul*, 346.
22. Kong sprul's receiving Karm chags med's *Ri chos mtshams kyi zhal gdams* is mentioned in Gardner, *Life of Jamgon Kongtrul*, 51; Karma chags med's role in Kong sprul's visionary life is mentioned, 66, 79, 90, 94, 310; Kong sprul as teacher of Karma nges don bstan skyes is mentioned, 82.

    A translation of a passage in which Kong sprul writes fondly about Karma chags med's ecumenism is given in *Jamgon Kongtrul's Retreat Manual*, 28.
23. Gardner, *Life of Jamgon Kongtrul*, 211–12.
24. Gardner, *Life of Jamgon Kongtrul*, 346–47, quoting 212. See also *Jamgon Kongtrul's Retreat Manual*, 55–56.
25. On this text, *Bod kyi gnas chen rnams kyi mdo byang dkar chags o rgyan gyi mkhas pa padma 'byung gnas kyis bkod pa*, see Gardner, "The Twenty-five Great Sites of Khams: Religious Geography, Revelation, and Nonsectarianism in Nineteenth-Century Eastern Tibet" (PhD diss., University of Michigan, 2006), 1–58; and 187–204, where it is translated in full. TsA 'dra is the twenty-third site on the list, discussed on 199.

    See also Ngawang Zangpo, *Sacred Ground: Jamgon Kongtrul on "Pilgrimage and Sacred Geography"* (Ithaca, NY: Snow Lion, 2001), where this text is referred to as *The Location List of the Twenty-Five Major Sacred Sites of Amdo and Kham*; and Rachel Pang, *Singer of the Land of Snows: Shabkar, Buddhism, and Tibetan National Identity* (Charlottesville: University of Virginia Press, 2024).
26. On this history, see Ngawang Zangpo, *Sacred Ground*, 97, 101–2, 104, and 190–91; this latter passage corresponds to 188.2–190.1 in *Thugs kyi gnas mchog chen po de bI ko TI tsA 'dra rin chen brag gi rtog pa brjod pa yid kyi rgya mtsho'i rol mo*, 159–227 in vol. 7 of *'Jam mgon kong sprul's Collected Works* (New Delhi: Shechen, 2002; BDRC W23723). This text translated in full in *Sacred Ground*, 167–221.

    On this history, see also *Jamgon Kongtrul's Retreat Manual*, 39–49, 144–46; Gardner, *Life of Jamgon Kongtrul*, 105–15, 165–82, 197–220.

    The reference to the time when the site is so empowered, in the 1859 text, is *Gsang thig snying po'i skor las thugs kyi gnas mchog tsA 'dra rin chen brag gi dkar chag*, 159–63 in vol. 30 of *The Treasury of Revelations and Teachings of Mchog gyur bde chen gling pa*, 39 vols. (Paro, Bhutan: Lama Pema Tashi, 1982; BDRC W22642), citing 161.5–6.
27. Gardner, *Life of Jamgon Kongtrul*, 282. The 1871, 1883, and 1895 letters are translated in full in Ngawang Zangpo, *Sacred Ground*, 233–35, 116–19, and 235–39.
28. 'Jam mgon kong sprul, *Dpal spungs yang khrod kun bzang bde chen 'od gsal gling gi sgrub pa rnams kyi kun spyod bca' khrims blang dor rab gsal phan bde'i 'byung gnas*, in *Collected Works*, 13 vols. (New Delhi: Shechen, 2002; BDRC W23723), 6: 1091–153, citing 1153.1–3 (*Jamgon Kongtrul's Retreat Manual*, 182). See also the opening of the text, *Phan bde'i 'byung gnas*, 1092.1–3 (*Retreat Manual*, 59).
29. Kong sprul's charter mentions that at the conclusion of the retreat, the meditators may "meet faces" (*gdong sprad*) with other people, indicating that they had been enjoined not to do so prior; 'Jam mgon kong sprul, *Phan bde'i 'byung gnas*, *Collected Works*, 6: 1108.5 (*Jamgon Kongtrul's Retreat Manual*, 114). Writing a letter: *Phan bde'i 'byung gnas*, 1136.1 (*Retreat Manual*, 162).
30. 'Jam mgon kong sprul, *Phan bde'i 'byung gnas*, *Collected Works*, 6: 1125.6–1126.2 (*Jamgon Kongtrul's Retreat Manual*, 151–52).
31. 'Jam mgon kong sprul, *Phan bde'i 'byung gnas*, *Collected Works*, 6: 1133.4–6 (*Jamgon Kongtrul's Retreat Manual*, 159).

7. THE TIBETAN ASCETIC SELF IN TIME 235

32. 'Jam mgon kong sprul, *Phan bde'i 'byung gnas, Collected Works*, 6: 1126.1–2 (*Jamgon Kongtrul's Retreat Manual*, 151–52), 1133.6–1134.6 (*Retreat Manual*, 159–60).
33. 'Jam mgon kong sprul, *Phan bde'i 'byung gnas, Collected Works*, 6: 1141.2–1142.1 (*Jamgon Kongtrul's Retreat Manual*, 166–67).
34. 'Jam mgon kong sprul, *Phan bde'i 'byung gnas, Collected Works*, 6: 1127.5 (*Jamgon Kongtrul's Retreat Manual*, 153).
35. *Jamgon Kongtrul's Retreat Manual*, 144. On the number of retreatants, see 18, 49, 56.
36. 'Jam mgon kong sprul, *Phan bde'i 'byung gnas, Collected Works*, 6: 1122.1–1125.5 (*Jamgon Kongtrul's Retreat Manual*, 144–50), 1127.5–6 (*Retreat Manual*, 153); Gardner, *Life of Jamgon Kongtrul*, 214.
37. 'Jam mgon kong sprul, *Phan bde'i 'byung gnas, Collected Works*, 6: 1127.6–1130.1 (*Jamgon Kongtrul's Retreat Manual*, 153–55).
38. Gardner, *Life of Jamgon Kongtrul*, 241–42, 280, 263, 316. See also 344.
39. 'Jam mgon kong sprul, *Phan bde'i 'byung gnas, Collected Works*, 6: 1093.3–1094.2 (*Jamgon Kongtrul's Retreat Manual*, 61–62).
40. Bad dreams: 'Jam mgon kong sprul, *Phan bde'i 'byung gnas, Collected Works*, 6: 1117.6–1118.1 (*Jamgon Kongtrul's Retreat Manual*, 123). Sick retreatant: *Phan bde'i 'byung gnas*, 1132.3–5 (*Retreat Manual*, 158); 1143.2–3 (*Retreat Manual*, 168).
41. The text clearly reads *ras bud*; this is typically spelled *ras phud*. 'Jam mgon kong sprul, *Phan bde'i 'byung gnas, Collected Works*, 6: 1109.4–1110.1 (*Jamgon Kongtrul's Retreat Manual*, 138). The text also states that once the retreatants begin practicing *gtum mo*, they may no longer wear *sha 'byar*, which would seem to mean leather, hides, or fur, and should therefore have *phyid 'gags* at their disposal, meaning felt or woolen clothes; *Phan bde'i 'byung gnas*, 1127.4–5 (*Retreat Manual*, 153).
42. 'Jam mgon kong sprul, *Phan bde'i 'byung gnas, Collected Works*, 6: 1095.2–1096.5 (*Jamgon Kongtrul's Retreat Manual*, 64–65). This corresponds to 'Jig rten gsum mgon, *Ri chos bdud rtsi'i bum chen*, in *'Bri gung bka' brgyud chos mdzod chen mo*, ed. A mgon rin po che and Ra se dkon mchog rgya mtsho, 151 vols. (Lhasa: Bri gung mthil dgon, 2004; BDRC W00JW501203), 26: 384–99, citing 384.4–386.1.
43. 'Jam mgon kong sprul, *Phan bde'i 'byung gnas, Collected Works*, 6: 1097.2–1098.4 (*Jamgon Kongtrul's Retreat Manual*, 67–70); Gardner, *Life of Jamgon Kongtrul*, 219.
44. Gardner, *Life of Jamgon Kongtrul*, 217; 'Jam mgon kong sprul, *Dpal spungs yang khrod kun bzang bde chen 'od gsal gling rten dang brten par bcas pa'i dkar chag zhing khams kun tu khyab pa'i sgra snyan, Collected Works*, 13 vols. (New Delhi: Shechen, 2002; BDRC W23723), 6: 697–949, citing 884.1–2, 885.4–6.
45. Gardner, *Life of Jamgon Kongtrul*, 268–70.
46. 'Jam mgon kong sprul, *Phan bde'i 'byung gnas, Collected Works*, 6: 1109.1–1116.3 (*Jamgon Kongtrul's Retreat Manual*, 130–43); Gardner, *Life of Jamgon Kongtrul*, 216.
47. 'Jam mgon kong sprul, *Phan bde'i 'byung gnas, Collected Works*, 6: 1131.4–1132.1 (*Jamgon Kongtrul's Retreat Manual*, 157–58).
48. *Jamgon Kongtrul's Retreat Manual*, 18; Gardner, *Life of Jamgon Kongtrul*, 218.
49. Lying down: Yang dgon pa, *Ri chos yon tan kun 'byung [ba] rin po che 'bar ba*, in *The Collected Works (gsung 'bum) of Yang dgon pa*, 3 vols. (Thimpu: Kunsang Topgey, 1976; BDRC W1KG17449), 1: 447–570, citing 477.2–3, 482.6, 511.4; sitting up: 473.3–6.
50. Quotation, Karma chags med, *Ri chos mtshams kyi zhal gdams*, 243.6 (Karthar 2: 153); dream yoga, 463.1–2 (Karthar 3: 139); alternating, 520.3–4 (Karthar 3: 274). See also 522.6–523.2 (Karthar 3: 278) and 550.2–3 (Karthar 3: 372).

After 1903, Brag dkar blo bzang dpal ldan bstan 'dzin snyan grags wrote favorably of the practice of "continually not lying down, but staying upright," so as to not fall into deep sleep and to remain more regularly engaged with one's practice; *Gnas dben par sdod pa'i chos mdzad mtha' dag la nye bar mkho ba'i ri chos mu tig gi phreng ba* (Gser rta rdzong: Gser thang bla rung lnga rig nang bstan slob gling, n.d.; BDRC W3CN4732), 130.14–16.

Perhaps related, in the early eighteenth century, Mi pham phun tshogs shes rab would prescribe assuming either of these two positions (*tsog pa'am seng ge'i nyal stabs*) as one prepares for the moment of death; *Ri chos zab mo grub pa'i bcud len sbrang rtsi'i snying po*, 432.5–433.1.

51. 'Jam mgon kong sprul writes about the need to remain in a meditative state throughout the night and thereby avoiding being "lost" in a state of ordinary sleep (*tha mal du ma shor ba*). It is unclear whether or not maintaining a state of practice is synonymous with remaining upright; *Phan bde'i 'byung gnas, Collected Works*, 6: 1121.4–5 (*Jamgon Kongtrul's Retreat Manual*, 128–29).

52. *Jamgon Kongtrul's Retreat Manual*, 175–76; all of the bracketed insertions, save for that regarding the Generation and Perfection phase practices, are in Ngawang Zangpo's translation. 'Jam mgon kong sprul, *Phan bde'i 'byung gnas, Collected Works*, 6: 1148.6–1149.3.

53. 'Jam mgon kong sprul, *Phan bde'i 'byung gnas, Collected Works*, 6: 1145.2–1146.3 (*Jamgon Kongtrul's Retreat Manual*, 169–71); *Phan bde'i 'byung gnas*, 1152.2–1153.3 (*Retreat Manual*, 181–82).

WORKS CITED

TIBETAN SOURCES

Karma nges don bstan rgyas (1849/1867/1879–1921/1942/1960). *Ri chos thar lam mdzub ston.* In *The Collected Works of Sman sdong mtshams pa rin po che Karma nges don bstan rgyas*, 3 vols., 3: 161–204. Reproduced from tracings from the collected blockprints impressed from the xylographs preserved at Sman dgon thub chen bde chen gling. Bir, H.P.: D. Tsondu Senghe, 1975. BDRC W10982.

———. *Collected Works.* 2 vols. Si khron bod yig dpe rnying bsdu sgrig khang, n.d. BDRC W3CN3402.

Karma chags med (1608/10/13–1678). *Ri chos mtshams kyi zhal gdams.* Printed based on impressions from the Rtsib ri blocks preserved at Brag dkar monastery in Solu. 840 folio sides. Brag dkar dgon pa, 1970. BRDC W23259.

———. *Sa dpyad rin chen gter mdzod.* In *Collected Works*, 60 vols., 58: 175–86. Nang chen rdzong: Gnas mdo gsang sngags chos 'phel gling gi dpe rnying nyams gso khang, 2010. BDRC W1KG8321.

Karma pa III Rang byung rdo rje (1284–1339). *Ri chos bdud rtsi'i nying khu.* In *Collected Works*, 13 vols., 4: 479–503. Lhasa: Dpal brtsegs bod yig dpe rnying zhib 'jug khang, 2013. BDRC W3PD1288.

———. *Collected Works.* 16 vols. Zi ling: Mtshur phu mkhan po lo yag bkra shis, 2006. BDRC W30541.

Klong chen pa dri med 'od zer (1308–1364). *Nags tshal kun tu dga' ba'i gtam.* In *Miscellaneous Writings (gsung thor bu)*, 2 vols., 1: 137–49. Reproduced from xylographic prints from the A 'dzom 'brug pa chos sgar blocks. Gangtok: Pema Thinley, Sikkim National Press, n.d. BDRC W23555.

———. *Rdzogs pa chen po ngal gso skor gsum.* Zhang kang then ma dpe skrun khang, 2005. BDRC W1GS60877.

Bka' brgyud pa'i gsung rab. 19 vols. Mtsho sngon mi rigs dpe skrun khang, 2004. BDRC W30023.

Bskal bzang bstan pa'i rgyal mtshan (1897–1959). *Shar rdza bkra shis rgyal mtshan gyi rnam thar.* Beijing: Krung go'i bod kyi shes rig dpe skrun khang, 1990. BDRC W14023.

Mkha' 'gro'i chos mdzod chen mo. Ed. Bla rung ar I ya tA re'i dpe tshogs rtsom sgrig khang. 53 vols. Bod ljongs bod yig dpe rnying dpe skrun khang, 2017. BDRC W3CN2459.

'Gos lo tsA ba gzhon nu dpal (1392–1481). *Deb ther sngon po.* 2 vols. Chengdu: Si khron mi rigs dpe skrun khang, 1984. BDRC W1KG5762.

Rgod tshang ras pa sna tshogs rang grol (1482–1559). *Gtsang smyon he ru ka phyogs thams cad las rnam par rgyal ba'i rnam thar rdo rje theg pa'i gsal byed nyi ma'i snying po.* Ed. Lokesh Chandra. New Delhi: Sharada Rani, 1969. BDRC W1KG9090.

Ngag dbang bstan 'dzin nor bu (1867–1940/49?). *Bca' yig ri chos zhal gdams.* Rewalsar, H.P.: Zigar Drukpa Kargyud Institute, 1985. BDRC W9674.

———. *Me tog bcud len gyi gdam pa skal bzang sna rgyan*. Woodblock print, in 11 folio sides. NGMPP L318/2.

Ngag dbang blo bzang bsam gtan (1687–1748/49). *Collected Works*. 4 vols. Lan kru'u: Kan su'u mi rigs dpe skrun khang, 2005. BDRC W29486.

Dngos grub dpal 'bar (1456–1527). *Rje btsun gtsang pa he ru ka'i thun mong gi rnam thar yon tan gyi gangs ri la dad pa'i seng ge rnam par rtse ba*. 1508 woodblock print, in 61 folio sides. BDRC W2CZ6647.

Lcang skya III Rol pa'i rdo rje (1717–1786). *Dben par dga' ba'i gtam chos glu ring mo*. In *Collected Works*, 7 vols., 4: 393–96. Beijing: Krung go bod brgyud mtho rim nang bstan slob gling nang bstan zhib 'jug khang, 1995. BDRC W28833.

Lce sgom shes rab rdo rje (1124–1204). *Ri khrod skal ldan sgron me*. In *Blo sbyong nyer mkho phyogs bsgrigs*, ed. Cha ris skal bzang thogs med and Ngag dbang sbyin pa, 675–88. Lan kru'u: Kan su'u mi rigs dpe skrun khang, 2003. BDRC W25275.

Chos rgyal lhun po. *ShAkya'i dge slong rdo rje 'dzin pa chen po/ nam mkha' rdo rje'i rnam par thar pa ngo mtshar gsal ba'i me long*. Undated woodblock print, in 103 folio sides. BDRC W3CN18491. NGMPP L18/5.

Mchog gyur bde chen gling pa (1829–1870). *Gsang thig snying po'i skor las thugs kyi gnas mchog tsA 'dra rin chen brag gi dkar chag*. In *The Treasury of Revelations and Teachings of Mchog gyur bde chen gling pa*, 39 vols., 30: 159–63. Paro, Bhutan: Lama Pema Tashi, 1982. BDRC W22642.

'Jam mgon kong sprul blo gros mtha' yas (1813–1899). *Collected Works*. 13 vols. Reproduced from a set of prints from the Dpal spungs xylographs from eastern Tibet. New Delhi: Shechen, 2002. BDRC W23723.

———, ed. *Gdams ngag mdzod*. 18 vols. Paro: Lama Ngodrup and Sherab Drimey, 1979–1981. BDRC W20877.

'Jig rten gsum mgon (1143–1217). *Khams gsum chos kyi rgyal po thub dbang rat+na shrI'i phyi yi bka' 'bum nor bu'i bang mdzod*. 12 vols. Ed. Drikung Kyabgon Chetsang VII. Delhi: Drikung Kagyu Ratna Shri Sungrab Nyamso Khang, 2001. BDRC W23743.

'Jigs med gling pa (1729/30–1798). *Ri chos zhal gdams ngo mtshar rgya mtsho*. In *Collected Works*, 9 vols., 8: 699–708. Sde dge: Sde dge dpar khang. BDRC W27300.

Dung dkar blo bzan 'phrin las (1927–1997). *Dung dkar tshig mdzod chen mo*. Beijing: Krung go'i bod rig pa dpe skrun khang, 2002.

Dol po pa shes rab rgya mtsho (1292–1361/62). *Ri chos nges don rgya mtsho zhes bya ba mthar thug thun mong ma yin pa'i man ngag*. Dharamsala: Library of Tibetan Works and Archives. Undated *dbu med* manuscript, in 922 pages. BDRC W23709.

Drung pa IV Kun dga' rnam rgyal (1567–1629). *Ri chos bai dUrya'i phreng ba zhes bya ba thar 'dod kyi mgul rgyan*. In *Gdams ngag mdzod*, ed. 'Jam mgon kong sprul blo gros mtha' yas, 18 vols., 9: 315–23. Paro: Lama Ngodrup and Sherab Drimey, 1979–1981. BDRC W20877.

Bdud 'joms rin po che 'jigs bral ye shes rdo rje (1904–1987). *Ri chos bslab bya nyams len dmar khrid go bder brjod pa grub pa'i bcud len*. In *Collected Works*, 25 vols., 13: 443–67. Kalimpong: Dupjung Lama, 1979–1985. BDRC W20869.

Sde srid Sangs rgyas rgya mtsho (1653–1705). *Bstan bcos Bai dūr Dkar po las Dri lan 'Khrul snang G.ya' sel Don gyi Bzhin ras Ston byed (The Eighteenth-Century Sde dge Redaction of the Sde srid Sangs rgyas rgya mtsho's Vai dūrya G.ya' sel with the Snyan sgron Nyis brgya brgyad pa)*. Reproduced from a print from the library of Tau Pon of Ga. Dehra Dun, 1976. 2 vols. BDRC W1KG12689.

Nam mkha' rdo rje (1486–1553). *Dpal ldan bla ma dam pa sprul sku nam mkha' rgyal mtshan dpal bzang po'i rnam par thar pa/ dgos 'dod kun 'byung nor bu'i 'phreng ba*. In *'Ba' ra bka' brgyud gser 'phreng chen mo*, 4 vols., 2: 394–521. Dehra Dun: Ngawang Gyaltsen and Ngawang Lungtok, 1970. BDRC W19231.

———. *ShAkya'i dge slong rdo rje 'dzin pa nam mkha' rdo rje'i mgur 'bum yid bzhin nor bu'i bang mdzod*. Undated woodblock print, in 47 folio sides. BDRC W3CN18491. NGMPP L18/5.

Gnubs chen sangs rgyas ye shes (ca. early 10th century). *Rnal 'byor mig gi bsam gtan or Bsam gtan mig sgron: A treatise on bhāvanā and dhyāna and the relationships between the various approaches to*

Buddhist contemplative practice. Reproduced from a manuscript made presumably from an eastern Tibetan print by 'Khor gdong gter sprul 'chi med rig 'dzin. Smanrtsis shesrig spendzod, vol. 74. Leh: Tashigangpa, 1974. BDRC W00EGS1016286.

PaN chen bla ma IV Blo bzang chos kyi rgyal mtshan (1567/68/70–1662). *Collected Works*. 5 vols. Gzhis ka rtse: Bkra shis lhun po par khang, n.d. BDRC W9848.

Dpa' bo gtsug lag phreng ba (1504–1564/66). *Chos 'byung mkhas pa'i dga' ston*. Beijing: Mi rigs dpe skrun khang, 2006. BDRC W8LS19006.

Pha dam pa sangs rgyas (d. 1117). *Phyag rgya chen po brda'i skor gsum and Zhal chems ding ri'i skor*. Two collections of instructions of Pha dam pa sangs rgyas on the Zhi byed practice. Reproduced from a rare manuscript from the National Library of Bhutan. Thimpu: National Library of Bhutan, 1985. BDRC W23993.

Phag mo gru pa rdo rje rgyal po (1110–1170). *Ri chos bdud rtsi bum pa'i gdams ngag*. In *'Bri gung bka' brgyud chos mdzod chen mo*, compiled by A mgon rin po che and Ra se dkon mchog rgya mtsho, 151 vols., 16: 281–87. Lhasa: Bri gung mthil dgon, 2004. BDRC W00JW501203.

Bod rgya tshig mdzod chen mo. 2 vols. Mi rigs dpe skrun khang, 1985.

Brag dkar ba chos kyi dbang phyug (1775–1837). *Grub pa'i gnas chen brag dkar rta so'i sgrub sde spong ba pa rnams kyi blang dor gyi rim pa gsal bar ston pa'i bca' yig mun sel nyin mor byed pa'i 'od snang*. In *Collected Works*, 12 vols., 12: 645–92. Swayambhunath, Kathmandu: Khenpo Shedup Tenzin, 2011. BDRC W1KG14557. Also available in an undated *dbu med* manuscript, in 59 folio sides; NGMPP L1224/7.

Brag dkar blo bzang dpal ldan bstan 'dzin snyan grags (1866–1928). *Collected Works*. 20 vols. Compiled in Chengdu. BDRC W23608.

———. *Gnas dben par sdod pa'i chos mdzad mtha' dag la nye bar mkho ba'i ri chos mu tig gi phreng ba*. Gser rta rdzong: Gser thang bla rung lnga rig nang bstan slob gling. Undated modern print, in 281 pages. BDRC W3CN4732. Also available in *Collected Works* 3: 649–926. All citations of this text refer to the modern reprint.

'Brug pa kun legs (b. 1455). *'Brug pa kun legs kyi rnam thar*. Beijing: Bod ljongs mi dmangs dpe skrun khang, 2005. BDRC W29517.

Mi pham phun tshogs shes rab (1654–1715). *Ri chos zab mo grub pa'i bcud len sbrang rtsi'i snying po*. In *Collected Works*, 2 vols., 1: 377–435. Darjeeling: Thub bstan gsang sngags chos gling 'brug sgar dpe mdzod khang, 2008. BDRC W2KG200924.

Smyug la paN chen ngag dbang grags pa (1458–1515) and Lha mthong lo tsA ba bshes gnyen rnam rgyal (b. 1512). *Dpal ldan bla ma dam pa grub pa'i khyu mchog phyogs thams cad las rnam par rgyal ba'i spyod pa can rje btsun kun dga' bzang po'i rnam par thar pa ris med dad pa'i spu long g.yo byed*, and its continuation *Rje btsun kun dga' bzang po'i rnam par thar pa ris med dad pa'i spu long g.yo byed ces bya ba las/ rim par phye ba gnyis pa phrin las rgyan gyi rnga sgra*. In *Bka' brgyud pa Hagiographies: A Collection of Rnam Thar of the Eminent Masters of Tibetan Buddhism*, ed. Khams sprul don brgyud nyi ma, 4 vols., 2: 383–660. Palampur, H.P.: Sungrab Nyamso Gyunphel Parkhang, Tibetan Craft Community, 1972. BDRC W20499.

Tsong kha pa blo bzang grags pa (1357–1419). *Byams pa gling na bzhugs pa'i dge 'dun rnams kyi spyi'i khrims su bya ba'i bca' yig chung ngu*. In *Collected Works*, 18 vols., 2: 698–713. New Delhi: Mongolian Lama Guru Deva, 1978–1979. BDRC W635.

Gtsang smyon he ru ka (1452–1507). *Rnal 'byor gyi dbang phyug chen po mi la ras pa'i rnam mgur*. Zi ling: Mtsho sngon mi rigs dpe skrun khang, 2005.

Zhabs dkar tshogs drug rang grol (1781–1851). *Chos bshad gzhan phan zla ba*. In *Collected Works*, 10 vols., 8: 1–283. Zi ling: Mtsho sngon mi rigs dpe skrun khang, 2002. BDRC W1PD45150.

Zhwa dmar II Mkha' spyod dbang po (1350–1405). *Ri chos gcig shes kun grol man ngag gi snying po*. Mtshur phu gdon gtsug lag dpe rnying phyogs sgrig khang. Undated modern print, in 36 pages. BDRC W3CN5081.

Zur mang legs bshad sgra dbyangs (b. 16th cent.). *Ri yi chos gtam kun tu bzang po'i sgra dbyangs*. Mtshur phu dgon gtsug lag dpe tshogs, n.d. 113 pages. BDRC W3CN5072.

Yang dgon pa rgyal mtshan dpal (1213–1258). *The Collected Works (gsung 'bum) of Yang dgon pa*. Reproduced from the manuscript set preserved at Pha jo ldings monastery. 3 vols. Thimpu: Kunsang Topgey, 1976. BDRC W1KG17449.

Rong tha che tshang blo bzang dam chos rgya mtsho (1865–1917). *Collected Works*. 6 vols. Reproduced from tracings from the extant set of prints from the Rong tha blocks. Delhi: Ngawang Sopa, 1975. BDRC W13528.

Bsod nams chos 'dzin (b. 1688). *Dben pa ri khrod 'grims pa'i gsal 'debs/ zhal gdam thar pa chen po'i gru sding*. Undated *dbu med* manuscript, in 11 folio sides. NGMPP AT146/3.

Lha btsun nam mkha' 'jigs med (1597–1650). *Ri chos rin po che gnad kyi phreng ba*. In *Rdo rje snying po sprin gyi thol glu*, 2 vols., 2: 609–68. N.p. BDRC W13780. A manuscript copy, in 51 folio sides, is preserved as NGMPP AT70/30.

Lha btsun rin chen rnam rgyal (1473–1557). *Grub thob gtsang pa smyon pa'i rnam thar dad pa'i spu slong g.yo ba*. In Gtsang smyon he ru ka, *Bde mchog mkha' 'gro snyan rgyud (Ras chung snyan rgyud): Two Manuscript Collections of Texts from the Yig cha of Gtsang smyon He ru ka*, 2 vols., 1: 1–129. Leh: Smanrtsis shesrig spendzod, 1971. BDRC W30124.

A mgon rin po che and Ra se dkon mchog rgya mtsho, eds. *'Bri gung bka' brgyud chos mdzod chen mo*. 151 vols. Lhasa: Bri gung mthil dgon, 2004. BDRC W00JW501203.

O rgyan gling pa (b. ca. 1323). *Rgyal po'i thang yig*. In *Bka' thang sde lnga*, Dga' ldan phun tshogs gling edition, ed. Lokesh Chandra, 105–287. New Delhi: International Academy of Indian Culture, 1982. BDRC W30450.

O rgyan rnam grol dbang po (b. ca. 1808). *Sbas mtha'i ri khrod du 'dug tshul dang rnams [=rnam] kun rang brgyud [=rgyud] chos dang bsre tshul gyi bslab bya zhal gyi gdams pa'i nying khu gsang ba bdud rtsi thig le*. A manuscript copy, in 10 folio sides, is preserved as NGMPP AT82/7.

WESTERN-LANGUAGE SOURCES

Ali, Daud. "Technologies of the Self: Courtly Artifice and Monastic Discipline in Early India." *Journal of the Economic and Social History of the Orient* 41, no. 2 (1998): 159–84.

———. *Courtly Culture and Political Life in Early Medieval India*. Cambridge: Cambridge University Press, 2004.

Allione, Tsultrim. *Women of Wisdom*. Ithaca, NY: Snow Lion, 2000.

Aris, Michael. *Bhutan: The Early History of a Himalayan Kingdom*. Warminster, England: Aris and Phillips, 1979.

———. *Hidden Treasures and Secret Lives: A Study of Pemalingpa (1450–1521) and the Sixth Dalai Lama (1683–1706)*. London and New York: Kegan Paul International, 1989.

Ashraf, Kazi K. *The Hermit's Hut: Architecture and Asceticism in India*. Honolulu: University of Hawai'i Press, 2013.

Barstow, Geoffrey. *Food of Sinful Demons: Meat, Vegetarianism, and the Limits of Buddhism in Tibet*. New York: Columbia University Press, 2019.

———, ed. *The Faults of Meat: Tibetan Buddhist Writings on Vegetarianism*. Somerville, MA: Wisdom, 2019.

Benson, H., J. W. Lehmann, M. S. Malhotra, R. F. Goldman, J. Hopkins, and M. D. Epstein. "Body Temperature Changes During the Practice of gTum mo Yoga." *Nature* 295 (1982): 234–36.

Bentor, Yael. "The Tibetan Practice of the Mantra Path According to Lce sgom pa." In *Tantra in Practice*, ed. David Gordon White, 326–46. Princeton, NJ: Princeton University Press, 2000.

Bhikku Ñāṇamoli, trans. *The Path of Purification (Visuddhimagga)*, by Bhadantācariya Buddhaghosa. Onalaska, WA: BPS Pariyatti Editions, 1999.

Blondeau, Anne-Marie, and Ernst Steinkellner, eds. *Reflections of the Mountain: Essays on the History and Social Meaning of the Mountain Cult in Tibet and the Himalaya*. Vienna: Verlag der Österreichischen Akademie der Wissenschaft, 1996.

Bourdieu, Pierre. *Outline of a Theory of Practice*. Trans. Richard Nice. Cambridge: Cambridge University Press, 1977.

———. *The Logic of Practice*. Trans. Richard Nice. Stanford, CA: Stanford University Press, 1990.

Cabezón, José Ignacio, and Penpa Dorjee. *Sera Monastery*. Somerville, MA: Wisdom, 2019.

Cabezón, José Ignacio, and Roger R. Jackson, eds. *Tibetan Literature: Studies in Genre*. Ithaca, NY: Snow Lion, 1996.

Campany, Robert Ford. *To Live as Long as Heaven and Earth: A Translation and Study of Ge Hong's "Traditions of Divine Transcendents."* Berkeley: University of California Press, 2002.

Cantwell, Cathy. "Reflections on Rasāyana, Bcud len, and Related Practices in Nyingma (Rnying ma) Tantric Ritual." *History of Science in South Asia* 5, no. 2 (2017): 181–203.

Chang, Garma C. C., trans. *The Hundred Thousand Songs of Milarepa*. Boulder, CO: Shambhala, 1977. Tibetan version first printed in 1488.

Childs, Geoff. *Tibetan Diary: From Birth to Death and Beyond in a Himalayan Valley of Nepal*. Berkeley: University of California Press, 2004.

Clements, Niki Kasumi. *Sites of the Ascetic Self: John Cassian and Christian Ethical Formation*. Notre Dame, IN: University of Notre Dame Press, 2020.

Collins, Steven. "Some Remarks on Hadot, Foucault, and Comparisons within Buddhism." In *Buddhist Spiritual Practices: Thinking with Pierre Hadot on Buddhism, Philosophy, and the Path*, ed. David Fiordalis, 21–69. Berkeley, CA: Mangalam Press, 2018.

Constitution of the Kingdom of Bhutan. 2008.

Copp, Paul. *The Body Incantatory: Spells and the Ritual Imagination in Medieval Chinese Buddhism*. New York: Columbia University Press, 2014.

Crislip, Andrew. "'I Have Chosen Sickness': The Controversial Function of Sickness in Early Christian Ascetic Practice." In *Asceticism and Its Critics: Historical Accounts and Comparative Perspectives*, ed. Oliver Freiberger, 179–209. New York: Oxford University Press, 2006.

Crosby, Kate. *Esoteric Theravada: The Story of the Forgotten Meditation Tradition of Southeast Asia*. Boulder, CO: Shambhala, 2020.

Czaja, Olaf. *Medieval Rule in Tibet: The Rlangs Clan and the Political and Religious History of the Ruling House of Phag mo gru pa*. Vienna: Verlag der Österreichischen Akademie der Wissenschaften, 2013.

David-Néel, Alexandra. *Magic and Mystery in Tibet*. Mansfield Centre, CT: Martino Publishing, 2014.

DiValerio, David M. *The Holy Madmen of Tibet*. New York: Oxford University Press, 2015.

———, trans. *The Life of the Madman of Ü*. New York: Oxford University Press, 2016.

Dorji, C. T. *A Concise Religious History of Bhutan*. Delhi: Prominent Publishers, 2008.

Dowman, Keith. *The Power-Places of Central Tibet: The Pilgrim's Guide*. London and New York: Routledge and Kegan Paul, 1988.

———, trans. *The Divine Madman: The Sublime Life and Songs of Drukpa Kunley*. 1982; reprint, Varanasi and Kathmandu: Pilgrims Press, 2000.

Dreyfus, Georges. *The Sound of Two Hands Clapping: The Education of a Tibetan Buddhist Monk*. Berkeley: University of California Press, 2003.

Dudjom Rinpoché. *Mountain Dharma: The Alchemy of Realization (Dudjom Rinpoche's Richo)*. Trans. and commentary by Keith Dowman. Dzogchen Now! Books, 2017.

Durkheim, Émile. *The Elementary Forms of Religious Life*. Trans. Karen E. Fields. 1912; reprint, New York: The Free Press, 1995.

Ehrhard, Franz-Karl. *Early Buddhist Block Prints from Mang yul Gung thang*. Lumbini: Lumbini International Research Institute, 2000.

———. "'Turning the Wheel of the Dharma in Zhing sa va lung': The Dpal ri sprul skus (17th to 20th centuries)." *Bulletin of Tibetology* 44, nos. 1–2 (2008): 5–29.

Elias, Norbert. *The Civilizing Process*, containing *The History of Manners* and *State Formation and Civilization*. Trans. Edmund Jephcott. 1939; reprint, Oxford: Blackwell, 1994.

Esler, Dylan. *The Lamp for the Eye of Contemplation: The* Samten Migdron *by Nubchen Sangye Yeshe, a 10th-century Tibetan Buddhist Text on Meditation*. Oxford: Oxford University Press, 2022.

Evans-Wentz, W. Y., trans. *Tibetan Yoga and Secret Doctrines*. 1935; reprint, New York: Oxford University Press, 2000.

Fiordalis, David, ed. *Buddhist Spiritual Practices: Thinking with Pierre Hadot on Buddhism, Philosophy, and the Path*. Berkeley, CA: Mangalam Press, 2018.

Flood, Gavin. *The Ascetic Self: Subjectivity, Memory and Tradition*. Cambridge: Cambridge University Press, 2004.

Foucault, Michel. *The Care of the Self: Volume 3 of the History of Sexuality*. Trans. Robert Hurley. New York: Vintage, 1986.

———. "On the Genealogy of Ethics: An Overview of Work in Progress." In *Ethics: Subjectivity and Truth, The Essential Works of Michel Foucault, 1954–1984*, vol. 1, ed. Paul Rabinow, trans. Robert Hurley et al., 253–80. New York: Penguin, 1987.

———. "Technologies of the Self." In *Technologies of the Self: A Seminar with Michel Foucault*, ed. Luther H. Martin, Huck Gutman, and Patrick H. Hutton, 16–49. Amherst: University of Massachusetts Press, 1988.

———. *The Use of Pleasure: Volume 2 of the History of Sexuality*. Trans. Robert Hurley. New York: Vintage, 1990.

———. *About the Beginning of the Hermeneutics of the Self; Lectures at Dartmouth College, 1980*. Trans. Graham Burchell. Chicago and London: University of Chicago Press, 2016.

Freiberger, Oliver, ed. *Asceticism and Its Critics: Historical Accounts and Comparative Perspectives*. New York: Oxford University Press, 2006.

Gamble, Ruth. *The Third Karmapa Rangjung Dorje: Master of Mahāmudrā*. Lives of the Masters. Boulder, CO: Shambhala, 2020.

Gardner, Alexander. "The Twenty-five Great Sites of Khams: Religious Geography, Revelation, and Nonsectarianism in Nineteenth-Century Eastern Tibet." PhD diss., University of Michigan, 2006.

———. *The Life of Jamgon Kongtrul the Great*. Boulder, CO: Snow Lion, 2019.

Gentry, James D. *Power Objects in Tibetan Buddhism: The Life, Writings, and Legacy of Sokdokpa Lodrö Gyeltsen*. Leiden: Brill, 2017.

Gerke, Barbara. "'Treating The Aged' and 'Maintaining Health': Locating bcud len Practices in the Four Medical Tantras." *Journal of the International Association of Buddhist Studies* 35, nos. 1–2 (2012): 329–62.

Germano, David. "Food, Clothes, Dreams, and Karmic Propensities." In *Religions of Tibet in Practice*, ed. Donald Lopez Jr., 293–312. Princeton, NJ: Princeton University Press, 1997.

Goldstein, Melvyn C. *A History of Modern Tibet, 1913–1951*. Berkeley: University of California Press, 1989.

Gorvine, William. "The Life of a Bönpo Luminary: Sainthood, Partisanship and Literary Representation in a 20th Century Tibetan Biography." PhD diss., University of Virginia, 2006.

———. *Envisioning a Tibetan Luminary: The Life of a Modern Bönpo Saint*. New York: Oxford University Press, 2019.

Greene, Eric. *Chan Before Chan: Meditation, Repentance, and Visionary Experience in Chinese Buddhism*. Honolulu: University of Hawai'i Press, 2021.

Guarisco, Elio, trans. *Secret Map of the Body: Visions of the Human Energy Structure*. Merigar, Italy: Shang Shung Publications, 2015.

Guenther, Herbert. *A Visionary Journey*. Boston and Shaftesbury: Shambhala, 1989.

Gyatso, Janet. "Down with the Demoness: Reflections on a Feminine Ground in Tibet." In *Feminine Ground: Essays on Women and Tibet*, ed. Janice Willis, 33–51. Ithaca, NY: Snow Lion, 1987.

———. *Apparitions of the Self: The Secret Autobiographies of a Tibetan Visionary*. Princeton, NJ: Princeton University Press, 1998.

———. *Being Human in a Buddhist World: An Intellectual History of Medicine in Early Modern Tibet*. New York: Columbia University Press, 2015.

Halkias, Georgios T. "Heavenly Ascents after Death: Karma Chags med's *Commentary on Mind Transference*." *Revue d'Études Tibétaines* 52 (2019): 70–89.

Hatchell, Christopher. *Naked Seeing: The Great Perfection, the Wheel of Time, and Visionary Buddhism in Renaissance Tibet*. New York: Oxford University Press, 2014.

Haynie, Eric. "Karma chags med's *Mountain Dharma*: Tibetan Advice on Sociologies of Retreat." MA thesis, University of Colorado, 2013.

Heimbel, Jörg. *Vajradhara in Human Form: The Life and Times of Ngor chen Kun dga' bzang po*. Lumbini: Lumbini International Research Institute, 2017.

Hoffmann, Helmut. *The Religions of Tibet*. Trans. Edward Fitzgerald. New York: Macmillan, 1961. First published as *Die Religionen Tibets*, 1956.

Hopkins, Jeffrey, trans. *Mountain Doctrine: Tibet's Fundamental Treatise on Other-Emptiness and the Buddha-Matrix*, by Döl bo ba Shay rap gyel tsen. Ed. Kevin Vose. Ithaca, NY, and Boulder, CO: Snow Lion, 2006.

Huber, Toni. "Where Exactly are Cārita, Devikoṭa, and Himavat? A Sacred Geography Controversy and the Development of Tantric Buddhist Pilgrimage Sites in Tibet." *Kailash* 14, nos. 3–4 (1990): 121–64.

———. "A Guide to the La Phyi Maṇḍala: History, Landscape and Ritual in South-Western Tibet." In *Maṇḍala and Landscape*, ed. A. W. Macdonald, 233–86. Emerging Perceptions in Buddhist Studies, no. 6. Delhi: D. K. Printworld, 1997.

———. *The Cult of Pure Crystal Mountain: Popular Pilgrimage and Visionary Landscape in Southeast Tibet*. New York: Oxford University Press, 1999.

IMAEDA, Yoshiro. *The Successors of Zhabdrung Ngawang Namgyel: Hereditary Heirs and Reincarnations*. Thimphu: Riyang Books, 2013.

Jackson, David P. *A Saint in Seattle: The Life of the Tibetan Mystic Dezhung Rinpoche*. Boston: Wisdom, 2004.

Jackson, Roger. "A Fasting Ritual." In *Religions of Tibet in Practice*, ed. Donald Lopez Jr., 271–92. Princeton, NJ: Princeton University Press, 1997.

Jamgön Kongtrül. *Jamgon Kongtrul's Retreat Manual*. Trans. Ngawang Zangpo. Boston: Snow Lion, 1994.

———. *The Treasury of Knowledge, Book One: Myriad Worlds*. Trans. the Kalu Rinpoché Translation Group. Boston: Snow Lion, 1995.

———. *The Treasury of Knowledge, Book Six, Part Four: Systems of Buddhist Tantra (The Indestructible Way of Secret Mantra)*. Trans. Elio Guarisco and Ingrid McLeod. Ithaca, NY, and Boulder, CO: Snow Lion, 2005.

———. *Manuel de retraite de Djamgœun Kongtrul*. Translated from Ngawang Zangpo's English translation by Pamela White. 1997; reprint, Ygrande, France: Éditions Yogi Ling, supported by the Tsadra Foundation, 2011.

Jansen, Berthe. *The Monastery Rules: Buddhist Monastic Organization in Pre-Modern Tibet*. Berkeley: University of California Press, 2018.

Jikmé Lingpa. "A Wonderous Ocean of Advice (For the Practice of Solitary Retreat)." Anonymous, undated translation of 'Jigs med gling pa's *Ri chos zhal gdams ngo mtshar rgya mtsho*. 7 pages. N.p.

Jones, Lindsay, ed. *Encyclopedia of Religion (Second Edition)*. 15 vols. Detroit: Macmillan Reference USA, 2005.

Jordan, Mark D. *Convulsing Bodies: Religion and Resistance in Foucault*. Stanford, CA: Stanford University Press, 2015.

Kapstein, Matthew. *The 'Dzam thang Edition of the Collected Works of Kun mkhyen Dol po pa Shes rab Rgyal mtshan: Introduction and Catalogue*. Majnu-Ka-Tilla, Delhi: Sherup Books, 1992.

———. "gDams ngag: Tibetan Technologies of the Self." In *Tibetan Literature: Studies in Genre*, ed. José Ignacio Cabezón and Roger Jackson, 275–89. Ithaca, NY: Snow Lion, 1996.

———. *The Tibetan Assimilation of Buddhism*. New York: Oxford University Press, 2000.

———. *The Tibetans*. Malden, MA: Blackwell, 2006.

———. "Tibetan Technologies of the Self, Part II: The Teachings of the Eight Conveyances." In *The Pandita and the Siddha: Tibetan Studies in Honor of E. Gene Smith*, ed. Ramon N. Prats, 110–29. Dharamsala: Amnye Machen Institute, 2007.

Karma Chagme and Rigdzin Kunzang Sherab. *Sky Dharma: The Foundations of the Namchö Treasure Teachings (The Life of Tertön Migyur Dorje and the Great Commentary to the Preliminary Practices)*. Trans. Khenpo Sonam Tsewang and Judith Amtzis. Boulder, CO: Snow Lion, 2022.

Khenpo Karthar Rinpoché. *Karma Chakme's Mountain Dharma*. Trans. Lama Yeshe Gyamtso, Chojor Radha, Namgyal Khorko. 4 vols. Woodstock, NY: Karma Triyana Dharmachakra Publications, 2004.

Kieffer-Pülz, Petra. "Rules for the *sīmā* Regulation in the *Vinaya* and its Commentaries and their Application in Thailand." *Journal of the International Association of Buddhist Studies* 20, no. 2 (1997): 141–53.

Kozhevnikov, Maria, James Elliott, Jennifer Shephard, and Klaus Gramann. "Neurocognitive and Somatic Components of Temperature Increases during g-Tummo Meditation: Legend and Reality." *PLoS ONE* 8, no. 3 (2013).

Kozhevnikov, Maria, Alina Veronika Irene Strasser, Elizabeth McDougal, Rupali Dhond, and Geoffrey Samuel. "Beyond Mindfulness: Arousal-Driven Modulation of Attentional Control During Arousal-Based Practices." *Current Research in Neurobiology* 3 (2022).

Lama Surya Das. *The Snow Lion's Turquoise Mane: Wisdom Tales from Tibet*. New York: HarperCollins, 1992.

Lindahl, Jared. "The Ritual Veneration of Mongolia's Mountains." In *Tibetan Ritual*, ed. José Ignacio Cabezón, 225–48. New York: Oxford University Press, 2010.

Longchen Rabjampa. "Song of the Enchanting Wildwoods." Trans. Timothy Hinkle. 2016. Distributed by Lotsawa House: https://www.lotsawahouse.org/tibetan-masters/longchen-rabjam/enchanting-wildwoods.

———. *Finding Rest in Meditation (The Trilogy of Rest, Volume 2)*. Trans. the Padmakara Translation Group. Boulder, CO: Shambhala, 2016.

Lopez, Donald, Jr., ed. *Religions of Tibet in Practice*. Princeton, NJ: Princeton University Press, 1997.

Martin, Dan. "The Woman Illusion? Research Into the Lives of Spiritually Accomplished Women Leaders of the 11th and 12th Centuries." In *Women in Tibet*, ed. Janet Gyatso and Hanna Havnevik, 49–82. New York: Columbia University Press, 2005.

McDougal, Elizabeth. "Coming Down the Mountain: Transformations of Contemplative Culture in Eastern Tibet." M.A. thesis, University of Sydney, 2016.

McMahan, David. "How Meditation Works: Theorizing the Role of Cultural Context in Buddhist Contemplative Practices." In *Meditation, Buddhism, and Science*, ed. McMahan and Erik Braun, 21–46. New York: Oxford University Press, 2017.

———. *Rethinking Meditation: Buddhist Meditative Practices in Ancient and Modern Worlds*. New York: Oxford University Press, 2023.

Melville, Herman. *Moby-Dick; Or, The Whale*. 1851; reprint, New York: Penguin, 2013.

Miller, Willa Blythe. "Secrets of the Vajra Body: Dngos po'i gnas lugs and the Apotheosis of the Body in the Work of Rgyal ba Yang dgon pa." PhD diss., Harvard University, 2013.

Molk, David, trans. *Lion of Siddhas: The Life and Teachings of Padampa Sangye*. Ithaca, NY: Snow Lion, 2008.

Monier-Williams, Sir Monier. *A Sanskrit-English Dictionary*. 1899; reprint, Springfield, VA: Nataraj Books, 2004.

Nattier, Jan. *Once Upon a Future Time: Studies in a Buddhist Prophecy of Decline*. Berkeley, CA: Asian Humanities Press, 1991.

Newman, John. "The Epoch of the Kālacakra Tantra." *Indo-Iranian Journal* 41, no. 4 (1998): 319–49.

Ngawang Zangpo. *Sacred Ground: Jamgon Kongtrul on "Pilgrimage and Sacred Geography."* Ithaca, NY: Snow Lion, 2001.

Oliphant, Charles Jamyang. "'Extracting the Essence': Bcud len in the Tibetan literary tradition." PhD diss., Faculty of Oriental Studies, Wolfson College, UK, 2015.

Olivelle, Patrick. "The Ascetic and the Domestic in Brahmanical Religiosity." In *Asceticism and Its Critics: Historical Accounts and Comparative Perspectives*, ed. Oliver Freiberger, 25–42. New York: Oxford University Press, 2006.

Olson, Carl. *Indian Asceticism: Power, Violence, and Play*. New York: Oxford University Press, 2016.

Pang, Rachel. *Singer of the Land of Snows: Shabkar, Buddhism, and Tibetan National Identity*. Charlottesville: University of Virginia Press, 2024.

Patrul Rinpoché. *The Words of My Perfect Teacher*. Trans. the Padmakara Translation Group. Boston: Shambhala, 1998.

Pettit, John Whitney. *Mipham's Beacon of Certainty: Illuminating the View of Dzogchen, the Great Perfection*. Boston: Wisdom, 1999.

Phuntsho, Karma. *The History of Bhutan*. Noida: Random House India, 2013.

Porter, Bill. *Road to Heaven: Encounters with Chinese Hermits*. Berkeley, CA: Counterpoint, 1993.

Quintman, Andrew. "Toward a Geographic Biography: Mi la ras pa in the Tibetan Landscape." *Numen* 55, no. 4 (2008): 363–410.

———, trans. *The Life of Milarepa*. New York: Penguin, 2010. Tibetan version first printed in 1488.

Ray, Reginald. *Buddhist Saints in India: A Study in Buddhist Values and Orientations*. New York: Oxford University Press, 1994.

———. *Secret of the Vajra World: The Tantric Buddhism of Tibet (The World of Tibetan Buddhism, Volume Two)*. Boston and London: Shambhala, 2001.

Roerich, George N., trans. *The Blue Annals*. 1949; reprint, Delhi: Motilal Banarsidass, 1996.

Roth, Harold D. *The Contemplative Foundations of Classical Daoism*. Albany: State University of New York Press, 2021.

Sandberg, Graham. *Tibet and the Tibetans*. London: Society for Promoting Christian Knowledge, 1906.

Schaeffer, Kurtis. *Himalayan Hermitess: The Life of a Tibetan Buddhist Nun*. New York: Oxford University Press, 2004.

———. *Buddhist Meditation: Classic Teachings from Tibet*. New York: Penguin, 2024.

Schaeffer, Kurtis, Matthew Kapstein, and Grey Tuttle, eds. *Sources of Tibetan Tradition*. New York: Columbia University Press, 2013.

Schneider, Nicola. "The Third Dragkar Lama: An Important Figure for Female Monasticism in the Beginning of Twentieth Century Kham." *Revue d'Études Tibétaines* 21 (2011): 45–60.

Schwerk, Dagmar. "Drawing Lines in a Maṇḍala: A Sketch of Boundaries Between Religion and Politics in Bhutan." *Working Paper Series of the HCAS "Multiple Secularities—Beyond the West, Beyond Modernities."* Leipzig University, 12 (2019).

———. *A Timely Message from the Cave: The Mahāmudrā and Intellectual Agenda of dGe bshes Brag phug pa dGe 'dun rin chen (192–1997), the Sixty-Ninth rJe mkhan po of Bhutan*. University of Hamburg, Department of Indian and Tibetan Studies, 2020.

Sernesi, Marta. "Writing Local Religious History: The *Abbatial History of Brag dkar rta so*." In *Unearthing Himalayan Treasures: Festschrift for Franz-Karl Ehrhard*, ed. Volker Caumanns, Sernesi, and Nikolai Solmsdorf, 387–415. Marburg: Indica et Tibetica Verlag, 2019.

———. "The *History of the Mountain Teachings*: 13th century Practice Lineages at rTsib ri." *Revue d'Études Tibétaines* 64 (2022): 479–515.
Shabkar Tsokdruk Rangdrol. *The Life of Shabkar: The Autobiography of a Tibetan Yogin*. Trans. Matthieu Ricard et al. Ithaca, NY: Snow Lion, 2001. Tibetan version written in 1837.
Shakabpa, Tsepon W. D. *Tibet: A Political History*. New Haven, CT, and London: Yale University Press, 1967.
Smith, Dennis. "*The Civilizing Process* and *The History of Sexuality*: Comparing Norbert Elias and Michel Foucault." *Theory and Society* 28, no. 1 (1999): 79–100.
Sonam Gyaltsen. *The Clear Mirror: A Traditional Account of Tibet's Golden Age; Sakyapa Sonam Gyaltsen's "Clear Mirror on Royal Genealogy."* Trans. McComas Taylor and Lama Choedak Yuthok. Ithaca, NY: Snow Lion, 1996.
Sørensen, Per. "The Prolific Ascetic Lce sgom Shes rab rdo rje *alias* Lce sgom Zhig po: Allusive, but Elusive." *Journal of the Nepal Research Centre* 11 (1999): 175–200.
Stagg, Christopher, trans. *The Hundred Thousand Songs of Milarepa*. Boulder, CO: Shambhala, 2017. Tibetan version first printed in 1488.
Stearns, Cyrus. *The Buddha from Dolpo: A Study of the Life and Thought of the Tibetan Master Dolpopa Sherab Gyaltsen*. Albany: State University of New York Press, 1999.
———. *Hermit of Go Cliffs: Timeless Instructions from a Tibetan Mystic*. Boston: Wisdom, 2000.
Steavu, Dominic. *The Writ of the Three Sovereigns: From Local Lore to Institutional Daoism*. Honolulu: University of Hawai'i Press, 2019,
Stein, R. A. *Tibetan Civilization*. Trans. J. E. Stapleton Driver. Stanford, CA: Stanford University Press, 1972.
———, trans. *Vie et chants de 'Brug pa Kun legs le yogin*. Paris: G.-P. Maisonneuve et Larose, 1972.
Sullivan, Brenton. *Building a Religious Empire: Tibetan Buddhism, Bureaucracy, and the Rise of the Gelukpa*. Philadelphia: University of Pennsylvania Press, 2021.
Sutherland, Patrick, and Tashi Tsering. *Disciples of a Crazy Saint: The Buchen of Spiti*. Oxford: Pitt Rivers Museum, 2011.
Taylor, Charles. *A Secular Age*. Cambridge, MA: Harvard University Press, 2007.
Thomas, Michael. "Mountains and Early Daoism in the Writings of Ge Hong." *History of Religions* 56, no. 1 (2016): 23–54.
Tsering Lama Jampal Zangpo. *A Garland of Immortal Wish-fulfilling Trees: The Palyul Tradition of Nyingmapa*. Trans. Sangye Khandro. Ithaca, NY: Snow Lion, 1988.
Valantasis, Richard. "Is the Gospel of Thomas Ascetical? Revisiting an Old Problem with a New Theory." *Journal of Early Christian Studies* 7, no. 1 (1999): 55–81.
Wallace, Vesna. *The Inner Kālacakratantra: A Buddhist Tantric View of the Individual*. New York: Oxford University Press, 2001.
White, David Gordon. *The Alchemical Body: Siddha Traditions in Medieval India*. Chicago: University of Chicago Press, 1996.

INDEX

alcohol, 61, 84, 100, 108–9
Amdo (*a mdo*), 23, 34, 50
animals. *See* birds; deer; dogs; lice; lions; meat, consumption of; monkeys; predatory animals; rhinoceroses; rodents
anuttarayoga tantra. See Unexcelled Yoga Tantra
approach–accomplishment (*bsnyen sgrub, sevāsādhana*), 4, 32–33, 72, 75, 150, 177
Atīśa Dīpaṃkara (982–1054), 35, 40–41, 50, 75, 103, 145
Avalokiteśvara, 4, 28, 31, 76, 130

bandits, 55, 61, 79, 114, 117, 129–31, 175, 184
Barawa Gyeltsen Pelzang (*'ba' ra ba rgyal mtshan dpal bzang*, 1310–1391), 41, 203n54
bardo, intermediate state, 26, 101, 152–53, 155
bcud len. See essence extraction
bedbugs. *See* lice
Bhutan, 7, 23, 160, 168, 194n9
birds, 52, 103–104, 107, 144, 151
Bön, 3–6, 34, 86, 164
Bourdieu, Pierre, 9–11
Buddhaghosa, 53

cairn. *See* retreat cairn
calendrical systems. 59, 162–63, 165, 195n14
Changkya III Rölpé Dorjé (*lcang skya rol pa'i rdo rje*, 1717–1786), 49, 191
channels, winds, and drops, 5, 25–27, 33, 54, 56–57, 66, 81, 96–97, 99–101, 110–111, 120, 123, 126, 163, 165

Chegom Sherap Dorjé (*lce sgom shes rab rdo rje*; Chegom Zhikpo, *lce sgom zhig po*; Chegom Dzongpa, *lce sgom rdzong pa*; Khakyong Drakpa, *mkha' skyong brag pa*, 1124–1204), 51–54, 74, 99, 120, 129, 139, 153–54, 158, 190
Chenga Drakpa Jungné (*spyan snga grags pa 'byung gnas*, 1175–1255), 25
Chenga Lodrö Gyeltsen (*spyan snga blo gros rgyal mtshan*, 1402–1472), 103
Chenga Rinchen Den (*spyan snga rin chen ldan*, b. 1202), disciple of Yangönpa, 25–26
Chimpu hermitage (*mchims phu*), 164
China, 3, 23, 34, 55, 58–59, 133–34, 164, 170, 196n26
Chödrak Yeshé. *See* Red Hat IV
Chokgyur Dechen Lingpa (*mchog gyur bde chen gling pa*, 1829–1870), 169, 173, 177
Chökyi Wangchuk. *See* Red Hat VI
Chöying Dorjé. *See* Karmapa X
Christianity, 10–12, 15, 48, 183, 193n2, 196n26, 225n19
circle of protection (*[b]srung 'khor*), 45, 81, 97, 130, 175, 213n4
clothing, 13, 36, 77, 90, 93–94, 99, 101–2, 104–5, 107, 111–12, 114, 129, 141, 150, 175, 179, 184, 235n41; geomancy of, 56; monastic robes, 94, 101, 107, 217n48; in connection to *tummo*, 111, 125–29, 175, 208n32, 219n6
Cutting (*gcod*), 5, 28–29, 31, 58–59, 79, 120–22, 124, 177

ḍākiṇīs, 60, 64, 81, 97, 112, 137
Dalai Lamas, 5, 7, 194n8, 233n19

dark retreat (*mun mtshams*), 4, 211n57
deer, 48, 52, 77, 99, 141
degenerate age (*snyigs dus*), 18, 79, 83, 90–91, 97, 114, 129, 138–39, 153–55, 157–59, 180–81
demonic entities, 26, 29, 45, 51, 55, 61, 63, 75, 84, 95, 99, 105, 108, 117, 119, 125, 134, 166, 175, 184, 186
dependent connection (*rten 'brel*), 56, 94, 97, 150
Dharma protectors, 5, 28–29, 32, 45, 58, 81, 97, 118, 137, 173, 176–77
Dingri (*ding ri*), 90
dkor, monastic property, 106–9, 141
dogs, 46, 112, 123, 151
Dolpopa Sherap Gyeltsen (*dol po pa shes rab rgyal mtshan*, 1292–1361/62), 177, 194n8, 201n41
Dordzin Namkha Dorjé (*rdor 'dzin nam mkha' rdo rje*), 1486–1553), 41–42, 217n48, 232n11
Drakar Jangchub Ling monastery (*brag dkar byang chub gling*), 34
Drakar Lozang Pelden Tenzin Nyendrak (*brag dkar blo bzang dpal ldan bstan 'dzin snyan grags*, 1866–1928), biographical details, 34, 39, 86; description of *Garland of Pearls*, 17, 34–37, 41, 191; on food, 104–5; on illness and healing, 118–19; on interpersonal relations, 74, 77, 118; on lineage, 139, 142, 144–45; on location for retreat, 46, 53; on other retreatants, 86–88, 92, 118; on retreat attendant, 80–81, 90
Drakar Taso hermitage (*brag dkar rta so*), 23, 39–40, 114
Drakarwa Chökyi Wangchuk (*brag dkar ba chos kyi dbang phyug*, 1775–1837), 114, 232n11
Drango (*brag 'go*), 34
dreams and dream yoga (*rmi lam*), 27–28, 31, 52, 55, 100, 121, 156, 168, 175, 178, 194n8, 202n50. *See also* Six Yogas of Naropa
Drepung Loseling monastery (*'bras spungs blo gsal gling*), 34
Drikung monastery, Drikung Kagyu (*'bri gung*), 23, 25, 49
Dromtönpa (*'brom ston pa*), 145
drops. *See* channels, winds, and drops
Drukpa Kagyu, 25, 45
Drukpa Künlé (*'brug pa kun legs*, b. 1455), 8
Durkheim, Émile, 1–2, 48, 206n18
Düsum Khyenpa. *See* Karmapa I
Dza Rongpu monastery (*rdza rong phu*), 23, 90, 112

eight worldly concerns, 104, 156–57
empowerment (*dbang, abhiṣeka*), tantric initiation, 4, 27–28, 32, 105, 128, 132, 136, 138, 144, 146–47, 150, 154, 156, 160, 172, 177, 222n42
essence extraction (*bcud len*), 18, 99–100, 109–13, 128, 184
extrasensory perception (*mngon shes*), 74, 100, 112, 152, 156

female meditators, 2–5, 34, 39–41, 114–15, 187
five Paths. *See* Grounds and Paths
fortnightly monastic confession (*gso sbyong, poṣadha*), 85, 89, 91, 104, 106
Foucault, Michel, 10–13, 72, 95, 145, 185
four meditation sessions (*thun bzhi*), 6, 28, 31–33, 35, 45, 70, 132, 134, 142, 172
Four Treatises (*rgyud bzhi*), 110, 122, 227n42
funerary rites, 29–30, 58–59, 75, 80, 153, 214n10
further improvement practices (*bogs 'don*), 25, 29, 96, 99, 111, 120, 130, 139–40, 143, 149, 178

Gampopa (*sgam po pa*, 1079–1153), 40, 146, 177
Ganzé (*dkar mdzes*), 23, 34
Geluk school, 3, 8, 24, 34–35, 37, 86
Generation and Perfection phase, 27, 33, 65, 111, 132, 150, 176, 179, 230n43
geomancy, 17, 54–62, 64–65, 67–68, 72, 80, 170
Geshé Kharakpa (*dge bshes kha rag pa*; Kharak Gomchung, *kha rag sgom chung*, tenth-eleventh cent.), 103
Getar Lung (*dge thar lung*), 34
Gö Lotsawa Zhönnu Pel (*'gos lo tsA ba gzhon nu dpal*, 1392–1481), 163
Götsangpa Gönpo Dorjé (*rgod tshang pa mgon po rdo rje*, 1189–1258), 25, 27, 232n7
Great Perfection, 4–5, 30, 196n28
Grounds and Paths (*lam, mārga*) 25, 112, 143, 151, 154
gtor ma. See ritual cake
guidebook literature (*gnas yig*), 63, 169–70
Guru Rinpoché. *See* Padmasambhava
guru yoga, 5, 27, 31, 122–24, 142, 144, 200n22

harmful taint (*grib*), 14, 61, 72, 78, 94, 96–97, 106–7, 127, 208n32, 220n18
herbs, 94, 99, 100, 111, 127
Hinduism, 3, 15, 22, 165, 193n2, 218n3
homa, fire pūja, 33, 96
hungry ghosts (*preta, yi dwags*), 32, 99, 132

illness and healing, 10, 18, 35, 51, 69, 75, 78–79, 81, 84, 96, 104–5, 112, 116–25, 129, 131, 134, 140, 156, 172–73, 175, 184

illusory body (*sgyu lus*), 27, 54, 101, 157. *See also* Six Yogas of Naropa
imaginal self, 18, 66, 117, 133–34, 147, 158, 175, 177, 184
initiation. *See* empowerment

Jamgön Kongtrül Lodrö Tayé (*'jam mgon kong sprul blo gros mtha' yas*, 1813–1899), 4, 19, 22, 157–58, 161, 167–82, 194n8
Jetsangpa Rinchen Peljor (*bye tshang pa rin chen dpal 'byor*), 112
Jikmé Lingpa (*'jigs med gling pa*, 1729/30–1798), 73, 80, 109, 191
Jikten Sumgön (*'jig rten gsum mgon*; Jikten Gönpo Rinchen Pel, *'jig rten mgon po rin chen dpal*, 1143–1217), 49, 65–66, 98, 175, 190
Jokhang (*jo khang*), 63
Jonang school, 3, 163, 167, 176–77, 201n41
Ju Mipam (*'ju mi pham*, 1846–1912), 34

Kachö Wangpo. *See* Red Hat II
Kadam school, 3, 24, 35, 51, 103, 107, 139–40, 145
Kailash. *See* Mount Kailash
Kālacakra tantra, 4–5, 110, 162–63, 165, 176–78, 208n33
Kalu Rinpoché (1905–1989), 22, 168, 170
Karma Chakmé (*karma chags med*, 1608/10/13–1678); biographical details, 28–29, 37–38, 69–70, 73, 140–42, 168, 173, 179; description of *Direct Advice on Retreat*, 17, 28–31, 34–35, 37, 42, 69–70, 168, 191; fundamentals of retreat, 30–34, 38, 45, 132, 149–51, 166, 178; on food, 102, 105–6, 109, 111; on healing and protection, 122–23, 129–30; on interpersonal relations, 72–73, 75–80, 82, 90–91, 134; on liberatory prospects, 150–55, 159; on lineage, 136–37, 140–42, 146; on location for retreat, 45, 57–61, 73, 81, 90; on monasticism, 81, 88–89, 106, 109; on retreat attendant, 80–81; on tummo, 127–29
Karma Ngedön Tenkyé (*karma nges don bstan rgyas*; Mendong Tsampa Rinpoché, *sman sdong mtshams pa rin po che*, b. late nineteenth cent.), 38, 62, 76–77, 82, 93, 106–7, 109, 128, 139, 168, 191
Karmapa I Düsum Khyenpa (*karma pa dus gsum mkhyen pa*, 1110–1193), 146
Karmapa III Rangjung Dorjé (*karma pa rang byung rdo rje*, 1284–1339), 46–47, 57, 102, 110, 112, 119, 138–39, 158, 177, 180, 190
Karmapa X Chöying Dorjé (*karma pa chos dbyings rdo rje*, 1604–1674), 28

Kelzang Tenpé Gyeltsen (*bskal bzang bstan pa'i rgyal mtshan*, 1897–1959), 86
Kham (*khams*), 23, 28, 34, 60, 168–69, 171
Khenpo Karthar Rinpoché, 57, 150, 153
Khyungpo Neljor (*khyung po rnal 'byor*, 1002–1064), 177
Kodrakpa Sönam Gyeltsen (*ko brag pa bsod nams rgyal mtshan*, 1182–1261), 25, 27, 54, 96
Kongpo (*kong po*), 14, 23, 148
Künzang Dechen Ösel Ling. *See* Tsadra Rinchen Drak
Kusali/Kusulu Accumulation. *See* Cutting

lam rim. *See* Stages of the Path
Lama Zhang (*bla ma zhang*, 1122–1193), 26, 50, 103
Lapchi (*la phyi*), 23, 66, 148
Latö (*la stod*), 25
Lhadong (*lha gdong*), 23, 25
Lhasa (*lha sa*), 7–8, 23, 34, 63, 193n6
Lhatsün Namkha Jikmé (*lha btsun nam mkha' 'jigs med*; Kunzang Namgyel, *kun bzang rnam rgyal*; Madman of Kongpo, *kong smyon*, 1597–1650), 14–15, 38, 61, 84–85, 105, 108, 118–19, 145, 165, 191
lice, bedbugs, 96, 131, 184
life-long retreat (*tshe mtshams*), 5, 33, 69, 150, 166, 202n52, 205n15, 232n7
lions, 28, 31, 86, 103, 128, 178, 206n16
lived deferential reverence, 16, 19, 63, 90–91, 95, 113, 137, 151, 159, 167, 178, 180–82, 184, 186
local deities, 28–29, 45, 47, 55, 63–65, 98–99, 173–74, 186
Longchenpa Drimé Özer (*klong chen pa dri med 'od zer*, 1308–1364), 49, 53, 65, 190
longevity practices, 28–29, 32, 173, 176
Lozang Chökyi Gyeltsen. *See* Panchen Lama IV
Lozang Jangchup Tenpé Drönmé (*blo bzang byang chub bstan pa'i sgron me*, 1504/05–1565/66), 110
luminosity (*'od gsal*), 27–28, 54, 157. *See also* Six Yogas of Naropa
lung. *See* reading transmission

Madman of Tsang (*gtsang smyon*, 1452–1507), 94, 194n8, 231n7
Mahāmudrā, 5, 25, 27, 30, 101, 120–21, 136, 146, 152, 154
mandala, 31–33, 55, 101, 132, 146, 151, 199n18
mantra, 4, 28, 31–33, 45, 72, 75–78, 109, 130–33, 138, 146, 171, 173

Marīcī, goddess, 130
Marpa (*mar pa*, 1012–1097), 62, 75, 145, 177
meat, consumption of, 104, 108–10, 114, 164, 179
Mendong Tsampa Rinpoché. *See* Karma Ngedön Tenkyé
Milarepa (*mi la ras pa*, 1028/40/52–1111/23), 8, 26, 50, 62, 64, 73, 75, 94, 103, 111, 114–15, 125, 129, 137, 140, 145, 172, 175, 181
Mingyur Dorjé (*mi 'gyur rdo rje*, 1645–1667), 29, 179
Mipam Püntsok Sherap (*mi pham phun tshogs shes rab*; Mendicant of Taktsé, *stag rtse bya bral ba*; Reincarnation of Taktsé, *stag rtse sku skye*, 1654–1715), 45, 61, 95, 105, 139, 142, 148–49, 166, 191
monastic charter (*bca' yig*), 39–40, 114–15, 123, 158, 168, 171–80
monastic scholasticism. *See* scholasticism
Mongolia, 25, 55, 57, 205n11
monkeys, 66, 140, 164
Mount Kailash, 23, 57, 66, 148

Namkha Ding hermitage (*nam mkha' ding*), 25
Nangchen (*nang chen*), 60
Naropa, 145, 151, 172. *See also* Six Yogas of Naropa
national identity. *See* Tibetan national identity
Nedo (*gnas mdo*), 23, 29, 228n11
nettles. *See* herbs
Ngawang Tenzin Norbu (*ngag dbang bstan 'dzin nor bu*, 1867–1940/49?), 90–91, 112–13, 191
nonobvious entities. *See* ḍākiṇīs, demonic entities, Dharma protectors, hungry ghosts, local deities, tutelary deity
Nupchen Sangyé Yeshé (*gnubs chen sangs rgyas ye shes*, ninth–tenth cent.), 41
Nyingma school, 3–4, 24, 28–30, 32, 34, 37, 41, 49, 73, 75–77, 84, 90, 110, 114, 168, 176

Orgyen Lingpa (*o rgyan gling pa*, b. ca. 1323), 164
Orgyen Namdröl Wangpo (*o rgyan rnam grol dbang po*; Chakbuk Rinpoché, *lcags sbug rin po che*, b. ca. 1808), 116, 139, 143, 191
Orgyenpa Rinchen Pel (*o rgyan pa rin chen dpal*, 1229/30–1309), 101, 138

Padmasambhava (Guru Rinpoché, *gu ru rin po che*, ca. eighth–ninth cent.), 7, 31, 57, 60, 62–63, 137, 164, 169, 171
Pakmodrupa Dorjé Gyelpo (*phag mo gru pa rdo rje rgyal po*, 1110–1170), 64, 98, 140, 190, 204n8

Panchen Lama IV Lozang Chökyi Gyeltsen (*paN chen bla ma blo bzang chos kyi rgyal mtshan*, 1567/68/70–1662), 85–86, 88, 90, 144, 190
Paths. *See* Grounds and Paths
Patrul Rinpoché (*dpal sprul rin po che*, 1808–1887), 40
Pawo II Tsuklak Trengwa (*dpa' bo gtsug lag phreng ba*, 1504–1564/66), 163
Pelpung monastery (*dpal spungs*), 23, 168–69, 174, 176
Pelyul lineage (*dpal yul*), 29
Pema Nyingjé Wangpo. *See* Tai Situ IX Pema Nyingjé Wangpo
Perfection phase. *See* Generation and Perfection phase
places of deviation (*gol sa*), 29, 152, 154, 218n3
poṣadha. *See* fortnightly monastic confession
Potowa Rinchen Sel (*po to ba rin chen gsal*, 1027/31–1105), 35–36, 86, 103, 144
Practice of the Observance. *See* Secret Practice
predatory animals, 61, 117, 119, 125, 129–30, 175
preliminary practices (*sngon 'gro*), 4, 27, 29, 31, 40, 138, 142, 176
protector deities. *See* Dharma protectors
Public Practice. *See* Secret Practice
pure land, 31, 33–34, 80, 153, 176
pure vision (*dag snang*), 65–66, 84–85, 144

Rangjung Dorjé. *See* Karmapa III
rasāyana. *See* essence extraction
Rdo rje lus kyi sbas bshad. *See* Karma Chakmé
reading transmission (*lung*), 32, 42, 105, 128, 143–44, 147, 168, 172, 177, 180
Rechungpa (*ras chung pa*, 1084–1161), 73
Red Hat II Kachö Wangpo (*zhwa dmar mkha' spyod dbang po*, 1350–1405), 66–67, 82, 88, 145, 190
Red Hat VI Chökyi Wangchuk (*zhwa dmar chos kyi dbang phyug*, 1584–1630), 28, 88
Reting monastery (*rwa sgreng*), 148
retreat attendant, 17, 71, 80–81, 84, 90–91, 173–75
retreat cairn or signboard (*mtshams [m]tho*), 45, 70, 77, 171, 177
rhinoceroses, 50, 91, 206n16
Rimé movement (*ris med*), 3–4, 167
ritual cake (*gtor ma*), 28, 32, 45, 98, 173
robbers. *See* bandits
rodents, 36, 66, 104

sādhana (*sgrub thabs*), 4, 29, 32, 65, 130, 132–33, 200n22
Sakya Paṇḍita (*sa skya paNDi ta*, 1182–1251), 25, 40
Sakya school, 3, 34
samaya vows (*dam tshig*), 36, 45, 55, 61, 66, 72, 81, 83, 91, 146, 208n32
Śāntideva, 50, 85
Sbas bshad. *See* Karma Chakmé
scholasticism, monastic, 3, 5, 8, 19–20, 34, 36, 145, 153, 186
Secret Practice, Public Practice, Practice of the Observance, 72, 99, 166, 209n35, 212n3, 214n10
Sera monastery (*se ra*), 8
Setsünpa (*se btsun pa*), 145
sevāsādhana. *See* approach–accomplishment
sexual yoga, 41, 96, 111, 123, 126, 131, 214n10
Shabkar Tsokdruk Rangdrol (*zhabs dkar tshogs drug rang grol*, 1781–1851), 64, 125, 140–41, 191; on food, 103–4, 107, 109, 112; on location for retreat, 50–51; on renouncing home and family, 74–75
Shangpa Kagyu, 173, 176–77
Shar Kelden Gyatso (*shar skal ldan rgya mtsho*, 1607–1677), 50
Shardza Tashi Gyeltsen (*shar mdza bkra' shis rgyal mtshan*, 1859–1933/35), 34, 86, 88
sickness. *See* illness and healing
siddhi, 55, 96, 112, 121, 138, 142–43, 153, 158, 179
signs of spiritual progress, 29, 36, 55, 96, 127, 131, 153–54, 158, 175, 179, 220n19, 226n38. *See also siddhi*
Sikkim, 23, 57
silence, 1, 75–77, 81, 84, 91, 184
Six Yogas of Naropa, 5, 25, 27, 125–26, 142
Sky Dharma (*gnam chos*), 29, 179
Sönam Chödzin (*bsod nams chos 'dzin*, b. 1688), 57, 93, 111, 116–17, 125, 128, 139, 191
spirit beings. *See* nonobvious entities
Stages of the Path literature (*lam rim*), 26, 40–41
starvation, 95–96, 102–3, 113, 117, 125, 224n3

Tai Situ IX Pema Nyingjé Wangpo (*ta'i si tu pad+ma snying rje dbang po*, 1774/75–1853), 177, 233n20
Tanak (*rta nag*), 23, 51
technologies of self, 10–12, 15, 68, 95, 117, 124–25, 130–35, 147, 178, 185
ten Grounds. *See* Grounds and Paths

Terdak Lingpa (*gter bdag gling pa*, 1646–1714), 177
Tewo Lungzang Nangwa (*the bo lung bzang nang ba*; Ngawang Lozang Samten, *ngag dbang blo bzang bsam gtan*, 1687–1748/49), 49
Theravada Buddhism, 3, 15, 45–46, 48–51, 53, 197n34
thieves. *See* bandits
three "bodies" of buddhahood (*sku gsum, trikāya*), 25, 91, 121, 155
Tibetan national identity, 7, 47, 63–64, 129, 164, 169
Tilopa, 138, 145, 151
torma. *See* ritual cake
transference of consciousness (*'pho ba*), 27, 75. *See also* Six Yogas of Naropa
treasure texts (*gter ma*), 5, 29, 73, 169, 173, 177, 179, 186, 203n52
Trisong Detsen (*khri srong lde btsan*, 742–797/804), 164
Trungpa IV Künga Namgyel (*drung pa kun dga' rnam rgyal*, 1567–1629), 37, 76, 190, 210n45
Tsadra Rinchen Drak hermitage (*tsA 'dra rin chen brag*; Künzang Dechen Ösel Ling, *kun bzang bde chen 'od gsal gling*), 158, 168–78
Tsang (*gtsang*), 23, 25, 41, 94
Tsangpa Gyaré (*gtsang pa rgya ras*, 1161–1211), 74
Tsari (*tsA ri*), 23, 50, 57, 66, 126, 148, 169–71
Tsöndrü Gyatso (*brtson 'grus rgya mtsho*), disciple of Karma Chakmé, 29, 57, 69–70, 73, 130, 140–42, 225n20
Tsongkhapa Lozang Drakpa (*tsong kha pa blo bzang grags pa*, 1357–1419), 35, 40–41, 75, 139, 213n5
Tsurpu monastery (*mtshur phu*), 23, 138
tummo (*gtum mo*), 27, 32, 54, 96, 111–12, 122, 124–29, 157, 175, 178, 181. *See also* Six Yogas of Naropa
tutelary deity (*yi dam*), 27, 29, 31–33, 65–66, 97, 112, 118, 123, 131–33, 137, 142, 146, 150, 177
twenty-four holy sites of India, 62, 65

Ü (*dbus*), 23, 28
Unexcelled Yoga Tantra, 27, 29, 81, 163, 165. *See also* Kālacakra tantra

Vinaya, 59, 85–86, 101, 172

winds. *See* channels, winds, and drops
women. *See* female meditators

Yangönpa Gyeltsen Pel (*yang dgon pa rgyal mtshan dpal*, 1213–1258), biographical details, 25, 41; description of *Blazing Jewel*, 17, 24–30, 34–35, 37, 41–42, 57, 190; fundamentals of retreat, 27–28, 37, 39, 71, 131, 165, 178; on food, 95–98, 101, 103, 107, 111, 117, 132; on healing and protection, 122–23, 129, 131; on interpersonal relations, 71–73, 76–77, 79, 81–82, 91; on liberatory prospects, 154–56, 158, 180; on lineage, 42, 139–40, 142, 148; on location for retreat, 14–15, 54–62, 65, 67; on monasticism, 27, 88; *Secret Explanation of the Vajra Body* (*rdo rje lus kyi sbas bshad*), 26, 165, 208n33; on *tummo*, 125–27, 129

Yeshé Tsogyel (*ye shes mtsho rgyal*), 7
yoga of eating (*zas kyi rnal 'byor*), 32, 96–98, 109, 132
yogic exercises (*'khrul 'khor*), 56, 123–24, 126–27

Zhabdrung Ngawang Namgyel (*zhabs drung ngag dbang rnam rgyal*, 1594–1651), 7
Zurmang Dutsi Til monastery (*zur mang bdud rtsi mthil*), 23, 37, 60
Zurmang Lekshé Drayang (*zur mang legs bshad sgra dbyangs*, b. sixteenth cent.), 37, 116, 129, 156–57, 190; on food, 99–102, 108, 110–11; on illness, 120–21, 124, 140; on location for retreat, 60–61; on relating to guru, 143–44; on other retreatants, 82–85, 90–91

GPSR Authorized Representative: Easy Access System Europe, Mustamäe tee
50, 10621 Tallinn, Estonia, gpsr.requests@easproject.com